CW00329456

Renault 30
Owners
Workshop
Manual

Ian Coomber

Models covered
Renault 30 TS and 30 TX, 2664 cc

ISBN 0 85696 682 7

ABCDE
FGHIJ
KLMNO
PQRST

Printed in England

THE
BOOK

HAYNES PUBLISHING GROUP
SPARKFORD YEOVIL SOMERSET BA22 7JJ ENGLAND
distributed in the USA by
HAYNES PUBLICATIONS INC
861 LAWRENCE DRIVE
NEWBURY PARK
CALIFORNIA 91320
USA

Acknowledgements

Thanks are due to Régie Renault for the supply of technical information and certain illustrations, to Castrol Limited who supplied lubrication data, and to the Champion Sparking Plug Company who supplied the illustrations showing the various spark plug conditions.

The bodywork repair photographs used in this manual were provided by Holt Lloyd Ltd who supply 'Turtle Wax', 'Dupli-color Holts' and other Holts range products. Sykes-Pickavant Ltd provided some of the workshop tools.

About this manual

Its aim

The aim of this manual is to help you get the best value from your vehicle. It can do so in several ways. It can help you decide what work must be done (even should you choose to get it done by a garage), provide information on routine maintenance and servicing, and give a logical course of action and diagnosis when random faults occur. However, it is hoped that you will use the manual by tackling the work yourself. On simpler jobs it may even be quicker than booking the car into a garage and going there twice, to leave and collect it. Perhaps most important, a lot of money can be saved by avoiding the costs a garage must charge to cover its labour and overheads.

The manual has drawings and descriptions to show the function of the various components so that their layout can be understood. Then the tasks are described and photographed in a step-by-step sequence so that even a novice can do the work.

Its arrangement

The manual is divided into twelve Chapters, each covering a logical sub-division of the vehicle. The Chapters are each divided into Sections, numbered with single figures, eg 5; and the Sections into paragraphs (or sub-sections), with decimal numbers following on from the Section they are in, eg 5.1, 5.2, 5.3 etc.

It is freely illustrated, especially in those parts where there is a detailed sequence of operations to be carried out. There are two forms of illustration: figures and photographs. The figures are numbered in sequence with decimal numbers, according to their position in the Chapter – eg Fig. 6.4 is the fourth drawing/illustration in Chapter 6. Photographs carry the same number (either individually or in related groups) as the Section or sub-section to which they relate.

There is an alphabetical index at the back of the manual as well as a contents list at the front. Each Chapter is also preceded by its own individual contents list.

References to the 'left' or 'right' of the vehicle are in the sense of a person in the driver's seat facing forwards.

Unless otherwise stated, nuts and bolts are removed by turning anti-clockwise, and tightened by turning clockwise.

Vehicle manufacturers continually make changes to specifications and recommendations, and these, when notified, are incorporated into our manuals at the earliest opportunity.

Whilst every care is taken to ensure that the information in this manual is correct, no liability can be accepted by the authors or publishers for loss, damage or injury caused by any errors in, or omissions from, the information given.

Introduction to the Renault 30

The Renault 30 was first introduced to the French market in February 1975 and became available in the UK in October of that year. The largest model in the Renault range of cars, it is powered by a 2.6 litre V6 engine which is water-cooled and has removable wet liners. The cylinder heads and crankcase are manufactured in aluminium; the valvegear is operated by chain-driven overhead camshafts (one to each cylinder bank).

A four or five-speed manual transmission is the standard fitting, depending on model, and automatic transmission is available as an option. The transmission is mounted in-line behind the engine, the transmission casing also housing the differential unit which transmits drive to the front wheels.

Independent suspension is used at the front and rear. The steering system is of rack-and-pinion type, power-assisted on all models.

Disc brakes are used at the front and rear, power-assisted by a servo unit. The handbrake is cable operated to the rear wheels only.

A comprehensive range of controls and equipment is fitted, again depending on model and optional requirements. A central door locking system is fitted to all models.

The Renault 30 offers spacious, comfortable transport readily adaptable to the needs of the business or family motorist and it provides proven reliability with a good performance.

Contents

Renault 30 TX

Renault 30 TS

General dimensions and weights

Dimensions
Length (overall)	14 ft 10 in (4.520 m)
Width (overall)	5 ft 8$\frac{3}{16}$ in (1.732 m)
Height (unladen)	4 ft 8$\frac{5}{16}$ in (1.431 m)
Front track	4 ft 8$\frac{7}{8}$ in (1.444 m)
Rear track	4 ft 8$\frac{5}{8}$ in (1.438 m)
Wheelbase	8 ft 9$\frac{5}{32}$ in (2.671 m)
Turning circle – between kerbs:	
Manual transmission models	33 ft 1$\frac{5}{8}$ in (10.10 m)
Automatic transmission models	34 ft 9$\frac{5}{16}$ in (10.60 m)
Turning circle – between walls:	
Manual transmission models	35 ft 9$\frac{1}{8}$ in (10.90 m)
Automatic transmission models	37 ft 4$\frac{13}{16}$ in (11.40 m)

Weights
Kerb weight (total):	
Manual transmission models	2910 lb (1320 kg)
Automatic transmission models	2956 lb (1340 kg)
Maximum permissible all-up weight (manual and automatic transmission models)	3837 lb (1740 kg)
Maximum trailer weight:	
With trailer braking	3527 lb (1600 kg)
Without trailer braking	1455 lb (660 kg)

Buying spare parts and vehicle identification numbers

Buying spare parts

Spare parts are available from many sources, for example: Renault dealers, other garages and accessory shops, and motor factors. Our advice regarding spare part sources is as follows:

Officially appointed Renault garages: This is the best source for parts which are peculiar to your car and are otherwise not generally available (eg complete cylinder heads, internal gearbox components, badges, interior trim etc). It is also the only place you should have repairs carried out if your car is still under warranty – non-Renault components may invalidate the warranty. To be sure of obtaining the correct parts it will always be necessary to give the storeman your car's vehicle identification number, and if possible, to take the old parts along for positive identification. It obviously makes good sense to go straight to the specialists on your car for this type of part for they are best equipped to supply you.

Other garages and accessort shops – These are often very good places to buy materials and components needed for the maintenance of your car (eg spark plugs, bulbs, drivebelts, oils and greases, filler paste etc). They also sell general accessories, usually have convenient opening hours, charge reasonable prices and can often be found not far from home.

Motor factors – Good factors will stock all the more important components which wear out relatively quickly (eg clutch components, pistons, valves, exhaust systems, brake cylinders/pipes/hoses/seals/pads etc). Motor factors will often provide new or reconditioned components on a part exchange basis – this can save a considerable amount of money.

Vehicle identification numbers

Modifications are a continuous and unpublicised process carried out by the vehicle manufacturers, so accept the advice of the parts storeman when purchasing a component. Spare parts lists and manuals are compiled upon a numerical basis, so individual vehicle numbers are essential to the supply of the correct component.

The vehicle identification plate and *body serial number plate* are located on the top right-hand side of the engine compartment above the headlights.

The body serial number is stamped onto the right-hand side of the engine compartment toward the rear. This should be quoted when ordering body parts.

The engine number plate is located on the cylinder block. This should be quoted when ordering engine parts.

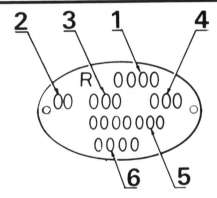

The oval plate gives the following information

1	Factory symbol		originally fitted
2	Vehicle details	5	Fabrication number
3	Equipment number	6	Model year
4	Optional equipment		

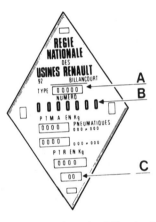

The lozenge plate gives the following information

A	Vehicle type	C	Model year
B	Chassis number		

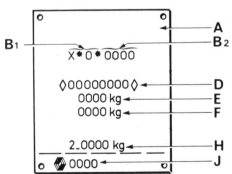

The rectangular plate (TX models only) gives the following information

A	Manufacturer		of loaded vehicle and trailer
B	EEC code number		
D	Chassis number	H	Maximum weight allowable over rear axle
E	Maximum all-up weight permissible		
F	Maximum permitted weight	J	Model year

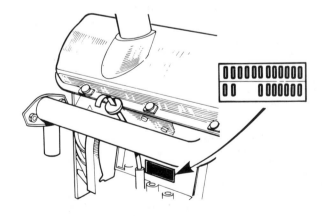

Engine number location

Tools and working facilities

Introduction

A selection of good tools is a fundamental requirement for anyone contemplating the maintenance and repair of a motor vehicle. For the owner who does not possess any, their purchase will prove a considerable expense, offsetting some of the savings made by doing-it-yourself. However, provided that the tools purchased are of good quality, they will last for many years and prove an extremely worthwhile investment.

To help the average owner to decide which tools are needed to carry out the various tasks detailed in this manual, we have compiled three lists of tools under the following headings: *Maintenance and minor repair*, *Repair and overhaul*, and *Special*. The newcomer to practical mechanics should start off with the *Maintenance and minor repair* tool kit and confine himself to the simpler jobs around the vehicle. Then, as his confidence and experience grow, he can undertake more difficult tasks, buying extra tools as, and when, they are needed. In this way, a *Maintenance and minor repair* tool kit can be built-up into a *Repair and overhaul* tool kit over a considerable period of time without any major cash outlays. The experienced do-it-yourselfer will have a tool kit good enough for most repair and overhaul procedures and will add tools from the *Special* category when he feels the expense is justified by the amount of use to which these tools will be put.

It is obviously not possible to cover the subject of tools fully here. For those who wish to learn more about tools and their use there is a book entitled *How to Choose and Use Car Tools* available from the publishers of this manual.

Maintenance and minor repair tool kit

The tools given in this list should be considered as a minimum requirement if routine maintenance, servicing and minor repair operations are to be undertaken. We recommend the purchase of combination spanners (ring one end, open-ended the other); although more expensive than open-ended ones, they do give the advantages of both types of spanner.

> Combination spanners - 10, 11, 12, 13, 14 & 17 mm
> Adjustable spanner - 9 inch
> Engine sump/transmission drain plug key
> Spark plug spanner (with rubber insert)
> Spark plug gap adjustment tool
> Set of feeler gauges
> Brake bleed nipple spanner
> Screwdriver - 4 in long x $\frac{1}{4}$ in dia (flat blade)
> Screwdriver - 4 in long x $\frac{1}{4}$ in dia (cross blade)
> Combination pliers - 6 inch
> Hacksaw (junior)
> Tyre pump
> Tyre pressure gauge
> Oil can
> Fine emery cloth (1 sheet)
> Wire brush (small)
> Funnel (medium size)

Repair and overhaul tool kit

These tools are virtually essential for anyone undertaking any major repairs to a motor vehicle, and are additional to those given in the *Maintenance and minor repair* list. Included in this list is a comprehensive set of sockets. Although these are expensive they will be found invaluable as they are so versatile - particularly if various drives are included in the set. We recommend the $\frac{1}{2}$ in square-drive type, as this can be used with most proprietary torque wrenches. If you cannot afford a socket set, even bought piecemeal, then inexpensive tubular box spanners are a useful alternative.

The tools in this list will occasionally need to be supplemented by tools from the *Special* list.

> Sockets (or box spanners) to cover range in previous list
> Reversible ratchet drive (for use with sockets)
> Extension piece, 10 inch (for use with sockets)
> Universal joint (for use with sockets)
> Torque wrench (for use with sockets)
> 'Mole' wrench - 8 inch
> Ball pein hammer
> Soft-faced hammer, plastic or rubber
> Screwdriver - 6 in long x $\frac{5}{16}$ in dia (flat blade)
> Screwdriver - 2 in long x $\frac{5}{16}$ in square (flat blade)
> Screwdriver - 1$\frac{1}{2}$ in long x $\frac{1}{4}$ in dia (cross blade)
> Screwdriver - 3 in long x $\frac{1}{8}$ in dia (electricians)
> Pliers - electricians side cutters
> Pliers - needle nosed
> Pliers - circlip (internal and external)
> Cold chisel - $\frac{1}{2}$ inch
> Scriber
> Scraper
> Centre punch
> Pin punch
> Hacksaw
> Valve grinding tool
> Steel rule/straight-edge
> Allen keys
> Selection of files
> Wire brush (large)
> Axle-stands
> Jack (strong scissor or hydraulic type)

Special tools

The tools in this list are those which are not used regularly, are expensive to buy, or which need to be used in accordance with their manufacturers' instructions. Unless relatively difficult mechanical jobs are undertaken frequently, it will not be economic to buy many of these tools. Where this is the case, you could consider clubbing together with friends (or joining a motorists' club) to make a joint purchase, or borrowing the tools against a deposit from a local garage or tool hire specialist.

The following list contains only those tools and instruments freely available to the public, and not those special tools produced by the vehicle manufacturer specifically for its dealer network. You will find occasional references to these manufacturers' special tools in the text of this manual. Generally, an alternative method of doing the job without the vehicle manufacturers' special tool is given. However, sometimes, there is no alternative to using them. Where this is the case and the relevant tool cannot be bought or borrowed, you will have to entrust the work to a franchised garage.

> Valve spring compressor
> Piston ring compressor
> Balljoint separator
> Universal hub/bearing puller
> Impact screwdriver
> Micrometer and/or vernier gauge
> Dial gauge
> Stroboscopic timing light

Dwell angle meter/tachometer
Universal electrical multi-meter
Cylinder compression gauge
Lifting tackle (photo)
Trolley jack
Light with extension lead

Buying tools

For practically all tools, a tool factor is the best source since he will have a very comprehensive range compared with the average garage or accessory shop. Having said that, accessory shops often offer excellent quality tools at discount prices, so it pays to shop around.

Remember, you don't have to buy the most expensive items on the shelf, but it is always advisable to steer clear of the very cheap tools. There are plenty of good tools around at reasonable prices, so ask the proprietor or manager of the shop for advice before making a purchase.

Care and maintenance of tools

Having purchased a reasonable tool kit, it is necessary to keep the tools in a clean serviceable condition. After use, always wipe off any dirt, grease and metal particles using a clean, dry cloth, before putting the tools away. Never leave them lying around after they have been used. A simple tool rack on the garage or workshop wall, for items such as screwdrivers and pliers is a good idea. Store all normal wrenches and sockets in a metal box. Any measuring instruments, gauges, meters, etc, must be carefully stored where they cannot be damaged or become rusty.

Take a little care when tools are used. Hammer heads inevitably become marked and screwdrivers lose the keen edge on their blades from time to time. A little timely attention with emery cloth or a file will soon restore items like this to a good serviceable finish.

Working facilities

Not to be forgotten when discussing tools, is the workshop itself. If anything more than routine maintenance is to be carried out, some form of suitable working area becomes essential.

It is appreciated that many an owner mechanic is forced by circumstances to remove an engine or similar item, without the benefit of a garage or workshop. Having done this, any repairs should always be done under the cover of a roof.

Wherever possible, any dismantling should be done on a clean, flat workbench or table at a suitable working height.

Any workbench needs a vice: one with a jaw opening of 4 in (100 mm) is suitable for most jobs. As mentioned previously, some clean dry storage space is also required for tools, as well as for lubricants, cleaning fluids, touch-up paints and so on, which become necessary.

Another item which may be required, and which has a much more general usage, is an electric drill with a chuck capacity of at least $\frac{5}{16}$ in (8 mm). This, together with a good range of twist drills, is virtually essential for fitting accessories such as mirrors and reversing lights.

Last, but not least, always keep a supply of old newspapers and clean, lint-free rags available, and try to keep any working area as clean as possible.

Spanner jaw gap comparison table

Jaw gap (in)	Spanner size
0.250	$\frac{1}{4}$ in AF
0.276	7 mm
0.313	$\frac{5}{16}$ in AF
0.315	8 mm
0.344	$\frac{11}{32}$ in AF; $\frac{1}{8}$ in Whitworth
0.354	9 mm
0.375	$\frac{3}{8}$ in AF
0.394	10 mm
0.433	11 mm
0.438	$\frac{7}{16}$ in AF
0.445	$\frac{3}{16}$ in Whitworth; $\frac{1}{4}$ in BSF
0.472	12 mm
0.500	$\frac{1}{2}$ in AF
0.512	13 mm
0.525	$\frac{1}{4}$ in Whitworth; $\frac{5}{16}$ in BSF
0.551	14 mm
0.563	$\frac{9}{16}$ in AF
0.591	15 mm
0.600	$\frac{5}{16}$ in Whitworth; $\frac{3}{8}$ in BSF
0.625	$\frac{5}{8}$ in AF
0.630	16 mm
0.669	17 mm
0.686	$\frac{11}{16}$ in AF
0.709	18 mm
0.710	$\frac{3}{8}$ in Whitworth; $\frac{7}{16}$ in BSF
0.748	19 mm
0.750	$\frac{3}{4}$ in AF
0.813	$\frac{13}{16}$ in AF
0.820	$\frac{7}{16}$ in Whitworth; $\frac{1}{2}$ in BSF
0.866	22 mm
0.875	$\frac{7}{8}$ in AF
0.920	$\frac{1}{2}$ in Whitworth; $\frac{9}{16}$ in BSF
0.938	$\frac{15}{16}$ in AF
0.945	24 mm
1.000	1 in AF
1.010	$\frac{9}{16}$ in Whitworth; $\frac{5}{8}$ in BSF
1.024	26 mm
1.063	$1\frac{1}{16}$ in AF; 27 mm
1.100	$\frac{5}{8}$ in Whitworth; $\frac{11}{16}$ in BSF
1.125	$1\frac{1}{8}$ in AF
1.181	30 mm
1.200	$\frac{11}{16}$ in Whitworth; $\frac{3}{4}$ in BSF
1.250	$1\frac{1}{4}$ in AF
1.260	32 mm
1.300	$\frac{3}{4}$ in Whitworth; $\frac{7}{8}$ in BSF
1.313	$1\frac{5}{16}$ in AF
1.390	$\frac{13}{16}$ in Whitworth; $\frac{15}{16}$ in BSF
1.417	36 mm
1.438	$1\frac{7}{16}$ in AF
1.480	$\frac{7}{8}$ in Whitworth; 1 in BSF
1.500	$1\frac{1}{2}$ in AF
1.575	40 mm; $\frac{15}{16}$ in Whitworth
1.614	41 mm
1.625	$1\frac{5}{8}$ in AF
1.670	1 in Whitworth; $1\frac{1}{8}$ in BSF
1.688	$1\frac{11}{16}$ in AF
1.811	46 mm
1.813	$1\frac{13}{16}$ in AF
1.860	$1\frac{1}{8}$ in Whitworth; $1\frac{1}{4}$ in BSF
1.875	$1\frac{7}{8}$ in AF
1.969	50 mm
2.000	2 in AF
2.050	$1\frac{1}{4}$ in Whitworth; $1\frac{3}{8}$ in BSF
2.165	55 mm
2.362	60 mm

A Haltrac hoist and gantry in use during a typical engine removal sequence

Jacking and Towing

Jacking

The jack supplied with the vehicle is not designed for service or repair operations, but purely for changing a wheel in the event of a puncture. A strong pillar or trolley type jack, supplemented with safety stands, should be employed for maintenance and repair tasks requiring the vehicle to be raised.

The jack point location is of particular importance on a vehicle of this type. Always locate a wood block between the jack and the underframe to protect the metal from deforming.

At the front, position the jack directly underneath the side-members and in line with the suspension arm centres. At the rear, position the jack under the triangular suspension arms so that the wood block straddles the two, locating in the holes as shown in the accompanying illustrations. At the side, position the jack and block as shown directly under the body valance under the front door.

Note: *Never lift the vehicle with the jack under the steering or suspension components or under the towing hooks.*

Towing

Should you have the misfortune to require the vehicle to be towed home or to a garage, it is essential that the correct procedure is adhered to.

Where possible, use a tow rope (in preference to chains) and ensure that it is of sufficient length. Towing hooks are provided at the front and rear of the vehicle as shown in the illustrations, and only these should be used for towing or when being towed. Never attach the tow rope to suspension or body parts.

When towing a vehicle equipped with automatic transmission, it must be remembered that the transmission fluid pump is driven directly by the engine. The front wheels must therefore be raised clear of the ground when towing. Under circumstances in which the maximum distance to be towed does not exceed 30 miles (50 km), the vehicle may be towed normally at a speed of 18 mph (30 km/h) or less, but an extra 4 pints (2 litres) of transmission fluid must be added to the transmission before commencing the journey. This additional oil must then be drained off on arrival at your destination.

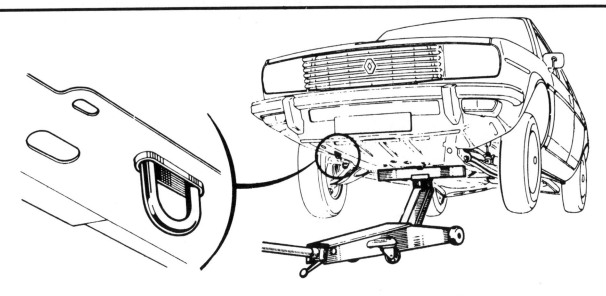

The towing eye location at the front of the vehicle – note jacking position

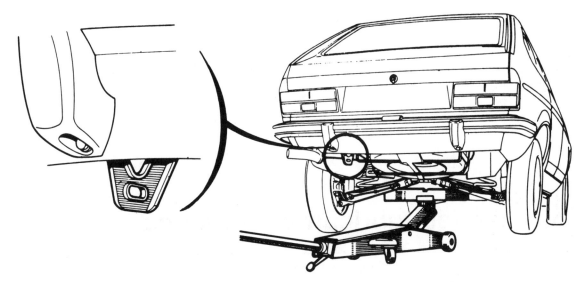

The towing eye location at the rear of the vehicle – note jacking position

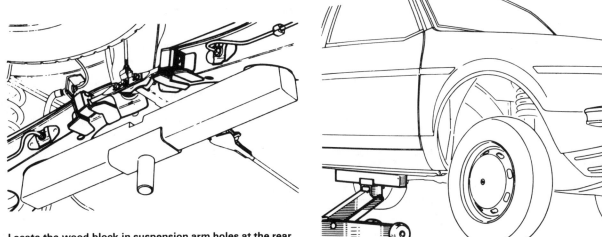

Locate the wood block in suspension arm holes at the rear

Jack location for side lifting

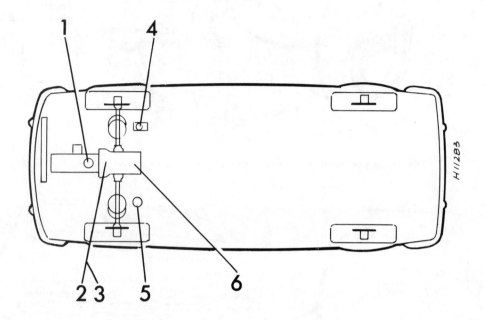

Recommended lubricants and fluids

Component or system	Lubricant type or specification	Castrol product
Engine (1)	20W/50 multigrade engine oil	GTX
Manual transmission (2)	SAE 80W hypoid gear oil to API GL4 or API GL5	Hypoy B EP80
Automatic transmission (3)	Automatic transmission fluid (Dexron type)	TQ Dexron® II
Brake fluid reservoir (4)	SAE J1703 hydraulic fluid	Castrol Girling Universal brake and Clutch Fluid
Power-assisted steering (5)	Automatic transmission fluid (Dexron type)	TQ Dexron® II
Final drive with automatic transmission (6)	SAE 80W hypoid gear oil to API GL5	Hypoid B EP80

Note: *The above are general recommendations only. Lubrication requirements may vary from territory to territory and according to operating conditions. Consult the operator's handbook supplied with the vehicle*

Safety first!

Professional motor mechanics are trained in safe working procedures. However enthusiastic you may be about getting on with the job in hand, do take the time to ensure that your safety is not put at risk. A moment's lack of attention can result in an accident, as can failure to observe certain elementary precautions.

There will always be new ways of having accidents, and the following points do not pretend to be a comprehensive list of all dangers; they are intended rather to make you aware of the risks and to encourage a safety-conscious approach to all work you carry out on your vehicle.

Essential DOs and DON'Ts

DON'T rely on a single jack when working underneath the vehicle. Always use reliable additional means of support, such as axle stands, securely placed under a part of the vehicle that you know will not give way.

DON'T attempt to loosen or tighten high-torque nuts (e.g. wheel hub nuts) while the vehicle is on a jack; it may be pulled off.

DON'T start the engine without first ascertaining that the transmission is in neutral (or 'Park' where applicable) and the parking brake applied.

DON'T suddenly remove the filler cap from a hot cooling system — cover it with a cloth and release the pressure gradually first, or you may get scalded by escaping coolant.

DON'T attempt to drain oil until you are sure it has cooled sufficiently to avoid scalding you.

DON'T grasp any part of the engine, exhaust or catalytic converter without first ascertaining that it is sufficiently cool to avoid burning you.

DON'T syphon toxic liquids such as fuel, brake fluid or antifreeze by mouth, or allow them to remain on your skin.

DON'T disconnect any air conditioning system hoses without first having the system discharged by a Renault dealer or refrigeration engineer.

DON'T inhale brake lining dust — it is injurious to health.

DON'T allow any spilt oil or grease to remain on the floor — wipe it up straight away, before someone slips on it.

DON'T use ill-fitting spanners or other tools which may slip and cause injury.

DON'T attempt to lift a heavy component which may be beyond your capability — get assistance.

DON'T rush to finish a job, or take unverified short cuts.

DON'T allow children or animals in or around an unattended vehicle.

DO wear eye protection when using power tools such as drill, sander, bench grinder etc, and when working under the vehicle.

DO use a barrier cream on your hands prior to undertaking dirty jobs — it will protect your skin from infection as well as making the dirt easier to remove afterwards; but make sure your hands aren't left slippery.

DO keep loose clothing (cuffs, tie etc) and long hair well out of the way of moving mechanical parts.

DO remove rings, wristwatch etc, before working on the vehicle — especially the electrical system.

DO ensure that any lifting tackle used has a safe working load rating adequate for the job.

DO keep your work area tidy — it is only too easy to fall over articles left lying around.

DO get someone to check periodically that all is well, when working alone on the vehicle.

DO carry out work in a logical sequence and check that everything is correctly assembled and tightened afterwards.

DO remember that your vehicle's safety affects that of yourself and others. If in doubt on any point, get specialist advice.

IF, in spite of following these precautions, you are unfortunate enough to injure yourself, seek medical attention as soon as possible.

Fire

Remember at all times that petrol (gasoline) is highly flammable. Never smoke, or have any kind of naked flame around, when working on the vehicle. But the risk does not end there — a spark caused by an electrical short-circuit, by two metal surfaces contacting each other, or even by static electricity built up in your body under certain conditions, can ignite petrol vapour, which in a confined space is highly explosive.

Always disconnect the battery earth (ground) terminal before working on any part of the fuel system, and never risk spilling fuel on to a hot engine or exhaust.

It is recommended that a fire extinguisher of a type suitable for fuel and electrical fires is kept handy in the garage or workplace at all times. Never try to extinguish a fuel or electrical fire with water.

Fumes

Certain fumes are highly toxic and can quickly cause unconsciousness and even death if inhaled to any extent. Petrol (gasoline) vapour comes into this category, as do the vapours from certain solvents such as trichloroethylene. Any draining or pouring of such volatile fluids should be done in a well ventilated area.

When using cleaning fluids and solvents, read the instructions carefully. Never use materials from unmarked containers — they may give off poisonous vapours.

Never run the engine of a motor vehicle in an enclosed space such as a garage. Exhaust fumes contain carbon monoxide which is extremely poisonous; if you need to run the engine, always do so in the open air or at least have the rear of the vehicle outside the workplace.

If you are fortunate enough to have the use of an inspection pit, never drain or pour petrol, and never run the engine, while the vehicle is standing over it; the fumes, being heavier than air, will concentrate in the pit with possibly lethal results.

The battery

Never cause a spark, or allow a naked light, near the vehicle's battery. It will normally be giving off a certain amount of hydrogen gas, which is highly explosive.

Always disconnect the battery earth (ground) terminal before working on the fuel or electrical systems.

If possible, loosen the filler plugs or cover when charging the battery from an external source. Do not charge at an excessive rate or the battery may burst.

Take care when topping up and when carrying the battery. The acid electrolyte, even when diluted, is very corrosive and should not be allowed to contact the eyes or skin.

If you ever need to prepare electrolyte yourself, always add the acid slowly to the water, and never the other way round. Protect against splashes by wearing rubber gloves and goggles.

Mains electricity

When using an electric power tool, inspection light etc, which works from the mains, always ensure that the appliance is correctly connected to its plug and that, where necessary, it is properly earthed (grounded). Do not use such appliances in damp conditions and, again, beware of creating a spark or applying excessive heat in the vicinity of fuel or fuel vapour.

Ignition HT voltage

A severe electric shock can result from touching certain parts of the ignition system, such as the HT leads, when the engine is running or being cranked, particularly if components are damp or the insulation is defective. Where an electronic ignition system is fitted, the HT voltage is much higher and could prove fatal.

Routine maintenance

Maintenance is essential for ensuring safety and desirable for the purpose of getting the best in terms of performance and economy from your car. Over the years the need for periodic lubrication – oiling, greasing and so on – has been drastically reduced if not totally eliminated. This has unfortunately tended to lead some owners to think that because no such action is required, components either no longer exist, or will last forever. This is a serious delusion. It follows therefore that the largest initial element of maintenance is visual examination. This may lead to repairs or renewals.

The summary below gives a schedule of routine maintenance operations. More detailed information on the respective items is given in the Chapter concerned. Before starting on any maintenance procedures, make a list and obtain any items or parts that may be required. Make sure you have the necessary tools to complete the servicing requirements. Where the vehicle has to be raised clear of the ground pay particular attention to safety and ensure that chassis stands and/or blocks supplement the jack. Do not rely on the jack supplied with the car – it was designed purely to raise the car for changing a wheel in the event of a puncture.

Check the coolant level in the expansion bottle and top up as detailed in Chapter 2, if necessary (photo)
Check the windscreen washer bottle fluid level and top up, if necessary (photo)
Check the battery electrolyte level (see Chapter 10)
Make a general inspection for oil, water or petrol leaks and repair as necessary
Check tyre pressures (photo)
Examine tyres for wear
Check the correct operation of all lights
Check the operation of the flasher units
Check the operation of the windscreen wipers and washer
Check the operation and efficiency of the horn

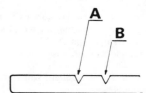

Maintain engine oil level between marks 'A' and 'B' on dipstick

Every 250 miles (400 km) or weekly – whichever comes first

Check the oil level in the sump and top up with the correct grade of oil if required (photo)

Topping up the engine oil

Check coolant level in expansion bottle

Check windscreen washer reservoir fluid level

Check the tyre pressures

Spark plug refitting using the special spanner supplied with the car. Tighten with one hand only

Every 5000 miles (8000 km) or six months – whichever comes first

Change the engine oil whilst it is hot
Remove, clean and gap the spark plugs – see Chapter 4 (photo)
Wipe the ignition leads clean and check their connections for security
Inspect the condition and tension of the alternator drivebelt
The power steering pump drivebelt must also be checked, as must the air conditioning compressor drivebelt (where fitted). Adjust or renew as necessary
On air conditioned models, check the respective system components and hoses for security and condition. Refer to Chapter 10 for precautionary details of working on air conditioning equipment
Check the oil level in the power steering reservoir and top up if necessary (refer to Chapter 11 for details). The constant need to top up indicates a leak from the system and this must be found and repaired as soon as possible
Check the fluid level in the brake master cylinder and top up if necessary (photo). The constant necessity to top up the fluid level indicates a fault in the brake circuit and this must be looked into without delay – see Chapter 9

Brake/clutch master cylinder fluid level check

Check the transmission oil level. On manual transmission, there is an oil level plug on the side of the housing, whilst on automatic transmission there is a dipstick. Full instructions for checking and topping up the automatic transmission are given in Chapter 7
Raise the vehicle and make a brief inspection of the steering and suspension components to ensure they are secure and in serviceable condition. Also check the exhaust system for condition and security whilst under the vehicle
On fuel injection models, check the system for signs of leaks and the respective components for condition and security

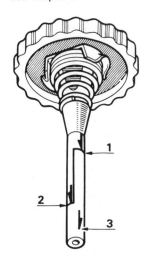

Power steering dipstick/filler cap showing level markings

1 Maximum level – system   cold
   hot   3 Minimum level
2 Maximum level – system

Every 10 000 miles (16 000 km) or yearly – whichever comes first

In addition to, or instead of, the work specified in the 5000-mile schedule
Renew the engine oil and oil filter. You will have to remove the engine undertray for access to the oil filter. Wipe the oil filter body with a dry rag to remove any oil, and grip firmly by hand and unscrew to remove. Allow for a certain amount of oil spillage and place a container or rag under the filter. It may be necessary to unscrew the filter using a strap wrench or other tool if it is

reluctant to move (photo). Lubricate the new seal and screw the new filter into position, tightening as described in Chapter 1, or according to the instructions on the filter

Refit the sump drain plug and then refill with the recommended lubricant to the correct level. Before refitting the undertray, start the engine and check for any signs of oil leakage around the filter joint

Renew the air filter element (carburettor and fuel injection models), referring to Chapter 3. (More frequent renewal may be needed in dusty conditions)

Check the carburettor linkages and adjustments as given in Chapter 3

Check the fuel lines for leaks and security. Clean fuel pump and filter gauge of sediment. Check that the inlet and exhaust manifolds are securely located

Remove distributor cap and check contact points adjustment (if applicable) and condition (photo). Also renew the spark plugs. Refer to Chapter 4 for ignition maintenance details

Check the clutch operating clearance as given in Chapter 5 and, if necessary, adjust

Make an inspection of all rigid and flexible brake hoses and connections, look for signs of leakage and/or deterioration, renew as applicable (Chapter 9)

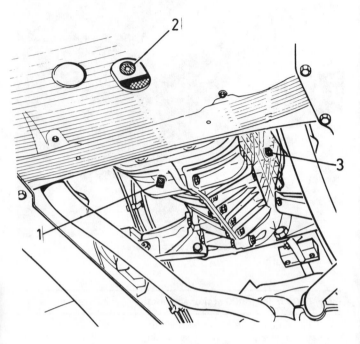

Drain/filler plug locations

1 Differential drain plug   3 Manual gearbox level/
2 Engine drain plug   filler plug

Removing the oil filter using a universal clamp

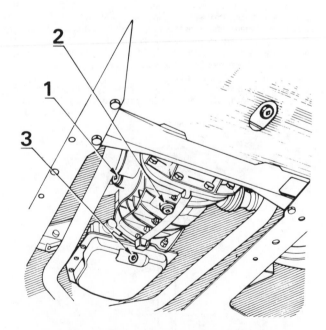

Automatic transmission drain/filler plug locations

1 Filler plug (differential)   3 Drain plug (automatic
2 Drain plug (differential)   transmission)

Check contact breaker points clearance (when applicable)

Check that the disc pad wear detector wiring connections are secure
Inspect the pads for wear and renew if necessary
Check the handbrake adjustment and take up any excess play, if necessary. Check the cable and linkages for wear or defects
Check the driveshafts for any signs of oil leakage and also for wear in the joint. Renew if necessary
Check the respective steering and suspension joints for signs of excessive wear. Check the shock absorbers for any signs of leakage and also for security
Check the wheel hubs for play and the wheel retaining nuts for security
Inspect the tyres for signs of excessive or uneven wear. If uneven wear is present, this is due to incorrect pressures or steering alignment. The latter should be checked and adjusted by your local Renault dealer
Check, and repair as necessary, the respective body fittings. In particular, pay attention to the bumpers and mountings, the door and tailgate hinges and catches
Where fitted, check the sunroof drainage channels
Check the seat belt mountings for security
Check around the underbody for signs of corrosion and repair as necessary. Minor repairs to bodywork and paintwork are dealt with in Chapter 12

Every 20 000 miles (32 000 km) or 2 years, whichever comes first

In addition to, or instead of, the work specified in the previous schedules

Drain and renew the transmission oil (manual or automatic), and refill with the correct grade and quantity of lubricant specified
Drain and renew the differential housing oil (automatic transmission only)
Renew the brake servo unit air filter (see Chapter 9)

Every 30 000 miles (45 000 km) or three years – whichever comes first

In addition to, or instead of, the work specified in the previous schedules

On fuel injection models, renew the fuel filter (in the fuel line – refer to Chapter 3 for details
Drain the cooling system completely and renew the antifreeze solution. Top up and bleed the system as given in Chapter 2
Renew the braking system hydraulic fluid. Consideration should be given to renewing all rubber seals, hoses etc at the same time

Fault diagnosis

Introduction

The vehicle owner who does his or her own maintenance according to the recommended schedules should not have to use this section of the manual very often. Modern component reliability is such that, provided those items subject to wear or deterioration are inspected or renewed at the specified intervals, sudden failure is comparatively rare. Faults do not usually just happen as a result of sudden failure, but develop over a period of time. Major mechanical failures in particular are usually preceded by characteristic symptoms over hundreds or even thousands of miles. Those components which do occasionally fail without warning are often small and easily carried in the vehicle.

With any fault finding, the first step is to decide where to begin investigations. Sometimes this is obvious, but on other occasions a little detective work will be necessary. The owner who makes half a dozen haphazard adjustments or replacements may be successful in curing a fault (or its symptoms), but he will be none the wiser if the fault recurs and he may well have spent more time and money than was necessary. A calm and logical approach will be found to be more satisfactory in the long run. Always take into account any warning signs or abnormalities that may have been noticed in the period preceding the fault – power loss, high or low gauge readings, unusual noises or smells, etc – and remember that failure of components such as fuses or spark plugs may only be pointers to some underlying fault.

The pages which follow here are intended to help in cases of failure to start or breakdown on the road. There is also a Fault Diagnosis Section at the end of each Chapter which should be consulted if the preliminary checks prove unfruitful. Whatever the fault, certain basic principles apply. These are as follows:

Verify the fault. This is simply a matter of being sure that you know what the symptoms are before starting work. This is particularly important if you are investigating a fault for someone else who may not have described it very accurately.

Don't overlook the obvious. For example, if the vehicle won't start, is there petrol in the tank? (Don't take anyone else's word on this particular point, and don't trust the fuel gauge either!) If an electrical fault is indicated, look for loose or broken wires before digging out the test gear.

Cure the disease, not the symptom. Substituting a flat battery with a fully charged one will get you off the hard shoulder, but if the underlying cause is not attended to, the new battery will go the same way. Similarly, changing oil-fouled spark plugs for a new set will get you moving again, but remember that the reason for the fouling (if it wasn't simply an incorrect grade of plug) will have to be established and corrected.

Don't take anything for granted. Particularly, don't forget that a 'new' component may itself be defective (especially if it's been rattling round in the boot for months), and don't leave components out of a fault diagnosis sequence just because they are new or recently fitted. When you do finally diagnose a difficult fault, you'll probably realise that all the evidence was there from the start.

Electrical faults

Electrical faults can be more puzzling than straightforward mechanical failures, but they are no less susceptible to logical analysis if the basic principles of operation are understood. Vehicle electrical wiring exists in extremely unfavourable conditions – heat, vibration and chemical attack – and the first things to look for are loose or corroded connections and broken or chafed wires, especially where the wires pass through holes in the bodywork or are subject to vibration.

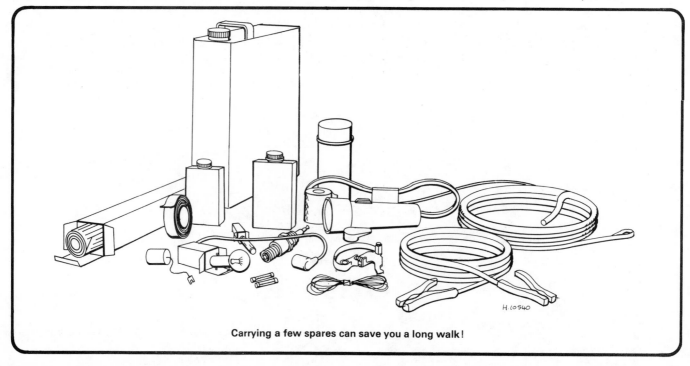

Carrying a few spares can save you a long walk!

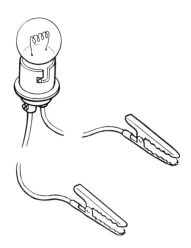

A simple test lamp is useful for tracing electrical faults

All metal-bodied vehicles in current production have one pole of the battery 'earthed', ie connected to the vehicle bodywork, and in nearly all modern vehicles it is the negative (–) terminal. The various electrical components – motors, bulb holders etc – are also connected to earth, either by means of a lead or directly by their mountings. Electric current flows through the component and then back to the battery via the bodywork. If the component mounting is loose or corroded, or if a good path back to the battery is not available, the circuit will be incomplete and malfunction will result. The engine and/or gearbox are also earthed by means of flexible metal straps to the body or subframe; if these straps are loose or missing, starter motor, generator and ignition trouble may result.

Assuming the earth return to be satisfactory, electrical faults will be due either to component malfunction or to defects in the current supply. Individual components are dealt with in Chapter 10. If supply wires are broken or cracked internally this results in an open-circuit, and the easiest way to check for this is to bypass the suspect wire temporarily with a length of wire having a crocodile clip or suitable connector at each end. Alternatively, a 12V test lamp can be used to verify the presence of supply voltage at various points along the wire and the break can be thus isolated.

If a bare portion of a live wire touches the bodywork or other earthed metal part, the electricity will take the low-resistance path thus formed back to the battery: this is known as a short-circuit. Hopefully a short-circuit will blow a fuse, but otherwise it may cause burning of the insulation (and possibly further short-circuits) or even a fire. This is why it is inadvisable to bypass persistently blowing fuses with silver foil or wire.

Spares and tool kit

Most vehicles are supplied only with sufficient tools for wheel changing; the *Maintenance and minor repair* tool kit detailed in *Tools and working facilities,* with the addition of a hammer, is probably sufficient for those repairs that most motorists would consider attempting at the roadside. In addition a few items which can be fitted without too much trouble in the event of a breakdown should be carried. Experience and available space will modify the list below, but the following may save having to call on professional assistance:

Spark plugs, clean and correctly gapped
HT lead and plug cap – long enough to reach the plug furthest from the distributor
Distributor rotor, condenser and contact breaker points (as applicable)
Drivebelt(s) – emergency type may suffice
Spare fuses
Set of principal light bulbs
Tin of radiator sealer and hose bandage
Exhaust bandage
Roll of insulating tape

Length of soft iron wire
Length of electrical flex
Torch or inspection lamp (can double as test lamp)
Battery jump leads
Tow-rope
Ignition waterproofing aerosol
Litre of engine oil
Sealed can of hydraulic fluid
Emergency windscreen
'Jubilee' clips
Tube of filler paste

If spare fuel is carried, a can designed for the purpose should be used to minimise risks of leakage and collision damage. A first aid kit and a warning triangle, whilst not at present compulsory in the UK, are obviously sensible items to carry in addition to the above.

When touring abroad it may be advisable to carry additional spares which, even if you cannot fit them yourself, could save having to wait while parts are obtained. The items below may be worth considering:

Throttle cables
Cylinder head gaskets
Alternator brushes

One of the motoring organisations will be able to advise on availability of fuel etc in foreign countries.

Engine will not start

Engine fails to turn when starter operated

Flat battery (recharge, use jump leads, or push start)
Battery terminals loose or corroded
Battery earth to body defective
Engine earth strap loose or broken
Starter motor (or solenoid) wiring loose or broken
Automatic transmission selector in wrong position, or inhibitor switch faulty
Ignition/starter switch faulty
Major mechanical failure (seizure)
Starter or solenoid internal fault (see Chapter 10)

Starter motor turns engine slowly

Partially discharged battery (recharge, use jump leads, or push start)
Battery terminals loose or corroded
Battery earth to body defective
Engine earth strap loose
Starter motor (or solenoid) wiring loose
Starter motor internal fault (see Chapter 10)

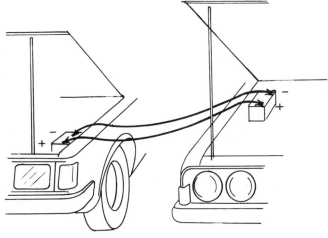

H.10541

Correct way to connect jump leads! Do not allow car bodies to touch!

Starter motor spins without turning engine
Flywheel gear teeth damaged or worn
Starter motor mounting bolts loose

Engine turns normally but fails to start
Damp or dirty HT leads and distributor cap (crank engine and check for spark)
Dirty or incorrectly gapped distributor points (if applicable)
No fuel in tank (check for delivery at carburettor) (photo)
Excessive choke (hot engine) or insufficient choke (cold engine)
Fouled or incorrectly gapped spark plugs (remove, clean and regap)
Other ignition system fault (see Chapter 4)
Other fuel system fault (see Chapter 3)
Poor compression (see Chapter 1)
Major mechanical failure (eg camshaft drive)

Engine fires but will not run
Insufficient choke (cold engine)
Air leaks at carburettor or inlet manifold
Fuel starvation (see Chapter 3)
Ballast resistor defective, or other ignition fault (see Chapter 4)

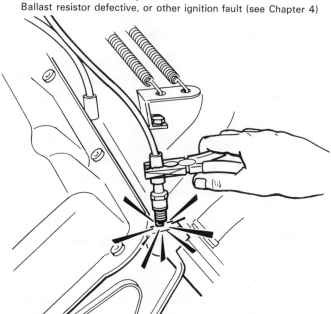

Crank engine and check for spark. Be sure to use an insulated tool, especially if electronic ignition is fitted

Remove fuel pipe from carburettor and check for fuel delivery. Do not try this on fuel injection models

---

Engine cuts out and will not restart

Engine cuts out suddenly – ignition fault
Loose or disconnected LT wires
Wet HT leads or distributor cap (after traversing water splash)
Coil or condenser failure (check for spark)
Other ignition fault (see Chapter 4)

Engine misfires before cutting out – fuel fault
Fuel tank empty
Fuel pump defective or filter blocked (check for delivery)
Fuel tank filler vent blocked (suction will be evident on releasing cap)
Carburettor needle valve sticking
Carburettor jets blocked (fuel contaminated)
Other fuel system fault (see Chapter 3)

Engine cuts out – other causes
Serious overheating
Major mechanical failure (eg camshaft drive)

Engine overheats

Ignition (no-charge) warning light illuminated
Slack or broken drivebelt – retension or renew (Chapter 2)

Ignition warning light not illuminated
Coolant loss due to internal or external leakage (see Chapter 2)
Thermostat defective
Low oil level
Brakes binding
Radiator clogged externally or internally
Electric cooling fan not operating correctly (if applicable)
Engine waterways clogged
Ignition timing incorrect or automatic advance malfunctioning
Mixture too weak

Note: *Do not add cold water to an overheated engine or damage may result*

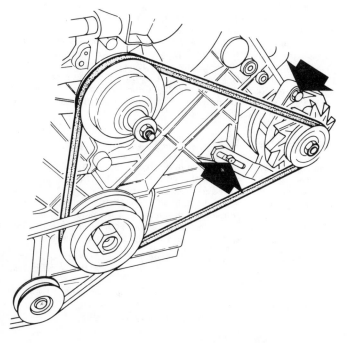

A slack drivebelt can cause overheating and battery charging problems. Slacken bolts (arrowed) to adjust

Low engine oil pressure

Gauge reads low or warning light illuminated with engine running
    Oil level low or incorrect grade
    Defective gauge or sender unit
    Wire to sender unit earthed
    Engine overheating
    Oil filter clogged or bypass valve defective
    Oil pressure relief valve defective
    Oil pick-up strainer clogged
    Oil pump worn or mountings loose
    Worn main or big-end bearings
Note: *Low oil pressure in a high-mileage engine at tickover is not necessarily a cause for concern. Sudden pressure loss at speed is far more significant. In any event, check the gauge or warning light sender before condemning the engine.*

Engine noises

Pre-ignition (pinking) on acceleration
    Incorrect grade of fuel
    Ignition timing incorrect
    Distributor faulty or worn
    Worn or maladjusted carburettor
    Excessive carbon build-up in engine

Whistling or wheezing noises
    Leaking vacuum hose
    Leaking carburettor or manifold gasket
    Blowing head gasket

Tapping or rattling
    Incorrect valve clearances
    Worn valve gear
    Worn timing chain
    Broken piston ring (ticking noise)

Knocking or thumping
    Unintentional mechanical contact (eg fan blades)
    Worn drivebelt
    Peripheral component fault (generator, water pump etc)
    Worn big-end bearings (regular heavy knocking, perhaps less under load)
    Worn main bearings (rumbling and knocking, perhaps worsening under load)
    Piston slap (most noticeable when cold)

Chapter 1 Engine

Contents

Specifications

General

Engine type	90° V6, dohc, water-cooled, aluminium alloy cylinder head and crankcase with removable wet liners
Renault type number:	
R1273	112
R1275	144
R1278	140
Bore	3.465 in (88 mm)
Stroke	2.874 in (73 mm)
Capacity	162.6 cu in (2664 cc)
Compression ratio:	
R1273	8.65 : 1
R1275	8.2 : 1, 8.65 : 1 or 9.2 : 1
R1278	9.2 : 1
Firing order	1–6–3–5–2–4
Location of No 1 cylinder	Left-hand bank, flywheel end

Valve clearances (cold)

Inlet	0.004 in (0.10 mm)
Exhaust	0.010 in (0.25 mm)

Cylinder heads

Maximum allowable contact face distortion	0.002 in (0.05 mm) in 4 in (100 mm)

Cylinder head height:
    Early models ...... 4.365 ± 0.006 in (110.87 ± 0.15 mm)
    Later models ...... 4.373 ± 0.006 in (111.07 ± 0.15 mm)

Valves, guides and springs
Stem diameter ...... 0.315 in (8 mm)
Seat angle:
    Inlet ...... 120°
    Exhaust ...... 90°
Valve head diameter:
    Inlet ...... 1.732 in (44 mm)
    Exhaust ...... 1.457 in (37 mm)
Valve seat widths:
    Inlet ...... 0.067 to 0.082 in (1.7 to 2.1 mm)
    Exhaust ...... 0.079 to 0.094 in (2.0 to 2.4 mm)
Valve guides:
    Bore ...... 0.315 in (8 mm)
    External diameter – nominal ...... 0.512 in (13 mm)
Valve springs free length (approx) ...... 1.858 in (47.2 mm)

Valve timing

	Left-hand	Right-hand
Inlet valve opens	9° BTDC	7° BTDC
Inlet valve closes	45° ABDC	43° ABDC
Exhaust valve opens	45° BBDC	43° BBDC
Exhaust valve closes	9° ATDC	7° ATDC

Camshafts
Endplay ...... 0.003 to 0.005 in (0.07 to 0.14 mm)
Number of bearings 4
Drive ...... Chain

Liners
Bore ...... 3.4646 in (88 mm)
Base location diameter ...... 3.6803 in (93.48 mm)
Liner protrusion ...... 0.006 to 0.009 in (0.16 to 0.23 mm)
Liner base seal thickness:
    Blue tag ...... 0.0034 in (0.087 mm)
    White tag ...... 0.0040 in (0.102 mm)
    Red tag ...... 0.0048 in (0.122 mm)
    Yellow tag ...... 0.0057 in (0.147 mm)

Pistons and piston rings
Piston type ...... Alloy – 3 rings
Gudgeon pin fitting ...... Press fit in small-end – free turning in piston
Piston fitting direction ...... Arrow to timing gear end
Piston ring thickness:
    Top compression ring ...... 0.059 in (1.5 mm)
    2nd compression ring ...... 0.079 in (2 mm)
    Oil scraper ring ...... 0.158 in (4 mm)
Ring gap ...... Supplied pre-adjusted

Gudgeon pins
Length ...... 2.8346 in (72 mm)
Diameter – external ...... 0.9252 in (23.5 mm)
Diameter – internal ...... 0.5906 in (15 mm)

Connecting rods
Side clearance ...... 0.008 to 0.015 in (0.20 to 0.38 mm)
Shell bearing material ...... Aluminium-tin

Crankshaft
Shell bearings material ...... Aluminium-tin
Number of main bearings 4
Endplay ...... 0.003 to 0.010 in (0.07 to 0.27 mm)
Thrust washer thickness available ...... 0.0905 in (2.30 mm), 0.0944 in (2.40 mm), 0.0964 in (2.45 mm) and 0.0984 in (2.50 mm)

Main bearing journal diameters:
    Nominal diameter ...... 2.7583 in (70.062 mm)
    Regrind diameter ...... 2.7465 in (69.762 mm)
    Regrinding tolerance ...... -0.0007 in (0.019 mm)
Crankpin diameters:
    Nominal diameter ...... 2.0588 in (52.296 mm)
    Regrind diameter ...... 2.0471 in (51.996 mm)
    Regrinding tolerance ...... -0.0004 to 0.0011 in (0.010 to 0.029 mm)

Engine lubrication

Oil pump type	Gear driven with integral pressure relief valve
Oil pressure at 80°C (176°F):	
Minimum at 900 rpm	32 lbf/in² (2.2 bar)
Minimum at 4000 rpm	64 lbf/in² (4.4 bar)
Oil capacity:	
With filter	10.1 Imp pints (5.75 litres)
Less filter	9.7 Imp pints (5.5 litres)

Torque wrench settings

	lbf ft	Nm
Camshaft sprocket bolts	58	78
Access plug to camshaft	23	30
Camshaft retaining plate bolts	11	15
Camshaft pulley bolt	71 to 78	96 to 105
Big-end cap nuts (must be renewed)	34	46
Main bearing cap nuts*	23	30
Sump bolts	11 to 15	15 to 20
Crankshaft pulley nut	135	183
Flywheel bolts (must be renewed)	34	46
Converter driveplate bolts (must be renewed)	49 to 52	66 to 71
Inlet manifold bolts	8 to 11	10 to 15
Cylinder head bolts†:		
1 – Initial tightening	15	20
2 – 2nd tightening	45	61
3 – Loosen off, then retighten to	15	20
4 – Angle tighten further 115°		
Oil pump drive sprocket bolts	4	6
Chain tensioner bolt	7 to 11	10 to 15
Timing cover bolts	7 to 11	10 to 15
Taper seat spark plugs (no washers)	13 to 15	17 to 20

Torque given plus further tightening of 75°
† Refer to Sections 41 and 51 for details

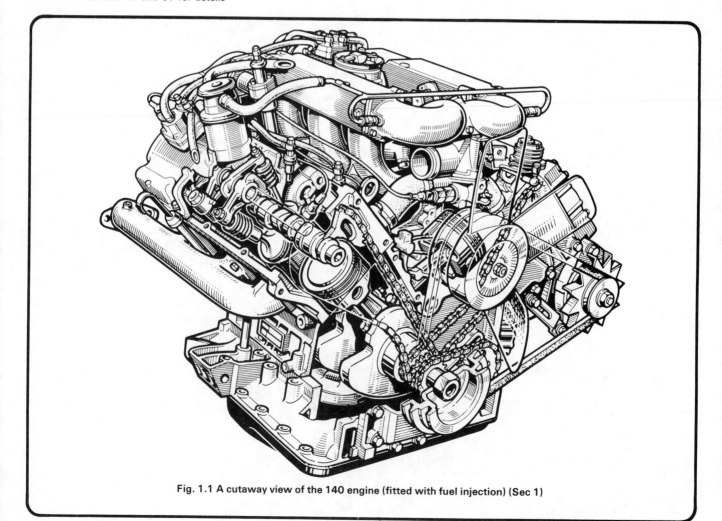

Fig. 1.1 A cutaway view of the 140 engine (fitted with fuel injection) (Sec 1)

1 General description and special notes

The V6 ohc engine fitted to the Renault 30 range of models is the product of collaboration between manufacturers Renault, Peugeot and Volvo. Its basic design is as follows.

The cylinder heads are of the crossflow type: that is to say, the inlet ports are on one side of the head and the exhaust ports on the other. There are separate alloy-cast iron valve seats fitted and the cylinder head bolts also retain the rocker arm mechanism.

The camshaft, journalled in four bearings of different sizes, are chain-driven from the front of the crankshaft; each chain being tensioned separately. The oil pump too is chain-driven off the crankshaft at the front end, and is located in the front of the block. The whole driving system is covered by a single section light alloy cover plate.

At the rear end of each camshaft there is an extra driving arrangement; on the right-hand side is a worm drive for the distributor and on the left, a cam for driving the mechanical fuel pump for cars with carburettors. The power steering pump unit is also driven from the rear end of the left-hand camshaft, by means of an external pulley.

The cylinder block has wet replaceable cast iron liners, which are class matched to the very light aluminium alloy pistons. These have two compression rings and one oil scraper ring.

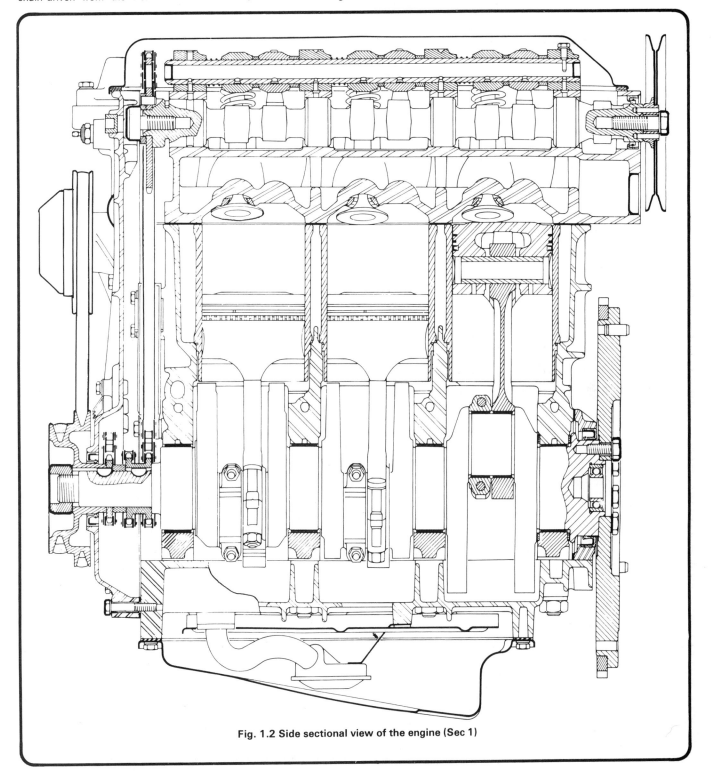

Fig. 1.2 Side sectional view of the engine (Sec 1)

The crankshaft is short, strong and has ground, surface-hardened bearing journals; it runs in four well-proportioned main bearings in the cylinder block. The main bearing caps and lower half of the crankcase are separate units, but the nuts for the main bearing caps are underneath (outside) the lower crankcase. This helps give added torsional strength to the light alloy engine construction. There are only three big-end crankpins, two connecting rods being mounted on each. The big-end bearings and main bearings run in renewable shells and all the crankpins can be ground to a limited undersize. The endfloat on the crankshaft is governed by variable size thrust washers.

The connecting rods are made of drop-forged steel; the gudgeon pins are pressed into them and journalled in the pistons.

In general, the information given in the following Sections refers to the most common models, having neither fuel injection nor air conditioning equipment fitted. On models fitted with these systems you will have to refer to the Chapters concerned (3 and 10) for details of the items in question. Particular care must be taken when working on air conditioned models.

2 Major operations possible with engine fitted

1   Where major overhaul or servicing is required it will be wise to remove the complete engine and obtain the ease of access provided by mounting the unit on a bench. However, the following components may be removed and refitted with the engine still in place in the vehicle:

(a) Cylinder head(s)
(b) Rocker shaft assembly
(c) Timing gear cover, camshaft sprockets and chains
(d) Oil pump
(e) Sump
(f) Pistons and connecting rods
(g) Cylinder liners
(h) Crankshaft front and rear oil seals
(j) Camshaft oil seal

3 Major operations requiring engine removal

1   With the engine removed from the vehicle, it is possible to achieve all of the items mentioned in the previous Section, plus the following:

(a) Crankshaft and main bearings – overhaul and refitting
(b) Crankcase – renewal or repair

4 Engine removal – general

1   Where only the engine is to be removed, there are few difficulties as it can be lifted direct from the engine compartment. If, however, the gearbox is also to be removed, it is not advisable to remove the two units combined, due to their size, weight and the gearbox location.
2   Ensure that the lifting tackle, sling and hoist support are up to the job, and that there is sufficient work area.
3   Remember to leave enough room to wheel the vehicle back out of the way once the engine is hoisted high enough. If a trolley hoist is used, it will not be necessary to move the vehicle, but the hoist will have to be moved back. Make sure it is on firm, level ground, with room to manoeuvre.
4   Whether one intends removing the engine on its own or the complete assembly of the engine and transmission, one must have an assistant. Read through the removal procedure completely before starting work and make sure you have all the equipment and help you require.
5   On air conditioned models it is **most important** that the system pipes and hoses are not disconnected unless the system has been depressurized. This should only be entrusted to your Renault dealer.
6   On models fitted with fuel injection, the detachment and where necessary removal of the system components is given more fully in Chapter 3.
7   When removing the engine, label or take a note of the respective hose and wiring connections to avoid confusion on reassembly. Do not trust to memory!

5 Engine – removal

1   Raise and support the bonnet. To provide further access, and prevent it being damaged during the removal operations, the bonnet should be detached and placed out of the way where it will not get knocked or scratched.
2   Unbolt and remove the engine undertray, then unscrew the sump drain plug and drain the engine oil into a suitable container.
3   On automatic transmission models, detach the oil cooler pipes at the radiator. Be prepared for spillage of oil.

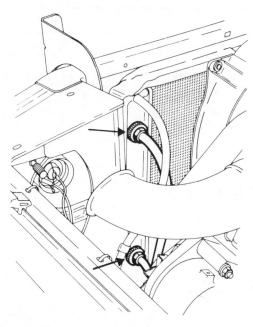

Fig. 1.3 Detach the oil cooler pipes – automatic transmission models (Sec 5)

4   On air conditioned models, remove the front grille panel to gain access to the condenser mountings on the radiator. Leaving the respective pipes connected, remove the compressor and place it to one side. Pivot the condenser out of the way and again do not disconnect the pipes. Refer to Section 40 of Chapter 10 for precautionary notes on the air conditioning system.
5   Referring to Chapter 2, drain the cooling system and remove the radiator with its shroud or (where applicable) the electric cooling fan motor unit. Detach the heater pipe hoses.
6   Disconnect the battery earth lead and then, taking note of their various positions, disconnect the respective ignition wires and associated engine wiring. Take particular note of the leads and wires to the starter motor. Remove or fold the wires back out of the way as applicable.
7   Remove the air filter (Chapter 3).
8   Remove the diagnostic socket from the rear of the right-hand cylinder bank and tie it back out of the way. Refit the engine lift bracket bolt.
9   Detach the fuel supply and vacuum hoses.
10 On fuel injection models, disconnect detach or remove as necessary the fuel feed pipe at the metering head, the fuel injectors, the auxiliary air device and the electromagnetic valve unit (refer to Chapter 3 for further details).
11 Loosen the power steering pump unit mountings, remove the drivebelt and then the pump unit, but leave the hoses attached. Rest the pump unit on the bulkhead in such a manner that it will not leak.
12 Remove the oil filter. This is necessary at this stage so that the starter motor can be withdrawn.
13 Remove the retaining bolts and withdraw the starter ring gear cover and the clutch or torque converter cover (as applicable) (photo).
14 On automatic transmission models, working through the exposed aperture, unscrew and remove each of the three converter-to-

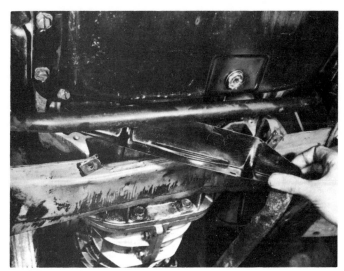

5.13 Remove the torque converter cover

5.14 Remove the driveplate bolts

5.15 The starter motor heat shield and spacers

5.20 Unbolt the engine mountings

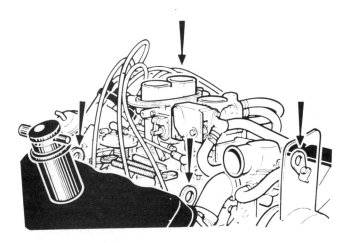

Fig. 1.4 Engine lifting eye positions (Sec 5)

driveplate bolts. Check that the plate-to-converter alignment mark is visible – mark accordingly if not, to ensure correct assembly. Rotate the engine, using a spanner located on the crankshaft pulley bolt, to position the converter bolts accordingly, and then jam the starter ring with a suitable screwdriver or similar, to prevent the engine turning whilst undoing each bolt (photo).

15 Remove the heat shield above the starter motor, noting the two spacers under the retaining bolts (photo). Remove the starter motor, referring to Chapter 10 if necessary.

16 Unbolt and detach the exhaust manifold-to-downpipe connections on each side.

17 Unscrew and remove the respective engine-to-transmission retaining bolts.

18 Position a jack under the transmission and raise it to support, **not** lift, the transmission. Use a block of wood or similar to spread the load.

19 Make a check around the engine, to see if any fittings are still attached, then arrange the lifting sling into position and check that it is secure. Lifting plates are fitted, and are shown in Fig. 1.4.

20 Raise and support the weight of the engine and transmission and remove the engine mountings, then lower the hoist so that the transmission is supported on the jack previously positioned underneath it (photo).

21 The engine can now be pulled carefully from the transmission unit, and when sufficiently clear, raised and removed (photo). On automatic

5.21A Lifting out the engine

5.21B Method of retaining the torque converter unit in position on automatic transmission models

transmission models, take additional care when withdrawing the engine, to avoid pulling out the torque converter as well. On removal of the engine, take precautions to prevent the converter from becoming dislodged from the transmission whilst the engine is out of the vehicle. Fabricate a suitable retaining plate to secure the converter (photo).

22 On removal of the engine, lower it and place it in an area where it can be cleaned externally, prior to dismantling.

6 Engine and transmission – removal

It is not generally recommended that the two units be removed together as both are relatively bulky. Therefore, unless suitable lifting gear, a couple of assistants and sufficient working clearance are available below the vehicle to disconnect and manoeuvre the transmission upwards when lifting the units out, they are best removed individually.

In addition to the normal engine/transmission removal tools, you will require the use of Renault spacer legs No T. Av. 603, with which to hold the front axle compressed – see paragraph 4 for details. You will also need a balljoint separator.

1   Following the procedures given in the preceding Section, disconnect the engine and its associate fittings as described in paragraphs 1 to 11, and 16.

2   Remove the drain plug and empty out the gearbox oil, or automatic transmission fluid as applicable, into a suitable container. On automatic transmission models remove the fluid level dipstick when draining.

3   On manual transmission models, unbolt and remove the clutch slave cylinder. Tie it up out of the way.

4   Fabricate a suitable pair of spacers, or if available, use Renault special spacer legs (tool number T. Av. 603). Position them between the front shock absorber lower mountings and the lower suspension arm pivot pins, as shown in Fig. 1.5. See Chapter 11 for details on spacer legs.

5   Now raise the front end of the vehicle and support it on stands or blocks to allow the front wheels to hang freely. When in this position, make a check to ensure that the spacer legs are securely located, before proceeding further.

6   Remove the front roadwheels.

7   Refer to Chapter 9 and remove the brake calipers, but do not disconnect the hydraulic brake hoses. Tie the calipers up out of the way.

8   Using a suitable punch, drive out the driveshaft roll pins on each side (Fig. 1.6).

9   Remove the retaining nuts and using a suitable balljoint separator, detach the upper suspension arm and steering arm balljoints.

10 Pivot the stub axle carriers and simultaneously withdraw the driveshaft from each side.

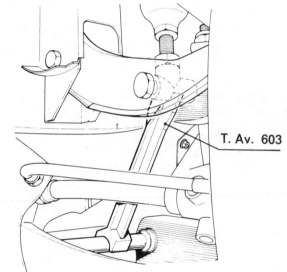

T. Av. 603

Fig. 1.5 Special Renault spacer leg T Av 603 in position (Sec 6)

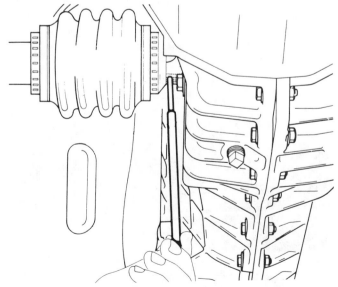

Fig. 1.6 Drive out the driveshaft roll pins (Sec 6)

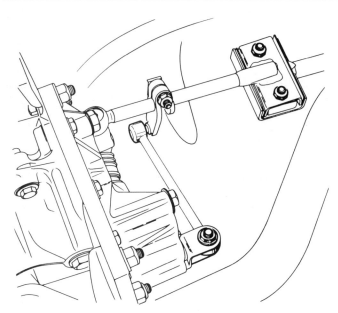

Fig. 1.7 Detach the gearchange control rod (Sec 6)

11 Unscrew and disconnect the speedometer cable at its gearbox connection.

12 Remove the retaining bolts and disconnect the right-hand and then the left-hand exhaust downpipes at their manifold connections.

13 On manual gearboxes, detach the gearchange control rod underneath (Fig. 1.7).

14 On automatic transmission models, refer to Fig. 1.8, loosen off the clamp nuts, detach the control rod and remove the linkage.

15 Disconnect and remove the oil cooler pipes at the automatic transmission.

16 Position a jack under the rear of the transmission unit (manual or automatic) and raise to support it. Use a suitable block of wood to spread the load.

17 Unbolt the transmission side mountings, remove the jack and allow the transmission to rest on the crossmember.

18 Loosen the cable clip nuts.

19 Check around the engine and transmission to ensure that all fittings are disconnected, then attach the engine lifting sling to each of the lift plates as shown in Fig. 1.4.

20 Take the weight of the engine by raising the hoist and, with the aid of an assistant, pull it forwards whilst simultaneously adjusting the

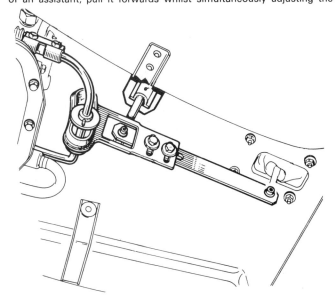

Fig. 1.8 Control rod and linkage of the automatic transmission (Sec 6)

jack under the gearbox, so that the engine is tilted to the necessary angle for withdrawal. Take care not to damage any of the surrounding components during the engine/transmission removal.

21 With the engine and transmission units removed from the car, first remove the oil filter, allowing for oil spillage, and then unbolt and remove the starter motor.

22 On automatic transmission models, remove the three converter-to-driveplate bolts as given in Section 5, paragraph 14.

23 Pulling the engine and transmission units apart requires an assistant. Check that all the engine-to-transmission retaining bolts are removed, then pull the two units apart. On automatic transmission models take care not to pull the torque converter from the transmission housing as the engine is withdrawn.

24 Having separated the two units it will be necessary with automatic transmission models to fabricate a retaining plate or means to prevent the converter from becoming detached whilst the transmission is removed. See Section 5, paragraph 21.

7 Engine dismantling – general

1 It is best to mount the engine on a dismantling stand, but if one is not available, stand the engine on a strong bench at a comfortable working height. Failing this, the engine can be stripped down on the floor.

2 During dismantling, the greatest care should be taken to keep the exposed parts free from dirt. As an aid to achieving this, it is a sound scheme to first clean down the outside of the engine, removing all traces of oil and congealed dirt.

3 Use paraffin or a good grease solvent. The latter will make the job much easier, as, after the solvent has been applied and allowed to stand for a time, a vigorous jet of water will wash off the solvent and all the grease and filth. If the dirt is thick and deeply embedded, work the solvent into it with a brush. Take care not to allow dirt, solvent or water to saturate the distributor if this is still in position. Other items to take particular care with in this respect are the alternator and the carburettor or fuel injection components, as applicable.

4 Finally wipe down the exterior of the engine with a rag and only then, when it is quite clean, should dismantling begin. As the engine is stripped, clean each part in a bath of paraffin.

5 Never immerse parts with oilways in paraffin, eg the crankshaft, but to clean, wipe down carefully with a solvent dampened rag. Oilways can be cleaned out with wire. If an air line is present all parts can be blown dry and the oilways blown through as an added precaution.

6 Re-use of old engine gaskets is false economy and can give rise to oil and water leaks. To avoid the possibility of trouble after the engine has been reassembled *always* use new gaskets throughout.

7 Do not throw the old gaskets away as it sometimes happens that an immediate replacement cannot be found and the old gasket is useful as a template. Hang up the old gaskets as they are removed on a suitable hook or nail.

8 To strip the engine it is best to work from the top down. The sump provides a firm base on which the engine can be supported in an upright position. When this stage where the sump must be removed is reached, the engine can be turned on its side and all other work carried out with it in this position.

9 Whenever possible, refit nuts, bolts and washers fingertight from wherever they were removed. This helps to avoid later loss and muddle. If they cannot be refitted, lay them out so that it is clear where they came from.

8 Engine dismantling – ancillaries

1 A word of warning at this stage is that you should always check that it is more economic to dismantle and overhaul a worn engine rather than simply to exchange it on the Renault Factory scheme. It is not always the case.

2 If you are intending to obtain an exchange engine complete, it will be necessary first of all to remove all those parts of the engine which are not included in the exchange. If you are stripping the engine completely yourself in the likelihood of some outside work being done by specialists, all these items will be taken off anyway.

3 Short engines are not available from Renault. It is as well to check with whoever may be supplying the replacement exchange unit what

it is necessary to remove, but as a general guide the following items will be supplied with a Renault Service exchange engine:

   (a) *Water pump and pulley*
   (b) *Crankshaft and camshaft pulleys*
   (c) *Oil filter and oil pressure switch*
   (d) *Coolant temperature switch*
   (e) *Spark plugs*
   (f) *Fuel pump*
   (g) *Flywheel and clutch assembly (manual transmission models)*
   (h) *Converter driveplate (automatic transmission models)*

4   It therefore follows that ancillary items not listed above such as the distributor, inlet/exhaust manifolds and carburettor etc should be removed from the old engine.
5   Refer to the respective Chapters concerned for removal procedures.

---

9   Cylinder head(s) – removal

   If the cylinder heads are to be removed for a complete engine overhaul or where the timing cover, chains and sprockets are also being removed, then it is better to remove the timing chain assemblies first. Follow paragraphs 4 to 11 in this Section, then remove the timing chains (Section 17); complete removal of the heads as described in paragraphs 14, 17 and 19 to 24 of this Section.

   If one or both cylinder heads are to be removed with the engine in the vehicle or where the rest of the engine is not being dismantled, you will need to keep the timing chain taut throughout the operation. If the chain tension is slackened for any reason you will have to remove the timing cover in order to reset the chain tensioner(s). A separate chain is used to drive each camshaft.

   To keep the chains taut you will need to use special Renault tool No. Mot. 589 (see Fig. 1.9) or be able to fabricate a similar support (photo 9.12) for the sprocket(s). The dummy bearing bracket (F) will only be required if the crankshaft has to be turned for any reason whilst the head(s) are removed, such as for pistons/connecting rods/liners removal, in order to maintain the valve timing.

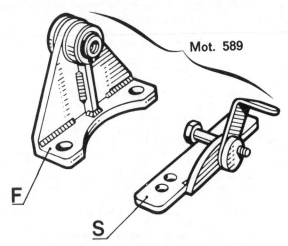

Fig. 1.9 Renault special tool Mot.589 (Sec 9)

F   *Dummy bearing to support sprocket if crankshaft has to be turned*
S   *Bracket to support the sprocket in fixed position*

1   Proceed as follows for each cylinder head in turn. The only difference between the two are the front end of the right-hand cylinder head camshaft bolt access aperture is covered by a plate secured by two bolts, and there is no drive pulley at the rear end (as with the left-hand camshaft) so this is also covered by a similar plate.
2   Where the engine is still in the vehicle, carry out the following preliminary operations:

   (a) *Drain the cooling system and disconnect the appropriate cooling and heating hoses as necessary, referring to Chapter 2 if required for further details. Note their respective connections*

   (b) *Disconnect the battery earth lead*
   (c) *Disconnect the ignition leads and other associated electrical wires from the cylinder head(s), noting their respective positions. Also detach the diagnostic socket and bracket for removal of the right-hand cylinder head*
   (d) *Remove the alternator (left-hand cylinder head)*
   (e) *On carburettor engines, remove the air cleaner unit and disconnect the throttle cable*
   (f) *On fuel injection engines, remove the air cleaner unit and disconnect the applicable fuel injection components (see Section 5, paragraph 10)*
   (g) *Detach the exhaust downpipe(s) from the manifold connection(s)*
   (h) *On the left-hand cylinder head, remove the power steering drivebelt and pump unit, but do not disconnect the hoses. Rest the pump unit on the bulkhead out of the way so that it does not leak*

3   The procedure with the engine fitted or removed is now the same.
4   On the left-hand cylinder head, unbolt and remove the fuel pump.
5   On the right-hand cylinder head, remove the distributor (see Chapter 4).
6   Remove the inlet manifold, referring to Chapter 3.
7   Remove the dipstick tube clip on the right-hand cylinder head.
8   Unbolt and remove the rocker cover(s).
9   On the left-hand cylinder head, unscrew and remove the camshaft sprocket bolt access plug using a 10 mm Allen key.
10   On the right-hand cylinder head, remove the cover plate from the front face of the timing case for access to the camshaft retaining bolt.
11   Turn the engine (using a spanner on the crankshaft pulley bolt) so that the left-hand camshaft sprocket drive pin is at the top as shown (Fig. 1.10).

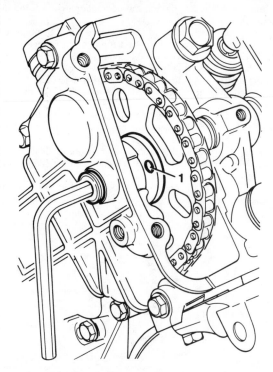

Fig. 1.10 Left-hand camshaft sprocket drive pin (1) to be positioned as shown (Sec 9)

12   Where the cylinder head(s) only are being removed, locate the camshaft sprocket support (Renault tool Mot. 589(S)) in position on the top face of the timing case, with the bolts holding it in position moderately tightened in the two rocker cover front fixing holes as shown in Fig. 1.13. In the event of this tool not being available, fabricate a suitable support from a piece of angled steel as shown. Cut it to size and drill the necessary holes for the retaining bolts (photos).
13   With the camshaft sprocket(s) suitably supported, loosen but do

9.12A The camshaft sprocket support fabricated in our workshop

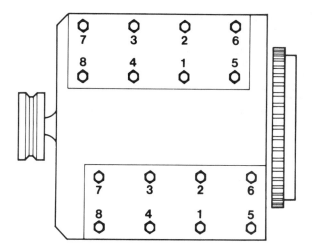

Fig. 1.11 Cylinder head bolt loosening and tightening sequence (Sec 9)

9.12B The camshaft sprocket support in position

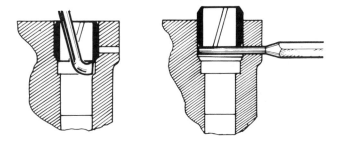

Fig. 1.12 Cylinder head location dowel removal using suitable hooked tool and punch (Sec 9)

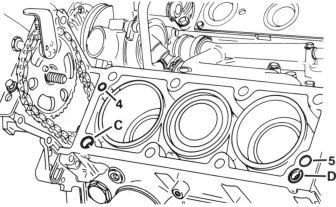

Fig. 1.13 Dowel positions (C and D). Also shown are the oil feed holes (4 and 5). Camshaft sprocket support is visible at left (Sec 9)

not remove the camshaft sprocket retaining bolt using a 10 mm Allen key.

14 Progressively loosen and remove the cylinder head retaining bolts in the sequence shown in Fig. 1.11, then lift clear the rocker assembly. Mark them accordingly to avoid confusion (right and left).

15 Unscrew and remove the camshaft flange bolt and remove the flange from its recess.

16 Slowly loosen off the camshaft sprocket bolt until the camshaft is disengaged from its sprocket.

17 Using a suitable rod (an old pushrod – from another engine! – is ideal) press down the cylinder head location dowels, the positions of which are shown in Fig. 1.13.

18 Unscrew and remove the timing cover-to-cylinder head retaining bolts. There are four bolts to each cylinder head.

19 The cylinder head(s) are now ready for removal. To prevent the cylinder liners being disturbed and unseated when removing the cylinder heads, lightly tap the head with a soft-faced mallet to unstick it from the gasket, then twist the cylinder head on its axis before lifting it free. **Do not** turn the engine to lift the cylinder head(s), or the liners will be unseated.

20 Remove the cylinder head gasket(s). Any coolant remaining in the cylinder block can be syphoned out.

21 Prise out the two cylinder head location dowels, taking care not to damage the cylinder block and gasket mating face – see Fig. 1.12.

22 The respective mating faces of both the cylinder block and cylinder head(s) must be cleaned prior to reassembly. Particular care must be taken when cleaning the cylinder block face to protect the two oil holes shown in Fig. 1.13. Plug these holes temporarily whilst cleaning, but don't forget to remove the plugs before refitting the new gasket!

23 For cylinder head dismantling and overhaul details, refer to Section 27. Prior to reassembly of the cylinder head check that the cylinder liner protrusions are as given in Section 39, then proceed as given in Section 41 or 42 as applicable.

24 When the cylinder head(s) only are removed from the engine it is important not to turn the engine unless:

(a) Liner clamp plates are fitted to prevent the cylinder liners from being disturbed, and

(b) Camshaft sprocket bearing bracket(s) are fitted – see the introduction to this Section

10 Rocker assembly – dismantling

1 Although the right-hand and left-hand bank rocker assemblies are identical, they should be dismantled separately and their respective components laid out in order of fitting and kept separate from each other (photo).
2 Unscrew the bolt from the end bearing pedestal and withdraw the pedestals, rocker arms, spacers and springs.
3 The oilway plugs at the end of each rocker shaft are press fitted and should not be removed. Note the direction of fitting of each rocker shaft to ensure correct reassembly. If refitted incorrectly, the oil feed holes will be blocked. Note that when fitted the oil holes face downwards.

11 Camshaft(s) – removal and refitting

Camshaft removal, inspection and refitting details are given in Section 27. The camshafts can only be removed from the cylinder heads when the heads are removed from the engine. Refer to Section 9 for the cylinder head removal details, and Section 41 or 42 as applicable for their refitting.

12 Sump and anti-emulsion plate – removal

1 If the engine is still in the car, unbolt and remove the engine undertray and then drain the engine oil into a suitable container.
2 Unscrew and remove the sump retaining bolts and lower the sump.

10.1 The rocker assembly cleaned and ready for dismantling

3 Remove the three retaining bolts and withdraw the suction pipe and gauze.
4 Remove the six retaining bolts and withdraw the anti-emulsion plate.

13 Pistons, connecting rods and cylinder liners – removal

1 If the pistons, connecting rods and cylinder liners are to be removed with the engine in position in the car remove the cylinder heads are given in Section 9. As mentioned in that Section, you will need to support the camshaft sprocket in order to keep the timing chain taut, and you will require special tool Mot. 589, dummy bearing 'F' for this purpose. This supports the camshaft sprocket whilst allowing the crankshaft to be turned for access to the respective big-end bolts. Note that when fitting the dummy bearing, it may be necessary to fit shims between the bearing support and the cylinder block in order to keep the timing chain taut, so have some shims at hand.
2 If all six piston and liner assemblies are to be removed or the engine is removed for general overhaul, remove the timing gear assemblies as described in Section 17. (In this case the camshaft sprocket support tool is not needed).
3 With the cylinder head(s) removed, unbolt and remove the sump and anti-emulsion plate as given in Section 12.
4 It is essential that where the existing liner, piston and connecting rod assemblies are to be refitted, they are marked for positional identification. If the engine has previously been dismantled then they should already be marked, in which case note the marking orientation relative to the cylinder block to ensure correct reassembly. If marking is necessary, use quick-drying paint and mark the piston, liner and connecting rod number (No 1 is in the left-hand bank at the flywheel end) in turn. Mark the piston crown and the top face of each liner in turn at corresponding points (Fig. 1.16) so that the angular position of each is aligned. Mark the big-end caps and rods numerically so that the bearing cap will be refitted the correct way round when the mating marks are adjacent (photo). To avoid confusion on reassembly, mark the caps and rods on the same side as the pistons and liners. Although each connecting rod and cap is die-stamped with a letter and number, they are numbered 1 to 6 from the rear of the engine. *These numbers relate only to the rod positions on the crankshaft and **not** to the cylinder numbers.*
5 The crankshaft will have to be turned during removal of the rods and this will cause the pistons to dislodge the cylinder liners. If some liners are not to be disturbed, for example if removing only one or two liner/piston assemblies, or possibly big-end bearing renewal with the cylinder head(s) removed, then the liners must be secured in position with suitable clamps. Use Renault clamps Mot 588, or fabricate suitable clamp plates. Secure them to the top face of the cylinder block

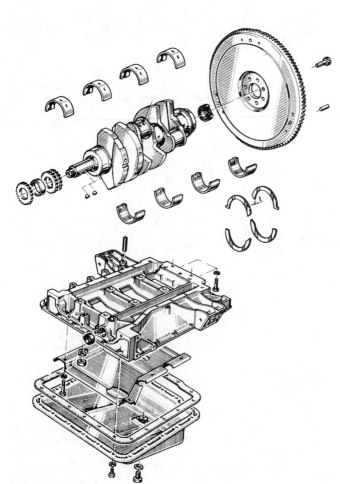

Fig. 1.14 Exploded drawing of the sump, anti-emulsion plate, bottom casing, crankshaft and associated components (Sec 12)

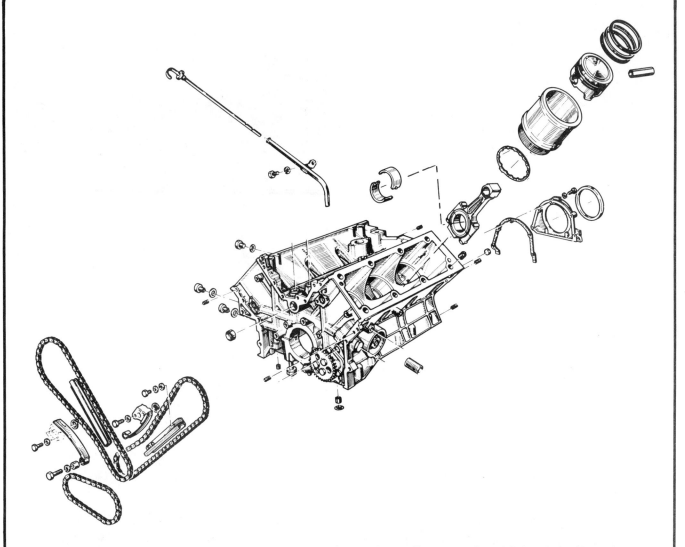

Fig. 1.15 Exploded drawing of the cylinder block, piston/connecting rod/liner assembly and timing chains (Sec 13)

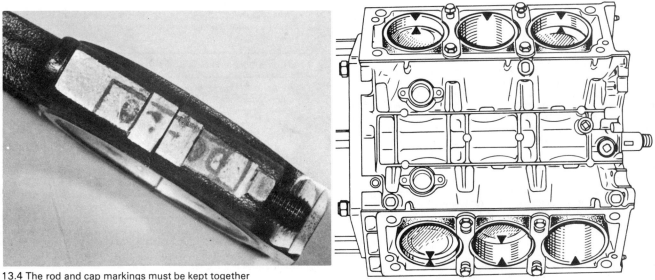

13.4 The rod and cap markings must be kept together

Fig. 1.16 Mark the piston crowns and cylinders for relative identification (Sec 13)

using 19 mm diameter bolts fitted to the cylinder head bolt holes as shown (Fig. 1.17).
6   Unscrew and remove the big-end bearing cap nuts.
7   Withdraw the big-end bearing caps complete with shell bearings.
8   Withdraw each cylinder liner/piston/connecting rod assembly upwards from the cylinder block. The liner seals will be broken during this operation and must be cleaned from the liner and block mating faces.
9   After removal of each connecting rod, temporarily refit its matching bearing cap and shell bearing.
10 Withdraw each connecting rod/piston assembly from its cylinder liner. Do not allow the piston rings to spring outwards during removal from the liners, but restrain them with the fingers to avoid breakage.

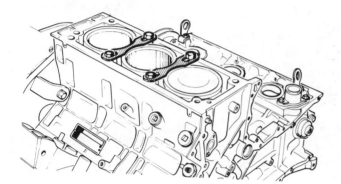

Fig. 1.17 Fit liner retaining clamps (Sec 13)

14 Piston rings – removal

1   Removal of rings from their grooves is an operation calling for care as they are of cast construction and will snap if opened too wide.
2   Cut three pieces of tin sheet (or use three old feeler gauges) and prise the open ends of the ring apart with the thumb nails just enough to permit the first strip of tin (or feeler) to be slid behind the ring. Slide in the other two pieces of tin and position them equidistantly round the periphery of the piston. The piston ring may now be drawn off as the strips will permit it to ride safely over the lands and other grooves of the piston.
3   The above information is not necessarily applicable if the rings are to be renewed in any case, but care should still be exercised to prevent damaging the pistons during removal.

15 Gudgeon pins – removal and refitting

The gudgeon pins fitted to these engines are an interference fit in the connecting rod small-end, but a running fit in the piston. It is preferable that the removal or fitting of gudgeon pins be left to a Renault agent as the connecting rod must first be heated to 250°C (482°F) and a press and special gauge tools employed.

16 Oil pump – removal

1   The oil pump is located in the front face of the cylinder block. Access to it is gained by removing the timing cover. The pump is driven by a chain from the crankshaft.

Engine in the car
2   Remove the sump drain plug and drain the engine oil.
3   Drain the cooling system and remove the radiator (see Chapter 2).
4   Remove the air filter unit (see Chapter 3).
5   Remove the respective front end drivebelts and the alternator adjusting strap.
6   Remove the rocker covers.
7   Unbolt and remove the engine undertray.

16.10 Method of jamming the flywheel (engine removed)

8   On air conditioned models, remove the cooling fan motor(s) and air conditioning compressor, but **do not** disconnect the pipes.
9   Unbolt and remove the starter ring gear cover (on the right-hand side).

Engine in or out of the car
10 Jam the starter ring gear to prevent the crankshaft turning (photo), then unscrew the crankshaft pulley nut using a 36 mm socket. When the nut is removed, unjam and rotate the crankshaft so that its pulley locating key is at the top and then withdraw the crankshaft pulley.
11 Remove the retaining bolts from the timing cover, noting their varying lengths and locations as they are removed. When all the bolts are removed withdraw the timing case. It may be stuck in position, in which case some careful light taps with a soft-headed mallet from the rear will help to unseal it.
12 Unscrew and remove the three oil pump sprocket securing bolts and then withdraw the sprocket and chain.
13 Unscrew the oil pump unit retaining bolts and withdraw the pump unit from the front end of the cylinder block. It may be tight, but do not attempt to free it by hammering or levering on the release valve boss (with the split pin through it).
14 Extract the pump driven gear.
15 It necessary remove the pump drive sprocket from the crankshaft.
16 For inspection and refitting of the pump unit, refer to Section 44.

17 Timing cover, chains and sprocket assemblies – removal

1   Refer to Section 16 and remove the timing cover, the oil pump drive chain and sprockets.
2   Before removing the respective timing chains and sprockets, first clean the chains and sprocket front faces and check that timing marks are visible. The chains and sprockets should be marked as shown in Fig. 1.18. Identify the right and left-hand chains and camshaft sprockets accordingly if they are to be re-used.
3   Loosen off bot chain tensioners by turning their ratchet mechanisms ani-clockwise using a suitable screwdriver.
4   Next remove the chain tensioners, by removing the two bolts that retain them.
5   Remove the gauze oil strainers behind the tensioners, then remove the tensioner blades. Unless there is a need to renew the straight guides (due to bad wear or damage), there is no need to remove them.
6   Remove the Allen bolt which retains the right-hand side camshaft sprocket and tap the gear off the camshaft. Remove it and the chain together. Jam the flywheel to prevent the engine turning when the camshaft Allen bolt is unscrewed.
7   Repeat this procedure and remove the left-hand side sprocket and chain.
8   Withdraw the double row sprocket from the crankshaft using a puller, and extract the Woodruff key from its groove.

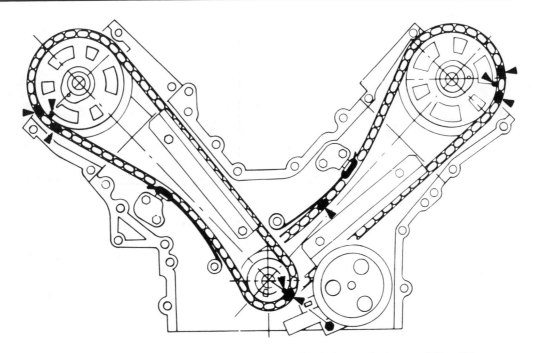

Fig. 1.18 Check timing chains and sprockets for timing marks (arrowed) (Sec 17)

18 Flywheel/driveplate – removal

1   On manual transmission models remove the clutch unit, referring to Chapter 5.
2   To prevent the crankshaft from turning when unscrewing the flywheel/driveplate retaining bolts, jam the ring gear teeth using a suitably shaped piece of metal.
3   Where applicable, bend over the retaining bolt locktabs (if fitted) and unscrew and remove the seven flywheel/driveplate retaining bolts (whilst supporting the flywheel driveplate), then lift it clear.
4   On automatic transmission models, note that a plate washer is fitted each side of the driveplate.

19 Bottom casing, main bearings and crankshaft – removal

1   It is assumed that the sump and anti-emulsion plate have been removed as given in Section 12, also the timing chain assemblies (Section 17) and the flywheel or driveplate (Section 18).
2   Unscrew and remove the bottom casing retaining bolts and nuts with washers, including the two smaller bolts from the rear main seal plate lower face.
3   Refer to Section 13 and mark and disconnect the connecting rods as given in paragraphs 4 to 7 inclusive (if not already done).
4   Before lifting out the main bearing caps, mark their relative positions (if not already marked) numerically.
5   Unscrew and remove the rear main bearing seal plate retaining screws using a 6 mm Allen key. Remove the main seal plate.
6   Lift out the main bearing caps and the lower halves of the end thrust washers.
7   Withdraw the crankshaft together with the upper halves of the end thrust washers.

20 Engine oil seals – renewal

All the engine oil seals can theoretically be renewed with the engine in the car. The seals should always be removed during an engine overhaul, since access to some of them is then considerably easier.

Crankshaft pulley oil seal

1   Raise the vehicle at the front end and support it on safety stands or ramps.

2   Unbolt and remove the engine undertray.
3   Loosen the air compressor unit and remove the compressor drivebelt (air conditioned models only).
4   Loosen the alternator and remove its drivebelt.
5   Remove the starter ring gear cover plate and then locate a locking plate to prevent the flywheel from turning. Unscrew the crankshaft pulley retaining nut, and then remove the flywheel (or driveplate) locking plate. Turn the crankshaft so that its keyway points to the top and then withdraw the pulley.
6   The oil seal is now accessible and can be prised free from the timing case using a screwdriver. Take care not to score or damage the housing (photo).
7   Lubricate the new seal prior to fitting. Carefully tap or press it into position, ensuring that it is inserted squarely and is not distorted once in position. A pipe drift of suitable diameter is ideal for seal fitment.
8   Reassembly of the crankshaft pulley and the respective drivebelt is a reversal of the removal process. Be sure to tighten the pulley retaining nut to the specified torque. The drivebelt tension must be adjusted (see Chapter 2).

20.6 The timing case oil seal shown with crankshaft pulley removed

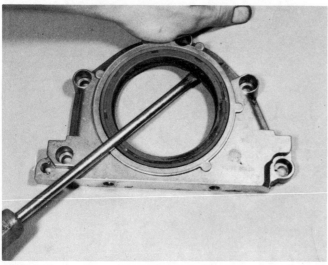

20.12 Prising out the main bearing rear seal (housing removed)

20.18 Power steering drive pulley removed to show camshaft rear seal

Main bearing oil seal – flywheel end

9   This seal is only accessible after removing the gearbox or automatic transmission (as applicable). Refer to Chapter 6 or 7 accordingly. In practice, therefore, it will probably be necessary to remove the engine.

10 On manual transmission models, remove the clutch unit and then unbolt and remove the flywheel. For clutch removal refer to Chapter 5.

11 On automatic transmission models, unbolt and remove the converter driveplate.

12 The oil seal is now accessible and can be eased out of the housing using a suitable screwdriver, taking care not to damage the housing (photo).

13 Lubricate the new seal before fitting and carefully drive it into position using a suitable diameter pipe drift.

14 When refitting the flywheel or driveplate, use new retaining bolts and smear the threads with thread locking compound. Tighten the bolts to the specified torque. Do not forget to locate a plate washer each side of the converter driveplate on automatic transmission models. Bend up the locktabs (where fitted).

15 Refit the clutch on manual transmission models, referring to Chapter 5.

16 Refit the normal gearbox or automatic transmission as applicable, referring to Chapter 6 or 7, or refit the engine.

Camshaft oil seal (at power steering pump pulley)

17 Loosen the power steering pump and remove its drivebelt.

18 Remove the camshaft pulley retaining bolt and then withdraw the pulley (photo).

19 The oil seal can now be carefully eased out of its housing using a screwdriver.

20 Lubricate the new seal before fitting and then insert it into its housing, using a suitable diameter tube drift to ensure that it is fitted correctly and without distortion. When in position the new seal should be flush with the cylinder head rear face.

21 Relocate the pulley and tighten its retaining bolt to the specified torque. Adjust the power steering pump drivebelt tension to complete.

21 Engine lubrication system – description

1   A diagram of the engine lubrication system is given in Fig. 1.19.

2   Oil from the sump is sucked into the circuit by the oil pump through a fitted suction pipe. From the oil pump, the oil passes through the oil filter from where it is pumped under pressure round the various oil galleries to the main bearings, big-end bearings, camshaft bearings and rocker assembly.

3   The oil pressure is limited by means of a relief valve fitted to the pump.

4   The main oil filter is of the disposable cartridge type and must be renewed at the specified intervals.

5   The oil pump is located in the front face of the cylinder block and is driven by a chain and sprockets from the crankshaft. The pump can be removed with the engine in the car after withdrawing the timing case (see Section 16).

6   The oil pressure transmitter, which lights up the oil warning light on the dashboard if pressure is low, is situated on the right-hand side of the cylinder block at the front.

22 Oil filter – renewal

1   The oil filter is located on the left-hand side of the cylinder block towards the front. Accessibility is poor and necessitates removal of the engine undertray. Alternatively, it may be possible to reach the filter from above.

2   If the old filter proves too tight to be removed by hand pressure, use a strap wrench to unscrew it. Alternatively, a large worm drive hose clip (or two joined together to make up the required diameter) strapped around the canister will provide a better grip point. If necessary, the canister can be tapped round using a small hammer.

3   Once the old filter is removed, wipe clean the joint area in the cylinder block and lubricate the new seal ring.

4   Screw the filter carefully into position by hand, ensuring that the seal does not twist or distort as it is tightened.

5   Do not overtighten the filter; it need only be tightened by firm hand pressure for half a turn after it seats against the block.

6   Check and top up the engine oil as required, then run the engine to check for any signs of leakage around the filter seal before refitting the engine undertray.

23 Engine components – cleaning and examination

1   Clean all components using paraffin and a stiff brush, except the crankshaft, which should be wiped clean and the oil passages cleaned out with a length of wire.

2   Never assume that a component is unworn simply because it looks all right. After all the effort which has gone into dismantling the engine, refitting worn components will make the overhaul a waste of time and money. Depending on the degree of wear, the overhauler's budget and the anticipated life of the vehicle, components which are only slightly worn may be refitted, but if in doubt it is always best to renew.

24 Crankshaft – examination and renovation

1   Clean out all the oil channels, using compressed air and thin wire.

2   Examine the bearing surfaces on the crankshaft for signs on scoring or scratches and check their ovality (or have them checked)

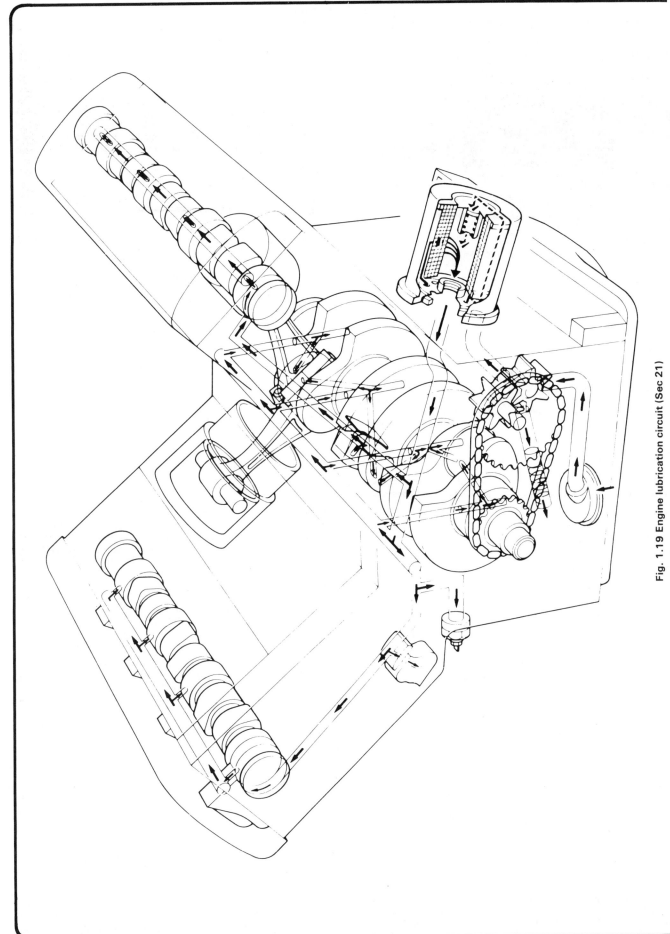

Fig. 1.19 Engine lubrication circuit (Sec 21)

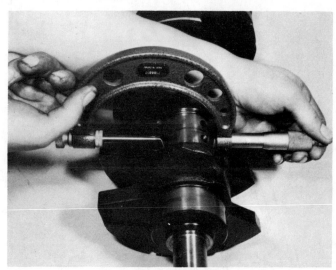

24.2 Measure the crankshaft journals for wear

with a micrometer. Take measurements at a number of positions on each surface, paying particular attention to the areas indicated by any wear shown on the bearing shells. If there are differences in diameter of more than 0.0003 in (0.007 mm) on the main bearing or the big-end surfaces, the crankshaft must be reground. It is probably worth-while regrinding the crankshaft if it is found that the bearings are worn and the crankshaft ovality is appreciably more than half these figures (photo).

3   The taper on the crankpins may not be greater than 0.0004 in (0.01 mm) for any one pin.

4   Where the crankshaft has to be reground, there are special undersize bearing shells available which must be used. These will normally be supplied by the firm doing the regrinding.

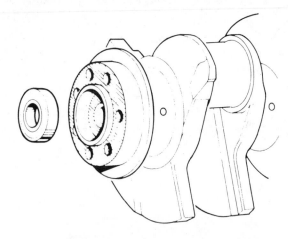

Fig. 1.20 Spigot bearing location in crankshaft – manual transmission models only (Sec 24)

5   Renew the spigot bearing if necessary (manual transmission models), and smear it with thread locking compound before fitting. If a new crankshaft is being fitted on manual transmission models, a new spigot bearing must be fitted as this is not supplied with the crankshaft.

25 Big-end and main bearings – examination and renewal

1   Inspect the bearing shells for signs of general wear, scoring, pitting and scratches. The shells should be a matt grey in colour. If any

trace of copper colour is noticed, it is an indication that the bearings are badly worn, because the white metal is plated onto a copper coloured underlay.

2   The bearing shells may have figures stamped on them to indicate their size. Naturally, ensure that the shells purchased are of the same size as the ones taken out, unless the crankshaft has been reground.

3   If you are in any doubt, or unless the engine has done less than 15 000 miles since the bearings were last renewed, buy a set of replacement shell bearings. This applies equally to the main bearings and the big-end bearings. Also obtain new thrust washers. The cost is not high when compared with the amount of work involved to strip the whole engine down yet again.

4   Never attempt to cure a noisy big-end by filing the bearing cap and/or grinding the bearing shell.

5   New big-end cap nuts must be used on reassembly.

26 Cylinder head(s) and piston crowns – decarbonisation

1   With the cylinder head(s) removed, the carbon deposits within the combustion spaces and ports can be cleaned using a suitable scraper and rotary wire brush. When cleaning, care must be taken not to score the respective chamber surfaces. As it is most likely that the valves will need removal for inspection and regrinding, full cylinder head cleaning is best left until the valves are removed as given in Section 27.

2   Having removed the worst of the carbon deposits that are readily accessible, clean the cylinder head with a suitable solvent and clean off any gasket or sealant solution from the respective mating surfaces.

3   When cleaning the piston crowns and cylinder liner bores with the pistons still in position it is essential that care is taken to ensure that no carbon gets into the cylinder bores as this could scratch the cylinder walls or cause damage to the piston and rings. To ensure this does not happen, first turn the crankshaft so that the piston to be worked on is at the top of its bore (having clamped the liners in position). Stuff rag into the other two bores or seal them off with paper and masking tape. The water jackets should also be covered with paper and masking tape to prevent particles of carbon entering the cooling system and damaging the water pump.

4   Press a little grease into the gap between the cylinder walls and the piston which is to be worked on. With a blunt scraper carefully scrape away the carbon from the piston crown, taking great care not to scratch the aluminium. Also scrape away the carbon from the surrounding lip of the cylinder wall. When all carbon has been removed, scrape away the grease which will now be contaminated with carbon particles, taking care not to press any into the bores. To assist prevention of carbon build-up the piston crown can be polished with a metal polish. Remove the rags or masking tape from the other cylinders and turn the crankshaft so that another piston is now at the top. Place rags in the cylinders which have been decarbonised and proceed as just described.

5   Repeat the above operations until all pistons are clean and bright.

27 Cylinder heads, valves and camshafts – overhaul

1   Remove the spark plugs and the injectors (if fitted).

2   Undo the two bolts and remove the rear cover plate on the rear end of the cylinder head (right-hand side). On the left-hand head, remove the power steering drivebelt pulley.

3   Remove the bolt and withdraw the camshaft retaining plate. This will of course have already been done if the cylinder head was removed with the engine still in the vehicle (photo).

4   The camshaft can now be fed out rearwards and be placed to one side for the moment.

5   Using a proprietary valve spring remover, remove all the valves and springs. Compress each spring in turn, remove the collets, then release the tool and remove the upper washer, spring, lower washer and valve (photos). If the valve seems a little stiff when pushing it through the guide, this is probably because it has carbon on the upper stem. This can easily be removed with fine emery cloth. Keep all the valves and their associated components in the correct order and together. A box divided into sections is ideal for this purpose. Alternatively punch a series of holes in a piece of cardboard and push each valve in order through the cardboard, stem upwards; finally, place the spring and washers over it.

27.3 Remove the bolt and withdraw the camshaft retaining plate

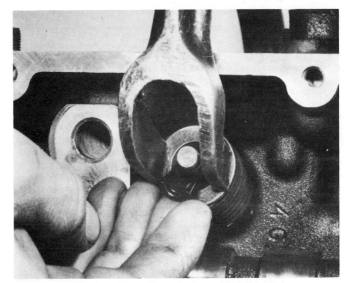
27.5A Compress the valve spring to remove the collets and ...

27.5B ... the upper washer and spring

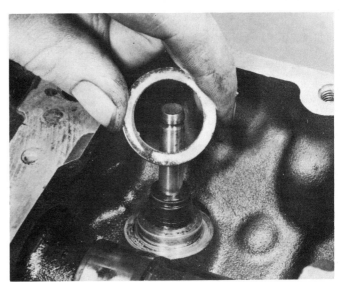
27.5C Remove the lower washer and ...

27.5D ... the valve stem seal

27.5E Remove the valve

6   Remove the valve stem seals from the valve guides and place them with their respective valves.

7   With the valves removed, clean out any carbon from the ports, the cylinder head face and the combustion chambers. Examine the valve seats; if they are only slightly pitted, it is possible to make them smooth again by grinding the valves against the seats, as described in Section 28. Where pitting is very deep, they will have to be recut: a job for the specialist with the necessary equipment.

8   Check the valve guides with the valve stems to ensure that they are a good fit: the stems should move easily in the guides without side play. Worn guides can be extracted and new ones refitted but this should be left to your Renault dealer.

9   Examine the valves, checking them for straightness and the condition of the face. Slight pitting can be removed by grinding-in, but if the pitting is deep the valve will have to be machine ground by a specialist. Grinding-in is covered separately in the next Section.

10   The camshaft and its bearings in the cylinder head are part of the Renault engine which seems virtually everlasting. If there should be noticeable play between the camshaft and its bearings, or if the bearings are damaged, the cylinder head will have to be renewed as the bearings are machined in the head. If very light scratches are present on the camshaft, these can be removed by gently rubbing down with a very fine grade emery cloth or oilstone. The greatest care must be taken to keep the cam profiles smooth.

11   Refit the camshaft in its journals and rotate it by hand. Check that it runs smoothly and that there is no trace of warping. Check the endfloat (see Specifications) with the camshaft retaining plate in position (photo). If it is excessive, fit a new retainer of different thickness. These are available from 0.1556 to 0.1565 in (3.952 to 3.976 mm).

12   If there is any doubt about the condition of the valve springs, renew them.

13   Check the cylinder heads and valve seats for cracks, or damage. Then check the surface condition of the cylinder head face. Use a straight-edge. The measurements must be made down the length of the block and diagonally across it. The maximum permitted deviation or warp is given in the Specifications. If the head is out of true to this sort of degree, it must be renewed.

14   Assuming the valves have been ground in as necessary, the cylinder head is ready for reassembly. Start by fitting new oil seals to the valve guides, then refit the valves. Place each valve in turn in its position, refit the lower washer, spring and upper washer, then compress the spring. Refit the collets and release the tool, ensuring that the collets stay in position correctly (photo).

15   When all the valves are refitted, slide the camshaft in from the rear. Note that the right-hand side camshaft has a worm drive on the rear end for driving the distributor. The left-hand side camshaft has an extra cam on the rear end for driving the fuel pump in carburettor-engined cars.

16   Lock the camshaft in position with the retaining plate and secure it with the bolt and washer.

17   The oil seal at the rear of the left-hand camshaft must be renewed before refitting the power steering pump drive pulley (see Section 20).

18   Use new O-ring seals when refitting the right-hand camshaft endplate.

27.11 Check the camshaft endfloat

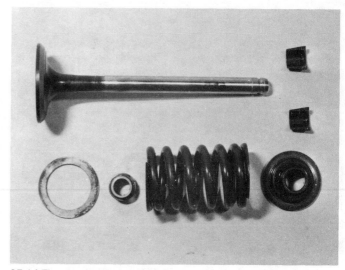

27.14 These components make up one complete valve assembly

28 Valves and valve seats – grinding in

1   Grinding in is essential when fitting valves whether these, or their seats, be new or old. As well as removing every trace of scoring, it ensures that the valve face and the seat have exactly the same slope and hence a reasonably wide area of contact. Where new valves are being fitted to correctly recut seats, grinding is still essential, because a valve face is cut to an angle which is very slightly less than that of the face in the cylinder head and consequently the contact area is very small. The correct area of contact is obtained by grinding.

2   Valve grinding is a simple matter, needing only fine and coarse carborundum paste, an inexpensive valve grinding tool and a great deal of patience. Place the cylinder head upside-down on a bench with a block of wood at each end to give clearance for the valve stems.

3   Smear a trace of coarse paste on the seat face, apply a suction tool to the valve head and insert the valve into the cylinder head. Press lightly on the tool using the palms of the hands, and rotate the tool with a to-and-fro motion (photo). Then lift the valve from the seat and give it a quarter or half a turn before repeating the process. When a

28.3 Grinding in a valve

dull, matt even surface finish is produced on both the valve seat and the valve, wipe off the coarse paste and carry on with the fine paste, lifting and turning the valve as before. When a smooth unbroken ring of light grey matt finish is produced on both valve and valve seat faces, the grinding operation is complete. Aim to get a seat width in accordance with the Specifications at the start of the Chapter. If the seat is too wide, reduce the width by carefully rounding off the corners with an oilstone.

4   When the grinding is complete, clean away every trace of grinding compound with paraffin or petrol. Take great care that none is left in the ports or the valve guides.

29 Rocker assemblies – examination and renovation

1   Having dismantled the respective rocker assemblies as given in Section 10, inspect the various parts for excessive wear or damage.
2   Check the rocker arm wear faces (where they contact the camshaft lobes). Where they are only slightly worn they can be refaced. More excessive wear will necessitate their renewal.
3   Inspect the rocker shafts for wear and renew if necessary. Do not try to remove the plugs on the end of each shaft.
4   Check the shafts for straightness by rolling them on a flat surface such as plate glass. They are unlikely to be bent, but if this is the case they must either be straightened or renewed. Check the oil feed holes and clear them out if blocked.
5   Check each rocker arm for wear on an unworn part of the shaft to check for excessive bore wear.
6   Check the spacer springs and spacer collars. There are collars of two widths fitted to each shaft, these being 5.35 mm (0.210 in) and 8.2 mm (0.322 in) wide respectively. Renew them if badly worn.
7   To reassemble each rocker shaft assembly ready for refitting, first ensure that all parts are clean and then as they are assembled lubricate them with clean engine oil.

8   Both shaft assemblies are identical.
9   If not already in position, locate the snap-ring into the end groove, then slide the bearing pedestal down the shaft with the flat on the boss to the snap-ring.
10   Locate a spacer spring, followed by a rocker arm located with its tappet adjuster screw on the left (from the snap-ring end).
11   Fit the thinner spacer into position followed by the next rocker arm, fitted with its tappet adjuster screw on the right (see Fig. 1.21).
12   Locate the thicker spacer collar, followed by the bearing pedestal with the flat on its boss towards the snap-ring end.
13   Repeat the above assembly sequence for the remaining pairs of rocker arms, spacers and springs.
14   Ensure that the respective rocker components are correctly fitted and that the shaft oil holes face downwards, then insert the end pedestal bolt with washer to secure.
15   Repeat this procedure with the second rocker shaft assembly.

30 Cylinder liners – examination and renovation

1   The cylinder bores must be examined for taper, ovality, scoring and scratches. Start by carefully examining the top of the cylinder bores. If they are at all worn a very slight ridge will be found on the thrust side. This marks the top of the piston ring travel. The owner will have a good indication of the bore wear prior to dismantling the engine, or removing the cylinder head. Excessive oil consumption accompanied by blue smoke from the exhaust is a sure sign of worn cylinder bores and piston rings.
2   Measure the bore diameter just under the ridge with a micrometer and compare it with the diameter at the bottom of the bore, which is not subject to wear. If the difference between the two measurements is more than 0.15 mm (0.006 in) then it will be necessary to fit new pistons and liner assemblies. If no micrometer is available remove the rings from a piston and place the piston in each bore in turn about ¾

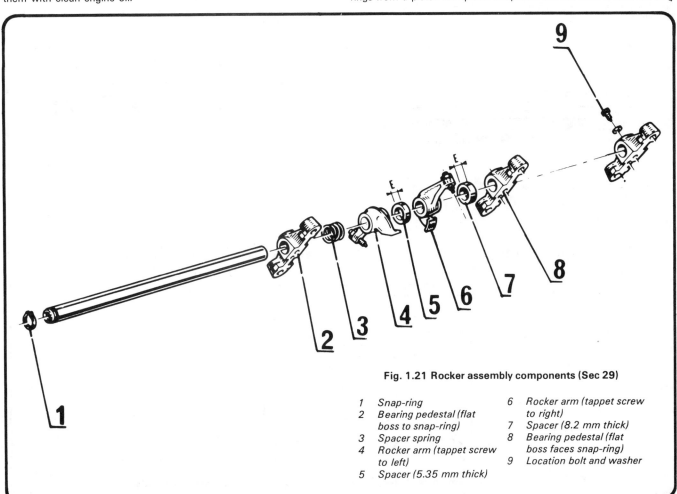

Fig. 1.21 Rocker assembly components (Sec 29)

1   Snap-ring
2   Bearing pedestal (flat boss to snap-ring)
3   Spacer spring
4   Rocker arm (tappet screw to left)
5   Spacer (5.35 mm thick)
6   Rocker arm (tappet screw to right)
7   Spacer (8.2 mm thick)
8   Bearing pedestal (flat boss faces snap-ring)
9   Location bolt and washer

in (18 mm) below the top of the bore. If a 0.25 mm (0.010 in) feeler gauge can be slid between the piston and the cylinder wall on the thrust side of the bore then remedial action must be taken.

3   If the liners are re-usable, deglaze the bores using coarse emery cloth. The upper ridge is best removed using a de-ridging tool. Clean all traces of abrasive from the bores on completion.

4   Should the liners have been disturbed they must be completely removed from the cylinder block and new seals fitted, otherwise once the seals have been disturbed the chances are that water will leak into the sump. Refer to Section 39 for cylinder liner installation details.

31 Pistons and rings – examination and renovation

1   If the old pistons are serviceable and are to be refitted, carefully remove the piston rings as given in Section 14.

2   With the rings removed from the pistons, clean out the grooves but take care not to scratch the aluminium in any way. Pieces of old piston ring are useful for this task, but protect your fingers – piston rings are sharp!

3   If new rings are to be fitted to the old pistons then the top ring should be stepped so as to clear the ridge left in the bore above the previous top ring. If a normal but unstepped new ring is fitted it will hit the ridge and break because the new ring will not have worn in the same way as the old, which will have worn in unison with the ridge. The piston rings are supplied pre-gapped for the particular liner diameter and it is not necessary to check them in the liners. It is not necessary to measure the side clearance in the piston ring grooves with the rings fitted as the groove dimensions are accurately machined during manufacture. When fitting new oil control rings to old pistons it may be necessary in this instance to have the groove widened by machining to accept the new wider rings.

4   If new pistons are to be fitted be sure to fit the correct type for your model. One of two piston types will be found, but where replacements are to be used, only the 'type 2' will be supplied by your Renault dealer (see Fig. 1.22).

5   Make sure that the new pistons will give the correct compression ratio. This can be checked by measuring the crown boss height as shown in Fig. 1.23. The respective boss heights are as follows:

> 9.1 : 1 compression ratio – 1.96 mm (0.077 in)
> 8.65 : 1 compression ratio – 1.80 mm (0.070 in)
> 8.2 : 1 compression ratio – 0.2 mm (0.007 in)

6   New pistons and liners are only supplied as complete sets. The respective components are carefully matched to each other during production. Accordingly, do not interchange components from one set to another.

32 Connecting rods and gudgeon pins – examination and renovation

1   A visual check only can be carried out to observe whether any movement or play can be seen when the piston is held still and the connecting rod pushed alternately.

2   If there has been evidence of small-end knock with the engine at normal working temperature, then the connecting rod/piston assembly should be taken to a Renault dealer as special tools are required to dismantle and refit these components.

3   Have the connecting rods checked for alignment whenever the gudgeon pins are renewed.

33 Timing chains, tensioners and timing cover – examination and renovation

1   After a considerable mileage the timing chains and sprockets will have worn and possibly be in need of renewal.

2   Clean and examine the camshaft sprockets and also the crankshaft and oil pump drive sprockets. If they are worn, indicated by hooked teeth, then they must be renewed. It is possible to renew the chains at time of major overhaul; if new sprockets are being fitted, new chains **must** be used.

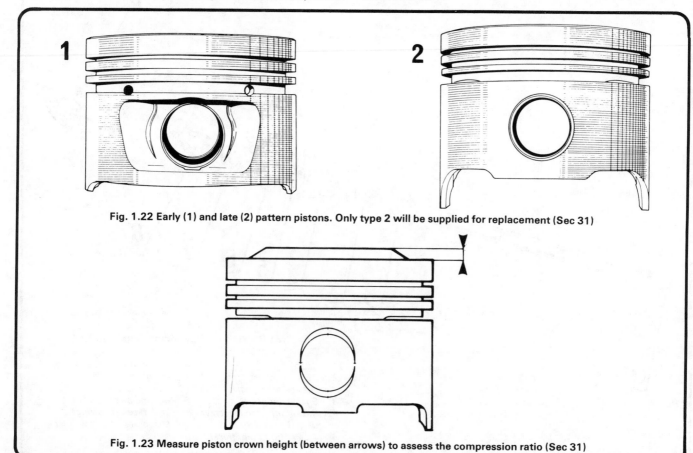

Fig. 1.22 Early (1) and late (2) pattern pistons. Only type 2 will be supplied for replacement (Sec 31)

Fig. 1.23 Measure piston crown height (between arrows) to assess the compression ratio (Sec 31)

3   Check the respective tensioner blades and pivots for wear. The tensioner block itself should not be dismantled; if suspect, renew it. If the retaining lock in the tensioner is accidentally removed then it must be renewed since there is no way of checking the lock finger position relative to the thrust ball during assembly, and it is possible to jam the tip of the finger with the spring – see Fig. 1.24.

4   On Type 112 engines from No 17029, the tensioner blades are of a modified type to strengthen the pivot. With this fitting, the cylinder block pivot pins are located 1.2 mm (0.047 in) further in compared with the earlier type, the timing cover stiffening ribs next to the tensioner blade pivots are reduced in size and the blade spacers are increased in width from 14 mm (0.551 in) to 20.5 mm (0.807 in). Longer blade retaining bolts are fitted (35 mm/1.38 in instead of 30 mm/1.18 in) and 1 mm (0.04 in) thick washers are used instead of the earlier 2 mm (0.08 in) thick washers.

5   With these modifications in mind, if a new cylinder block is being fitted in place of the earlier engine type, then the later tensioners, bolts and washers must also be fitted. If fitting the original timing cover to the later block, the bosses (A and B in Fig. 1.25) will have to be reduced by 3.5 mm (0.138 in) near the tensioner pivots. Your Renault dealer should be entrusted with this task.

6   The new chain tensioner blades are not interchangeable with the earlier type. Make sure you get the correct type when buying new ones.

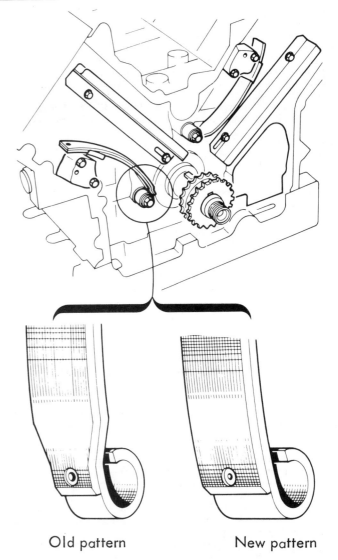

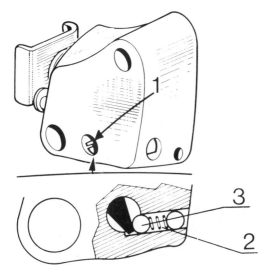

Fig. 1.24 Chain tensioner details (Sec 33)

1   Retaining lock   3   Ball
2   Spring

Old pattern   New pattern

Fig. 1.26 The early and late type chain tensioner blade identification features (Sec 33)

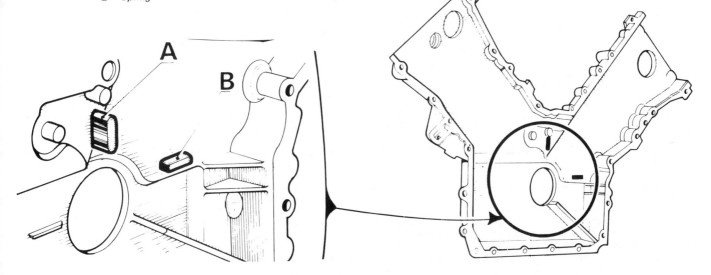

Fig. 1.25 Timing cover showing boss position (A and B) (Sec 33)

34 Cylinder block – examination and renovation

1   Check for cracks. The cost of welding the alloy material must be weighed against a new casing. Threaded holes which have stripped, may have proprietary thread inserts installed to rectify, the only exception to this being the oilway plug in the cylinder block next to the oil filter (Fig. 1.27).
2   If a new cylinder block is to be fitted, refer to Section 33 concerning its interchangeability with regard to chain tensioners and the timing case.
3   Ensure that the location flanges for liner base seals are perfectly clean prior to reassembly.

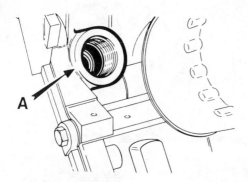

Fig. 1.27 Cylinder block oilway plug location (A) (Sec 34)

35 Flywheel/driveplate and starter ring gear – examination and renovation

1   If the starter ring gear teeth on the flywheel (manual transmission) or torque converter driveplate (automatic transmission) are excessively worn, it will be necessary to obtain complete new assemblies. It is not possible to obtain separate ring gears.
2   On manual transmission models, examine the clutch mating surface of the flywheel and renew the flywheel if scoring or cracks are evident.
3   On automatic transmission models, the driveplate face should be checked for run-out, using a dial gauge. The maximum permissible run-out is 0.3 mm (0.012 in). Renew the plate if this figure is exceeded.
4   The flywheel/driveplate retaining bolts must be renewed on assembly, as must the flywheel bolt locking washers (where fitted).

36 Engine mountings – inspection

The engine mounting rubbers are often ignored simply because they do not normally present any problems. However their work rate is probably equal to any other engine component and therefore if the engine is removed at any time, it is worthwhile checking the condition of the mounting rubbers. If they shows signs of deterioration due to oil impregnation, heat or simply age, they should be renewed. Mountings that have lost their resistance to shocks will cause engine/transmission vibrations and increase the fatigue rate of other associated engine/transmission connections, as well as that of the driver and occupants of the car.

37 Engine reassembly – general

1   To ensure maximum life with minimum trouble from a rebuilt engine, not only must everything be correctly assembled, but all the parts must be spotlessly clean, all the oilways must be clear, locking washer and spring washers must always be fitted where indicated and all bearing and other working surfaces must be thoroughly lubricated during assembly. Before assembly begins renew any bolts or studs, the threads of which are in any way damaged, and whenever possible use

new spring washers. **Note**; *Before fitting the cylinder head bolts check that the holes and threads in the block are clean and free of oil – this is most important.*
2   Apart from your normal tools, a supply of clean rags, an oil can filled with engine oil (an empty plastic detergent bottle, thoroughly cleaned and washed out, will do just as well), a new supply of assorted spring washers, a set of new gaskets and a torque wrench should be collected together.
3   A torque wrench is essential during reassembly. This is because the various housings are manufactured from aluminium alloy and whilst this gives the advantage of weight reduction it also means that the various components must be accurately fitted and tightened to the specified torque settings or serious distortion or damage could result. Distorted or cracked housings are not cheap to renew so beware!
4   Apart from the gaskets, seals and applicable engine components, it is essential that the following be renewed when assembling the engine:

   (a)   *Flywheel or converter driveplate retaining bolts*
   (b)   *Flywheel bolt lockplates (where fitted)*
   (c)   *Big-end cap nuts*

5   Take your time during reassembly. Some operations, for example the establishment of correct liner protrusion, require care and patience if good results are to be obtained.

38 Crankshaft and main bearings – refitting

1   Make sure that the crankcase is thoroughly clean and that all the oilways are clear. Inject oil into the oilways at several points with a forcefeed oil can or plastic bottle: this will have the two-fold benefit of checking that the oilways are clear and getting oil into them before you start assembly. Do the same with the crankshaft – it is particularly important to get as much oil as possible into the crankshaft oilways. Then place the cylinder block upside down on the workbench ready for reassembly.
2   Remove every trace of protective grease from new bearing shells.
3   Wipe the seats of the main bearing seals in the crankcase clean and fit the appropriate shells in them. Fit the thrust washers to the rear bearing. Note that the bearing shells have tabs on them which fit into grooves in the casing, so they can only be fitted the one way. If the old bearings are being refitted, be sure to place them in their original positions. Remember that the inner shells have oil holes in them (photos).
4   Oil the shells generously and place the crankshaft on top of them – be sure that it is the right way round (photos).
5   When refitting the thrust washers to the rear end bearing housing, note that there are four halves in all and that the upper two halves have tags. When fitted, the oil grooves in the thrust washers must face away from the cap on each side. Oil the thrust washers before refitting them; not only does it help the general lubrication process, but it also helps them stay in position.
6   Wipe the bearing cap housings and fit their shells into them, keeping an eye on the order if necessary. The caps fit as numbered 1 to 4, from rear to front, with the number stamped on the cap facing towards the front of the engine. Also, the bearing shell tags must marry up to ensure accurate refitting (photo).
7   Oil the bearing surfaces of the crankshaft generously and fit the front and rear bearing caps over them, ensuring that they locate properly. The mating surfaces must be spotlessly clean or the caps will not seat correctly (photo).
8   When the two end main bearing caps have been refitted, hold them in position temporarily by fitting some spacers (sockets will do as shown in photo 38.9) under the retaining nuts which should be tightened to the specified torque. Check that the crankshaft rotates freely. Some stiffness is normal with new shells, but there should be no binding or tight spots.
9   Lever the crankshaft forwards and backwards, checking the amount of endfloat with the Specifications given at the beginning of this Chapter (photo). The clearance can be reduced or increased by altering the thickness of the thrust washers which are available in three different oversizes, apart from the standard size, as quoted in the Specifications.
10 When satisfied that the endfloat is acceptable, leave the two end main bearing caps bolted in position temporarily until you are ready to

38.3A Insert the main bearing shells ...

39.3B ... and locate the rear bearing upper half thrust washers with oil grooves outwards

38.4A Lubricate the bearings ...

38.4B ... and fit the crankshaft

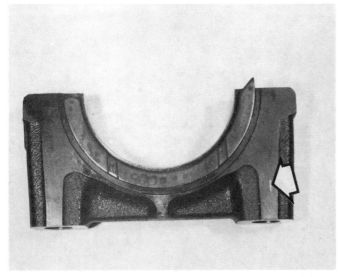
38.6 The number on the bearing cap (arrowed) faces the front of the engine

38.7 Refit the main bearing cap together with the lower half thrust washers

38.9 Check the crankshaft endfloat (note bearing cap temporary retainers)

39.3 Liner seal fits over the base section

refit the bottom casing. Locate the connecting rod big-end bearings before refitting the bottom casing, to avoid having to work through its confined access apertures.

39 Cylinder liners, pistons and connecting rods – refitting

1   Before fitting the piston and connecting rod assemblies into the liners, the liners must be checked in the cylinder block for depth of fitting. This is carried out as follows.
2   Although the cylinder liners fit directly onto the cylinder block flange, base seals are fitted between the flanges in the cylinder block and the cylinder liners. New seals must always be used once the liners have been disturbed from the cylinder block.
3   Varying thicknesses of liner base seals are available in order to obtain the correct liner protrusion above the top face of the cylinder block faces on each bank. The liner base seals are available in four thicknesses (see Specifications) and are colour tagged for identification (photo).
4   Selection of the base seal thicknesses required is made by inserting the respective liners into position in the cylinder block without the base seals fitted. The respective liner protrusions in each cylinder block bank face in turn are then checked. Lay a straight-edge across the top face of a liner and measure the gap to the top face of the cylinder block with feeler gauges. Repeat this with the two other liners in the bank concerned and make a note of the respective protrusions (photos).
5   Now subtract the largest measurement reading taken from 0.009 in (0.23 mm) to determine the theoretical seal thickness requirement.
6   Seal thickness equal to, or just less than, the calculated thickness should then be selected. As an example, if the maximum reading taken from a liner protrusion is 0.004 in (0.10 mm), subtract this from 0.009 in (0.23 mm) to give 0.005 in (0.13 mm). In this instance a red tag base seal is required, which has a thickness of 0.0048 in (0.122 mm).
7   One seal of the same thickness is fitted to each liner. When in position the seal castellations must be engaged in the recess as shown (Fig. 1.28).
8   When the liners are refitted into the cylinder block, locate them so that the base seal tags are visible as shown (Fig. 1.29), then recheck their protrusions above the cylinder block face.
9   The protrusional difference between adjacent liners when fitted must not exceed 0.0016 in (0.04 mm). In addition, the protrusional differences (where applicable) must be stepped in one direction as shown (Fig. 1.30). Where necessary, change the thickness of one or more liner seals acordingly whilst keeping the protrusions within the permitted tolerance.
10   When the respective liner positions and base seals are selected, mark their positions accordingly. When re-using the original liners this should not be necessary, since they should have been marked for position when dismantling. It is essential that they be refitted with

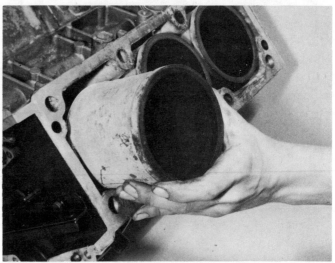

39.4A Insert the liner into the cylinder block

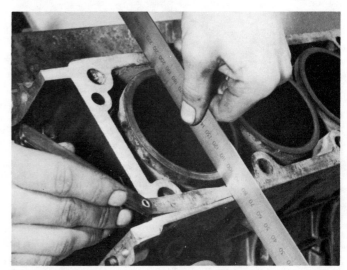

39.4B Check the liner protrusion above the cylinder block top face

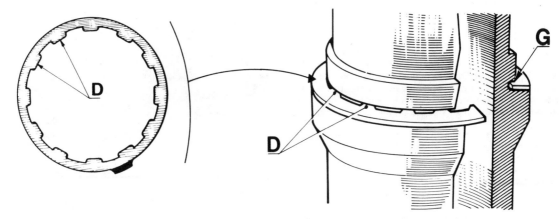

Fig. 1.28 Locate the seal castellations (D) within the groove (G) (Sec 39)

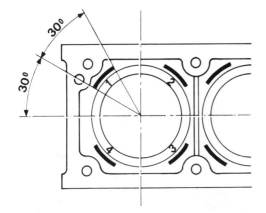

Fig. 1.29 Liner seal tags to be positioned in one of the four locations shown (Sec 39)

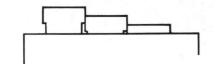

Fig. 1.30 Step cylinders as shown where there are protrusional differences (1 to 3, 4 to 6, or vice versa) (Sec 39)

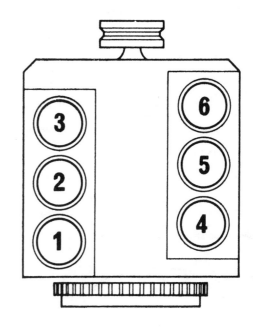

Fig. 1.31 Cylinder numbering sequence (Sec 39)

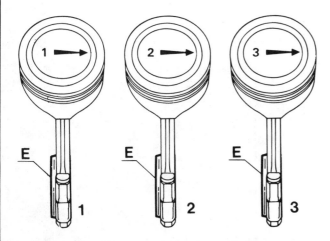

Fig. 1.32 Piston and connecting rod orientation with extended rod flange (E) offset to the rearwards on left-hand bank (Sec 39)

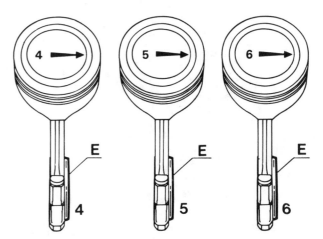

Fig. 1.33 Piston and connecting rod orientation with extended rod flange (E) offset to the front on right-hand cylinder bank (Sec 39)

their respective pistons and connecting rods. The assemblies are numbered 1 to 6 as shown in Fig. 1.31.

11 Each cylinder liner is now ready for fitment of the connecting rod and piston assemblies.

12 As previously explained, the fitting of the pistons to the connecting rods will have been carried out by the Renault agent due to the difficulty of removing and inserting the gudgeon pin. Check that the pistons have been fitted correctly, however, by noting that the arrows on the piston crowns will face towards the timing gear end, and that the connecting rod/cap number markings are on the side noted during dismantling.

13 If new piston and liner assemblies have been supplied, they must be cleaned off the anti-rust coating. Soak them in a suitable solvent to remove the protective coating – do not scrape it off.

14 Keep the respective pistons and rings with their mating cylinder. They are carefully matched sets.

15 Fit the piston rings to each piston in turn, reversing the process for removal as described earlier in this Chapter. Where new ring sets are being fitted to old pistons and liners, follow the manufacturer's instructions supplied with the rings. *It is most important that the rings are assembled in the correct manner.* Once fitted into their ring grooves, check that the rings are free to rotate around the piston and that they do not bind in the groove when fully compressed. If they do, then it is likely that a piece of carbon still remains on the ring land and it needs further cleaning.

16 Liberally oil the rings and ring grooves and turn the rings so that the gaps are at three different points of circle, as shown in Fig. 1.34.

17 Locate the shell bearings in the connecting rod and cap big-end bearings (photos).

18 Lubricate each liner bore and piston assembly in turn as they are assembled.

19 Make sure the piston ring gaps are still correctly spread out around the piston. Fit the piston ring clamp around the piston and tighten it up (photo). Take care not to scratch the piston.

20 Offer the piston (and connecting rod) to its respective bore, noting that it can only fit one way round. The arrow on the top of the piston must face towards the front of the engine (photo). It is easy therefore to check whether the pistons have been refitted correctly; the arrows on the pistons must point uniformly. Progressively press the piston/connecting rod assembly into position in each cylinder liner in turn. Excessive force should not be required, firm hand pressure only being necessary.

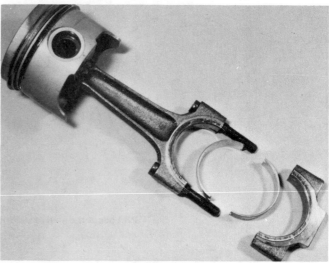

39.17A Piston, connecting rod, end cap and shell bearings ready for fitting

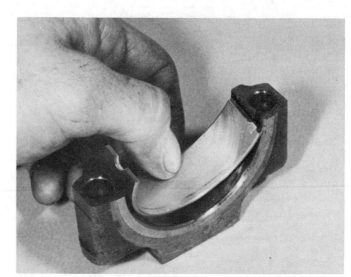

39.17B Insert the bearing shells so that the tag is located correctly

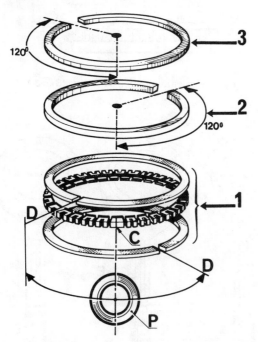

Fig. 1.34 Fit piston rings with gaps as shown (Sec 39)

1	Oil scraper ring	C	Scraper expander gap
2	Lower compression ring	D	Scraper rail gaps
3	Top compression ring	P	Gudgeon pin

39.19 Refit the piston into its cylinder using a ring compressor

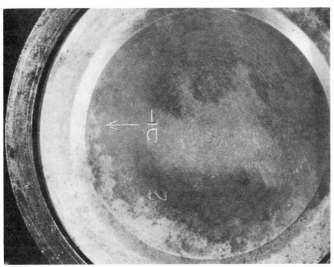

39.20 Arrow on top of piston to point to front (timing case) end

21 Assemble each bank in turn, starting with No 1 cylinder. As each piston and connecting rod in turn is fitted into its liner, engage the big-end cap and bearing over the the crankshaft journals (photo). Hand tighten the bearing cap nuts for the moment. Remember to use new nuts.

22 As each assembly in turn is fitted, check that the orientation and alignment markings are correct, then fit the temporary liner clamps to prevent the liners from moving during subsequent operations requiring the crankshaft to be turned.

23 When all the pistons and connecting rods are fitted, tighten the big-end bearing cap retaining nuts to the specified torque (photo). On completion, check that the crankshaft rotates without excessive binding or tight spots (but not if the timing chains are in position, unless the dummy camshaft bearing is fitted – see Section 9.

24 Leave the liner clamps in position for subsequent operations until the cylinder heads are ready to be fitted.

---

40 Bottom casing and sump – refitting

1 Remove the nuts and spacers from the front and rear main bearing cap studs.

2 Lubricate the No 2 and 3 main bearing cap shells and the bearing journal, and fit the respective caps into position. The peak casting on each cap must point towards the timing cover (photos).

39.21 Locate connecting rod and cap, ensuring that the mating marks are aligned

39.23 Tighten the connecting rod big-end nuts to the specified torque setting

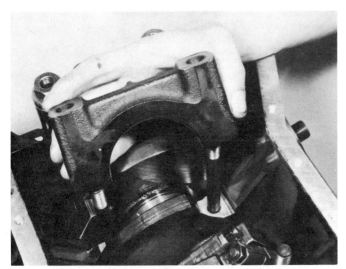

40.2A Locate the number 2 and number 3 main bearing caps

40.2B Bearing cap orientation must be as shown

3　Locate the rear seal cover gasket, smearing it with grease to hold it in position, then fit the seal housing so that its bottom face is flush with the cylinder block bottom face (photos). Fit and tighten the Allen screws (photo).

4　Trim off the gasket ends protruding from the lower facings, and check that they are flush by placing a straight-edge across them.

5　Locate a new O-ring seal in the channel between the cylinder block and bottom casing.

6　Check that the mating surfaces of both the cylinder block and lower casing are clean and oil free.

7　Apply a thin layer of RTV sealant to the cylinder block mating surface, then lower the bottom casing into position (photos).

8　Locate the main bearing cap washers and nuts, but do not tighten them yet (photo).

9　Check the alignment of the cylinder block with the bottom casing rear face, and the alignment of the bellhousing retaining brackets, using a straight-edge (photo). It is essential that they be aligned, or

distortion could result when refitting the transmission. Align if necessary and then tighten the two Allen screws which secure the rear of the bottom casing to the rear seal housing.

10　Tighten the main bearing cap nuts to the specified torque in the sequence shown in Fig. 1.35 (photo). Each nut must then be further tightened (in the sequence given) a further 75°. To do this, first make a protractor or angle template using a piece of stiff cardboard. Mark one edge as the 0° line and then using a geometrical protractor, mark a line or cut the cardboard at an angle of 75° from the 0° line. Locate the socket onto the nut to be tightened and mark a line on the socket in alignment with the 0° line, then tighten the nut until the socket line is in alignment with the 75° line. An assistant will be required to hold the cardboard template in position whilst the nut is being tightened, as the template must not move at all (photo).

11　Repeat this procedure on each nut in turn until the eight main bearing cap nuts are tightened correctly.

12　Fit the bottom casing retaining bolts and tighten them evenly.

40.3A Locate the rear seal and its housing

40.3B Check that housing bottom face is flush with crankcase lower face ...

40.3C ... then fully tighten the retaining screws

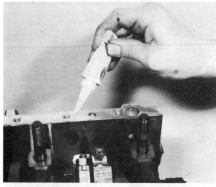
40.7A Apply liquid sealant (RTV) to crankcase lower face ...

40.7B ... then fit the bottom casing

40.8 Locate the main bearing cap washers and nuts, and hand tighten them

40.9 Check the end faces of the bottom casing, the rear seal housing and the cylinder block for alignment

40.10A Tighten the main bearing nuts to the specified torque ...

40.10B ... then a further 75°. Use a fabricated template as shown to assess this arc

40.13 Refit the anti-emulsion plate and tighten its retaining bolts

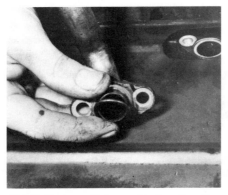
40.14A Fit a new O-ring seal to the oil suction pipe

40.14B Refit the oil suction pipe unit

40.15A Refit the sump using a new gasket ...

40.15B ... and tighten the securing bolts

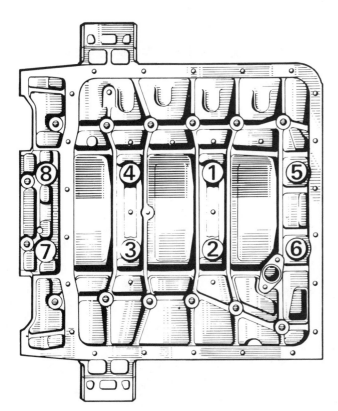
Fig. 1.35 Main bearing cap nuts to be tightened in sequence shown (Sec 40)

13 Relocate the anti-emulsion plate and secure with bolts and washers (photo).

14 Locate a new O-ring onto the bottom end of the oil suction pipe, then refit the suction pipe assembly into position (photos).

15 Fit the new sump gasket into position and then refit the sump. Locate and tighten its retaining bolts to the specified torque (photos). Make sure that the sump drain plug is tight.

41 Cylinder heads, refitting – timing components not yet fitted

1 With the bottom half of the engine rebuilt, it is time to turn the engine over and rest it on the sump. To make working on it more pleasant, place a block under the rear end of the lower crankcase to bring it level.

2 Refitting both the cylinder heads is basically the same operation performed twice. Start by rotating the crankshaft so that the No 1 cylinder piston is 0.59 in (15 mm) before the peaks of its compression stroke (TDC). Keep the crankshaft in this position whilst fitting the cylinder heads and rocker assemblies to avoid the possibility of the pistons touching the valves during the subsequent operations.

3 Prise up the cylinder head location dowels so that a $\frac{1}{8}$ in (3 mm) rod or drill shank can be located underneath them through the access holes in the side of the cylinder block. This should keep them in the raised position until the head has been refitted (photos).

4 Remove the liner retaining plates from the side of the engine on which you are working, and wipe over the cylinder block mating face.

5 Check that you have the correct gasket for the side on which you are working – they are different. Place it in position and make sure all the bolt holes and oil holes line up (photo). The two tongues should follow the profile of the block at the front end. Do not use any jointing compound.

6 If the camshaft is still removed from the cylinder head being fitted, lubricate its bearings and locate it into position in the cylinder head, referring to Section 27.

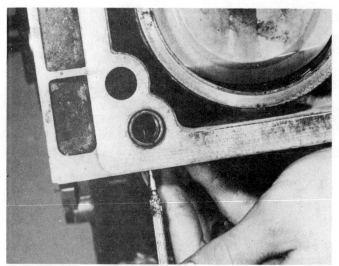

41.3a Raise the cylinder head location dowels at the front ...

7   Place the cylinder head in position, having first checked that its face is completely clean (photo). Locate it on the dowels and make sure it seats correctly. The drill bits (or rods) can then be removed from the side of the block.
8   Now pick up the correct rocker assembly for the side of the engine you are working on. They were marked appropriately when they were removed. Remember the assemblies are similar, but that when refitting them, the circlip on the end of the rocker shaft is at the front of the engine for the left-hand side assembly, and at the rear of the engine for the right-hand side assembly. Place the assembly in position on the head.
9   Oil the cylinder head bolts and screw them loosely into position (photo).
10 Check that the camshaft and rocker arms are correctly lined up. With the left-hand side cylinder head, the camshaft should be lined up so that the valves for No 1 cylinder (at the rear) rock (exhaust closing, inlet opening). If rebuilding the right-hand side cylinder head, the camshaft should be rotated to a position where the valves for No 6 cylinder (front) rock.
11 The cylinder head bolts can now be tightened in the sequence shown in Fig. 1.11. Initially tighten them in the sequence given to the first stage specified torque, then give them a second tightening to the second stage torque.

41.3B ... and at the rear

41.5 Locate a cylinder head gasket

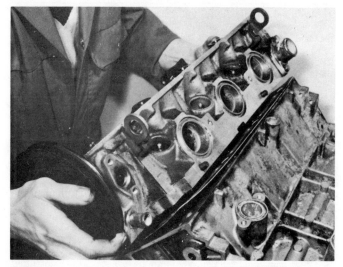

41.7 Lower a cylinder head into position, locating it over the protruding dowels

41.9 Refit the rocker assembly and loosely screw in the bolts

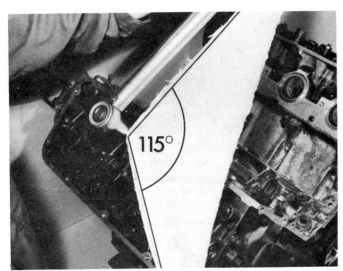

41.12 Tighten the cylinder head bolts to the recommended torque, then through a further 115°, using template to assess the arc

12 Now that the gasket is evenly compressed, loosen off bolt number 1. Retighten it to the third stage torque, then further tighten it by moving the torque wrench through an arc of 115° as shown in Fig. 1.36. To angle tighten the bolts correctly make a cardboard template, mark one side as the 0° line and using a geometrical protractor mark off or cut at an angle of 115° from the 0° line. Get an assistant to hold the template in position whilst you tighten the bolt through an arc of 115° (photo).
13 Repeat this procedure with each of the remaining cylinder head bolts in turn in the sequence given.
14 When one cylinder head has been completed, the other can be refitted in exactly the same way. Go back to paragraph 3 and follow the instructions through.

42 Cylinder heads, refitting – timing components fitted

1 Where the cylinder head(s) are being refitted with the timing chains and sprockets in position, it is assumed that the camshaft sprockets are supported as described in Section 9 in order to maintain the timing chain tension and the valve timing.
2 Remove the liner retainers.
3 Where the cylinder liners have not been removed, their respective protrusions above the top face of the cylinder block must be checked before refitting the cylinder head(s).
4 To do this, place a rule across the top of the liners and check the clearance between the rule lower edge and the cylinder block top face using feeler gauges. The liner protrusions must be within the limits given in the Specifications. The nearer the protrusion is to 0.009 in (0.23 mm) the better.
5 If the liner protrusions are outside this tolerance, the liner base seals require renewal so that the correct protrusion can be attained. Refer to Sections 13 and 39 for details.
6 Refit one cylinder head at a time in the following manner, taking care not to allow the timing chain to become slack at any time during assembly. If it does, you will have to remove the timing cover after the head has been fitted in order to reset the chain tension and check the valve timing – see Section 43. A separate tensioner is fitted to each timing chain.
7 New timing cover-to-cylinder head gasket sections must be used. Clean off any of the old gasket still remaining and then cut to size and locate new gasket sections as shown in Fig. 1.37. Stick them in position by smearing with a thin layer of RTV sealant.
8 Refer to the previous Section and complete the procedures given in paragraphs 3 to 7 inclusive.
9 Locate the timing cover-to-cylinder head retaining bolts, but hand tighten them only at this stage.
10 Align the camshaft drive peg hole and mate the camshaft with the sprocket. Relocate the camshaft retaining plate and fit and tighten the securing bolt.
11 Fit and hand tighten the camshaft sprocket retaining bolt.
12 Refer to the previous Section and complete the operations given in paragraphs 8 to 14 inclusive.

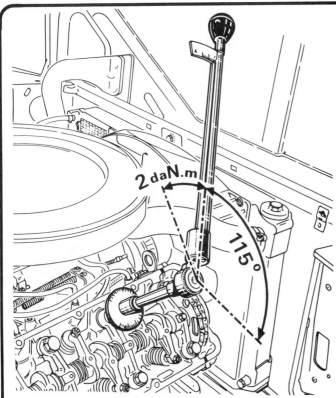

Fig. 1.36 Cylinder head bolt tightening method (Sec 41)

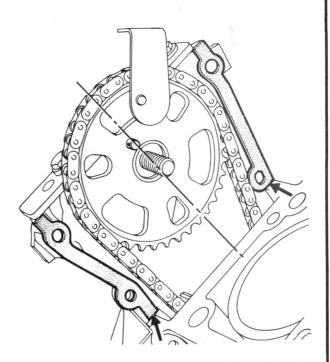

Fig. 1.37 Locate the new timing case-to-cylinder head gasket sections (arrowed) (Sec 42)

42.13 Tighten the camshaft sprocket retaining bolt

13 With the cylinder head(s) tightened down, tighten the timing cover-to-cylinder head bolts and the camshaft sprocket bolt to the specified torque settings (photo).
14 Refit the access plug into the front of the left-hand bank timing cover. When assembling the right-hand bank, refit the front cover plate using a new seal (photo).
15 Drive the oil seal into position in the rear end of the left-hand cyiinder head (if not already fitted – see Section 20). Refit the power steering pump drive pulley.
16 Refit the right-hand camshaft endplate to that cylinder head, again using a new seal (photo).
17 Before refitting the rocker covers, the valve clearances must be adjusted as given in Section 45.

43 Timing chains, sprockets and tensioner assemblies – refitting

1   Relocate the timing chain tensioner oil filter gauzes (photo).
2   Refit the chain guides and tensioners into position on the cylinder block front face.
3   Locate and bolt the tensioner blades into position.
4   Engage the timing sprocket key into its keyway in the crankshaft and then refit the timing sprocket so that its timing mark faces outwards (photo).

42.14 Refit the end plug into front of the timing case on the left-hand bank

42.16 Refit the cover and seal on the right-hand bank

43.1 Insert the tensioner oil filter gauzes

43.4 Refit the crankshaft timing chain sprocket

5   The left-hand side timing chain assembly is fitted first. Rotate the crankshaft so that its keyway is facing upwards to the centre-line of the left-hand cylinder bank.

6   Fit the left-hand camshaft sprocket into the chain so that the timing mark on the sprocket front face is between the two marked links of the chain (photo). Supporting the chain and sprocket in this position, fit the chain lower end over the camshaft sprocket and align the single marking on the chain link with the timing mark on the front face of the sprocket. The chain is fitted over the rear teeth of the double timing sprocket (photos).

7   If the cylinder head and camshaft are in position, then the camshaft sprocket can be fitted to the camshaft so that the driving pin engages its slot in the shaft flange. Locate the camshaft retaining bolt and tighten it to the specified torque whilst preventing the crankshaft from turning.

8   Where the cylinder head and/or camshaft are not in position then you will have to support the camshaft sprocket temporarily on a dummy bearing as given in Section 9.

9   To fit the right-hand timing chain assembly, first turn the crankshaft through 150° so that the timing mark on the crankshaft sprocket aligns with the oil pump cover lower retaining bolt (photo).

10   Now fit the right-hand camshaft sprocket into its chain so that its timing mark is between the twin markings on the chain links. Supporting the chain and sprocket in this position, fit the chain over the crankshaft sprocket so that the single marking on the chain link

43.6A Chain to camshaft gear relative positions – left-hand bank

43.6B Crankshaft sprocket and left-hand bank timing chain marks to align

43.6C The left-hand cylinder bank timing chain and sprockets assembled

43.9 Align the crankshaft sprocket timing mark as shown

43.10 With the right-hand bank timing chain assembly fitted, chain timing marks should be at positions shown

43.13 Set the chain tensioners

43.15A Locate the timing cover gaskets ...

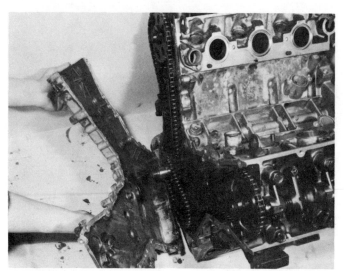

43.15B ... then refit the covers and bolts. Note that the cover bolts are of different lengths

aligns with the crankshaft sprocket timing mark. This chain is fitted over the front teeth of the crankshaft sprocket (photo).

11 As with the left-hand sprocket, if the cylinder head and camshaft are in position then the camshaft sprocket can be fitted to the camshaft, engaging its drive pin into the flange slot. The camshaft sprocket retaining bolts should then be refitted. Prevent the crankshaft from turning and tighten the retaining bolt to the specified torque setting.

12 If the cylinder head/camshaft is not fitted, then the camshaft sprocket must be supported temporarily as given in Section 9.

13 The timing chain tensioners can be reset when the respective camshaft sprockets are bolted in position on their camshafts and the chains fitted. On earlier models the tensioners are set by turning them clockwise using a suitable screwdriver as shown (photo). On later models, press the tensioner shoe in so that it touches the tensioner body, then release the shoe but do not assist the spring action. Lock the tensioner by pressing the shoe in and turning the ratchet anti-clockwise.

14 Refit the oil pump as given in Section 44. New cylinder blocks are always fitted with a new oil pump, but the sprockets and drive chain have to be assembled.

15 Locate the timing gear cover gaskets (dry) and then refit the timing cover, engaging it over the location dowels. When fitting the cover

retaining bolts, the lower section bolts should be smeared with a thread sealing compound. Trim off any protruding gasket from the cylinder head faces (photos).

16 Using a suitable diameter drift, carefully drive the crankshaft pulley oil seal into position. Lubricate the seal prior to fitting.

17 Refit the crankshaft pulley and then fit the retaining bolt. Jam the flywheel to prevent the crankshaft from turning and tighten the pulley nut to the specified torque (photos).

44 Oil pump – inspection and refitting

1 Having removed the oil pump from its location on the front lower face of the cylinder block (Section 16), it can be cleaned in petrol or solvent for inspection.

2 Check the pump rotor and its housing for any signs of wear or damage. The complete pump assembly must be renewed if found to be defective.

3 To inspect the oil pressure relief valve, extract the split pin and withdraw the spring seat, spring and release valve plunger (photo). Check the end face of the plunger and its contact face within the body for signs of scoring or damage, and renew if necessary.

4 The drive chain and sprockets shouldl also be checked for wear and renewed if worn.

5 Reassembly of the pump unit is a reversal of the dismantling procedure.

6 When assembling the relief valve plunger, ensure that it is fitted the correct way round.

7 Locate the driven gear and pump cover and tighten the retaining bolts to the specified torque. Rotate the sprocket flange to ensure that the pump gear rotates freely (photos).

8 Prime the pump on completion by squirting some engine oil through the aperture shown (photo) with the oil filter removed.

9 The pump driven sprocket bolt threads should be smeared with thread locking compound when fitting the sprocket.

10 Ensure that the drive sprocket distance piece is in position on the crankshaft before refitting the sprocket and chain (photos).

11 Refit the timing cover and the crankshaft pulley as described in Section 43.

12 If the engine is in the vehicle, the remaining reassembly details are a reversal of the removal sequences.

45 Valve clearances – adjustment

1 Remove the retaining screws and lift each rocker cover clear.

2 The clearances given in the Specifications are for a cold engine. To check the clearances you will need a set of feeler gauges, whilst for adjustment a 13 mm spanner (preferably a ring spanner) and a

43.15C Tighten the cover bolts to secure ...

43.15D ... and trim off any protruding gasket at the top face

43.17A Locate the crankshaft pulley ...

43.17B ... tighten the pulley nut to the specified torque

44.3 The oil pump and relief valve components

44.7A Insert the driven gear ...

44.7B ... the drivegear and cover

44.8 Prime the oil pump through the side aperture within the oil filter mounting location in the cylinder block

44.10A Locate the distance piece ...

44.10B ... the sprocket key ...

44.10C ... and the sprocket

44.10B Oil pump drive chain and sprockets fitted

screwdriver are required. Note that different clearances are specified for inlet and exhaust valves.

3   The precise adjustment of the valve/rocker clearances is of utmost importance for two main reasons. First, to enable the valves to be opened and closed at the precise moments required by the cycle of the engine. Second, to ensure quiet operation and minimum wear of the valvegear components.

4   Settings made when the engine is on the bench will require rotation of the crankshaft and this may be done by turning the crankshaft pulley bolt. If the engine is in the car and a manual gearbox fitted, select top gear, then jack up the front so that a front wheel is clear of the ground and can be turned. With automatic transmission, this method is not possible and 'inching' the engine using the starter motor will have to be resorted to.

5   Turn the engine by means of one of the methods described until No 1 piston is rising on the compression stroke. This may be ascertained by placing a finger over No 1 plug hole and feeling the build-up of pressure. Carry on turning until the TDC position is reached, when the 'A' mark shown in Fig. 1.38 is aligned with the 'O' line on the clutch/torque converter housing. There are two sets of timing marks on the flywheel or driveplate, the details of which are explained in Chapter 4. The valves of No 5 cylinder should be 'rocking' – ie exhaust valve closing, inlet valve opening.

45.9A Refit the rocker cover(s) ...

Fig. 1.38 Appearance of manual (left) and automatic (right) timing marks on transmission housing with No 1 piston at TDC (Sec 45)

6   Check and adjust as necessary the following valve clearances. Inlet valves are nearest the middle of the engine, exhaust valves on the outside:

No 1 cylinder inlet
No 2 cylinder inlet
No 4 cylinder inlet
No 1 cylinder exhaust
No 3 cylinder exhaust
No 6 cylinder exhaust

7   If the clearance requires adjustment, loosen the locknut, and with the feeler in position turn the adjuster screw until the feeler blade is nipped and will not move. Now unscrew the adjuster until the feeler blade is a firm sliding fit. Tighten the locknut without moving the screw and recheck the clearance (photo).

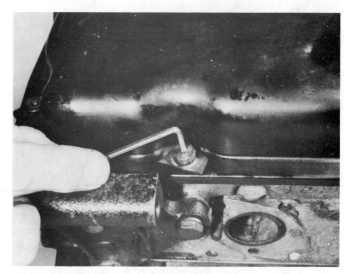
45.9B ... and tighten the retaining screws

8   Now rotate the crankshaft by one complete turn so that the flywheel 'A' mark is again aligned with the 'O' mark on the housing. Check that No 1 cylinder rocker arms are 'rocking' and then check/adjust the following valves:

No 3 cylinder inlet
No 5 cylinder inlet
No 6 cylinder inlet
No 2 cylinder exhaust
No 4 cylinder exhaust
No 5 cylinder exhaust

9   When all the valve clearances have been checked and where necessary adjusted, refit the rocker covers, renewing the gaskets if the old ones are damaged or are brittle. Ensure that each cover retaining screw has the special flat washer fitted (photos).

10 When the engine is restarted check around the rocker cover edges for any signs of oil leaks.

45.7 Valve clearance adjustment

---

46 Flywheel/driveplate – refitting

1   On manual gearbox models if the spigot bearing was removed or if a new crankshaft has been fitted, the spigot bearing must be fitted into position.

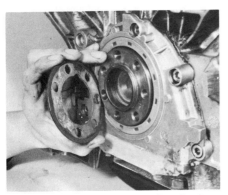

46.6 Don't forget the spacer washers for the converter driveplate on automatic transmission models

46.7 Tighten the retaining bolts to the specified torque

47.5 Fit new O-rings for the cooling pipe connections

2 Grease the bearing with heat-resistant grease, but do so sparingly.

3 Clean out the bearing housing in the end of the crankshaft, though this should already be clean if the engine has been fully dismantled and thoroughly cleaned.

4 Place the bearing squarely in the flange and tap it firmly home into position.

5 New flywheel or driveplate retaining bolts must always be used when refitting to the crankshaft. The bolt lockplates (where fitted) must also be renewed.

6 Locate the flywheel or driveplate into position on the crankshaft rear flange so that the respective bolt holes are aligned. In the case of the driveplate a spacer washer must be fitted on each side of the plate as shown (photo).

7 Smear the retaining bolt threads with thread locking compound before fitting. Tighten the bolts progressively to the specified torque (photo).

8 On manual transmission models, reassemble the clutch unit to the flywheel as given in Chapter 5.

47 Engine reassembly – ancillary equipment

1 The refitting of all the ancillary equipment to the engine, before it is itself refitted, is mainly a matter of following in reverse order the procedure laid down in Section 8.

2 However, there are one or two points that should be mentioned before the refitting procedure begins. Firstly, when refitting the exhaust manifolds, always use new gaskets and make sure they are the correct way round. When refitting the right-hand manifold also refit the engine dipstick guide tube. Where the engine only has been removed, the exhaust manifold on the left-hand cylinder bank is best fitted after the engine is installed and the starter motor located in its transmission housing aperture, as access is restricted.

3 Do not refit the oil filter until after the starter motor is fitted.

4 Set the crankshaft so that No 1 cylinder is about to fire and then

refit the distributor so that it is correctly timed. See Chapter 4 for full details.

5 Locate new O-rings for the cooling pipe flange connections to the cylinder block on each side (photo).

6 Refit the Y-pipe and its associated coolant hose connections.

7 The water pump and its associated pipe fittings can now be fitted to the front end of the cylinder block (photo). Ensure that all the hose connections are secure, also the pump mounting bolts.

8 Refit the cooling hoses at the rear (photo).

9 Having checked that all the hose connections are secure, locate the heat shield into position between the cylinder banks as shown (photo) to cover up what by now resembles a smoke pit!

10 Fit the inlet manifold O-rings into position and then locate the spacer gasket on each side.

11 The inlet manifold can now be refitted and bolted down. Connect the coolant hose. Particular care must be taken if the carburettor(s) are attached to the manifold not to damage them. On fuel injection models, refer to Chapter 3 for refitment of the inlet air manifold and associated fittings.

12 Refit the fuel pump into position at the rear of the left-hand bank cylinder head, using a new gasket. Reconnect the fuel supply hose to the carburettor.

13 If removed, refit the cooling fan/pulley assembly to the water pump drive spindle.

14 If not yet refitted, refer to Chapter 5 and locate the clutch unit on the flywheel.

15 The engine is now ready for refitting to the car. If refitting complete with the transmission unit, assemble the two as given in the following Section.

48 Engine to gearbox/automatic transmission – refitting

Manual gearbox

1 If not already fitted, refer to Chapter 5 and refit the clutch unit to

47.7 Refit the water pump and coolant pipes

47.8 Relocate the rear cooling hoses

47.9 Refit the heat shield

the flywheel. Check that the release bearing and lever are correctly located and lubricate the clutch shaft splines sparingly with grease.

2   Adequately support the engine and gearbox at the same relative height so that the gearbox primary shaft will slide horizontally into the splined hub of the friction disc.

3   The help of an assistant to keep the engine still will be useful. Keep the gearbox quite level and push it into engagement with the engine. In order to engage the primary shaft of the gearbox with the driven plate splines and finally with the flywheel bush, it may be necessary to turn the gearbox slightly or to raise or lower it fractionally, but on no account allow the weight of the gearbox to hang upon the clutch assembly while the primary shaft is passing through it, and support it at all times.

4   Refit the bellhousing attachment bolts. Refit the starter motor and its heat shield at this stage, rather than when the engine is in the car.

Automatic transmission

5   Remove the temporary retaining plate holding the torque converter in its housing.

6   Smear the converter-to-driveplate location housing with grease before re-engaging the two.

7   Couple the two assemblies together and fit the retaining bolts.

8   Align the torque converter and driveplate bolt holes and insert the bolts, observing any alignment marks. Turn the crankshaft by means of a spanner on the crankshaft pulley and as each bolt hole becomes accessible, insert the bolt through the aperture underneath. Jam the starter ring gear and tighten the securing bolts to the specified torque.

9   Refit the starter motor and its heat shield at this stage, rather than when the engine is in the car.

49 Engine – refitting

1   First check that all of the engine ancillary items are fitted and secure, that is at least, those which you have intended to fit before the installation of the engine. Clean the engine compartment and tie back any cables and wires which might interfere with the refitting of the engine.

2   Prior to commencing refitting, check the condition of the engine mountings (and gearbox/transmission mountings as applicable). If the rubber mountings show any signs of deterioration or are oil soaked, renew them.

3   Locate and arrange the lifting sling so that when the engine (and transmission as applicable) are lowered into position, they can be suitably angled for easy refitting.

4   Using the hoist, lift the unit(s) into the engine compartment, and carefully lower and guide into position. It will be particularly useful to have an assistant during this operation. Raise or lower the transmission accordingly as the unit(s) are refitted. Where the gearbox

is already in the car, pay particular attention to paragraphs 1 to 3 or 5 to 8 (as applicable) in the previous Section.

5   Where the engine is to be refitted on its own, refit the starter motor after the engine is installed, but before refitting the oil filter and engine undertray.

6   Once the engine is refitted into the car, the reassembly of the various fittings and associated attachments is basically a reversal of the removal procedures. The following special points should be noted.

7   When refitting the torque converter housing lower cover plate on automatic transmission models, don't forget to locate the power steering hose clip under the retaning bolt on the left-hand side (photo).

8   If not already fitted, locate the starter motor (three bolts) and reconnect the wires. Refit the heat shield.

9   Before refitting the oil filter, inject some engine oil through the oil hole to prime the oil pump (see Section 44).

10   Reconnect the exhaust manifold downpipes on each side, applying some exhaust pipe sealant to the joint surfaces to prevent leakage.

11   Refit the alternator and retension the drivebelt as given in Chapter 2.

12   Relocate the diagnostic socket into its location bracket on the rear of the right-hand cylinder bank and reconnect the wires, one of which is the earth wire (yellow) and fits under the head of the socket bracket retaining bolt with a shakeproof washer.

13   Reconnect the throttle cable to the quadrant mechanism and adjust if necessary (Chapter 3).

14   Reconnect the servo vacuum hose to the inlet manifold, and (where applicable) the vacuum pipe to the automatic transmission.

15   Reconnect the fuel supply and return hoses (photo).

16   Refit the radiator and fan shroud.

17   Reconnect the heater hoses, and the radiator-to-water pump and thermostat hoses.

18   Reconnect the oil cooler hoses (automatic transmission models).

19   Reconnect the governor control cable and adjust it as given in Chapter 7 (automatic transmission models).

20   On models with fuel injection, refer to Chapter 3 for details on refitting the system components.

21   Reconnect the coolant temperature sender and the oil pressure switch wires.

22   Refit the diagnostic socket pick-up unit plate. If the pick-up has been withdrawn from the plate, it must be readjusted before tightening its clamp screw. Refer to Fig. 1.40 and adjust the pick-up so that it is 0.020 to 0.040 in (0.5 to 1 mm) from the flywheel/converter driveplate face. If a new pick-up unit is being fitted, set it so that the three lugs are in contact with the flywheel/converter driveplate face and then retighten the clamp screw.

23   Reconnect the ignition HT and LT wires. The respective HT lead positions are marked on the top of the distributor cap adjacent to each lead. The numbers refer to the lead fitted positions – not nessarily the firing order. See Chapter 4 for full details.

24   Check for any other ancillary engine wiring yet to be connected.

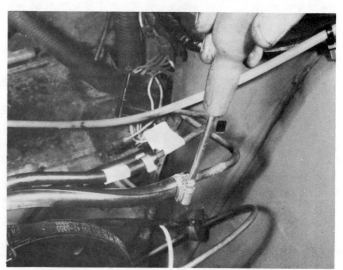

49.7 Locate the power steering hose clip under the bolt head for the lower cover plate

49.15 Reconnect the fuel supply and return hoses

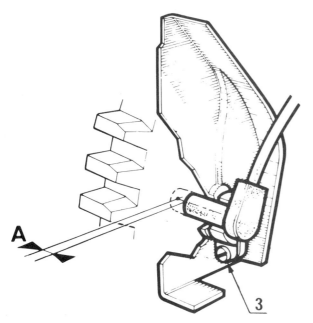

Fig. 1.39 Adjust the clearance (A) before fully tightening the TDC pick-up clamp screw (3) (Sec 49)

25 Refit the power steering pump and adjust the drivebelt.
26 Reconnect any air conditioning components where applicable.
27 Before refitting the air filter, check around the engine to ensure that all fittings and components are reconnected and secure.
28 Top up the engine with the recommended grade and quantity of engine oil. If the gearbox/automatic transmission was also removed, this should also be topped up with the specified lubricant.
29 Refill and bleed the cooling system as given in Chapter 2.
30 Do not refit the engine undertray yet, as on restarting the engine you will need to check it thoroughly for any signs of leaks, the source of which may only be detectable from underneath.
31 Refit the bonnet and check it for alignment before fully tightening the hinge bolts.
32 Finally make sure that all tools, rags, etc have been removed from the engine compartment before attempting to restart the engine.

50 Engine – initial start-up after overhrual or major repair

1 Make sure the battery is fully charged – it may have to work hard before the engine starts. Check oil and coolant levels.

2 If the fuel system has been dismantled, it will require quite a lot of engine revolutions to get the petrol up to the carburettors. With the fuel injection engines, of course, this problem will not arise. If there is doubt about the state of charge of the battery, take the plugs out and the petrol will be pumped up with far less effort.
3 As soon as the engine fires and runs, keep it going at a fast tickover only (no faster) and bring it up to normal working temperature.
4 As the engine warms up, there will be odd smells and some smoke from parts getting hot and burning off oil deposits. Look for water or oil leaks which will be obvious if serious, particularly as the engine is clean.
5 Check the ignition timing as described in Chapter 4.
6 When the engine running temperature has been reached, adjust the idling speed as described in Chapter 3.
7 Once the car has been used on the road it will be possible to check that the ignition timing is correct and gives the necessary smoothness and power. Do not forget that although the old pistons and crankshaft may still have been used, new bearing shells will have been fitted. Treat it as a new engine and run-in at reduced revolutions for at least 500 miles (800 km).
8 After the first 500 miles or so, retighten the cylinder head bolts as described in the next Section. If new bearings etc have been fitted, it will be advantageous to change the engine oil and filter at the same time.

51 Cylinder head bolts – check/tightening procedure

1 The cylinder head bolts must be further check-tightened after an initial mileage is covered, 300 to 500 miles (500 to 800 km) is recommended by Renault. This check must always be made whenever a cylinder head has been removed or when a service exchange engine has been fitted. On new models it should be checked by your Renault dealer on a free of charge basis within the warranty period.
2 To make this check the air filter and rocker covers must be removed and the carburettor-to-inlet manifold and timing cover-to-cylinder head bolts loosened off.
3 The engine must be cold when making this check, Renault specify at least 2 hours after it has been run.
4 Referring to Fig. 1.11, loosen cylinder head bolt No 1 and then retighten it to 15 lbf ft (20 Nm). Repeat this procedure on each bolt in turn on the cylinder head concerned, in the numerical sequence given.
5 Now starting with the No 1 bolt, further tighten each bolt in sequence, a further 115°. The method of achieving this is discussed in Section 41.
6 When all the bolts are tightened to the specified amount, retighten the inlet manifold and timing cover bolts. Before refitting the rocker covers, check and if necessary adjust the valve clearances as given in Section 45.
7 On completion refit the rocker covers and any ancillary items which were disturbed for this check.

52 Fault diagnosis – engine

Symptom	Reason(s)
Engine will not turn when starter switch is operated	Flat battery Bad battery connections Bad connections at solenoid switch and/or starter motor Starter motor jammed Defective solenoid Starter motor defective
Engine turns normally but fails to start	No spark at plugs No fuel reaching engine Too much fuel reaching the engine (flooding)
Engine starts but runs unevenly and misfires	Ignition and/or fuel system faults Incorrect valve clearances Burnt out valves Worn out piston rings

Symptom	Reason(s)
Lack of power	Ignition and/or fuel system faults Incorrect valve clearances Burnt out valves Worn out piston rings
Excessive oil consumption	Oil leaks from gaskets or seals Worn piston rings or cylinder bores resulting in oil being burnt by engine Worn valve guides and/or defective valve stem seals
Excessive mechanical noise from engine	Wrong valve clearances Worn crankshaft bearings Worn cylinders (piston slap) Slack or worn timing chain and sprockets
Poor idling	Leak in inlet manifold gasket Ignition timing incorrect Fuel system fault General wear in moving components
Oil contaminated by coolant	Cylinder head gaskets blown Cylinder liner base seal leaking Cylinder liner cracked Cylinder block cracked

Note: *When investigating starting and uneven running faults, do not be tempted into snap diagnosis. Start from the beginning of the check procedure and follow it through. It will take less time in the long run. Poor performance from an engine in terms of power and economy is not normally diagnosed quickly. In any event, the ignition and fuel systems must be checked first before assuming any further investigation needs to be made.*

Chapter 2 Cooling system

Contents

Specifications

General
System type .... Sealed and pressurised, centrifugal pump, electric cooling fan on some models

System capacity:
    Standard .... 17.2 Imp pints (9.8 litres)
    With air conditioning .... 17.9 Imp pints (10.2 litres)
Blow-off pressure:
    Metal expansion tank valve .... As stamped on valve
    Plastic expansion tank valve (white) .... 11.5 lbf/in^2 (0.8 bar)
    Plastic expansion tank valve (brown) .... 17 lbf/in^2 (1.2 bar)

Thermostat
Type .... Wax
Opening commences .... 180°F (82°C)
Fully open by .... 201°F (94°C)

Cooling fan thermoswitch (when fitted)
Cuts in at .... 198° ± 9°F (82° ± 5°C)
Cuts out at .... 179° ± 9°F (82° ± 5°C)
Minimum difference between cut-in and cut-out .... 11°F (6°C)

Drivebelt deflection adjustments
Water pump/alternator .... 0.21 to 0.25 in (5.5 to 6.5 mm)
Air conditioning compressor .... 0.11 to 0.15 in (3 to 4 mm)
Power steering pump .... 0.09 to 0.11 in (2.5 to 3 mm)

Torque wrench settings

	lbf ft	Nm
Alternator pivot bolt	30	40
Alternator adjusting link nuts and bolts	14	20

1 General description

A sealed type cooling system is used on engines fitted to the Renault 30 series. The engine coolant is circulated by a thermo-syphon, water pump assisted system, and the coolant is pressurised. This is primarily to prevent premature boiling in adverse conditions and to allow the engine to operate at its most efficient running temperature, this being just under the boiling point of water.

With this type of cooling system, the overflow pipe from the radiator is connected to an expansion tank, which makes topping-up virtually unnecessary. The coolant expands when hot, and instead of being forced down an overflow pipe and lost, as with the earlier systems, it flows into the expansion tank. As the engine cools, the coolant contracts and because of the pressure differential, flows back into the radiator.

The cap on the expansion tank is set at a pressure which will increase the boiling point of the coolant to just above that at normal atmospheric pressure.

The cooling system comprises the radiator, top and bottom hoses, the expansion tank, the water pump, the fan and the thermostat. A drain tap is provided on the right-hand side of the cylinder block and there is also one on the left-hand side of the left-hand side cylinder block. The radiator does not have a conventional cap as the system is filled through the expansion tank. The radiator is of the horizontal type, having the tanks standing along the sides of the matrix.

The system functions as follows: cold coolant from the radiator circulates up through the lower radiator hose to the water pump,

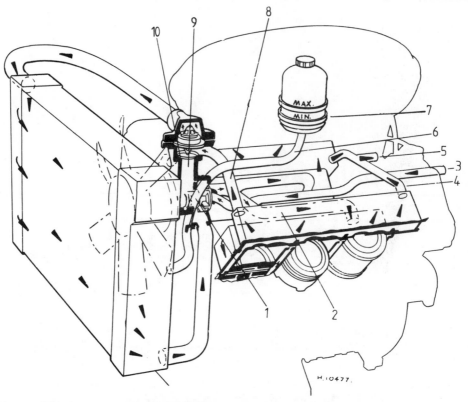

Fig. 2.1 The cooling system layout (Sec 1)

1   Coolant pump
2   Inlet pipe (Y-pipe)
    between pump and cylinder
    block
3   Return pipe for

4   Inlet pipe for
    compartment heater
5   To compartment heater
6   Filler hose between
    compartment heater

    radiator and expansion
    tank
7   Expansion tank
8   Return hoses between

    cylinder heads and
    thermostat housing
9   Bypass
10 Thermostat housing

helping to keep the cylinder bores and pistons cool. The coolant then
travels up into the cylinder heads and circulates around the
combustion spaces and valve seats. Then, when the engine is at its
normal operating temperature, the water flows out of the cylinder
heads, past the now open thermostat, through the top hose and into
the radiator. The coolant flowing down through the radiator matrix is
cooled by the time it reaches the bottom hose when the cycle is
repeated.

   When the engine is cold, the thermostat (a valve which opens and
closes according to coolant temperature), maintains the circulation of
the same coolant in the engine and only when the correct minimum
temperature is reached, as given in the Specifications, does the
thermostat begin to open, allowing coolant to return to the radiator.

2   Cooling system – draining

1   If the coolant is known to be in clean condition and of the correct
constituency of antifreeze mixture, arrange suitable containers to hand
before commencing draining.
2   Where one object of draining is to flush the system then it is to be
recommended that the engine is at normal operating temperature as
sludge and dirt will then be in suspension and more readily removed.
If the engine is drained hot, flush with hot water *not* cold, or distortion
or cracking of internal engine components may occur.
3   Set the facia heater control to 'hot'.
4   Remove the air vent valve from the expansion bottle.
5   Open the drain tap at the bottom rear face of the radiator and
drain. The coolant will flow slowly at first and as the expansion bottle
empties it will flow faster. At this stage, unscrew and remove the
radiator filler cap (photo).
Note: *Where there is no drain plug or tap fitted to the radiator base,
unscrew and detach the radiator bottom hose connection to drain the
system. Due to the uncontrolled flow of coolant when the hose is
disconnected, extra care must be taken when the coolant is hot.*

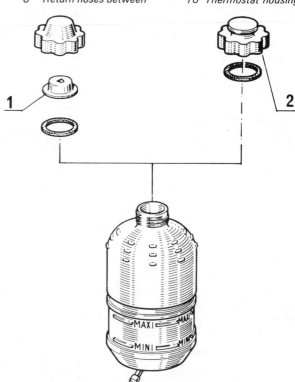

**Fig. 2.2 Expansion tank showing the two types of air vent valve
caps fitted (Sec 2)**

1   Metal valve

2   Plastic valve (white or
    brown)

2.5 Radiator drain plug (arrowed)

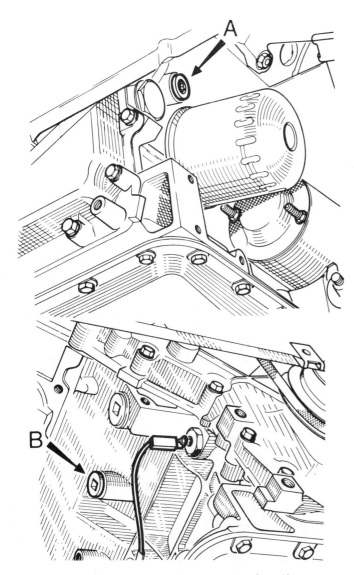

Fig. 2.3 The cylinder block drain plugs (Sec 2)

A   Left-hand side   B   Right-hand side

6   To drain the cylinder block, remove the drain plug each side as shown in Fig. 2.3 and open the bleed screws (on the thermostat housing and heater return hose).

3   Cooling system – flushing

1   Remove the thermostat from its water pump location as described in Section 12.
2   Temporarily reconnect the hose to the water pump outlet.
3   Check that the drain plugs are open and that the heater control is on 'hot'.
4   Insert a hose in the radiator filler cap and flush through until the water emerges clean. Use hot water if the engine was drained hot.
5   The accumulation of sludge or scale may necessitate removal of the radiator (Section 6) and reverse flushing. This is carried out by inverting the radiator matrix and placing a hose in the outlet pipe so that water flows in a reverse direction to normal.
6   Chemical descaler should only be used in a cooling system if scale and sludge formation are severe. Adhere strictly to the manufacturer's instructions.
7   Leakage of the radiator or cooling system may be temporarily stopped by the use of a proprietary sealant but in the long term, a new cylinder head or other gasket, water pump, hoses or radiator matrix must be installed (as applicable).

4   Cooling system – filling and bleeding

1   Have ready a sufficient quantity of coolant mixture as described in Section 5. Close the radiator and block taps and/or reconnect the bottom hose.
2   Turn the heater control lever to 'hot'.
3   Check that the bleeder screws on the thermostat housing and heater return hose are fully open.
4   Loosen the expansion bottle clip and lift the bottle temporarily as high as possible (whilst still connected to the hose).
5   Next refill the radiator to the 'full' mark and refit the radiator cap (photo). Complete the filling of the system by the expansion bottle.
6   When the coolant exits from the bleed screws they can be retightened.
7   The level of the coolant in the expansion bottle should be roughly 70 mm ($2\frac{3}{4}$ in) above the 'MAXI' mark.
8   Refit the expansion bottle cap (with valve and seal).
9   Run the engine at a fast tickover for a couple of minutes to warm up the coolant and enable the thermostat to commence opening. Next, open up the bleed screws again, and when the coolant flows out of them, retighten the bleed screws and stop the engine.

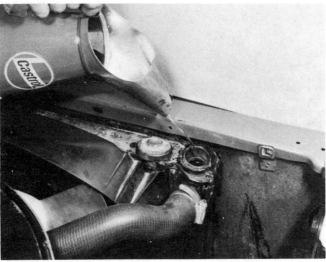

4.5 Refilling the radiator

10 Refit the expansion bottle into position and make secure with the clip. After a short period (once the engine has cooled down) recheck the coolant level in the expansion bottle and, if necessary, top up the level given in paragraph 7. If coolant passes through the expansion bottle valve at any time then the valve must be renewed.

5 Coolant and antifreeze mixture

1 The original coolant in the sealed system is of 'long-life' type and with antifreeze characteristics. It is preferable to mix a new coolant solution every two years, however, as apart from the antifreeze properties, rust and corrosion inhibitors (essential to a light alloy engine) will, after this period of usage, tend to lose their effectiveness.
2 Mix the antifreeze with either distilled water or rain-water in a clean container. Drain and flush the system as previously described and pour in the new coolant. Do not allow antifreeze mixture to come in contact with vehicle paintwork, and check the security of all cooling system hoses and joints as antifreeze has a 'searching' action.
3 The following amounts of antifreeze (as a percentage of the total coolant – see Specifications) will give protection down to the specified temperatures:

Percentage of antifreeze	Protection to (°C)
50%	−37
40%	−25
30%	−16
25%	−13
20%	−9
15%	−7
10%	−4

A mixture of less than 20% strength is not recommended as anti-rust and anti-corrosion action is not effective.

6 Radiator (and electric cooling fan, where fitted) – removal and refitting

1 On models fitted with an electric cooling fan, disconnect the battery earth lead.
2 Assuming only the radiator (and electric cooling fan, where fitted) is being removed, it is not necessary to drain the complete cooling system. Instead, locate clamps at the position indicatated in Fig. 2.4 and tighten to compress the top and bottom hoses, thereby retaining the coolant in the engine and heater systems. A pair of G-clamps and some flat pieces of wood will do the job. The hoses must of course be in good condition or they will crack when compressed. If no clamps are available, drain the system.

3 Drain the radiator coolant through the drain plug or detach the bottom hose from the radiator connection, as applicable.
4 Where an electric cooling fan is fitted, detach the wires from the connectors, and unclip from the hose. Also disconnect the leads from the thermal switch in the base of the radiator.
5 Disconnect the expansion bottle-to-radiator hose, and the radiator top and bottom hoses (photo).
6 On automatic transmission models, detach the oil cooler pipes from the left-hand side of the radiator (photo).
7 On models fitted with air conditioning, detach the condenser pipe retaining clamps and remove the front grille to gain access to the condenser mountings. **Do not** under any circumstances open the condenser pipes.
8 Remove the retaining screws and lift the fan shroud clear from the radiator (models with conventional fan),

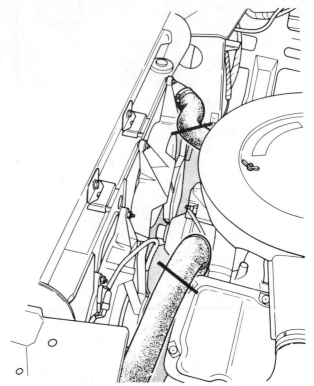

Fig. 2.4 Clamp hoses at points indicated (Sec 6)

6.5 Disconnecting the radiator bottom hose

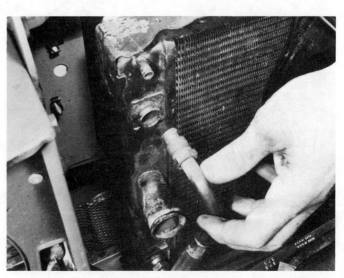

6.6 Disconnect the automatic transmission oil cooler pipes from the radiator

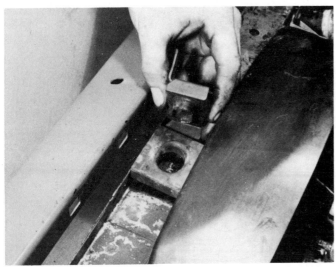

6.9 Radiator retaining clamp

6.10 Lifting the radiator into position – note that the fan shroud is preassembled

9   Remove the radiator retaining bolt and carefully lift the radiator clear (photo).

10 Refitting is a reversal of the removal procedure, but check before fitting that the location mountings are in good condition and renew if necessary (photo).

11 When the radiator is in position and the hoses reconnected, top up the radiator with coolant before releasing the hose clamps. Run the engine and bleed the system (see Section 4) to complete, and check for leaks. On automatic transmission models, check the transmission oil level.

7   Radiator – inspection and cleaning

1   With the radiator out of the car, any leaks can be repaired by soldering (as below) or using a fibreglass paste. Clean out the inside of the radiator by flushing with clean water, turn it upside-down and reverse flush the matrix. Clean the exterior of the radiator by hosing down with a strong jet of water to clean away road dirt and dead flies, etc which may be lodged in the matrix.

2   Inspect the radiator hoses for cracks, internal or external perishing and damage caused by over-tightening of the hose clips. Renew defective hoses. Examine the hose clips and renew them if they are rusted or distorted.

3   Do not attempt to solder a radiator yourself. The amount of local heat required will almost certainly melt adjacent joints. Take the radiator to a specialist or exchange it for a reconditioned unit.

8   Electric cooling fan unit – removal and refitting

1   Disconnect the battery earth lead.

2   Detach the cooling fan motor wires at the connectors.

3   Unscrew and remove the unit-to-radiator retaining nuts whilst supporting the unit, then lift it clear.

4   Measure the fan retaining bolt (or nut on some types), noting that it has a *left-hand thread*.

5   Remove the fan motor retaining bolts or nuts and withdraw the unit. One type of motor is secured to the fan guard/support by pop rivets, and these must be drilled through to remove. A defective motor must be renewed; no repair is possible.

6   Refitting of the fan unit is a reversal of the removal process. When in position ensure that all fastenings are secure, then run the engine and check that the fan becomes operational to maintain the normal engine operating temperature once it is reached.

7   Before condemning a suspect fan motor, remember that the thermoswitch could be faulty. Refer to Section 11 for thermoswitch details.

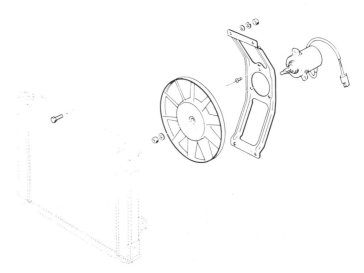

Fig. 2.5 Engine cooling fan – electric type (Sec 8)

9   Drivebelts – adjustment and renewal

1   The water pump, alternator and (where fitted) air conditioning compressor are all driven from the crankshaft pulley, a double-track pulley being used on air conditioning equipped models. The power steering pump is driven from the rear end of the left-hand cylinder bank camshaft.

2   The respective drivebelts must be correctly tensioned at all times. A tight fitting will reduce the belt life and also that of the drive bearings of the component concerned. A loose fitting will also reduce the belt life, and the belt will slip and consequently also reduce the efficiency of the unit it drives.

3   The belts can be adjusted independently, but the water pump and alternator drivebelt can only be removed after withdrawal of the air conditioning compressor drivebelt (where fitted).

4   Inspect the condition of the belts occasionally and renew them if they show any signs of fraying, or have stretched so that available adjustment has been fully used.

5   Belts are correctly adjusted when there is a total deflection of the specified amount (see Specifications), under a moderate thumb pressure at the centre of the longest run of the belt concerned as shown in Figs. 2.6, 2.7 and 2.8.

6   To make adjustment to the drivebelt of a particular system, loosen the alternator/pump/compressor (if applicable) and pivot the unit

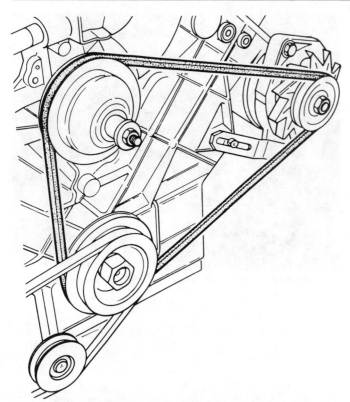

Fig. 2.6 Alternator/water pump drivebelt (Sec 9)

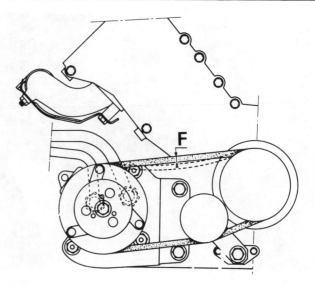

Fig. 2.7 Air conditioning compressor drivebelt (Sec 9)

F   Deflection

Fig. 2.8 Power steering drivebelt. Deflection check point arrowed (Sec 9)

inwards or outwards to slacken or tighten the belt respectively. Retighten the mounting bolts of the unit concerned and recheck the tension of the belt.

7   Whenever a new belt has been fitted, its tension should be rechecked after the engine has been run for a short initial period. New belts normally stretch a fraction during the early stage of usage and will probably be in need of further adjustment after a short time.

8   To remove and refit a belt, loosen the mounting bolts of the alternator/power assisted steering pump/compressor, as applicable, and slacken off the adjustment of the belt for removal. Refitting of the belt is a reversal of the above procedure and it must, of course, be adjusted for tension.

10 Engine coolant temperature transmitter – testing

1   Where an engine coolant transmitter unit is suspected of being faulty, the only simple way to test it is by substitution.

2   The transmitter unit is located in the front of the thermostat housing.

3   Removal necessitates partial draining of the cooling system, whilst the gauge removal necessitates removal of the instrument panel (see Chapter 10).

4   It is not possible to repair the gauge or sender unit and they must therefore be renewed if faulty.

5   A simple test of the gauge may be made by touching the sender unit wire to earth (ignition on) whilst an assistant observes the gauge. The gauge should read 'hot'; if not, either there is a break in the wiring or the gauge itself is at fault.

11 Radiator electric cooling fan temperature switch – testing

1   The thermal switch which regulates the operation of the electric cooling fan is fitted into the radiator. Ideally, tests to the switch should be carried out after it has been removed from its location. If this is done, the cooling system will have to be drained and refilled, but the following alternative method may be submitted.

2   Connect a test light to the fan switch. Where the engine is cold (ie switch contacts open), it should not light up.

3   Start the engine and blank off the radiator to ensure quick warming up.

4   Hold a thermometer in contact with the radiator. When the temperature reaches the cut-in point (see Specifications), the lamp should light.

5   Switch off the engine and allow the temperature of the radiator to drop. When the cut-out temperature is reached (see Specifications), the lamp should go out.

6   If the switch does not operate within the test limits, renew it.

7   If the switch does not operate correctly, then the fault must lie in the fan assembly or the connecting wiring or relay.

12 Thermostat – removal, testing and refitting

1   To remove the thermostat, start by lowering the coolant level in the system. When draining, collect the coolant in a container for re-use.

2   Disconnect the wire from the coolant temperature sender.

3   Disconnect the thermostat-to-radiator hose at the thermostat.

12.4A Lift clear the cover ...

12.4B ... and lift out the thermostat

4   Unscrew and remove the two thermostat housing cover bolts and then lift clear the cover. The thermostat can now be withdrawn from its housing (photos).
5   To check the performance of a suspect thermostat, suspend it in a container of water which can be heated. As the water warms up, note the temperature at which the thermostat begins to open and also that at which the fully open position is reached. Compare these with the figures in the Specifications at the beginning of this Chapter.
6   Generally speaking, when the thermostat fails to remain shut, this leads to overheating, and if for any reason you are unable to renew the thermostat you should remove it and run the car without it. This is alright as a temporary measure, but in this situation the engine takes longer to warm up on starting and also there is no regulation of the coolant system to keep the engine at its optimum operating temperature. Therefore, always renew the thermostat at the first opportunity.
7   Before inserting the new thermostat into position, prise free the cover O-ring seal and clean its location groove.
8   Locate a new O-ring seal, followed by the thermostat and its top cover.
9   Relocate and tighten the retaining bolts. Reconnect the hose and the temperature sender unit.
10 Refill and bleed the cooling system as given in Section 4.

13 Water pump – removal, overhaul and refitting

1   Disconnect the battery earth lead, then detach the coolant temperature switch wire at its sender unit connection at the thermostat housing.

2   Drain the cooling system as given in Section 2.
3   Remove the air filter unit, followed by the inlet manifold assembly, referring to Chapter 3. This is necessary in order to gain suitable access to the pipe connections at the rear of the water pump.
4   Detach and remove the cooling fan shroud (with the cooling fan on electrically operated types).
5   Disconnect the thermostat-to-radiator hose.
6   Loosen the alternator mountings and remove the drivebelt.
7   Disconnect the water pump/radiator hose (at the pump), and the heater hose from the thermostat housing.
8   Disconnect the hose on each side to the cylinder heads, and also the inlet manifold hose if still attached to the pump (photo).
9   Unscrew and remove the water pump retaining bolts and withdraw the pump unit forwards to disconnect it from the rear hoses.
10 Before inspecting and overhauling the pump, check that the two short hoses at the rear of the pump are in good condition; this is the best time to change them. In fact, it is best to change them anyway so you will not get a problem later. Also, check the two flange joints at the rear end of the Y-pipe. If these show any traces of leakage at all, it is a simple task to remove the two bolts on each flange and renew the O-rings.
11 To remove the fan/pulley assembly from the water pump, remove the retaining nut and washer and carefully withdraw them from the drive spindle (photos).
12 Remove the rear casing of the pump in order to inspect the working parts, and detect whether play can be felt in the impeller shaft and bearings. This casing is held in place by five Allen bolts (photo).
13 If the impeller, shaft or bearings are worn the unit will have to be renewed. The bearings and shaft cannot be renewed on their own; as a replacement assembly, you will get the main pump housing including

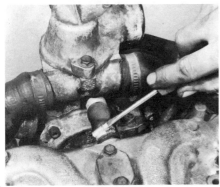

13.8 Disconnecting the hose from the inlet manifold

13.11A Fan retaining nut

13.11B Remove the special washer

13.12 Pump unit shown with rear casing removed

13.14A Relocate the pump and ...

13.14B ... tighten its retaining bolts

13.14C Retighten the respective hose clips

13.14D Locate the key into the impeller shaft ...

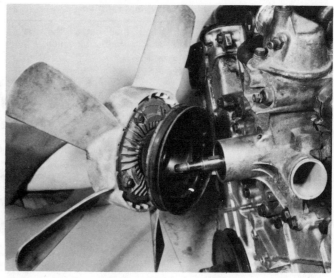

13.14E ... and refit the pulley and fan assembly

the impeller and shaft but without the rear casing, thermostat or elbow. These parts will have to be removed from the old unit, as will the temperature transmitter. They can all be transferred to the new unit, but make sure that new gaskets are employed for the water housing elbow and the rear casing.

14 Once the pump has been reassembled, it can then be refitted to the vehicle. Refitting is basically the reverse procedure to removal, but it can be difficult to get the side pipes onto the pump and cylinder head stubs. Make sure that the key is properly located in the impeller and that the drivebelts are fitted over the pulley and rest on the hub behind the fan while the pulley is refitted (photos).

15 When the inlet manifold is refitted make sure that new O-rings are used for the inlet port and remember to refit the heat shield.

16 Finally, check the tension of the drivebelts and adjust them as described in Section 9. Then refill the whole system with coolant, as described in Section 4, and check for leaks.

14 Fault diagnosis – cooling system

Symptom	Reason(s)
Excessive rise in coolant temperature	Broken or loose drivebelts Low coolant level in system Faulty thermostat Ignition too far retarded Incorrect fuel mixture Blocked radiator tubes Brakes binding Faulty electric cooling fan or sender unit switch (if fitted)
Loss of coolant	Leaking radiator or drain tap Leaking hoses or joints Expansion tank cap defective Defective cylinder head gasket
Over-cooling	Thermostat jammed open Thermostat missing Incorrect thermostat fitted

Note: *Unlike an open cooling system, the sealed system loses little or no coolant unless there is a definite leak somewhere, or overheating is so pronounced that it would be detected quite apart from its effect on the coolant level.*

Chapter 3 Fuel and exhaust systems

Contents

Specifications

Part A: Carburettor models

Carburettor type
R1273 .... Solex 34 TBIA single choke and 35 CEEI twin choke
R1275 .... Weber 38 DGAR twin choke

Idling adjustment
Idle speed (all models, automatic in 'N') .... 900 rpm, ± 25 (R1273), ± 50 (R1275)
CO level at idle .... 2.0 to 2.5%

Solex carburettor specifications

	34 TBIA	35CEEI (each choke)
Choke tube (mm)	28	27
Main jet	130 (127.5*)	145
Air compensating jet	145	150
Idle jet	42	47.5
Accelerator pump jet	50	60
Needle valve (mm)	1.5	1.7
Float weight (g)	5.7	–
Accelerator pump stroke (mm)	5	By cam

Automatic transmission models

Weber carburettor specifications

	Each choke
Choke tube (mm)	27
Main jet	155 (152*)
Air compensation jet	155
Idle jet	50 (57*)
Mixture centralizer	3.5
Emulsifier	F80
Initial throttle opening (extreme cold)	0.75 (0.80*)
Float level below joint face (mm)	40
Float travel (mm)	10
Accelerator pump jet	60

Automatic transmission models

Fuel pump

Type	Diaphragm
Drive	From left-hand camshaft

Fuel tank capacity

14 Imp gallons (64 litres)

Fuel octane rating

97 RON minimum (UK 4-star)

Part B: Fuel injection models

System type

Bosch K-Jetronic

Idling adjustment

Idle speed:
Manual transmission	900 ± 50 rpm
Automatic transmission (in 'N' or 'P')	975 ± 50 rpm

CO level at idle:
Manual transmission	$1\frac{1}{2}$ to $2\frac{1}{2}$%
Automatic transmission	1 to $1\frac{1}{2}$%

Test data

Fuel injectors opening pressure	39.1 to 53.6 lbf/in² (2.7 to 3.8 bar)

Feed pressure:
Checking	65.2 to 75.4 lbf/in² (4.5 to 5.2 bar)
Setting	68.1 to 71.0 lbf/in² (4.7 to 4.9 bar)

Minimum residual pressure:
After 10 minutes	24.6 lbf/in² (1.7 bar)
After 20 minutes	21.7 lbf/in² (1.5 bar)

Control pressure (engine hot):
Vacuum disconnected	39.1 to 44.9 lbf/in² (2.7 to 31. bar)
Vacuum connected (idling)	49.3 tp 53.6 lbf/in² (3.4 to 3.8 bar)

Main fuel pump

Type	Electric rotor
Delivery pressure	72.5 lbf/in² (5.0 bar)

Fuel tank capacity

14 Imp gallons (64 litres)

Fuel octane rating

97 RON minimum (UK 4-star)

PART A: CARBURETTOR MODELS

1 General description

The fuel system of the Renault 30 models fitted with a carburettor is basically conventional in principle. The fuel tank is mounted on the underside of the car, just forward of the rear suspension assembly. From the tank the fuel is drawn to the carburettor via a mechanically operated diaphragm pump, mounted on the engine. The pump also incorporates a filter to prevent any sediment drawn from the tank reaching the carburettor.

The carburettor(s) fitted to all models incorporate an automatic choke system. This utilises redirected engine coolant which is used to warm up the carburettor inlet manifold and autochoke device.

The type 112 engine fitted to the R1273 model has two Solex carburettors fitted. These are mounted in line and provide a two-stage fuel supply system to the engine. The Solex 34 TB1A is the primary carburetor whilst the 35 CEEI is the secondary carburettor. Their operation is described in Section 3.

The R1275 model is fitted with a Weber 38 DGAR carburettor, the details of which are given in Section 8.

All carburettor models are fitted with an air filter containing a disposable type element, which must be renewed at the specified intervals, or more frequently in exceptionally dusty conditions.

2 Air cleaner – renewal, servicing and refitting

1 To renew the air cleaner element, unscrew and remove the air cleaner top cover retaining screws and lift the cover clear (photo).

2 Wipe clean the inside of the air cleaner body before inserting the new element and refitting the top cover.

3 If the air cleaner complete is to be removed, then the top cover and element must first be removed as previously described.

2.1 Air cleaner element removal

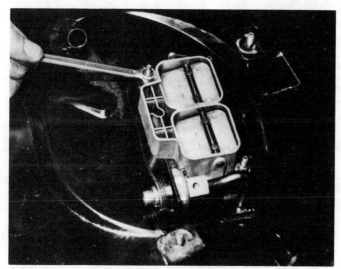

2.4 Air cleaner-to-carburettor retaining bolts

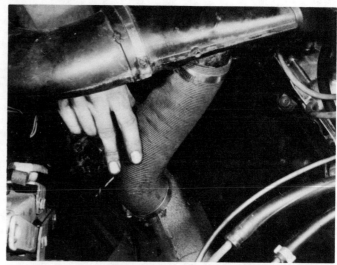

2.6 Air cleaner intake/exhaust manifold hot air ducting

4   Unscrew and remove the cleaner unit-to-carburettor retaining nuts, also the front retaining nut from the thermostat housing location stud (photo).
5   Detach the HT leads from the container.
6   Disconnect the hot air duct from the exhaust manifold and then remove the air cleaner unit (photo).
7   Refitting is a reversal of the removal procedure.

3   Solex carburettors (type 112 engine) – general description

The R1273 has two Solex carburettors fitted, these being the 34 TBIA and 35 CEEI models.
The 34 TBIA carburettor is a single choke type and feeds the engine fuel during the initial stages of acceleration, after which the second carburettor (the 35 CEEI) becomes operational. The 35 CEEI is of the twin choke type.
Cold starting is assisted by means of an automatic choke,

thermostatically operated by a wax type element, which expands as the engine coolant warms up. The automatic choke is integral with the 34 TBIA carburettor.
When the engine is idling, the 34 TBIA carburettor supplies 80% of the fuel mixture to the engine by means of a constant richness circuit. This allows the idle speed to be adjusted by a single adjuster screw.
The twin throttle butterflies in the 35 CEEI carburettor open simultaneously and are controlled by means of a pneumatic diaphragm which is vacuum-operated from each choke tube. The throttle control of the 34 TBIA carburettor is fitted with a moving stop; this prevents the throttle butterflies in the twin choke carburettor opening during the first 30° of throttle travel.
When the engine is idling, the twin choke carburettor supplies 20% of the engine fuel mixture requirements so that the carburettor is primed for operation on acceleration.
The carburettor locations and their mixture supply routes through the inlet manifold are shown in Figs. 3.1 and 3.2.

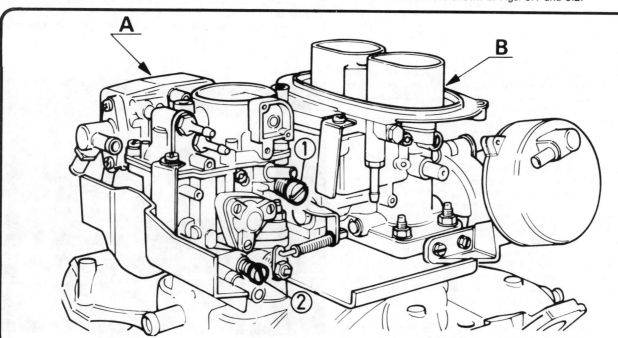

Fig. 3.1 Solex TBIA (A) and 35 CEEI (B) carburettors fitted to the 112 engine showing the two main adjusters (Sec 3)

1   Idle speed adjuster (volume) screw   2   Idle mixture adjuster screw

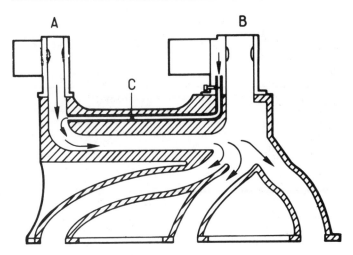

Fig. 3.2 Manifold circuit for the Solex twin carburettor model (Sec 3)

A   34 TBIA mounting   C   Idle/primer circuit
B   35 CEEI mounting

Solex 34 TBIA operating description

Starting with the idling circuits, refer to Fig. 3.3. There are two idle jets fitted, the first jet supplies the progression hole (8) and part (7) with the fuel mixture. A factory set mixture flow control screw is fitted to part (7). The second idle jet is fitted internally and this supplies the second circuit with the necessary airflow and has its own adjuster screw. This is the main idle speed adjuster.

The main circuit is also shown in Fig. 3.3, and comprises the jet assembly to the venturi and the supply jet from the float chamber.

The accelerator pump circuit is also supplied from the float chamber, via the diaphragm to the supply jet in the throttle butterfly opening.

A mixture enrichment circuit is also shown in Fig. 3.3. In this circuit the enrichment valve movement is regulated by the inlet manifold vacuum (which depends on engine loading and speed) and by the coil spring, which under certain operating conditions will push the valve back, having overcome the vacuum. Fuel is then allowed to pass through the metering jet and into the main jet circuit, enabling the mixture to be enriched as required.

The choke flap control mechanism components are shown in Fig. 3.4. When the engine is cold the choke thermostat is contracted so that roller (7) on lever (6) is set in its lowest position. The deflooding lever is held by the initial throttle opening cam so that the accelerator lever enables the throttle butterfly to open partially. When the engine starts, the vacuum below the butterfly increases and the capsule diaphragm is sucked outwards and pulls the rod, which in turn partially opens the choke flap.

As the engine coolant warms up, the choke thermostat expands. This progressively opens the choke flap (by means of the roller and lever), and the initial throttle opening cam moves back up following the roller. The throttle butterfly is closed down to its normal idling operation position by the accelerator lever and the influence of the return spring.

When the spring stops, it cools and the system operation is reversed by means of the counter spring.

To overcome flooding, a deflooding mechanism is built into the system. The accelerator must be fully open to push back the butterfly link; the deflood lever will then pivot onto the lever cam, causing the choke flap to open.

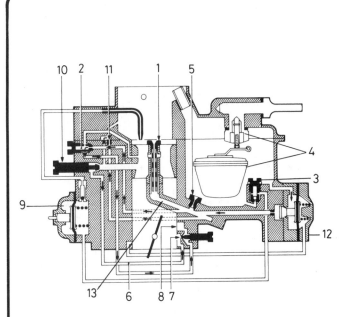

Fig. 3.3 The Solex 34 TBIA carburettor – sectional diagram (Sec 3)

1 Main jet enrichener to venturi	8 Progression hole
2 First idle jet	9 Diaphragm (accelerator pump)
3 Pump valve	10 Adjuster screw (idle speed)
4 Float and needle valve unit	11 Second idle jet
5 Main jet	12 Enrichment vacuum assembly
6 Idle feed circuit	13 Main jet circuit
7 Port	

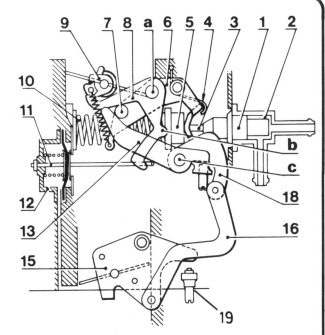

Fig. 3.4 Choke flap mechanism components (Sec 3)

1 Wax thermostat	11 Rod
2 Engine coolant	12 Pneumatic capsule
3 Thermostat piston	13 Initial throttle opening cam lever
4 Spring	15 Accelerator lever
5 Piston stop	16 Link
6 Lever	18 Deflooding lever (pivot c)
7 Roller	19 Fixed idle stop
8 Lever and hinge (a)	
9 Cam control (cam b)	
10 Counter spring	

Solex 35 CEEI operating description

A sectional view of this carburettor is shown in Fig. 3.5. There are three principal circuits, these being the main circuit, the accelerator pump circuit and the idle circuit.

In the main circuit, a jet in each barrel supplies an emulsified mixture which is dispersed into each venturi through the respective diffusers.

In the accelerator pump circuit, the pump spring is compressed by the pump lever when the butterflies are closed. The pump lever is actuated by the throttle opener diaphragm. When the lever is released, the accelerator pump diaphragm is pushed back and fuel is delivered through the one-way valve, up to the dual jet and into each barrel.

The idle circuit is fed by a jet in each barrel. The idle mixture is controlled by a single adjustment screw, the position of which is preset at manufacture.

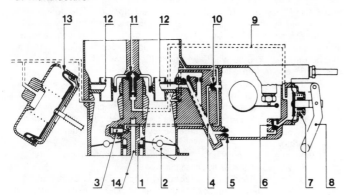

Fig. 3.5 The Solex 35 CEEI carburettor – sectional diagram (Sec 3)

1 Progression holes	8 Lever (accelerator pump)
2 Accelerator pump cam	9 Fuel delivery channel
3 Idle channel jet	10 Idle jet (one of two)
4 Main jet well (one of two)	11 Dual jet
5 Main jet (one of two)	12 Diffusers
6 One-way valve	13 Throttle opener diaphragm
7 Diaphragm (accelerator pump)	14 Idle channel

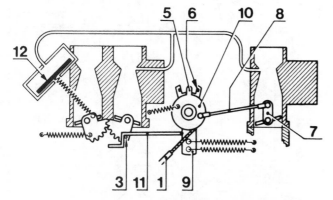

Fig. 3.6 Accelerator controls – Solex carburettors (Sec 3)

1 Accelerator cable	8 Connecting arm
3 Stop peg	9 Lever
5 Roller stop	10 Roller
6 Lever	11 Butterfly control arm
7 Link	12 Pneumatic diaphragm

Throttle linkages

To synchronise the throttle action of the two carburettors a combination of mechanisms is employed. Refer to Fig. 3.6.

As the accelerator cable is actuated, the roller to which it is attached pivots and the connecting arm operates the 34 TBIA carburettor butterfly. When the roller is turned beyond 30°, the roller stop contacts and actuates the lever face (9). This then actuates the

butterfly control arm (11), releasing its stop peg and allowing the 35 CEEI carburettor butterflies to open. Vacuum in the two carburettor choke tubes operates on the throttle opener to open the butterflies.

On releasing the accelerator, the movements are reversed and the butterflies close.

4 Solex carburettors – idle speed adjustment

1 Run the engine up to its normal operating temperature. The air filter must be in position and the filter element known to be in a serviceable condition.

2 Check that the vacuum advance and (where applicable) automatic transmission vacuum capsule hoses are securely connected and in good condition before making any adjustments. The ignition system must also be correctly adjusted.

3 The idle adjustment screws are shown in Fig. 3.1. Normal adjustment should be confined to the idle speed adjuster (volume) screw; the idle mixture adjuster screw should not require adjustment except after carburettor overhaul.

4 If available, a tachometer should be used to check the idle speed settings, but if not your own judgement will have to suffice and a further check made by your Renault dealer at the earliest opportunity.

5 To set the idle speed, simply turn the volume screw in the desired direction to increase or decrease the engine speed accordingly to the specified value.

6 If the idle speed or quality is not satisfactory then further adjustment of both the volume and mixture screws is probably required. The adjustment of both screws is usually only required after a carburettor has been dismantled or overhauled. A tamperproof cap may be fitted over the mixture screw, however, and to make any adjustment of this screw you will have to break the cap and remove it. Make sure that you are not breaking any laws by so doing.

7 To adjust, proceed by screwing in the two adjuster screws so that the engine speed is reduced to 680 to 700 rpm, but do not fully tighten either screw to achieve this.

8 Starting with the volume screw, adjust each screw in turn to increase the engine speed in stages of 50 rpm until the range of 960 to 980 rpm is reached. Then screw in the mixture screw to reduce the idle speed to within the specified range whilst giving an even running engine.

9 Ideally, final adjustment should be made using an exhaust gas analyser (CO meter) to make sure that the exhaust CO level at idle is within the specified range. In some countries this may be required by law.

10 Fit a new tamperproof cap where regulations require it.

5 Solex carburettors – removal and refitting

1 Disconnect the battery earth lead.

2 Remove the air filter assembly as given in Section 2.

3 Disconnect the fuel feed and return hoses. Clamp or plug them to prevent leakage.

4 Partially drain the cooling system and then clamp the hoses to and from the thermo choke unit. Unclip the hoses to detach them.

5 Disconnect the respective accelerator controls (as required).

6 Disconnect the vacuum hose(s).

7 Unscrew and remove the carburettor-to-inlet manifold flange retaining bolts and carefully lift the carburettor(s) clear.

8 Refitting is a reversal of the removal procedure. Use new flange gaskets and do not overtighten the retaining nuts.

9 When all of the components and associated fittings and controls are reattached, top up the cooling system and bleed the system as given in Chapter 2. Check the fuel lines and coolant hoses for signs of leaks when the engine is started. Once the engine has run up to its normal operating temperature, make any necessary adjustments.

6 Solex 34 TBIA carburettor – dismantling, reassembly and adjustments

1 With the carburettor removed from the engine, clean it externally and prepare a clean work area where it can be dismantled and the various parts laid out for inspection.

2   Unscrew and remove the float chamber upper body retaining screws and detach the upper body. Take care as the upper body is lifted clear not to damage the gasket, as a new one may not be readily available.
3   Empty the float chamber. To remove the float, extract the hinge pin, then unhook the needle valve.
4   Do not dismantle the choke butterflies or spindles unless essential.
5   The respective jets and associated components can now be removed from the carburettor. As each component is removed, take a note of its location to ensure correct refitting or refer to Fig. 3.7 for identification of jets.
6   To remove the accelerator pump unit, unscrew the four retaining screws and carefully withdraw the cover and diaphragm.
7   When the pump unit is removed, check the diaphragm for splits or pin-holes. Renew if necessary.
8   Clean the respective components, blowing through the jets with a tyre pump – never use a wire to probe them.
9   Reassembly is a reversal of dismantling, but use new gaskets and check that any interconnecting linkage is correctly located. The following checks/adjustments must be made during reassembly.

Float level check
10 Invert the float chamber top cover and locate its gasket in position on the mating face (Fig. 3.8). Now measure the distance from the bottom of the float to the gasket face (distance 'B'). This should be 1.515 ± 0.040 in (38.5 ± 1 mm). When measuring this distance the

needle valve/float clip closed end should be facing the choke unit and the needle valve should be fully seated. If necessary, adjust the float level setting by carefully bending the float hinge piece using a pair of long-nosed pliers.

Choke flap pneumatic opening
11 The extent of the choke flap pneumatic opening depends on the ambient temperature at the time of checking. You will need a gauge rod or drill shank with which to measure the choke flap opening. The diameter of the rod should be as follows:

Ambient temperature	Gauge rod diameter
15°C (59°F)	4.6 mm (0.181 in)
20°C (68°F)	5.5 mm (0.216 in)
25°C (77°F)	6.6 mm (0.259 in)
30°C (86°F)	7.9 mm (0.311 in)

Insert the appropriate gauge rod down between the choke flap and the carburettor bore and push the control rod into the capsule using suitable pliers (Fig. 3.9). Should the choke flap opening need adjustment, turn the capsule screw in or out as necessary to give the correct setting.

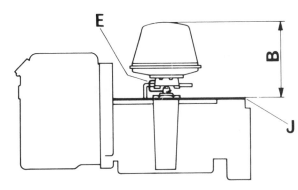

Fig. 3.8 Float level adjustment – Solex carburettors (Sec 6)

E   Needle/float clip   gasket face clearance
    (closed end to choke)   J   Gasket
B   Measure float base to

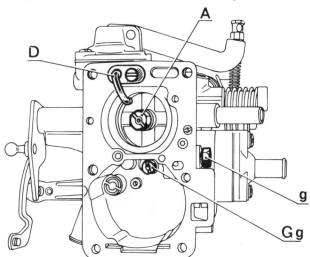

Fig. 3.7 Solex 34 TBIA carburettor (Sec 6)

g   Idle jet   D   Accelerator pump
Gg Main jet   discharge tube
A   Air compensator jet

Fig. 3.9 Choke flap pneumatic opening clearance check (Sec 6)

A   Gauge rod   S   Control rod
R   Stop screw

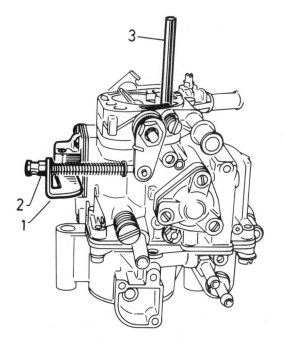

Fig. 3.10 Accelerator pump stroke check (Sec 6)

1   Lever   3   Gauge rod
2   Adjustment screw

Accelerator pump stroke

12 Insert a gauge rod or drill shank of 5 mm (0.196 in) diameter down between the carburettor bore and the throttle butterfly and then referring to Fig. 3.10, check that the pump lever is at the end of its stroke. With the lever pressed against the stop, turn the adjuster screw as necessary until it is just touching the lever.

Initial throttle opening

13 Referring to Fig. 3.11, measure dimension 'x' with a vernier gauge. This measurement will depend on the ambient temperature at the time of measuring, and should be as follows:

Ambient temperature	Dimension 'X'	Initial throttle opening (mm)
15°C (59°F)	28.5 mm (1.12 in)	0.85 (0.95*)
20°C (68°F)	27.9 mm (1.09 in)	0.80 (0.90*)
25°C (77°F)	27.3 mm (1.07 in)	0.75 (0.85*)
30°C (86°F)	26.6 mm (1.04 in)	0.70 (0.80*)

*Figures in brackets refer to automatic transmission models

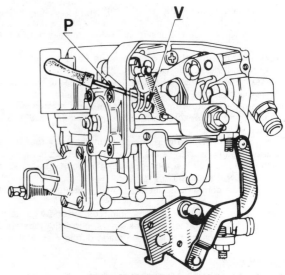

Fig. 3.12 Adjust initial throttle opening screw (V) with screwdriver (P) passing through coil spring as shown (Sec 6)

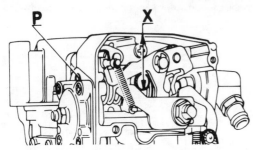

Fig. 3.11 Initial throttle opening check (Sec 6)

P   Access aperture for adjustment screw
X   Measure between points shown

Should adjustment be necessary, insert a screwdriver through the aperture shown in Fig. 3.12 and turn the screw (V) in the desired direction.

14 Check the initial throttle opening with a suitable gauge rod according to temperature (see above) and if necessary adjust by turning the stop screw shown (Fig 3.13).

7 Solex CEEI carburettor – dismantling and reassembly

1   Clean the external components of the carburettor before dismantling. Clean and prepare a work area where the various components can be laid out.
2   Remove the retaining screws and carefully lift off the float chamber cover. Try not to damage the cover gasket as it is removed, in case a replacement is not readily available.
3   From the float chamber cover, unscrew and remove the fuel line union and plug. Withdraw the hinge pin and remove the float.
4   When dismantling the main body/float chamber, do not remove or readjust the position of the compensator jets. These are shown in Fig. 3.14.
5   Unscrew and remove the float body plugs, the main jets, idle jets, the accelerator pump valve, the spray jets holder, the accelerator pump and the vacuum capsule.
6   Clean the various components in petrol and blow them dry with an air line (a tyre pump will suffice). **Do not** probe or clean blocked jets with wire.
7   Check the condition of all parts, in particular the accelerator pump and vacuum capsule diaphragms. Renew any defective components.
8   Reassembly is a reversal of the dismantling procedure. Ensure that all parts are perfectly clean as they are refitted.
9   Before refitting the float chamber cover, check the float level by inverting the cover and locating the gasket. Measure the distance from the float outer tip to the gasket face. This should be 1.515 ± 0.040 in (38.5 ± 1 mm). Adjust the level accordingly if necessary by bending the float arm in the desired direction (See Fig. 3.8).
10   When the carburettor is reassembled, refit it to the manifold and make the following checks before refitting the air filter unit.

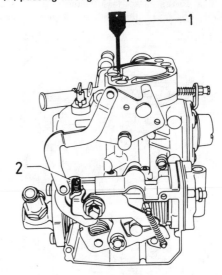

Fig. 3.13 Check throttle opening with gauge rod (1). Adjust with stop screw (2) if necessary (Sec 6)

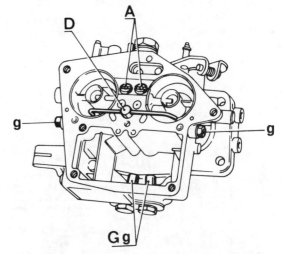

Fig. 3.14 The Solex 35 CEEI carburettor (Sec 7)

g	Idle jets		do not remove
Gg	Main jet	D	Accelerator pump
A	Air compensator jets –		discharge tube

11 Check the 1st barrel butterfly angle adjustment by inspecting the butterfly position. It should just mask the progression slit, but not go beyond it. If necessary adjust accordingly by altering the adjuster screw (C) shown in Fig. 3.15.

12 Now repeat the butterfly angle check in the same manner for the 2nd barrel and if necessary adjust by altering the setting of screw (D).
13 If on completion of the above adjustments the throttle butterfly actions are suspect when in operation, have your Renault dealer check the pneumatic diaphragm throttle opening action. This check requires the use of a special vacuum gauge which your Renault dealer should have.

8 Weber 38 DGAR carburettor – general description

1   This carburettor is fitted to the R1275 model Renault 30. It is a twin barrel downdraught carburettor, fitted with a semi-automatic choke which is regulated according to the engine coolant temperature by means of a bimetal spring. The throttle butterfly action in each barrel is simultaneous.
2   The principal features in the operation of this carburettor are as follows.

Cold start mechanism

3   As mentioned, this carburettor has a semi-automatic choke to assist in starting and running a cold engine. It is semi-automatic in that the accelerator pedal needs to be pressed fully down once then slowly released when starting the engine from cold. This action sets the choke; only after this has been done should the ignition be switched on and the starter actuated. When the engine is running, the accelerator pedal should be pressed down quickly and released to enable the cold start mechanism to reduce the idling speed. This is particularly important on automatic transmission models prior to moving the selector lever.

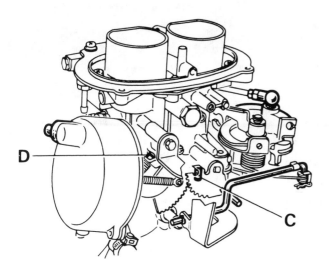

Fig. 3.15 Solex 35 CEEI carburettor 1st barrel adjustment (Sec 7)

    C   1st barrel butterfly angle adjuster screw
    D   2nd barrel butterfly angle adjuster screw

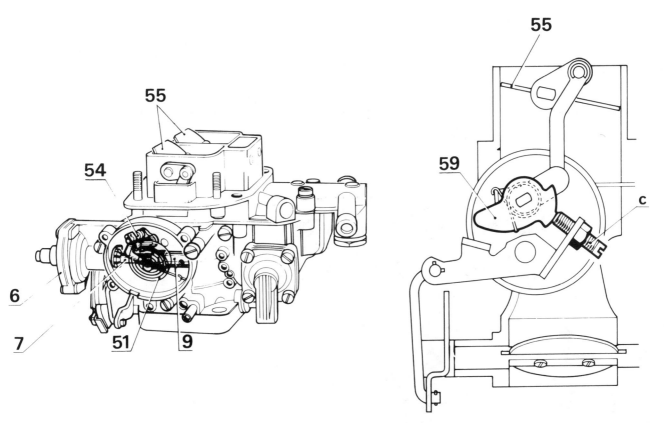

Fig. 3.16 The Weber 38 DGAR carburettor semi-automatic choke device (Sec 8)

6	Diaphragm	51 Bimetal spring	55 Choke flaps	C Throttle butterfly
7	Rod	54 Lever	59 Cam lever	setting screw
9	Compensation spring			

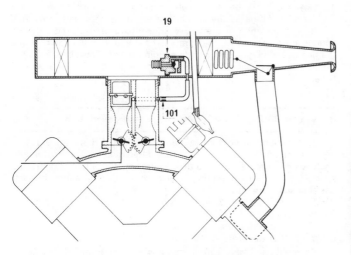

Fig. 3.17 Low temperature enrichment device thermostat (19) and calibrated air jet (101) (Sec 8)

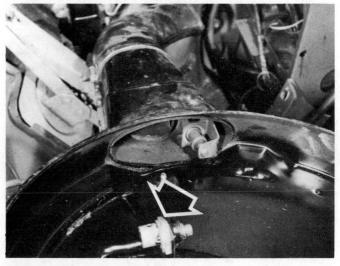

8.8 Air cleaner low temperature enrichment device (arrowed)

4   When the engine is started from cold the bimetal spring (see Fig. 3.17) prevents the choke flaps from opening so that an enriched mixture is supplied. Once the engine is running, vacuum in the diaphragm unit adjoining the bimetal spring housing causes the diaphragm rod to rotate the bimetal spring lever against the spring action, relieving the choke setting accordingly.

5   As the engine runs and the coolant temperature rises, the bimetal spring expands and its action against the cam lever corresponding reduces the choke action. Once the normal operating temperature is reached, the bimetal spring will have expanded sufficiently to open the choke flaps fully. The cam lever will have turned so that the throttle setting screw will not be in contact with it. This allows the throttle butterflies to return to their normal idle position.

6   When the engine is turned off and allowed to cool down, the bimetal spring contracts and closes the choke flaps, whilst the cam lever returns to hold the throttle butterflies in the partially open setting (Fig. 3.1).

7   If when starting from cold flooding occurs, the accelerator pedal should be pressed down fully so that the choke flaps are opened to allow the flooding to clear.

8   Before passing on from the choke system, it should be mentioned that there is a 'low temperature enrichment device' fitted into the air filter unit on models fitted with automatic transmission (photo). Shown in Fig. 3.17, this device is a wax thermostat which in cold climatic conditions (below 59°F (15°C)) closes a small air inlet. With the air supply restricted to the calibrated jet in the central idle circuit, the mixture is richened until the engine warms up, causing the thermostat to reopen the air inlet.

Idle and progression circuits

9   Refer to Fig. 3.18 for a diagram of the idle and progression circuits, which are more or less self-explanatory. In the first circuit, fuel from the wells passes to the idle jets and is then emulsified with air entering the circuit through the calibrated orifices. The fuel/air mixture

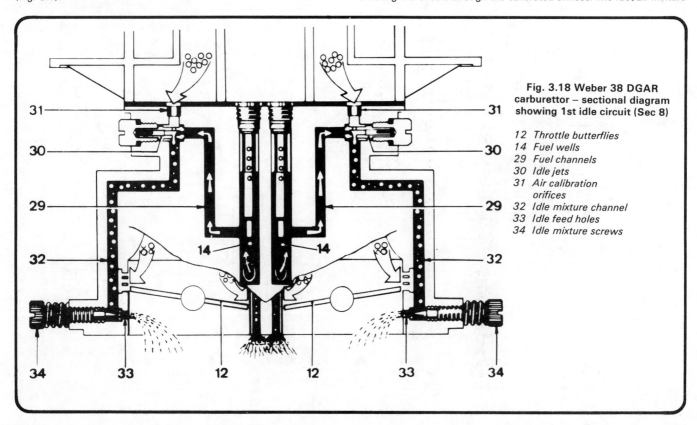

Fig. 3.18 Weber 38 DGAR carburettor – sectional diagram showing 1st idle circuit (Sec 8)

12 Throttle butterflies
14 Fuel wells
29 Fuel channels
30 Idle jets
31 Air calibration
    orifices
32 Idle mixture channel
33 Idle feed holes
34 Idle mixture screws

then passes on to the idle feed holes, where it is dispersed into the carburettor barrel.

10 The second idle circuit operates in a similar manner; this is shown in Fig. 3.19. Note that the volume control screw is preset at the factory.

Main circuit

11 Fuel is delivered to the carburettor through an intergral filter (removable for cleaning) and is then metered into the float chamber. The float and needle valve maintain the correct level of fuel.

12 From the float chamber the fuel is delivered through the main jets in the base of the float chamber, into the fuel wells, whence it passes through the emulsion tubes, mixes with air from jets and is delivered into the centralizers in the barrel.

13 A low pressure vacuum enrichment device is incorporated, located in the base of the float chamber. Its purpose is to feed fuel through a calibrated jet and into the main fuel supply channel whenever the throttle is opened suddenly. This is necessary to overcome the effect on the extra vacuum which would otherwise cause a fuel shortage in the main fuel supply. The main circuit diagram is shown in Fig. 3.20.

14 An accelerator pump is fitted and the details of this are shown in Fig. 3.21. This unit is actuated by the throttle spindle pivot lever and

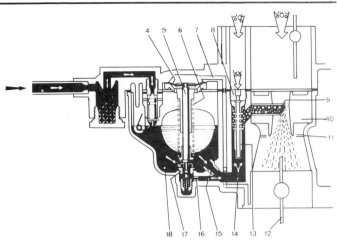

Fig. 3.20 The Weber 38 DGAR carburettor main circuit diagram (Sec 8)

4 Enrichment device	11 Diffuser
5 Rod	12 Throttle butterfly
6 Spring	13 Emulsion tube
7 Channel	14 Well
8 Air correction jet	15 Main jet
9 Delivery nozzle	16 Calibrated jet
10 Centralizer	17 Needle valve

supplies additional fuel through a ball valve into a supply jet in each barrel simultaneously. Any excess fuel from the pump is redirected to the float chamber.

9 Weber 38 DGAR carburettor – idle speed adjustment

1 Before any adjustment to the idle speed setting is made, the ignition system should be correctly adjusted and known to be in good condition.

2 Run the engine up to its normal operating temperature. On automatic transmission models the selector lever should be in the 'P' or 'N' position throughout this adjustment.

3 The ambient temperature must be at least 68°F (20°C) when making adjustment; if not, the low temperature enrichment hose must be disconnected at the carburettor on automatic transmission models (Fig. 3.17).

4 An independent tachometer should be connected to the engine in accordance with its makers instructions. Ideally, an exhaust gas analyser (CO meter) should also be available. Adjustment of the idle mixture without an exhaust gas analyser should be regarded as at best a temporary measure, and may be forbidden by local or national anti-pollution laws.

5 Adjustment of the idle speed is carried out by turning the throttle stop screw (photo). Unless the carburettor has been overhauled, or idle

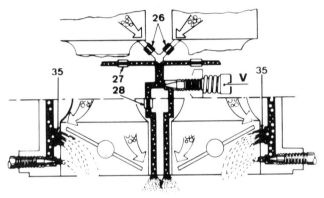

Fig. 3.19 Weber 38 DGAR carburettor – sectional diagram showing 2nd idle circuit (Sec 8)

26 Calibration orifices (air)	28 Calibration orifice (fuel/air)
27 Calibration orifices (fuel)	V Mixture screw (preset)

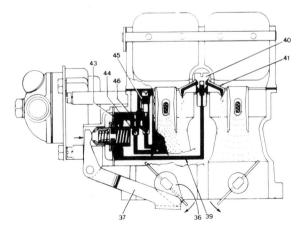

Fig. 3.21 Accelerator pump components (Weber 38 DGAR) (Sec 8)

36 Cam	43 Spring
37 Throttle pivot lever	44 Ball valve
39 Channel	45 Fuel return channel
40 Ball valve	46 Calibrated sleeve
41 Jet	

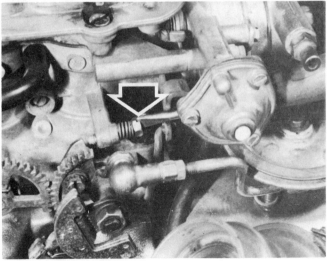

9.5 Throttle stop screw (arrowed) adjustment

quality at the specified speed is unsatisfactory, there should be no need to touch the idle mixture adjusting screws.

6   If idle mixture adjustment is necessary, locate the adjuster screws (Fig. 3.18). They may be hidden behind tamperproof caps, which will have to be prised out before adjustment can take place. Satisfy yourself that you are not breaking any laws by so doing.

Idle mixture adjustment using an exhaust gas analyser

7   Screw both mixture adjuster screws fully home without forcing them, then back off each screw one complete turn.

8   Start the engine and bring the idling speed to 950 rpm using the throttle stop screw.

9   Read the exhaust gas CO level on the analyser. Tighten each mixture screw by the same amount to bring the CO level to within the specified limits.

10 Use the throttle stop screw to bring the idle speed to within the specified range.

11 Recheck the CO level and readjust if necessary, turning each mixture adjustment screw by the same amount.

12 When adjustment is satisfactory, disconnect the test gear. Fit new tamperproof plugs to the idle mixture screws where this is required by law.

Idle mixture adjustment without an exhaust gas analyser

13 Screw the mixture adjusting screw on the choke housing side fully home without forcing it.

14 Start the engine and allow it to idle. Adjust the mixture screw on the side opposite the choke housing to obtain the maximum possible idle speed. (It may be necessary to unscrew the screw a considerable amount).

15 Using the throttle stop screw, adjust the engine speed to 850 rpm.

16 Screw in the mixture screw on the side opposite the choke housing to reduce the engine speed to 700 rpm.

17 Unscrew the mixture screw on the choke housing side to bring the engine speed above 900 rpm. If this is not possible, turn the screw to achieve the highest possible engine speed, then increase this to 900 rpm using the throttle stop screw.

18 Screw in the mixture screw on the choke housing side to reduce the engine speed to 875 rpm.

19 Adjustment is now complete. Have the adjustment checked using an exhaust gas analyser at the earliest opportunity.

10 Weber 38 DGAR carburettor – removal and refitting

1   Remove the air cleaner unit as given in Section 2.

2   Detach the throttle rod balljoint (photo).

3   On automatic transmission models, disconnect the kickdown cable.

10.2 Throttle rod balljoint (1) and kickdown switch cable connection (2)

10.6 Lifting the carburettor clear

4   Disconnect the fuel supply hose and also the vacuum hose. Plug the fuel hose (or clamp it) to prevent fuel leakage.

5   Clamp the automatic choke coolant hoses, then disconnect the hoses from the choke housing.

6   Unscrew and remove the four carburettor flange retaining nuts and carefully lift the carburettor clear of the inlet manifold (photo). Try not to break the flange gasket as the carburettor is removed, in case a replacement is not available, in which case the existing one can be reused, or at least used as a pattern to make a new one.

7   Refitting is a reversal of the removal process, but use a new flange gasket if possible. With the coolant hoses reconnected, remove the clamps and check the coolant level. Top up and bleed if necessary (see Chapter 2).

8   Readjust the carburettor when the engine has been restarted and warmed up.

9   To adjust the automatic transmission kickdown cable refer to Chapter 7, Section 6.

11 Weber 38 DGAR carburettor – dismantling, reassembly and adjustment

1   Having removed the carburettor from the engine (as described in the previous Section), clean it externally and prepare a suitable clean work area where it can be dismantled and the parts laid out for inspection.

2   Remove the petrol inlet filter plug and extract the filter. Detach the choke valve connecting rod (photo).

3   Remove the retaining screws and carefully lift clear the float chamber cover, together with its gasket. Try not to damage the gasket as the cover is lifted, as a replacement gasket may not be readily available (photo).

4   Withdraw the float pivot pin and remove the float, then unscrew and remove the float needle valve unit.

5   Turning to the main carburettor body assembly, unscrew and remove the main jets, the air compensation jets and the idle jets, the respective positions of which are shown (photo). Note the fitted position of each jet in turn as it is removed and mark or segregate them so that they can be refitted to their original locations when reassembling.

6   Remove the four accelerator pump cover retaining screws and carefully withdraw the cover (photo). Take care not to damage the pump diaphragm. Withdraw the coil spring.

7   Unscrew the choke housing cover retaining screws and withdraw the cover, noting its alignment mark with that on the main body (photo).

8   Remove the three retaining screws to enable the choke vacuum diaphragm cover and diaphragm to be removed. Again take care not to damage the diaphragm on removal.

11.2 Detach the choke valve connecting rod, prising free the clip (arrowed)

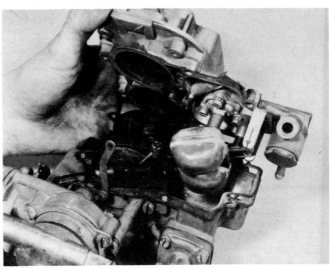

11.3 Float chamber cover removal

11.5 Weber carburettor with float chamber removed showing mixture centralisers (1), air compensation jets (2), idle jets (3) and main jets (4)

11.6 Accelerator pump cover removal

9   Remove the compensator unit screws and withdraw the cover and spring. Take particular care when removing the diaphragm.
10   The main components of the carburettor are now dismantled and can be cleaned and inspected. An air line is useful here to blow through the jet and internal parts of the carburettor – a tyre pump will do the job. **Do not** use wire or any other similar methods to probe or unblock any jets and parts, as it will damage the finely machined surfaces.
11   Renew any components that are damaged or appear worn or defective in any way. Check the diaphragms for splits or pinholes.
12   Reassembly is a reversal of the dismantling procedure. Take care to seat the diaphragms correctly, do not force any components into position and do not overtighten fastenings or jets when assembling. The following items must be checked for adjustment during assembly.

Float level check and adjustment

13   Locate the gasket into position on the float chamber cover and then support the cover as shown in Fig. 3.22, so that it is held vertically but without the weight of the float pressing the ball into the needle valve. Now measure the dimension (A) between the gasket joint face and the float lower edge. This should be as shown. Should adjustment be necessary to achieve this, carefully bend the float support arm accordingly, but ensure that it remains square to the valve centre-line.
14   Pivot the float and check its travel as shown by the dotted line (B) in Fig. 3.22. Adjust as required by bending the lug accordingly.

11.7 Choke housing alignment marks (arrowed)

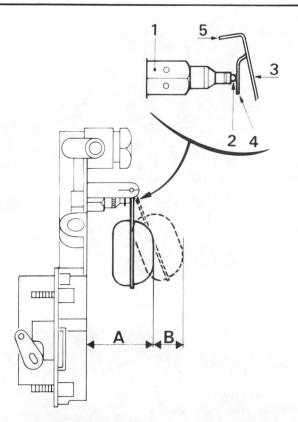

Fig. 3.22 Float level check (Weber) (Sec 11)

1	Needle valve	5	Lug
2	Ball	A	1.575 in (40 mm)
3	Arm	B	0.394 in (10 mm)
4	Tongue		

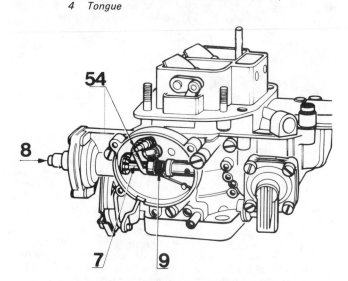

Fig. 3.23 Choke unit adjustment (Weber) (Sec 11)

7	Rod	9	Compensator
8	Stop screw	54	Lever

Choke unit adjustment

15 Check that the respective jets are repositioned in the carburettor and then refit the float chamber cover. Reattach the choke valve connecting rod.

Choke unit adjustment

16 Before refitting the choke housing cover, check the choke adjustment. Shut off the choke flaps by pushing on the butterfly spindle, then referring to Fig. 3.23, move the rod to the left so that it is resting

against the capsule stop screw, whilst holding the lever against the rod.

17 Measure the choke flap part open setting, which should be 10 mm (0.394 in). Insert a drill shank of this diameter between the carburettor body and the choke valve to check this clearance, and adjust if necessary by turning the capsule stop screw the amount required. When making this check, take care not to compress the compensator spring.

18 On refitting the choke housing cover, ensure that the spring hooks onto the operating lever and then locate the cover, aligning the reference marks of the cover and housing.

Throttle butterflies synchronisation

19 During this check, the choke flaps must be held open. Start by loosening off the throttle stop screw, then similarly unscrew each mixture adjusting screw (B) so that their tips are withdrawn from the throttle butterflies. Use a suitable spanner and loosen off the synchroniser screw (C) in the 1st barrel (photo).

20 Adjust the 1st barrel throttle stop screw so that the butterfly clearance is 0.1 mm (0.004 in), measured between the butterfly edge and the bore on the progression side of the carburettor. Use a narrow feeler gauge or rod to measure the clearance.

21 Holding the accelerator cable cam with one hand to retain the 1st barrel butterfly in position, open the 2nd barrel butterfly slightly more than 0.1 mm (0.004 in) and then screw in (but don't tighten) the synchroniser screw. Insert the 0.1 mm feeler gauge into position on the progression side of the bore for the 2nd barrel and lightly tap the 2nd barrel toothed quadrant to give the clearance required to even up the butterfly openings to 0.1 mm (0.004 in). When this is achieved, retighten the synchroniser screw and then recheck that the butterfly to carburettor body gap is the same in each barrel. If not, repeat the above procedure until it is.

Deflooding device check

22 Engage the choke mechanism and then fully open the throttle. Now check the choke flap part open setting as given in paragraph 17. If necessary bend the connecting rod (Fig. 3.24) accordingly to achieve the correct part open setting.

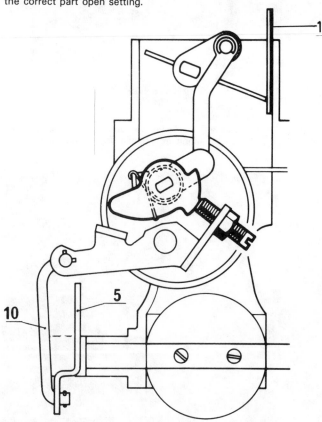

Fig. 3.24 Deflooding device check showing the gauge rod (1), the throttle lever (5) and rod (10) (Sec 11)

11.19 Throttle stop screw (A), one of the two mixture adjusting screws (B) and the synchroniser screw (C)

12.2 Detaching the accelerator cable

13.10 Remove the inlet manifold retaining bolts

13.11 Locate the O-seals into the inlet ports

12 Accelerator cable – removal and refitting

1   Extract the split pin from the pedal attachment pivot and disconnect the cable from the pedal.
2   Working at the engine end of the cable, detach the cable from the accelerator control quadrant (photo).
3   Pull the cable through from within the car and remove it.
4   Refit in the reverse order to removal, adjusting the cable fitting at the quadrant end if necessary. Check the throttle action on completion, ensuring that the throttle can open and close fully.

13 Inlet manifold – removal and refitting

1   Disconnect the battery earth lead.
2   Refer to Section 2 and remove the air cleaner unit.
3   Drain the cooling system as given in Chapter 2.
4   Disconnect the accelerator control cable at the quadrant.
5   Detach the automatic transmission kickdown cable (if applicable).
6   Unclip and detach the fuel supply and return hoses. Plug or clamp the hoses to prevent leakage.
7   Detach the coolant hoses from the choke housing.
8   Disconnect the vacuum hose at the distributor.

9   If the carburettor(s) are to be removed at this stage, unbolt the throttle control plate and remove it. On twin carburettor models, detach the connecting links between the two carburettors if they are being removed individually. Remove the carburettor(s) from the manifold.
10   Unbolt the manifold retaining bolts and then lift the manifold clear (photo). Remove the gaskets and sealing rings from each inlet bank of the cylinder heads.
11   Refitting is a reversal of the removal process. Renew the manifold-to-cylinder head and (if applicable) carburettor-to-manifold gaskets and seals (photo) and ensure that all joint faces are clear before reassembling.
12   When reassembled, top up the cooling system and bleed it as given in Chapter 2.
13   Check the adjustments of the accelerator cable and (where applicable) the automatic transmission kickdown cable before refitting the air cleaner unit.
14   Check for petrol and coolant leaks on restarting the engine.

14 Fuel tank – removal and refitting

1   The fuel tank is located underneath the car, attached to the floor directly in front of the rear suspension area. Access for removal leaves

a lot to be desired, so therefore run the car onto ramps or over a pit if available. Failing this, rate it as high as possible at the rear and ensure that the vehicle is secure on chassis stands or similar.

2   The tank should preferably be removed when the fuel level is very low; if not, syphon the contents into a suitable container and store in a safe place.

3   Disconnect the battery earth lead. Raise the rear seat and detach the fuel gauge sender unit wire from the top of the tank (photo).

4   Working underneath, first detach and remove the handbrake cable assembly situated directly underneath the tank (see Chapter 9).

5   Unbolt and remove the diagonal crossmembers from the rear suspension central mounting (Fig. 3.25).

6   Disconnect the fuel supply and return hoses and plug them to prevent leakage.

7   Disconnect the filler and vent pipes through the rear wheel arch.

8   The tank can now be unbolted around its retaining flange. **Note:** *One of the bolts secures the earth wire.* Support the tank as it is unbolted, then carefully lower it, detach the earth wire and remove the tank.

9   Should the fuel tank be in need of repair, consult your Renault dealer or a fuel tank repair specialist. **Do not** attempt to repair the tank yourself by welding or similar methods requiring heat; even if the tank is empty the fumes are highly explosive!

10   Refitting of the tank is a reversal of the removal procedure. Check

that all pipe connections are secure and when the tank is refilled check for any signs of leakage.

11   Reconnect the suspension arms and handbrake cable. Readjust the handbrake as given in Chapter 9.

15 Fuel tank – cleaning

1   With time it is likely that sediment will collect in the bottom of the fuel tank. Condensation, resulting in rust and other impurities will usually be found in the fuel tank of any car more than three or four years old.

2   When the tank is removed it should be vigorously flushed out turned upside down and, if facilities are available, steam cleaned. The fuel gauge sender unit should be removed first.

3   To remove the tank, see Section 14.

16 Fuel pump – description and testing

1   Carburettor equipped engines are fitted with a mechanical diaphragm fuel pump. It is mounted on the inside of the left-hand side cylinder bank and is driven off the rear end of the camshaft for that side of the engine.

2   It has one major difference from most fuel pumps of the diaphragm type in that it is fitted with a restricted fuel return feed to the tank. This means that surplus fuel flows through the restriction and back of the fuel tank via a small feed pipe.

3   The fuel pump is of the continuous operation type. This is necessary so that the fuel in the pump is circulating continuously and does not become too warm at any stage. The possibility of air locks occurring in the fuel supply is also thereby avoided.

4   If the fuel pump is suspected of malfunction, a simple test can be carried out by detaching the fuel feed pipe at the carburettor. Place the disconnected pipe end into a clean container or piece or rag and disable the ignition system. Having ensured that the car is not in gear, turn the engine on the starter motor. Assuming that there is fuel in the fuel tank, there should be a good flow of petrol from the pipe. If there is very little or no flow, remove the pump for inspection.

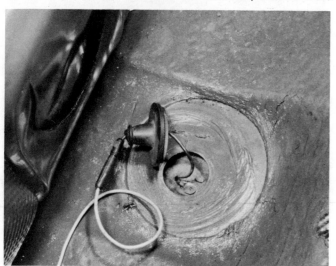

14.3 Detach the fuel tank sender unit wire

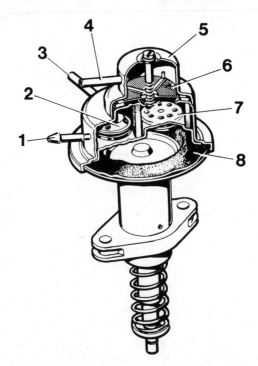

Fig. 3.26 Cutaway view of the fuel pump (Sec 16)

1	*Return line*	*5*	*Cover*
2	*Outlet valve*	*6*	*Strainer*
3	*Outlet*	*7*	*Inlet valve*
4	*Inlet*	*8*	*Diaphragm*

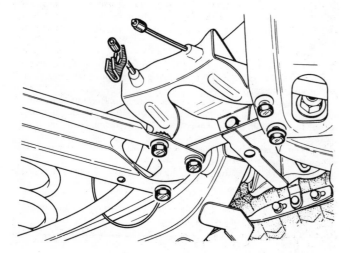

Fig. 3.25 Detach the handbrake cable and unbolt the diagonal crossmembers (Sec 14)

17 Fuel pump – removal, inspection and refitting

1   Remove the inlet and outlet pipes from the fuel pump and the surplus fuel return pipe. Plug the ends of the pipes to stop dirt entering them or fuel escaping.
2   Undo the bolts holding the fuel pump to the left-hand side cylinder head and lift it away.
3   Due to the design of this type of pump there is very little that can be done to it. It is not possible to strip it down in the same way as other diaphragm type pumps: the diaphragm is sealed in. If therefore it goes wrong mechanically, a complete new pump must be fitted.
4   The only maintenance that can be carried out on this type of pump is to clean the filter gauze or strainer which can become blocked with sediment sucked up from the fuel tank.
5   To do this, remove the screw in the centre of the top of the pump. Then carefully ease off the top section complete with inlet pipe, and place it carefully to one side (photos).
6   Prise the filter away carefully and wash any sediment off it in a petrol bath. Do not scrub it; damage may result.
7   Refit the filter gauze and cover in the reverse order to that in which they were removed and then check the operation of the pump. If any doubt still exists as to its efficiency, it must be renewed. Do not forget to check that fuel is getting through from the tank.

8   Clean the old gasket remains from the cylinder head and place a new gasket in position.
9   Fit a new fuel pump in the reverse order to that which was used to remove the old one (photo).

18 Exhaust system – removal and refitting

1   The exhaust system comprises an exhaust manifold from each cylinder bank, and twin downpipes, each of which incorporates a primary expansion box. These are joined to a joint secondary expansion box; from this a single intermediate pipe takes the exhaust gas to the silencer at the rear.
2   One of two system types will be fitted, depending on production date and model. Both systems are shown in the accompanying diagrams (Figs. 3.27 and 3.28).
3   The complete system or just part of it can be removed for repair or renewal. The respective pipe section joints will either be of the flanged type, such as the manifold-to-downpipe joint, or a collared sleeve and clamp joint such as the downpipe-to-secondary expansion box pipe joint (photo).
4   The flanged type joints can normally easily be separated by simply removing the clamping nuts of the joint and withdrawing the pipe from the manifold or mating pipe as the case may be. It may however be

17.5A Remove the pump cover and seal ...

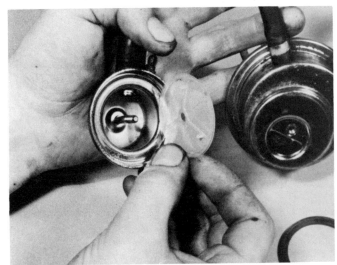
17.5B ... then remove the filter

17.9 Refit the pump using a new flange gasket

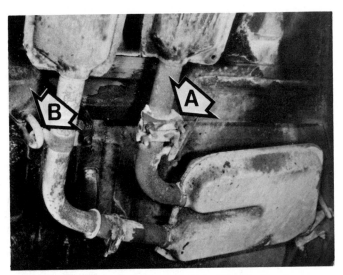
18.3 Exhaust system showing a sleeved joint (A) and rubber hanger ring location (B)

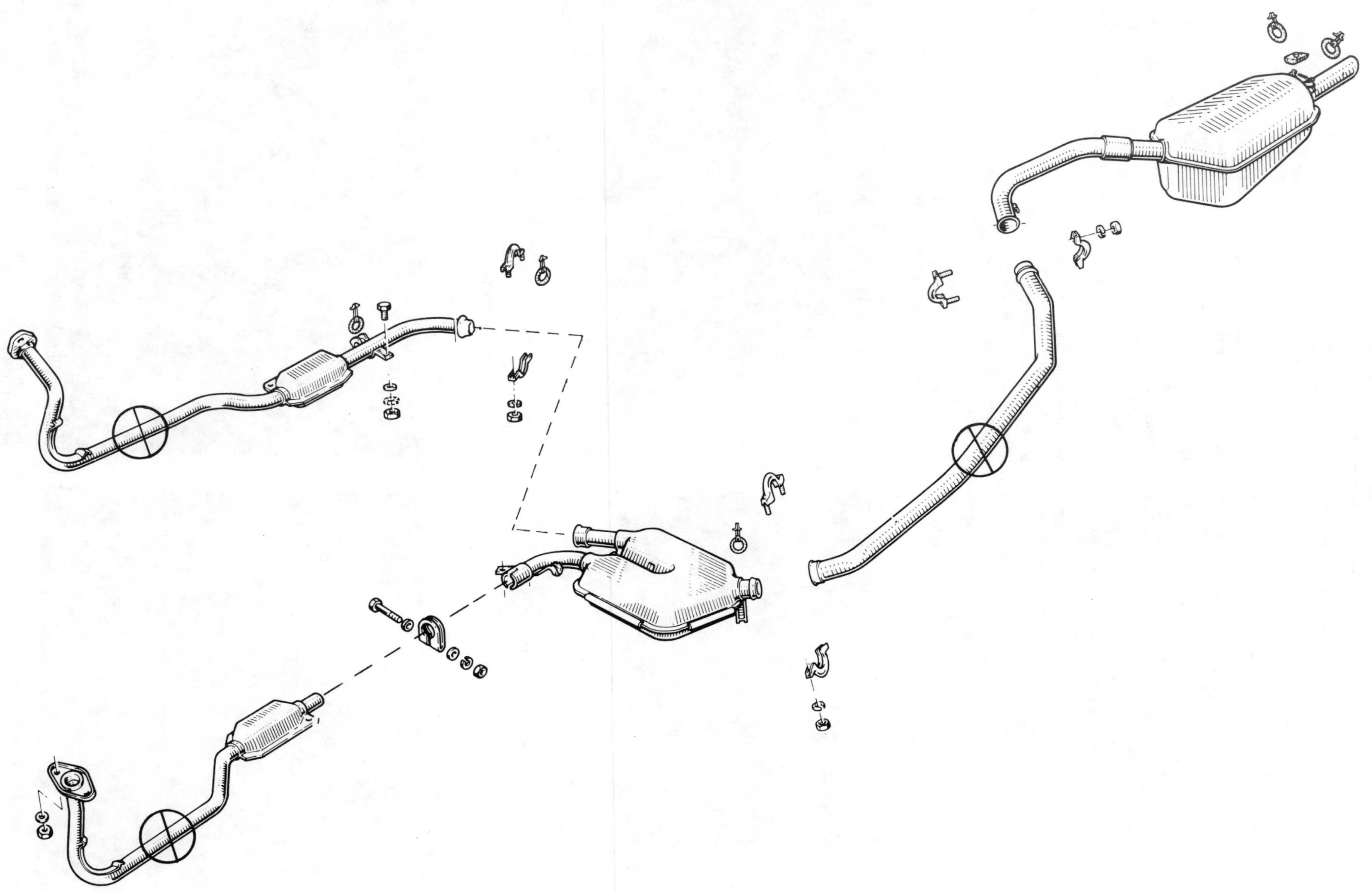

Fig. 3.27 Exhaust system components – early models (Sec 18)

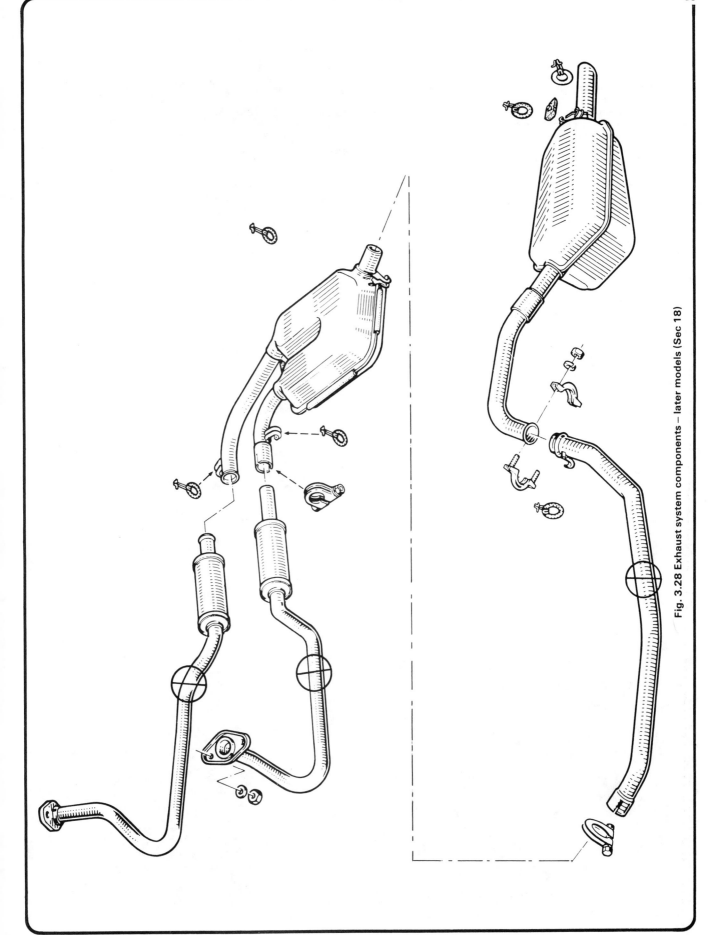

Fig. 3.28 Exhaust system components – later models (Sec 18)

necessary to apply some rust penetrating fluid to the nuts and joints to ease removal.

5   The collared sleeve joint is not so easily separated and normally requires a certain amount of heat from a gas torch to separate the two pipes after the clamp has been removed. In this instance special care must be taken to guard against fire whenever working underneath the vehicle, particularly at the petrol tank end or near fuel lines!

6   If a pipe section is being renewed it is usually far quicker to cut it through close to the joint concerned to ease removal.

7   The system is suspended in position by means of brackets and rubber mounting straps or rings and these can be levered from their mounting brackets when necessary.

8   The foregoing operations should be followed if only certain sections of the system are to be renewed. If the complete system must be renewed, then it will be much easier if the old pipes are sawn through with a hacksaw in short lengths for removal.

9   When fitting the new system, de-burr the connecting sockets and smear the pipe ends with an exhaust system sealant. New mounting clips and rubber suspension rings should be fitted, also new pipe clamps.

10 Do not fully tighten the retaining clamps and joint clamp/flange nuts until the complete system is in position and fully suspended. Check that the pipes do not foul any electrical leaks or other components before final tightening of the fastenings.

11 Run the engine on completion and check for any signs of leakage.

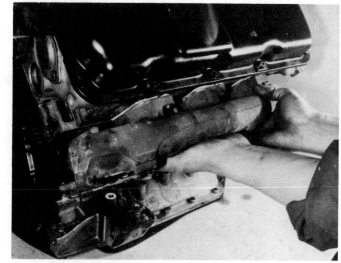
19.5B Fit the manifold

19 Exhaust manifolds – removal and refitting

1   If the left-hand exhaust manifold is being removed, disconnect the hot air duct between the manifold and the air cleaner intake.

2   Unbolt and detach the manifold-to-downpipe connection.

3   Unscrew and remove the manifold retaining nuts and withdraw the manifold(s) and the gaskets. To remove the rearmost gasket on the right-hand side, you will have to unscrew and remove the engine oil dipstick guide tube upper location bracket bolt and spacer.

4   Refitting is a reversal of the removal procedure, but note the following points.

5   Ensure that the mating surfaces are clean and use new gaskets (photo). To retain the gaskets in position on the studs whilst the manifold is being fitted, smear the head side of the gasket with a light even coating of exhaust sealant or failing this use grease. Refit the manifold(s) (photo).

6   Once the right-hand manifold is in position, relocate the dipstick guide tube and spacer (photos). Relocate the air duct on the left-hand manifold.

7   The downpipe connection flange joints must also be clean and smeared with exhaust sealant prior to assembling.

8   Check the system for any signs of leaks when the engine is restarted.

19.6A Locate the spacer collar ...

19.5A Locate the manifold gaskets over the studs

19.6B ... and fit the bolt to secure the guide tube

20 Fault diagnosis – fuel system (carburettor models)

We give in the following table a few of the symptoms of carburettor or fuel system trouble with reasons for their occurrence. Always bear in mind that it is difficult to distinguish between ignition faults and carburettor faults in many cases. The golden rule should be – before starting on the carburettor, make 100% certain of the ignition. Ignition faults are easy to check, ignition adjustments, when required, are easy to make, and furthermore when adjustment is required as a result of normal wear and tear this adjustment is much more likely to be in the ignition than in the carburettor. The following table, therefore, assumes that all is in order in the ignition system.

Symptom	Reason(s)
Smell of petrol when engine is stopped	Leaking pipes or unions Leaking fuel tank
Smell of petrol when engine is idling	Leaking fuel lines or unions between pump and carburettor Overflow of fuel from float chamber due to wrong level setting, ineffective needle valve or punctured float
Excessive fuel consumption not covered by leaks or float chamber faults	Worn jets Choke defect Brakes binding
Difficult starting, uneven running, lack of power, cutting out	Blockages in carburettor jet(s) Float chamber fuel level too low or needle valve sticking Fuel pump not delivering sufficient fuel Intake manifold gaskets leaking or manifold fractured

PART B: FUEL INJECTION MODELS

21 Fuel injection system – description and operation

The fuel injection system is of the continuous injection (CI) type in which the injection valves are always open. Unlike some other fuel injection systems, the amount of fuel supplied is not controlled by injection time variation but by the variation of fuel flow through the injectors.

The CI system principle is to measure continuously the airflow into the engine and let this airflow control the amount of fuel fed to the engine. The measuring of the induced air and the control of the fuel flow is provided by an air-fuel control unit which is the 'heart' of the CI system. The air-fuel control unit consists of an airflow sensor and a fuel distributor or metering head, and these are mounted directly on top of the airflow casing located between the inlet manifolds of each cylinder bank. An air cleaner unit is fitted to the venturi of the airflow sensor unit in a similar manner to that of a conventional carburettor.

The airflow sensor consists of a plate in the air inlet venturi. As air passes through the venturi, the plate is raised or lowered in accordance with the amount of airflow.

The airflow sensor plate movement is transferred by a lever to a control plunger or piston in the fuel metering head. A balance weight on the end of the lever equalizes the weight of the plate and the lever.

The fuel metering piston is housed within a cylinder which has six rectangular slots in it, one for each cylinder, known as metering slots. These slots are uncovered according to piston movement which as mentioned, is dictated by the airflow sensor plate (FTS).

To provide satisfactory operation under certain temperatures, starting and full load conditions, a control circuit is fitted to supply a variable pressure to the other end of the piston according to operating conditions.

The left-hand distributor supplies the mixture to the right-hand cylinder bank, and the right-hand distributor supplies the left-hand cylinder bank. This is because the inlet manifold tracts cross over (see Fig. 3.31).

A priming pump within the fuel tank supplies fuel to the main fuel pump. The main pump is located on the right-hand chassis member next to the fuel tank and is an electric pump of permanent roller, magnetic type. The pump has a check valve fitted which ensures that the circuit pressure is maintained when the engine stops. As a safety measure the pump switches off automatically when the engine stops, even though the ignition may still be switched on.

Fuel from the pump is pressure fed through an accumulator (mounted alongside the pump), to the line filter and then to the metering head. Fuel is also supplied to the cold start injector. This device is electro-magnetically controlled and is fed by a thermotime switch (actuated by engine coolant temperature) and the starter solenoid.

As fuel is supplied to the injectors from the metering head they open under fuel pressure (Fig. 3.32).

The cold start injector works in conjunction with an auxiliary air device to regulate the mixture requirement to the cylinders during cold starts. The auxiliary air device is actuated by an electrically heated bimetallic blade which opens the air passage according to the temperature in it, and supplements the air supply by drawing air from the air inlet upstream of the throttle butterflies. The auxiliary air circuit closes as soon as the engine reaches its normal operating temperature.

A compensating pressure regulator, sensitive to the inlet manifold vacuum, regulates the mixture when the engine is cold or operating under full loading. When the engine is cold, a bimetallic strip resistance in the regulator, is activated when the ignition is switched on. The bi-metallic strip progressively bends, releases the regulator spring and restores normal pressure as normal temperature is reached.

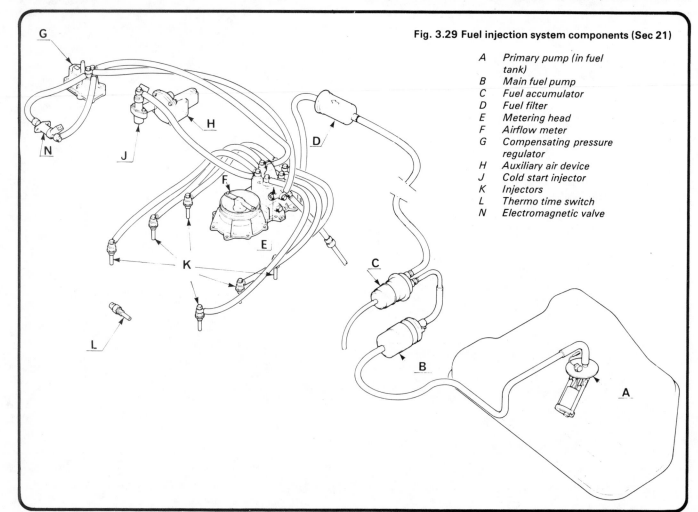

Fig. 3.29 Fuel injection system components (Sec 21)

A	Primary pump (in fuel tank)
B	Main fuel pump
C	Fuel accumulator
D	Fuel filter
E	Metering head
F	Airflow meter
G	Compensating pressure regulator
H	Auxiliary air device
J	Cold start injector
K	Injectors
L	Thermo time switch
N	Electromagnetic valve

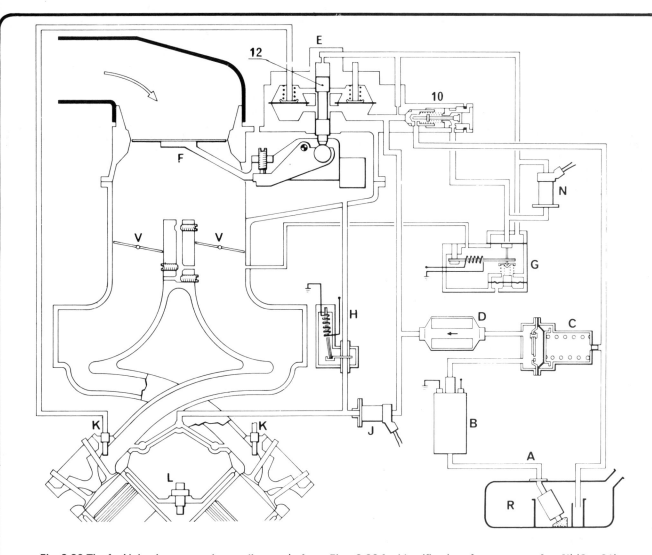

Fig. 3.30 The fuel injection system layout diagram (refer to Figs. 3.29 for identification of components A to N) (Sec 21)

R   Fuel tank   V   Throttle butterflies   10   Fuel pressure regulator   12   Control plunger

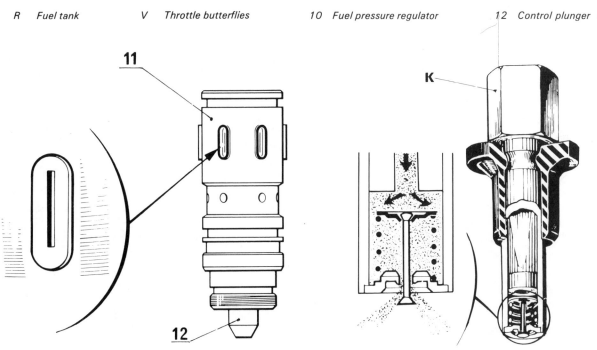

Fig. 3.31 The control plunger (12) showing the injector feed slots (11) (Sec 21)

Fig. 3.32 Cutaway view of an injector (K) showing fuel flow past opened valve (Sec 21)

When the throttle is opened fully there is a low manifold vacuum and the regulator control pressure drops accordingly.

To prevent the effects of fuel feed percolation when starting a hot engine, an electro-magnetic control valve operates in conjunction with the pressure control regulator inlet and outlet supplies to reduce the control pressure whilst increasing the injection pressure. This control valve operates in parallel with the starter solenoid.

A fuel pressure regulator within the metering head enables a steady pressure of fuel to be supplied, excess fuel being returned to the fuel tank. The pressure regulator also prevents vapour locks forming by maintaining a residual pressure.

Diagrams of the system layout, showing its major components, are given in Figs. 3.30 and 3.31.

The fuel supply electrical circuit diagram is shown in Chapter 10. The inversing relay is located under the steering column; its function is to cut out the feed to the fuel pump resistance wire when the starter motor is operated. A pump resistance wire is necessary to reduce the main pump output to match that of the primary pump within the fuel tank.

The RPM relay is fitted to cut out the fuel pumps as soon as the engine is stopped, even though the ignition may still be on. This is a safety feature. This relay too is fitted beneath the steering column.

22 Fuel injection system – maintenance and repairs

1   As mentioned in the previous Section, the fuel injection system is made up of a number of individual units or components, each of which is of equal importance and a matched part of the system. Because of the relative complexity of the system, repairs to most of the components are not advisable (or in some instances possible) for the owner/driver working on a DIY basis. Therefore apart from routine maintenance and the detachment of some components when working on the engine, it is advisable to entrust any fuel injection system repairs to your Renault dealer. He will be familiar with the system and will have the special tools and equipment necessary for testing the system components.
2   Where removal and dismantling procedures are possible for the DIY mechanic, we have given the details in the following Sections.
3   Whenever working on the fuel injection system, particular attention must be paid to ensure that no dirt enters the system.
4   The following maintenance procedures can easily be undertaken

by the home mechanic at the specified intervals (if not before).

(a)   Air filter element: renew at 10 000 miles (15 000 km) referring to Section 23. Renew the filter element more frequently if the vehicle is used in dusty conditions
(b)   In-line fuel filter: renew at 30 000 miles (45 000 km) referring to Section 24
(c)   Regular checks must be made to ensure that the respective fuel and air/vacuum line hoses and connections are in good condition, securely fitted and free of leaks

5   Remember that fuel lines in the fuel injection system may contain fuel under pressure, even if the engine has not been running for some time. **Do not** smoke or allow any naked flame nearby when there is any risk of fuel spillage. Take care to avoid spilling fuel onto a hot engine, and keep a fire extinguisher handy.

23 Air cleaner unit – removal, element renewal and refitting

1   To renew the air filter element, the cleaner unit complete must be removed.
2   Detach the breather pipe connection and then unscrew the three bolts to enable the unit to be lifted clear (Fig. 3.33).
3   To renew the element, unclip the case snap fasteners and separate the unit upper and lower halves. Extract the old element, clean out each half casing and locate the new element. Reassemble the casings.
4   Refit the air cleaner unit in the reverse order of removal, renewing the O-ring seal of the inlet port to the airflow meter should it be unserviceable.

24 Fuel line filter – renewal

1   The fuel line filter is shown in Fig. 3.34.
2   Before removing the old filter, clean the connections. Then remove the fuel lines from the filter. Be prepared for some spillage. Undo the clamp and remove the filter itself.
3   Transfer the nipples, seals and clamp to the new filter. Ensure that the seals are in good order first.
4   Take note of which way the arrow is positioned on the filter and fit the new filter with the arrow following the direction of flow.
5   Reconnect the fuel lines and ensure that there are no leaks.

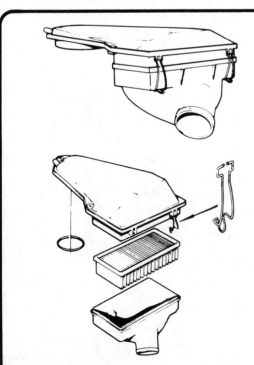

Fig. 3.33 Air filter assembly components (Sec 23)

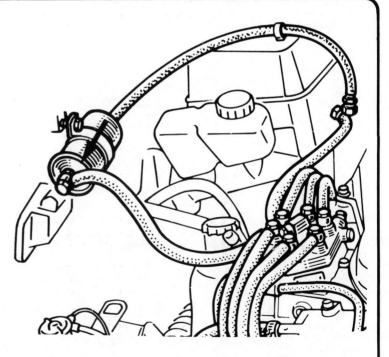

Fig. 3.34 Fuel line filter – arrow indicates direction of fuel flow (Sec 24)

25 Fuel injector(s) – removal and refitting

1   Clean round the fuel injector and fuel pipe. Disconnect the fuel pipe (Fig. 3.35). Be prepared for some spillage.
2   Remove the injector retainer and the injector.
3   When refitting the injector, fit a new rubber seal.
4   Reconnect the fuel pipe. Start the engine and check for leaks.

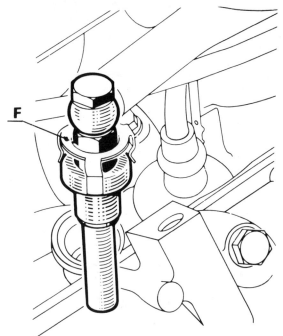

Fig. 3.35 Fuel injector retaining clip (F) and pipe connection (Sec 25)

26 Fuel metering head – removal, inspection and refitting

1   Disconnect the battery earth lead and remove the air filter.
2   Referrring to Fig. 3.36, disconnect the following pipe unions to the metering head unit:

   (a) fuel inlet pipe
   (b) injector feed pipes
   (c) control pressure inlet
   (d) fuel return pipe (to fuel tank)
   (e) control pressure return
   (f) cold start injector feed

3   Unscrew and remove the three fuel metering head retaining screws and remove the metering head. Lift it partially to enable your fingers to slide underneath and support the control piston, otherwise it will drop (refer to Fig. 3.37). If the metering assembly complete has been removed simply invert it and remove the head to prevent the piston from dropping out.
4   To inspect the unit, clean it only with petrol and blow dry with a foot pump. Remove the control piston and inspect it for any signs of gum deposits or possibly seizure. Rotate and oscillate the piston and and ensure that it moves freely in its bore. Should it be defective in any way it must be renewed together with the head, so they are matched during manufacture.
5   The pressure regulator assembly can be removed by unscrewing the retaining plug and withdrawing the discharge valve, spring, regulating piston and setting washers. You will probably need a suspended magnet to extract the piston.
6   Renew any defective components. The O-ring seals must be renewed on reassembly; should the regulating piston be in need of renewal, the metering head must also be renewed, as again these are a matched pair.
7   With all parts perfectly clean, reassemble in the following order: regulating piston, spring, discharge valve and washers. The washers must make the same total thickness as when removed, as they

determine the operating pressure. Refit the plug to retain the assembly, using a new seal.
8   Refitting of the metering head unit is a reversal of the removal procedure. Hold the piston in position as the head is lowered to prevent it dropping.
9   Ensure that the respective hoses are correctly refitted and are secure at their unions. Check for any signs of leakage when the engine is restarted.

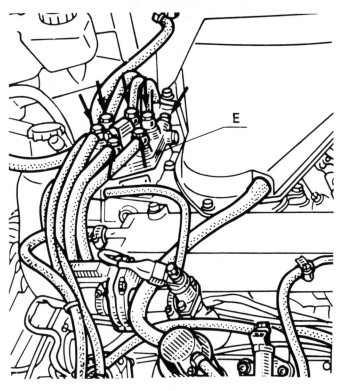

Fig. 3.36 Detach items indicated from the fuel metering head (E) (Sec 26)

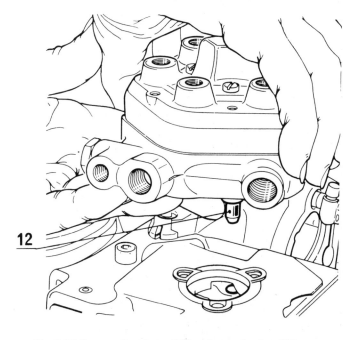

Fig. 3.37 Support the piston (12) underneath when lifting or lowering the metering head (Sec 26)

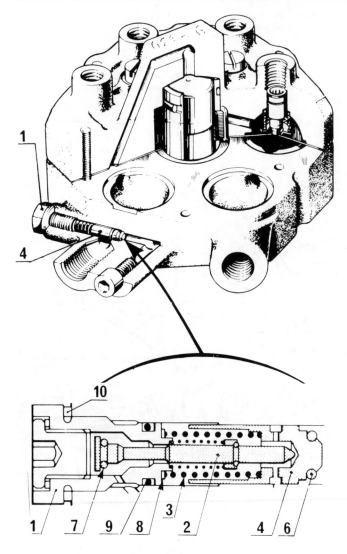

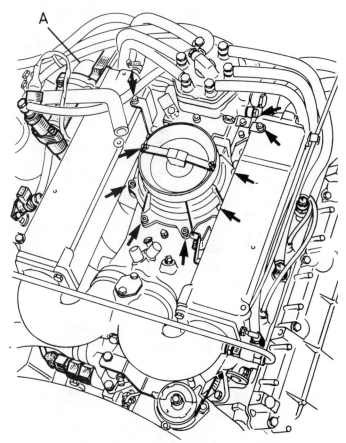

Fig. 3.39 Airflow meter retaining screws (arrowed). Also shown is the air hose to lower casing location (A) (Sec 27)

Fig. 3.38 Pressure regulator assembly (Sec 26)

1	*Plug*
2	*Discharge valve and washers*
3	*Spring*
4	*Regulating piston*

6	*O-ring*
7	*O-ring*
8	*Setting washers*
9	*O-ring*
10	*Seal*

27 Airflow meter – removal, inspection and assembly

1   Remove the air filter unit and disconnect the battery earth lead.
2   Detach the respective fuel pipes at the metering head as detailed in the previous Section.
3   Unscrew and remove the airflow meter retaining screws shown in Fig. 3.39 and lift the regulator clear.
4   With the metering head removed, check that the sensor plate is free and that the lever pivot pin is not binding. Renew the lever and pin if they are defective.
5   If renewing the lever pivot pin, remove the circlip, washer, seal, ball and spring (see Fig. 3.40). Then unscrew the retaining bolt and withdraw the pivot pin, the lever and adjuster arm. The bushes cannot be renewed.
6   If required withdraw the circlip, washer, seal and ball from the other side of the pin.
7   On reassembly, lubricate the balls and spring with a molybdenum grease, then assemble in the reverse order to dismantling.
8   When refitting the sensor plate it must be centralised before tightening the retaining bolts securing the lever to the pin.
9   Apart from being concentric when fitted, the sensor plate height setting must also be correct.

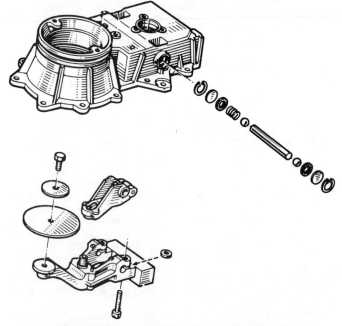

Fig. 3.40 Airflow meter pivot pin assembly (Sec 27)

10 When assembling, check the sensor plate top face to air funnel rib height clearance (see Fig. 3.41), this should be zero ± 0.020 in (± 0.5 mm).
11 Should it be found that the sensor plate is too high, adjust it by inserting a suitable punch through the hole shown in Fig. 3.42 and tapping very lightly so that the guide spindle spring blade is pushed down to obtain the specified setting. Do not repeatedly adjust the

guide spindle, as this may weaken it, and do not over-adjust as it is difficult to raise the plate.

12 Check the sensor plate for centralisation and if necessary proceed as follows to make adjustment.

13 Remove the anti-return stop bracket, loosen off the plate centre screw and centralise the plate. Retighten the bolt to the specified torque of 5 Nm (4 lbf ft).

14 Before refitting the air filter unit, check that the meter lever moves freely and also that the sensor plate cannot touch the venturi. Note however that the airflow meter must not be pressed unless the engine is stopped and the fuel pumps are known to be deactivated, otherwise if the injectors are fitted they will supply unwanted fuel and the engine may not restart. If the injectors are not connected, petrol will be pumped over the engine!

15 Should the meter lever not move freely, this is probably due to a defective sensor plate pivot pin or a defective meter head control plunger.

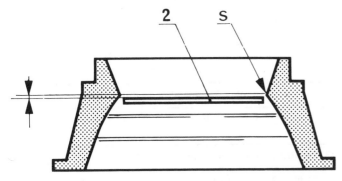

Fig. 3.41 Airflow meter sensor plate height check (Sec 27)

2 Plate   S Rib

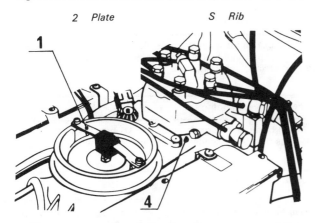

Fig. 3.42 Anti-return stop bracket (1) and the punch entry hole (4) (Sec 27)

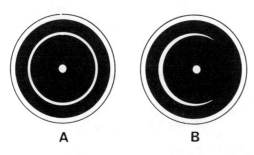

Fig. 3.43 Airflow meter sensor plate – check for centralisation (Sec 27)

A Correct   B Incorrect

28 Lower air casing – removal and refitting

1 Disconnect the battery earth lead and remove the air filter unit.

2 Disconnect the respective fuel unions from the metering head, noting their locations.

3 Loosen off the air inlet pipe to auxiliary air valve hose clip, then turn the pipe to free the air valve hose. Pull and separate the air hose from the lower air casing. (Fig. 3.39).

4 Remove the cap screw and bolt securing the air casing to the inlet manifold on each side.

5 Detach the connecting arm from the throttle linkage balljoint connection by rotating the securing clip a half turn to release it, the sliding it along the joint to enable the ball to be unlocked, so releasing the arm.

6 Disconnect the distributor HT leads (noting their respective locations).

7 Detach and pull the lower air casing to the rear so that it is clear of the intake elbow rings, then lifting it at the rear so that it clears the distributor cap, withdraw the casing and detach the vacuum pipes from the distributor.

8 Refitting is a reversal of the removal procedure, but be sure to renew the seals. There is one located in the port which the auxiliary air valve hose fits into, and a plastic seal is also fitted at the end of the air channel. Another O-ring seal is fitted at the lower casing end in the connection rings.

9 With the vacuum pipes connected, fit the casing and locate the control bolt at the front end first, followed by the cap-screw and bolt on each side.

10 When refitting the auxiliary air pipe into the lower casing, ease its fitting by greasing the O-ring.

11 Ensure that the distributor HT lead connections and the fuel unions at the metering head are secure.

12 On restarting the engine check the respective fuel hose connections for any signs of leakage.

29 Air inlet manifold – removal and refitting

1 Refer to the previous Section and remove the lower air casing.

2 Unscrew and remove the four manifold retaining bolts (Fig. 3.44) and lift it clear.

3 Remove the gaskets and seals as they must be renewed on reassembly.

4 Before refitting ensure that all mating faces are perfectly clean. Refit in the reverse order to removal.

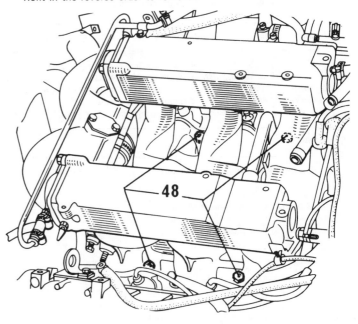

Fig. 3.44 Inlet air manifold retaining bolt locations (48) (Sec 29)

5   Refit the inlet sleeves and reconnect the distributor vacuum pipe.
6   When the airflow meter unit has been refitted, do not forget to pass the throttle control arm under the bracket.
7   Reconnect the following items:

(a) *The auxiliary air pipe*
(b) *The fuel pipes and injectors*
(c) *The HT leads*
(d) *The crankcase rebreathing and vacuum hoses*
(e) *The thermal switch to auxiliary air valve lead*

8   Ensure that all connections are correctly and securely made. On restarting the engine recheck the connections and inspect for any signs of fuel leakage.

30 Fuel pump/accumulator – removal and refitting

1   Disconnect the battery earth lead.
2   Working underneath the vehicle at the rear detach the wires to the

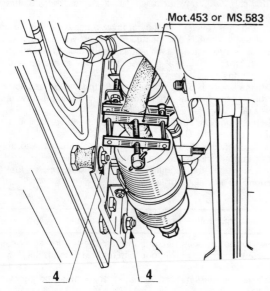

Mot.453 or MS.583

4   4

Fig. 3.45 The pump/accumulator unit showing position of retaining nuts (4) and hose clamps used when removing (Renault special tool numbers given) (Sec 30)

fuel pump unit. The pump is fitted to the side-member on the right-hand side, opposite the fuel tank.
3   To save draining the fuel tank, clamp the fuel inlet pipe to the pump unit. A suitable G-clamp and two pieces of flat wood will do the job (Fig. 3.45).
4   With the pipe clamped, disconnect the inlet and outlet pipes at the pump.
5   Remove the pump/accumulator unit retaining clamp nuts and then lift away the combined units.
6   Refitting is the reverse of the removal procedure. Take care to reconnect the wires correctly and securely and cover them with their insulators.

31 Accelerator cable – removal and refitting

1   Refer to Section 12; the procedure is basically the same.
2   If it is wished to remove the throttle linkage connecting arm, refer to Section 28, paragraph 5.
3   On refitting, adjust the cable length so that the compensating spring is compressed by approximately 2 mm (0.08 in) when the throttle is wide open.

32 Exhaust manifolds – removal and refitting

Refer to Section 19; similar considerations apply.

33 Exhaust system – removal and refitting

Refer to Section 18. The procedures are the same.

34 Fuel tank – removal and refitting

The procedure is as given in Section 14, with the additional point that the low pressure fuel pump electrical wires must be disconnected and reconnected accordingly.

35 Fuel tank – cleaning

The procedure is as given in Section 15, but remove the fuel pump as well as the gauge sender unit before commencing cleaning.

36 Fault diagnosis – fuel injection system

We give in this Section a table detailing a few of the symptoms of fuel system trouble, with reasons for their occurrence. Always bear in mind that it is difficult to distinguish between ignition faults and fuel system faults in many cases. The golden rule should be – before starting on the fuel system – make 100% certain of the ignition. Ignition faults are easy to check, ignition adjustments, when required, are easy to make. Furthermore, when adjustment is required as a result of normal wear and tear, this adjustment is much more likely to be in the ignition than in the fuel system. The following table assumes that all is in order in the ignition department.

Symptom	Reason(s)
Smell of petrol when engine is stopped	Leaking fuel pipes or unions Leaking fuel tank
Smell of petrol when engine is idling	Leaking fuel lines or unions in the fuel distribution system
Difficult starting with cold engine	Leak in the intake system Airflow sensor plate maladjusted Fuel distributor or airflow sensor sticking or binding Line pressure too low Control pressure too high Auxiliary air valve not opening Cold start injector faulty Thermotime switch faulty Blocked fuel lines or filters

Chapter 4 Ignition system

Contents

Specifications

General

System type:	
R1273, R1275 with manual gearbox, R1275 with automatic transmission up to 1978	Conventional distributor, twin contact breakers and coils, taper seat spark plugs
R1275 with automatic transmission from 1978 and R1278	Transistorised ignition (no contact breaker points), single coil, taper seat spark plugs
Distributor rotation	Clockwise
Firing order (all models)	1–6–3–5–2–4
Location of No 1 cylinder	Flywheel end, left-hand bank (viewed from rear)
HT lead connections (counting clockwise round cap):	
Conventional distributor	1–4–3–6–2–5
Transistorised distributor	As firing order

Spark plugs

Make and type	AC 42-5LTS, Champion BN9Y, or equivalent
Electrode gap	0.022 to 0.026 in (0.55 to 0.65 mm)

Contact breaker adjustment (conventional distributor)

Gap setting (initial adjustment only)	0.015 in (0.4 mm) nominal
Dwell angle (percentage):	
Group A (left-hand bank)	76 ± 3° (63 ± 3%)
Group B (right-hand bank)	76 ± 5° (63 ± 5%)

Ignition timing (static or idle)

All models, except R1275 with low compression (8.2:1) engine	10° BTDC ± 1°
R1275 with low compression (8.2:1) engine	6° BTDC ± 1°

Diagnostic socket

TDC pick-up up flywheel/driveplate face clearance	0.020 to 0.040 in (0.5 to 1.0 mm)

Torque wrench setting

	lbf ft	Nm
Spark plugs	13 to 15	17 to 20

1 General description

In order that the engine may run correctly it is necessary for an electrical spark to ignite the fuel/air mixture in the combustion chambers at exactly the right moment in relation to engine speed and loading. The ignition system is based on feeding low tension voltage from the battery to the coil(s) where it is converted to high tension voltage. The high tension voltage is powerful enough to jump the gap between the electrodes of the sparking plugs in the cylinders many times a second under high compression, providing that the system is in good condition and all the adjustments are correct.

One of two system types are used on the Renault 30 depending on model, these being either a contact breaker type ignition or a transistorised ignition system. The operating details of the transistorised ignition system are given in Section 2, together with some special precautions concerning it.

On engines fitted with contact breaker type ignition, dual contact breaker points are used, both housed in the same distributor. Two coils are also used. Note that the HT lead connection positions on this type of distributor differ from the engine firing order.

The system is divided into two circuits; the low tension and high tension. The low tension (sometimes called primary) circuit consists of the battery, the wire to the starter solenoid, the wire from the starter

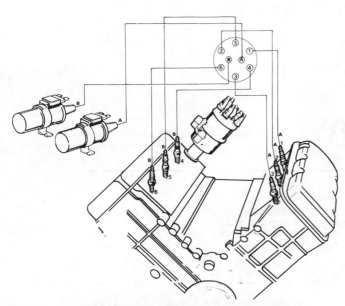

**Fig. 4.1 Ignition HT lead diagram on models fitted with the
mechanical contact breaker points distributor (Sec 1)**

A   Left-hand cylinder bank   B   Right-hand cylinder bank

solenoid to the ignition switch, the wires from the ignition switch to
the coil low tension windings (SW or + terminal) and from the coil low
tension windings (CB or – terminal) to the distributor contact breaker
points and condenser.

The high tension (HT) circuit comprises the HT or secondary coil
windings, the heavily insulated lead from each coil to the distributor
cap centre contacts, the rotor arm and the leads from the distributor
cap six outer contacts to the spark plugs.

Low tension voltage is stepped up by the coil windings to high
tension voltage intermittently by the operation of the contact points
and the condenser in the low tension circuit. High tension voltage is
then fed via the centre contact in the distributor cap to the rotor arm.

As the rotor arm rotates it aligns with each cap outer HT lead
contact segment in turn, the contact points open and the high voltage
is discharged, jumping the gap from rotor arm to contact and thence
along the plug lead to the centre electrode of the spark plug. Here it
jumps the other gap – sparking in the process – to the outer plug
electrode and hence to earth.

The timing of the spark can be adjusted by moving the outer body
of the distributor in relation to the distributor shaft. This alters the
position at which the points open in relation to the position of the
crankshaft.

The timing is also altered automatically by a centrifugal device,
which further alters the position of the complete points mounting
assembly in relation to the shaft when engine speed increases, and by
a vacuum control working from the inlet manifold which varies the
timing according to the position of the throttle and consequently the
load on the engine. Both of these automatic alterations advance the
timing of the spark at light loads and high speeds.

The mechanical advance mechanism consists of two weights,
which move out from the distributor shaft due to centrifugal force as
engine speed rises. As they move out, so the cam is rotated relative to
the shaft and the contact breaker opening position is altered. The
degree to which the weights move out is controlled by springs, the
tension of which significantly controls the extent of the advance.

The vacuum advance device is a diaphragm and connecting rod
attached to the contact breaker plate. When the diaphragm moves in
either direction the plate is moved, thus altering the timing. The
diaphragm is actuated by depression (vacuum) in the inlet manifold
and is connected by a small bore pipe to the carburettor body.

A diagnostic socket is fitted to enable Renault mechanics to
quickly pinpoint any problem within the ignition system and also to
time it accurately. Unfortunately, without the necessary associate
equipment, the diagnostic socket is of little use to the home mechanic.

2 Transistorised ignition system – general description

R1278 models, and R1275 models fitted with automatic transmission from 1978, have a breakerless type distributor which operates
with a single coil of special design. The main advantage of this system
is that no routine maintenance adjustments are required, apart from
checking the ignition timing at the specified intervals.

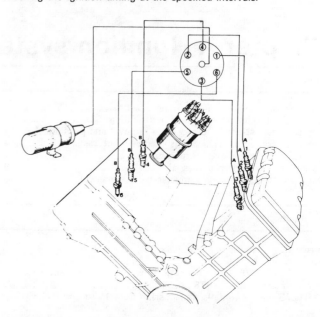

**Fig. 4.2 Ignition HT lead diagram on transistor ignition models
Firing order is 1-6-3-5-2-4 (Sec 2)**

The main components of the system are shown in Fig. 4.3.

An impulse goes from the distributor to the control unit. This
makes and breaks the current to the ignition coil with the help of
impulses from the impulse sender. The dwell angle is regulated
electronically. From the ignition coil, the high tension impulse goes as
usual to the spark plugs via the distributor rotor arm.

The ignition advance is still controlled by means of centrifugal
weights and a vacuum chamber.

The impulse sender opens and closes a magnet, as opposed to an
electrical, circuit. This induces impulses in the magnetic pick-up or coil.
The impulse sender is made up of four main parts: the stator, the
magnetic pick-up (or coil), the rotor and the magnet. Whilst the stator,
pick-up and magnet are connected to the distributor housing, the rotor
is connected to, and rotated with, the distributor shaft.

The control unit, or electronic module, is of a solid state design
employing transistors. It converts and amplifies the impulses from the
impulse sender and sends them on to the coil. It also performs a
second function, control of the dwell angle.

The rotor each has six teeth and the stator has three teeth. The
magnet creates a magnetic field which passes through the stator.
When the pole teeth are opposite each other, the magnetic circuit is
closed; when the teeth are apart, the circuit is open. In this way the
rotor opens and closes the magnetic field as it rotates; this generates
the current pulses in the magnetic pick-up. The pole teeth have in
effect a similar function to that of the cam lobes in a conventional
distributor.

Special precautions

Particular care must be taken whenever any work or checks are
being performed on the ignition system or associated engine components necessitating the detachment of the HT leads.

Do not attempt to run the engine with any HT lead disconnected
or serious damage to the system could result. If a spark plug is
removed for testing with the lead attached ensure tht it is properly
earthed.

Take care to avoid receiving electric shocks from the HT system.
The HT voltage is higher than in conventional ignition systems and
could be hazardous to people in poor health.

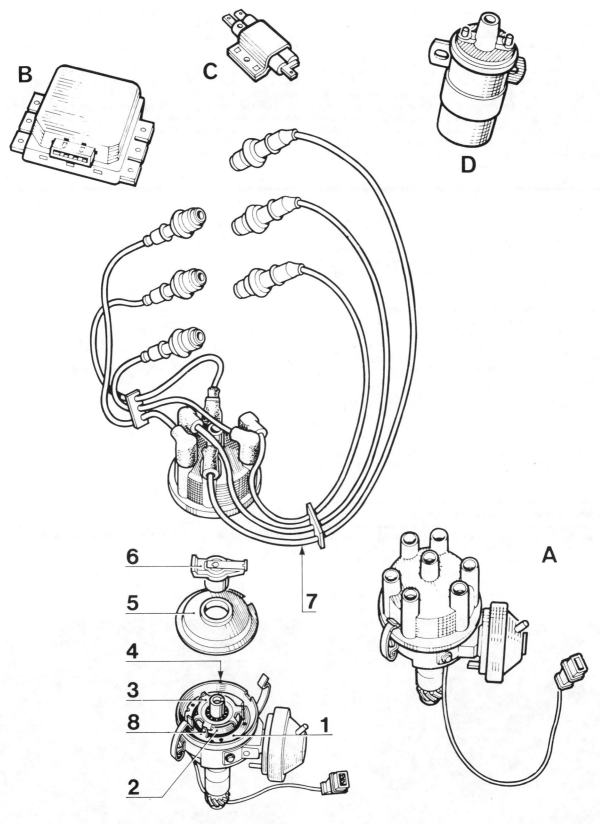

Fig. 4.3 The main components of the transistorised ignition system (Sec 2)

1	Permanent magnet		point	8	Inpulse sender segment	B	Electronic control unit
2	Pick-up coil	5	Dustproof cover	A	Distributor (inductive	C	Resistors
3	Rotor	6	Rotor arm		pick-up unit)	D	Coil (special)
4	No 1 cylinder firing	7	HT lead harness				

3 Routine maintenance

1   More engine breakdowns and problems are probably attributable to ignition faults than to any other cause. To safeguard against such problems, routine maintenance checks and (where necessary) adjustments should be made at the specified intervals.

2   *Spark plugs:* Remove the plugs and thoroughly clean away all trace of carbon. Examine the porcelain insulation round the central electrodes inside the plug, and if damaged discard the plug. Reset the gap between the electrodes. Do not use a set of plugs for more than 10 000 miles. It is false economy. At the same time check the plug caps. Always use the straight tubular ones normally fitted. Good replacements are normally available at your local Renault agency. For further information refer to Section 12.

3   *Distributor (contact breaker type):* Every 10 000 miles remove the cap and rotor arm and put one or two drops of engine oil into the centre of the cam recess. Smear the surfaces of the cam itself with petroleum jelly. Do not over-lubricate as any excess could get onto the contact breaker points surfaces and cause ignition difficulties. Every 10 000 miles also examine the contact breaker point surfaces. If there is a build-up of deposits on one face and a pit in the other it will be impossible to set the gap correctly and they should be refaced or renewed. Set the gap when the contact surfaces are in order – refer to Section 4.

4   *Distributor (breakerless):* The only lubrication necessary with a breakerless type distributor is a couple of drops of engine oil on the felt wick in the centre of the distributor shaft (photo). To do this, remove the distributor cap and rotor. Note that it may not be possible to remove the distributor cap when the rotor is in a certain position. If so, turn the engine so that the rotor is in a different position (pointing towards the centre of the engine).

5   *General:* Examine all leads and terminals for signs of broken or cracked insulation. Also check all terminal connections for slackness or signs of fracturing of some strands of wire. Partly broken wire should be renewed. The HT leads are particularly important as any insulation faults will cause the high voltage to 'jump' to the nearest earth and this will prevent a spark at the plug. Check that no HT leads are loose or in a position where the insulation could wear due to rubbing against part of the engine.

4 Distributor contact breaker points – adjustment

1   There are two sets of contact points fitted to the distributor, one being for the left-hand cylinder bank which is adjustable by means of a fastening screw on the baseplate. The other set of points is for the right-hand cylinder bank and is adjustable externally by an adjuster screw.

2   The two contact points sets are mounted parallel to each other,

each side of the rotor shaft, and their pivot pin positions must be kept symmetrical relative to the cam spindle. An eccentric adjuster is fitted to alter the moving contact points positions, but this is preset during manufacture and it is most unlikely that it will need further adjustment during the life of the distributor.

3   Assuming that the contact points are clean and in good condition, proceed as follows to check their adjustment, having removed the cap, rotor arm and dust shield.

4   Turn the crankshaft slowly to the point where one of the cam lobes has fully opened the left-hand bank contact points (see Fig. 4.4). The crankshaft can be turned by engaging a gear and moving the car accordingly. On automatic transmission models, turn the crankshaft by hand using a suitable spanner on the crankshaft pulley nut at the front. Removal of the spark plugs makes this task much easier.

5   Select a feeler gauge of the specified thickness and insert it between the contact faces. The blade should be a firm sliding fit. If adjustment is necessary to this set of points, loosen the clamp screw (photo) and adjust the fixed contact accordingly to open or close the clearance as required, then retighten the screw.

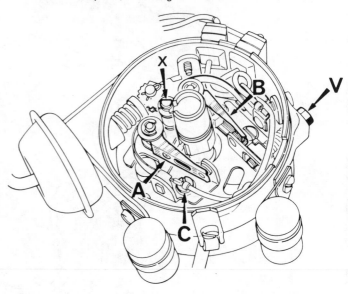

Fig. 4.4 Distributor contact breaker points and adjusters (Sec 4)

A   *Contact points for left-hand cylinder bank (group A)*
B   *Contact points for right-hand cylinder bank (group B)*
C   *Contact points adjuster screws for group A*
V   *Contact points adjuster screw for group B (external)*
X   *Eccentric adjuster (preset – do not alter the setting)*

3.4 Lubricating the transistorised distributor wick

4.5 Adjusting the contact breaker points – left-hand cylinder bank

6 Check the right-hand cylinder bank points clearance in a similar manner, and adjust if required by turning the external adjustment screw indicated in Fig. 4.4.

7 Setting the contact breaker gaps as described above should be regarded as an initial adjustment only. For best results, the dwell angle must be checked and adjusted if necessary. Dwell angle is the amount (expressed in degrees) through which the distributor cam turns between the instants of closure and opening of one set of contact breaker points.

8 Various proprietary instruments are available for measuring the dwell angle; unless specific instructions are given to the contrary, use the 6-cylinder scale on the instrument and *multiply the reading by two*. This is because, with two sets of contact points and a three-lobed cam, we are effectively measuring dwell on two 3-cylinder engines – but you are unlikely to find a dwell meter with a 3-cylinder scale!).

9 Connect the dwell meter, in accordance with the maker's instructions, to the group A (left-hand cylinder bank) LT circuit. Crank the engine on the starter motor, or allow it to idle, again according to the meter maker's instructions. Read the dwell angle (see above) and compare it with the value given in the Specifications.

10 If the dwell angle is too large, increase the points gap as described in paragraph 5. If the angle is too small, reduce the points gap. Recheck and repeat until adjustment is correct.

11 Connect the dwell meter to the group B (right-hand cylinder bank) LT circuit. Measure the dwell angle again, but if adjustment is necessary, proceed as described in paragraph 6. Note that a greater variation from the specified dwell angle is permitted on this set of contacts – see Specifications.

12 If the specified dwell angle cannot be obtained on both sets of contact breakers, the distributor may be worn or the eccentric adjuster may be at fault. Consult your Renault dealer if the latter is suspected.

13 On completion, check the ignition timing and adjust if necessary – see Section 10.

5 Contact breaker points – removal and refitting

1 Unclip and remove the distributor cap.

2 Bend out the retaining tabs of the rotor arm securing screw washer and then remove the screw with its washer. Lift the rotor arm away from the shaft (photo), also the dust shield.

3 Unscrew and remove the external adjuster screw and withdraw its coil spring (Fig. 4.4).

4 Prise free the respective contact-to-pivot retaining clips and washers (photo). Take care as the clips are removed not to lose them.

5 Unscrew and remove the contact retaining screws.

6 Detach the low tension wires and lift out the contact breaker points.

7 Examine each of the contact point faces in turn. Look for a 'pip' on one face and a corresponding pit on the other, and/or possibly uneven wear. The faces of both contacts, where this is apparent, should be cleaned and resurfaced using an oilstone. Keep the faces to their original contour and remove all surface deformity on each contact.

8 Where severe burning has occurred (usually caused by a defective condenser or poor earth connections), or possibly severely worn contact faces, they must be renewed.

9 Clean the faces of both contacts, whether old or new, prior to refitting, using methylated spirit. This removes any oil or protective coating that may be present.

10 Refitting is a reversal of the removal procedure, but ensure that the fibre washer located above the moving contact breaker is relocated.

11 Adjust the contact breaker points as described in Section 4.

12 When refitting the dust shield, be sure to align its slotted section with the corresponding slot of the distributor body (photo).

6 Condenser(s) – removal and refitting

1 Fault ignition resulting in misfiring and uneven running can be caused by a faulty condenser which is mounted externally on the body of the distributor (contact breaker type).

2 Should one or possibly both pairs of contact breaker points show signs of excessive burning and pitting on the faces of the contacts, it is an indication that the condenser(s) are in a defective condition and in need of renewal.

5.2 Removing the rotor arm

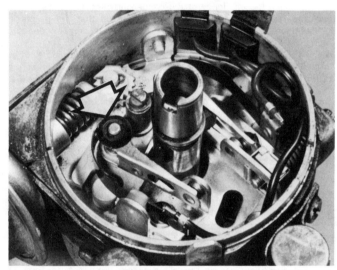

5.4 Moving contact pivot retaining clip and washer (arrowed)

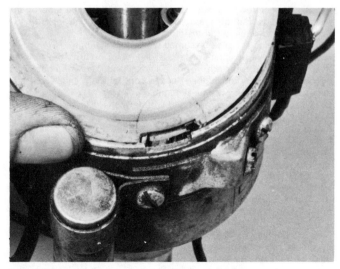

5.12 Align slots of dust shield and distributor body

6.6 One condenser and its retaining screw

7.6 Removing the distributor (engine removed for clarity)

3   To check the efficiency of the condenser remove the distributor cap and rotor arm. Then rotate the engine so that the points in question are closed – that is with the breaker arm resting between two high points on the cam.
4   Switch on the ignition and with a non-conductive article such as a splinter of wood, move the contacts open by levering on the spring of the moving breaker. If there is a strong blue spark it indicates that the condenser has probably failed.
5   If a condenser fails so that it is short-circuiting the contact breaker points, the points will be unable to interrupt the LT circuit and ignition failure on the respective cylinder bank will occur accordingly.
6   To renew a condenser, detach the wire from the terminal post, remove the mounting screw and replace the old unit with a new one (photo). Check that arcing has been virtually eliminated by testing as already described.

7   Distributor – removal and refitting

1   The removal and refitting details for both the contact breaker and breakerless (transistorised) ignition distributors is basically the same. However, on fuel injection models it will be necessary to remove the fuel metering head assembly to gain access to the distributor (refer to Chapter 3).
2   Detach the HT lead connectors from the spark plugs, and also the coil HT lead(s).
3   Disconnect the LT lead(s) from the terminal on the side of the distributor body. Pull off the hose from the vacuum unit (photo).
4   Unclip and remove the distributor cap.
5   If the engine is not to be turned whilst the distributor is removed, mark the relative positions of (a) the distributor body to the cylinder head and (b) the rotor arm to the cylinder head. This will enable the distributor to be repositioned exactly on refitting and avoid the necessity of having to retime the ignition.
6   Unscrew the retaining nut and withdraw the distributor (photo).
7   Refitting is the reversal of the removal procedure. Realign the marks made on removal before retightening the distributor clamp nut. Ensure that the respective lead connections are secure. Check the ignition timing and adjust if necessary (Section 10).
8   If a new or overhauled distributor is being fitted, or if the engine has been turned since the distributor was removed, then proceed as follows when fitting to ensure the correct timing.
9   Turn the engine to set it at the TDC position with No 1 cylinder firing. To do this remove No 1 cylinder spark plug (left-hand bank, rear) and place your finger over the hole. Turn the engine until you feel the pressure building up in that cylinder. Now turn your attention to the flywheel timing mark aperture on the transmission housing. On manual gearbox models the flywheel has a single line timing mark on its periphery to denote TDC, No 1 cylinder (left bank) firing. There is also a double line marking, which is the timing mark for checking the

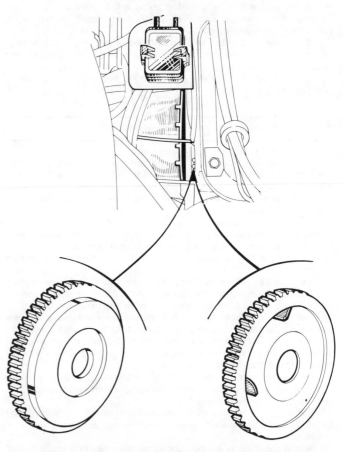

Fig. 4.5 The flywheel (left)/converter driveplate (right) timing mark lines/lugs (Sec 7)

ignition timing of the right-hand cylinder bank, but this can be ignored at the moment (Fig. 4.5). On automatic transmission models these timing marks are in the form of lugs attached to the converter driveplate. The timing mark lug for the No 1 cylinder (left-hand bank) is triangular, whilst that for the right-hand bank is a sector shaped lug.
10 Align the single timing line/triangular lug with the O mark on the calibrated scale for the TDC setting.

Conventional distributor
11 Now preset the distributor, so that when it is lowered into

Measuring plug gap. A feeler gauge of the correct size (see ignition system specifications) should have a slight 'drag' when slid between the electrodes. Adjust gap if necessary

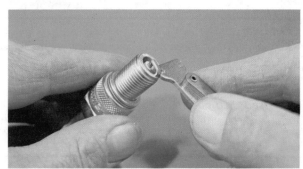

Adjusting plug gap. The plug gap is adjusted by bending the earth electrode inwards, or outwards, as necessary until the correct clearance is obtained. Note the use of the correct tool

Normal. Grey-brown deposits, lightly coated core nose. Gap increasing by around 0.001 in (0.025 mm) per 1000 miles (1600 km). Plugs ideally suited to engine, and engine in good condition

Carbon fouling. Dry, black, sooty deposits. Will cause weak spark and eventually misfire. Fault: over-rich fuel mixture. Check: carburettor mixture settings, float level and jet sizes; choke operation and cleanliness of air filter. Plugs can be re-used after cleaning

Oil fouling. Wet, oily deposits. Will cause weak spark and eventually misfire. Fault: worn bores/piston rings or valve guides; sometimes occurs (temporarily) during running-in period. Plugs can be re-used after thorough cleaning

Overheating. Electrodes have glazed appearance, core nose very white – few deposits. Fault: plug overheating. Check: plug value, ignition timing, fuel octane rating (too low) and fuel mixture (too weak). Discard plugs and cure fault immediately

Electrode damage. Electrodes burned away; core nose has burned, glazed appearance. Fault: pre-ignition. Check: as for 'Overheating' but may be more severe. Discard plugs and remedy fault before piston or valve damage occurs

Split core nose (may appear initially as a crack). Damage is self-evident, but cracks will only show after cleaning. Fault: pre-ignition or wrong gap-setting technique. Check: ignition timing, cooling system, fuel octane rating (too low) and fuel mixture (too weak). Discard plugs, rectify fault immediately

position, the driven gear will align correctly with the gear on the camshaft. To do this, refit the distributor rotor arm without the shield, and line it up as shown in Fig. 4.6.
12 Lower the distributor into position with the adjustment bracket over the stud (Fig. 4.7).

Transistorised distributor
13 On R1275 models fitted with transistorised ignition, align the rotor arm with the No 1 cylinder mark on the distributor body and then fit the distributor so that the vacuum capsule is as shown in Fig. 4.8.

14 On R1278 models, position the rotor arm so that it turns to align with the No 1 cylinder mark on the distributor body when in its fitted position – see Fig. 4.9.

All models
15 With the distributor fitted in position, refit the washer and retaining nut to secure it.
16 Remove the rotor arm and refit the shield. Note that there is a tab which fits in the small recess in the distributor body.

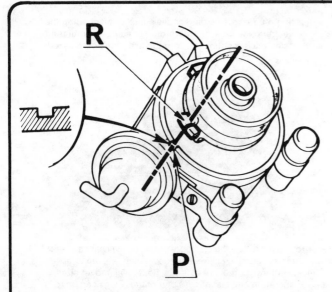

Fig. 4.6 Align correct rotor segment marking (B) with distributor body timing mark (P) (conventional distributor) (Sec 7)

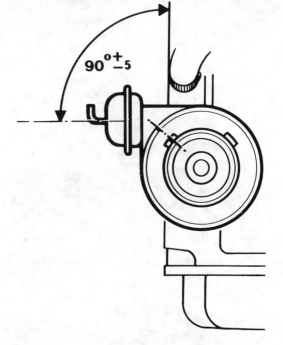

Fig. 4.7 Distributor and rotor alignment positions at firing point of No 1 cylinder when fitted (conventional distributor) (Sec 7)

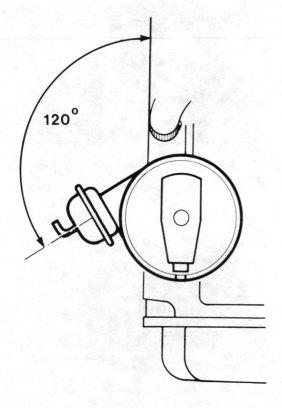

Fig. 4.8 The fitted position of the transistorised distributor on the R1275 model (Sec 7)

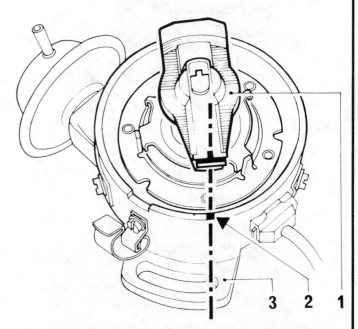

Fig. 4.9 The fitted position of the transistorised distributor on the R1278 models

1   Rotor arm   3   Clamp plate
2   Alignment mark

17 Refit the rotor arm, and turn the engine so the rotor arm points towards the centre of the engine. If this is not carried out, the distributor cap will not go back on.
18 Refit the distributor cap and vacuum hose. Make sure the clips are locked securely in place.
19 Run the engine and adjust the timing, if necessary, with a stroboscope. See Section 10 for details.

8 Distributor (transistorised) – impulse sender renewal

1 Unclip and remove the distributor cap, then tuck it out of the way. Also remove the rotor arm and shield.
2 Remove the two screws securing the vacuum control unit in place on the distributor body, and lift the unit away (photo).
3 Remove the screw securing the contact (and impulse sender lead to the control unit) in place and remove the contact, pulling it carefully straight out (photo).
4 Next, remove the circlip, spring washer and shims (if any) holding the rotor itself in place (photo).
5 The rotor and locking pin can then be removed. Use two screwdrivers on opposite sides of the rotor to ease it up the shaft (Fig. 4.10).
6 Now you can reach the three screws in the outer edge of the

baseplate which hold the impulse sender and baseplate assembly in place. Unscrew them and also remove the retaining circlip (photo). Pull the whole assembly out.
7 To detach the impulse sender from the baseplate remove the three screws in the centre of the baseplate and separate the two parts (photo).
8 When refitting the impulse sender to the baseplate, note that the connector points should be placed opposite to and above the attachment lug for the baseplate. Then secure it in position with the three screws through the baseplate.
9 Refit the assembly to the distributor body. Ensure that the connector pins are opposite the hole in the body so that the contact and lead, when refitted, can engage them. Secure the baseplate in position with the three screws and refit the circlip (photo).
10 Refit the rotor and line up the groove on its inside edge with the slot in the distributor shaft.
11 Refit the rotor locking pin and ensure that the slot in the roll pin faces the shaft (photo). If this is not done, the pin can be liable to shear off.
12 Refit the star washer and any shims that may have been fitted, then refit the circlip (photo).
13 Now refit the impulse sender contact and lead. Secure it in position with the single small screw.

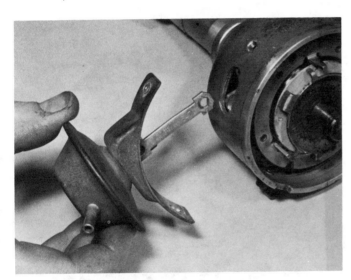
8.2 Withdrawing the vacuum control unit

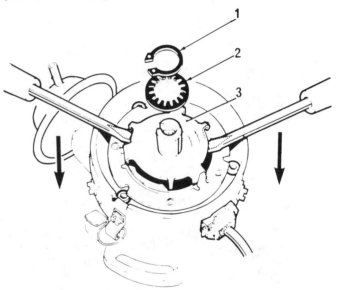
Fig. 4.10 Rotor removal method (Sec 8)
1 Circlip   2 Star washer   3 Rotor

8.3 Extract the impulse sender lead connector from the distributor

8.4 Remove the rotor retaining circlip

8.6 Remove the three Allen screws around the edge of the baseplate

8.7 Remove the impulse sender

8.9 The baseplate refitted with the circlip in position

8.11 The rotor and locking pin refitted

8.12 Refit the star washer

14   Refit the vacuum control unit and secure it in place with the two small screws.

15   Refit the distributor cap clips, if they were removed, and refit the vacuum pipe.

16   Refit the shield and rotor arm, then refit the distributor cap and lock it securely in place.

17   If the distributor has been taken out to change the impulse sender, check, when the task is completed, that the shaft turns freely in both directions. Hold the body in one hand and turn the driven gear with the other. The only resistance which may be felt is caused by the magnet when the teeth pass each other.

18   If the distributor has been removed from the car, refer to Section 7 for the relevant refitting instructions and setting up procedures.

9   Distributor – inspection and repair

Transistorised distributor

1   Thoroughly wash all mechanical parts in petrol or paraffin and wipe dry using a clean non-fluffy rag, having stripped the distributor as described in Section 8. Once the impulse sender and baseplate assembly has been removed, you can reach the centrifugal weights.

2   Check the distributor cap for signs of tracking, indicated by a thin black line between segments of the cap. Renew the cap if this is

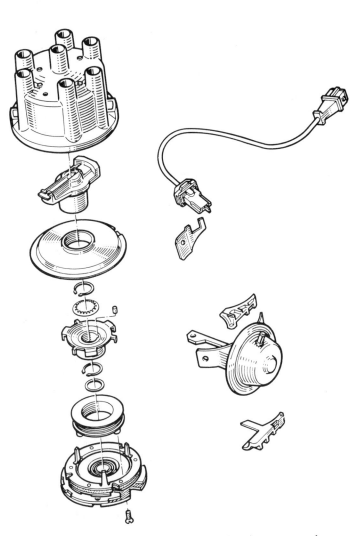

Fig. 4.11 Transistorised distributor showing the upper section components (Sec 9)

9.4 The centrifugal springs and weights

10 Ignition timing – checking and adjustment

1   It is necessary to check the ignition timing whenever the contact breaker gaps have been altered or the contact breaker points renewed (conventional distributors), whenever the distributor has been removed and refitted, and after engine overhaul (all distributors). It is also good practice to check the timing at normal service intervals, in case wear in the timing chain or other distributor drive components has caused a deviation from the correct setting.

2   The only satisfactory method for checking the timing on these engines is to use a stroboscopic timing light. This method is known as dynamic timing, since it is done with the engine running. It is also the only method possible on engines fitted with transistorised ignition. The static timing method given below should be regarded as an initial adjustment only, to enable the engine to be started.

3   Generally, if the distributor has been fitted correctly (Section 7) and the contact breaker points are in good condition and correctly gapped (where applicable), the engine will run and the static timing procedure may be omitted.

Static timing (conventional distributor only)

4   Remove the spark plugs and turn the crankshaft (see Section 4) until the single line on the flywheel (manual transmission) or the triangular lug on the driveplate (automatic transmission) is aligned with the correct graduation on the timing scale on the bellhousing aperture. See Fig. 4.12 and Specifications. The rotor arm must be aligned as shown in Fig. 4.7 – otherwise, rotate the crankshaft a further 360°.

5   With the timing marks so aligned, the contact breaker points for the left-hand bank of cylinders (group A) should be *just* opening. To see if this is so, connect a 12 volt test lamp between the group A coil LT terminal (the one connected to the distributor) and earth. With the points open, the lamp will be lit if the ignition is switched on.

6   Slacken the distributor clamp bolt and rotate the distributor body slightly, first one way and then the other, and check that the contact breaker points are opening as described. Tighten the clamp bolt when adjustment is correct.

7   Turn the crankshaft one-third of a revolution in the normal direction of rotation, to bring the double line (manual transmission) or the sector shaped lug (automatic transmission) into line with the correct graduation on the timing scale. With the test lamp connected to the group B coil LT terminal and the ignition on, the lamp should just come on as the timing marks come into alignment. Adjust if necessary using the external adjuster screw for the group B contacts, but remember that this will also alter the dwell angle, which must remain within the specified limits. **Do not** adjust by moving the distributor body, since this will upset the previously set group A timing.

8   If it is found impossible to achieve correct timing on both sets of contacts, the fault may lie in the distributor (assuming that the dwell

evident. Check that the carbon brush moves freely in the centre of the distributor cap and renew it if it is worn or in bad condition.

3   If the metal portion of the rotor arm is badly burned or loose, renew the arm. Slight burning can be cleaned up with a fine file.

4   Examine the centrifugal weight and pivot pins for wear. In particular, the holes in the centrifugal weights should not be oval or deformed in any other way. The importance of the springs has already been mentioned and these should be checked and renewed if necessary (photo).

5   The play between the distributor housing and the driveshaft should not exceed 0.008 in (0.2 mm). If the play is excessive, renew the bushes and if this is insufficient, also the shaft.

6   Renewing the bushes is a matter of driving or pulling them out and pressing or gently tapping the new ones in, one from each end with the felt lubricator between them. The lubricator and the bushes should be soaked in oil for at least half an hour before fitting. The fibre washers at each end of the shaft should be next to the housing. The endplay in the shaft should lie between 0.004 and 0.010 in (0.1 and 0.25 mm). If necessary, this can be adjusted by altering the number of spacing washers on the distributor shaft. **Note:** *avoid using any form of cleaning spirit on the electrical components.*

Conventional distributor

7   No overhaul procedures are laid down by the manufacturer, and it is unlikely that spare parts will be available. The procedures given above for the transistorised distributor may be found helpful if it is wished to dismantle the conventional distributor for examination.

angles are correct). As a temporary measure it may be wise to 'split the difference' between the two sets in order to avoid the imbalance between the cylinder banks which will occur if one side is correctly timed and the other side is not.

9   With the static timing correct, proceed to time the engine dynamically as described below.

Dynamic timing (all distributor types)

10 If necessary, highlight the timing marks on the flywheel/driveplate and the relevant graduation on the timing scale (Fig. 4.12) with quick-drying white paint. Typist's correcting fluid is ideal.

11 The engine must be at normal operating temperature and (where applicable) the contact breaker points must be correctly adjusted and in good condition. Disconnect and plug the distributor vacuum pipe.

12 Connect a timing light (strobe) to No 1 spark plug HT lead in accordance with the maker's instructions. Some timing lights connect in series with the spark plug; others require additional connections to a 12 volt battery or to an external power supply. Position all leads clear of moving parts, and make sure that you do not get articles of clothing,

long hair etc, caught in engine moving parts during subsequent operations.

13 Start the engine and allow it to idle. Point the timing light at the timing marks, they will appear stationary and, if the timing is correct, in alignment.

14 If the marks are not aligned, slacken the distributor clamp bolt and move the distributor body slightly to bring the marks into alignment accordingly. Tighten the clamp bolt and recheck.

Conventional distributor only

15 Stop the engine and transfer the timing light to No 6 spark plug lead. Start the engine and check that the mark for the right-hand bank of cylinders is aligned correctly. If adjustment is necessary, use the external adjuster screw for the group B contact breakers. **Do not** adjust by moving the distributor body, or the previously set timing for the left-hand cylinder bank will be upset.

All distributor types

16 Accurate checking of the centrifugal and vacuum advance mechanisms is beyond the scope of the DIY mechanic. A rough check may be made by increasing engine speed and checking that the timing mark appears to move away from the pointer on the timing scale. If the

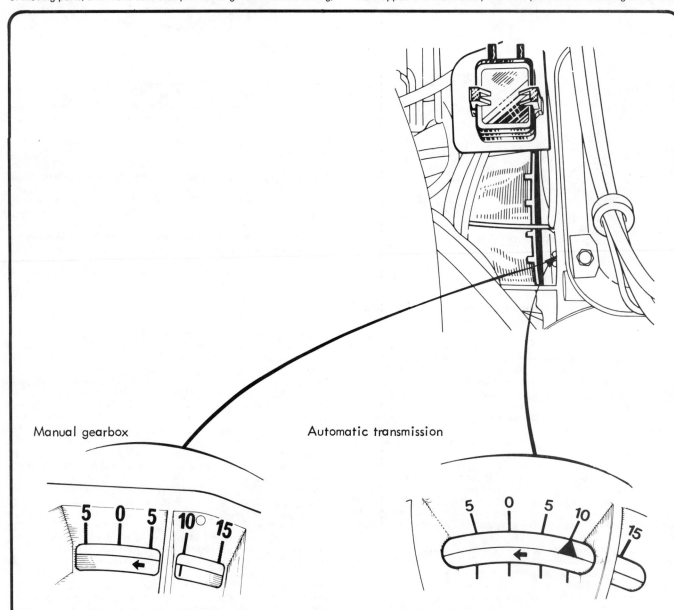

Manual gearbox

Automatic transmission

Fig. 4.12 The flywheel/torque converted driveplate timing marks and timing gradations. In this instance the markings are shown opposite the 10° BTDC gradation and are for the left-hand cylinder tank (Sec 10)

vacuum pipe is reconnected, a further advance should be observed. Jerky movement of the timing mark, or flutter, suggests that the automatic advance mechanisms are worn or sticking.

17   When adjustment is complete, switch off the engine, disconnect the timing light and remake the original connections.

11 Diagnostic socket and TDC pick-up – removal and refitting

1   Detach the battery earth lead from its terminal.
2   Remove the diagnostic socket from its bracket and the earth wire from the bracket retaining bolt (photo).
3   Disconnect the low tension wire and ignition coil wires.
4   Working underneath the car, unbolt and remove the engine protector plate. Raise and support the car with axle stands to provide sufficient space when working underneath.
5   The TDC pick-up unit is located in the support plate on the right-hand side of the cylinder block to the rear (Fig. 4.13). The pick-up unit is retained in the plate by the clamp screw. Remove this screw and withdraw the pick-up unit (photo).
6   Refit in the reverse order to removal. When the pick-up is being fitted, adjust it so that it is 0.020 to 0.040 in (0.5 to 1.0 mm) from the flywheel or driveplate face. If a new pick-up unit is being fitted, it has

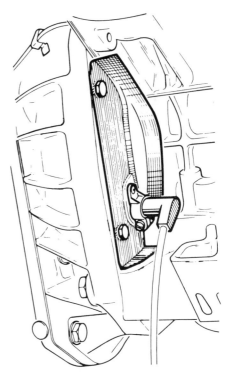

Fig. 4.13 The diagnostic socket pick up unit location (Sec 11)

three lugs which must be just in contact with the flywheel or driveplate when fitted.
7   Tighten the pick-up clamp screw when the pick-up unit is in its set position.

11.2 The diagnostic socket, retaining bracket and earth wire location under bracket bolt head

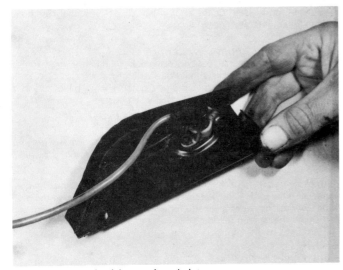

11.5 The diagnostic pick-up unit and plate

12 Spark plugs and HT leads – general

1   With the development of modern technology and materials, spark plugs are generally very reliable and require minimal attention. When they are due for checking and cleaning it is good practice to have them thoroughly sand blasted, gapped and checked under pressure on the machine that most garages have installed.
2   They can also be used as good indications of engine condition, particularly as regards the fuel mixture being used and the state of the pistons and cylinder bores. Check each plug as it is possible that one cylinder condition is different from the rest. Plugs come in different types to suit the particular type of engine. A 'hot' plug is for engines which run at lower temperatures than normal and a 'cold' plug is for the hotter running engines. If plugs of the wrong rating are fitted they can either damage the engine or fail to operate properly. Under normal running conditions a correctly rated plug in a properly tuned engine will have a light deposit of brownish colour on the electrodes. A dry, black, sooty deposit indicates an over-rich fuel mixture. An oily, blackish deposit indicates worn bores or valve guides. A dry, hard, whitish deposit indicates too weak a fuel mixture. If plugs of the wrong heat ranges are fitted they will have similar symptoms to a weak mixture together with burnt electrodes (plug too hot) or to an over-rich mixture caked somewhat thicker (plug too cold). Do not try to economise by using plugs beyond 10 000 miles. Unless the engine remains in exceptionally good tune, reductions in performance and fuel economy will outweigh the cost of a new set.
3   The standard plug recommended for the Renault 30 models is a washerless type which has a conical seating. It is important when fitting these plugs that the seating faces are clean and the plugs are tightened to the specified torque or with the special spanner supplied with the vehicle (Fig. 4.14).
4   The spark plug gap is of considerable importance, as, if it is too large or too small the size of the spark and its efficiency will be seriously impaired. The spark plug gap should be set to the value given in the Specifications.
5   To set it, measure the gap with a feeler gauge, and then bend

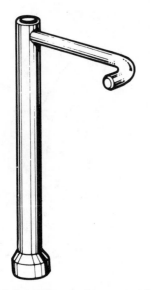

Fig. 4.14 Special spark plug spanner (Sec 12)

open, or close, the outer plug electrode until the correct gap is achieved. The centre electrode should never be bent as this may crack the insulation and cause plug failure, if nothing worse.

6   When renewing the plugs refit the leads from the distributor cap in the correct positions as shown in Fig. 4.1 or 4.2 as applicable.

7   The HT leads and their connections at both ends should always be clean and dry and, as far as possible, neatly arranged away from each other and nearby metallic parts which could cause premature shorting in weak insulation. The metal connections at the ends should be a firm and secure fit and free from any signs of corrosive deposits. If any lead shows signs of cracking or chafing of the insulation it should be renewed. Remember that radio interference suppression is required when renewing any leads.

Note: *It is advisable when removing spark plugs from this engine to use a fully cranked 'short' spark plug spanner. Be especially careful when refitting plugs to do so without force and screw them up as far as possible by hand first. Do not over-tighten. The aluminium head does not take kindly to thread crossing and extra force. The proprietary non-cranked plug caps should always be used to ease fitting and to ensure against HT lead shorting.*

13 Fault diagnosis – ignition system

1   Engine troubles normally associated with, and usually caused by faults in, the ignition system are:

   (a) *Failure to start when the engine is turned*
   (b) *Uneven running caused by misfiring or mistiming*
   (c) *Even running at low engine speed and misfiring when engine speeds up or is under load*
   (d) *Even running at higher engine speeds and misfiring or stoppage at slow speed*

Standard ignition system (contact breaker type)

2   Because there are separate contact breaker points and coils for each cylinder bank, test each circuit in turn to find which circuit the fault is in.

3   For (a), failure to start, first check that all wires are properly connected and dry. If the engine fails to catch when turned on the starter do not continue turning or the battery will be flattened and the

problem made worse. Remove one spark plug lead from a plug and turn the engine again and see if a spark will jump from the end of the lead to the top of the plug or the engine block. Hold the lead with an insulated tool. It should jump a gap of $\frac{1}{4}$ in with ease. If the spark is there ensure that the static ignition timing is correct and then check the fuel system.

4   If there is no spark at the plug lead, proceed further and remove the HT lead from the centre of the distributor which comes from the coil. Try again by turning the engine so see if a spark can be obtained from the end. If there is a spark the fault lies between the contact in the distributor cap and the plug. Check that the rotor arm is in good condition and making proper contact in the centre of the distributor cap and that the plug leads are properly attached to the cap. The terminals inside the cap should be intact, clean and free from corrosion.

5   If no spark comes from the coil HT lead, check next that the contact breaker points are clean and the gap is correct. If there is still no spark obtainable it may be assumed that the low tension circuit is at fault. To check the low tension circuit properly it is best to have a voltmeter handy or a 12V bulb in a holder with two wander leads attached. The procedure now given is arranged so that the interruption in the circuit – if any – can be found.

6   Starting at the distributor, put one of the two leads from the tester (be it lamp or voltmeter) to the moving contact terminal of the circuit concerned and the other to earth. A reading (or light) indicates that there is no break in the circuit between the ignition switch and the contact point (which should be open). Check next that the condenser is OK as described in Section 6. If this is satisfactory it means that the coil is not delivering HT to the distributor and must therefore be renewed.

7   If there is no LT reading on the first check point, repeat the test between the CB (–) terminal of the coil and earth. If a reading is now obtained there must be a break in the wire between the CB (–) terminal and the distributor.

8   If there is no reading at this second check point repeat the test between the SW (+) terminal of the coil and earth. If this produces a reading then the low tension post of the coil windings must be open-circuited and the coil must be renewed.

9   If there is no reading at this third check point there must be a break between the ignition switch and the coil.

10   For (b), uneven running and misfiring, check first by ensuring that all HT wires are dry and properly connected. Ensure also that the leads are not short circuiting to earth against metal or the engine itself. If this is happening an audible click can usually be heard from the place where the unwanted spark is being made.

11   For (c), misfiring occurs at high speeds, the points gap is too small or the spark plugs need renewal due to failure under more severe operating pressures. The contact points spring may also be weak.

12   For (d), if misfiring is occurring at low engine speeds and the engine runs satisfactorily at high speeds, the points gap is probably the cause – being too great. If not, check the slow running adjustment of the carburettor (see Chapter 3). Also check that the centrifugal advance weights are not binding.

Transistorised ignition system

13   As with the mechanical contact breaker ignition system, should faults occur, basic checks should be made of the HT and LT circuits. however, the following precautionary notes should be observed to avoid causing damage to the transistorised system:

   (a) *When an HT lead has been detached for testing, ensure that it is earthed before starting the engine*
   (b) *Do not disconnect an HT lead whilst the engine is running*
   (c) *Due to the relatively high current which it draws, a test light should not be used for checks*

14   More detailed checks of the transistorised ignition system require specialised electrical knowledge and testing equipment, and therefore your Renault dealer or local automotive electrician should be entrusted to check the system for fault diagnosis and repairs as necessary.

Chapter 5 Clutch

Contents

Specifications

General
Clutch type	Single dry plate with diaphragm spring pressure plate; hydraulic operation
Disc diameter	9.25 in (235 mm)
Disc lining thickness (new)	0.303 in (7.7 mm)

Adjustment data
Free play at release arm	0.07 to 0.11 in (2 to 3 mm)
Pushrod to master cylinder clearance	0.008 to 0.020 in (0.2 to 0.5 mm)
Slave cylinder travel (minimum)	0.472 in (12 mm)

Torque wrench settings
	lbf ft	Nm
Flywheel securing bolts (must be renewed)	34	46

1 General description

The clutch is actuated hydraulically. The clutch unit itself is of the dry disc type with a diaphragm spring pressure plate.

The pendant clutch pedal is connected to the clutch master cylinder by a short pushrod. The master cylinder is mounted on the engine side of the bulkhead, in front of the driver. The hydraulic reservoir is shared with the brake master cylinder.

Depressing the clutch pedal moves the piston in the master cylinder forwards, so forcing hydraulic fluid through the hydraulic pipe to the slave cylinder. The piston in the slave cylinder moves forward on the entry of the fluid and actuates the clutch release arm by means of a short pushrod and the clutch becomes disengaged. As the pedal is released so the process is reversed.

The gearbox input shaft runs in line with the crankshaft and locates in the end of the crankshaft within a pilot bearing. The clutch friction disc locates on the input shaft splines between the flywheel and pressure plate contact surfaces. Pressure plate actuation is by means of the diaphragm spring and clutch release (thrust) bearing. This release bearing is in turn actuated by a withdrawal lever (release arm) attached to the flywheel housing.

When in the drive condition, the clutch friction disc is sandwiched under spring pressure between the flywheel and pressure plate. When the pressure plate is drawn back, the friction disc is no longer sandwiched between the flywheel and the pressure plate and ceases to be driven by the flywheel.

The release bearing is concentric with the gearbox input shaft, but in no way connected to it. The front part of the bearing revolves when it is in contact with the spring; the back part is stationary, being attached to the release arm which is also stationary. When the clutch is engaged, the front of the bearing is not in contact with the spring and so does not revolve.

The central hub of the clutch friction disc is sprung in order to absorb transmission shocks and to help ensure a smooth take-off.

2 Clutch – adjustment

1   The clutch is hydraulically actuated and the clearance of the pushrod must be periodically checked. The clearance between the end of the pushrod and the piston in the master cylinder must be between 0.2 to 0.5 mm (0.008 to 0.020 in). This is shown more clearly in Fig. 5.2.

2   This clearance is obtained by checking the distance from the end of the pushrod to the pushrod-to-pedal clevis pin, which should be about 115 mm (4.5 in). If adjustment is necessary, loosen the pushrod locknut away from the clevis, rotate the pushrod accordingly to set the clearance, then retighten the locknut.

3 Clutch unit – removal, examination and refitting

1   Access to the clutch unit for its removal is only available on removing the engine or gearbox from the car. Refer to Chapter 1 for details of engine removal, or Chapter 6 for gearbox removal instructions.

2   With the clutch unit now accessible, mark the position of the clutch pressure plate cover in relation to its location on the face of the flywheel.

3   Unscrew the clutch cover securing bolts (shown in Fig. 5.3). These should be unscrewed in diametrically opposite sequence, a few turns at a time, until the diaphragm spring pressure is released and the pressure plate assembly can be withdrawn. During withdrawal of the pressure plate assembly, do not let the driven plate fall.

4   Examine the driven plate friction linings for wear and loose rivets. Check the disc for distortion, cracks, broken hub springs or worn splines in its hub. The surface of the linings may be highly glazed but provided the woven pattern of the friction material can be seen clearly then the plate is serviceable. Any signs of oil staining will necessitate

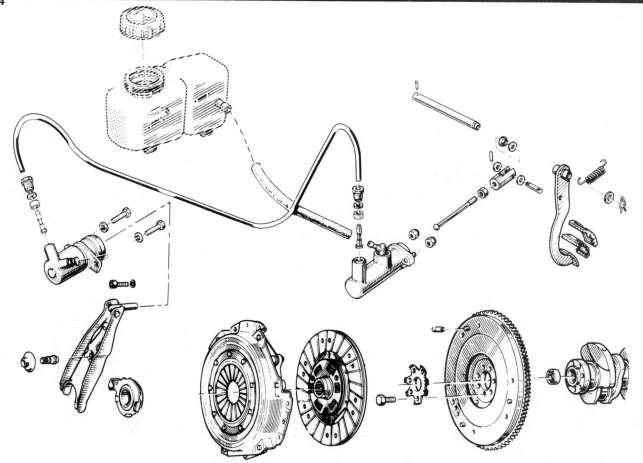

Fig. 5.1 Clutch hydraulic system and clutch unit assembly components (Sec 1)

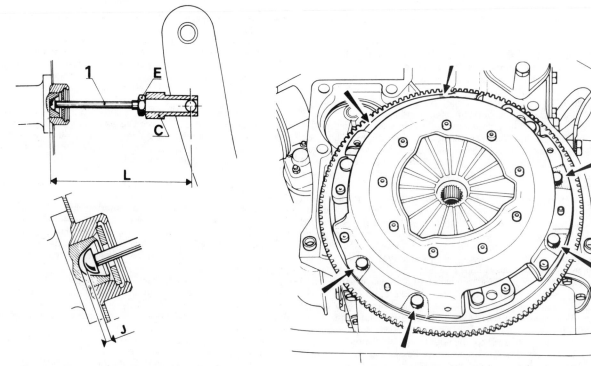

Fig. 5.2 Clutch pushrod adjustment (Sec 2)

1   Pushrod
E   Locknut
C   Clevis
L   115 mm (4.5 in)
J   0.2 to 0.5 mm (0.008 to 0.020 in)

Fig. 5.3 Clutch unit retaining bolt positions (arrowed) (Sec 3)

renewal of the driven plate. Investigation and rectification of the oil leak (probably crankshaft rear main bearing seals) will be required.

5   Check the amount of wear which has taken place on the friction linings. If they are worn level with or to within 1.6 mm (0.06 in) of the heads of the securing rivets, the driven plate should be renewed as an assembly. Do not attempt to reline it yourself as it is rarely successful.

6   Examine the machined faces of the flywheel and the pressure plate. If scored or grooved, renew both components on a factory exchange basis. Note that if the flywheel is removed, new bolts must be used on reassembly.

7   Check the segments of the pressure plate diaphragm spring for cracks and renew the assembly if apparent.

8   Where clutch engagement has been fierce or clutch slip has occurred in spite of the driven plate being in good condition, renew the pressure plate assembly complete.

9   Check the clutch release bearing which is located in the fork of the release lever. See that it spins freely without shake or slackness and that its pressure face is not scored or chipped. Renew it as a matter of course at time of major overhaul.

10 Before refitting the clutch unit, check that all friction contact faces are clean and free from oil and grease. Clean the machined face of the flywheel with a petrol-soaked rag.

11 Locate the driven plate on the face of the flywheel so that the longer projection of the splined hub is on the gearbox side.

12 Locate the pressure plate assembly on the flywheel (sandwiching the driven plate) so that the cover/flywheel mating marks are in alignment.

13 Screw in the securing bolts in diametrically opposite sequence until they are slightly more than finger tight.

14 The driven plate must now be centralised by inserting either an old gearbox first motion shaft, or a suitably stepped mandrel or dowel which will pass through the hub of the driven plate and engage with the spigot bolts have not yet been tightened, the insertion of the

centralising tool will cause the driven plate to move sideways or up and down as necessary until it is centralised. Try the tool in two or three different positions to ensure perfect centralising and to enable the gearbox first motion shaft to pass through the clutch driven plate during refitting of the gearbox to the engine.

15 Fully tighten the pressure plate-to-flywheel bolts in diametrically opposite sequence.

16 Refit the gearbox to the engine in the reverse sequence to removal and tighten the respective retaining bolts to the specified torque wrench settings (where given).

17 Readjust the clutch operating clearance to complete.

4   Clutch withdrawal mechanism – removal and refitting

1   Remove the gearbox or engine from the car as given in Chapter 6 or 1 respectively.

2   Free the withdrawal lever from the release bearing, then disconnect the lever from the ball head in the clutch housing by withdrawing it outwards initially. When detached, extract the lever from within the housing.

3   Withdraw the release bearing.

4   Check the bearing for wear and/or binding and renew if necessary.

5   Grease the ball and fork fingers prior to reassembly.

6   Refitting is a reversal of the removal procedure.

5   Clutch master cylinder – removal and refitting

1   Remove the brake master cylinder reservoir filler cap and syphon off some fluid so that the level is just below the clutch master cylinder feed pipe connection on the side. Do not allow any dirt to enter the

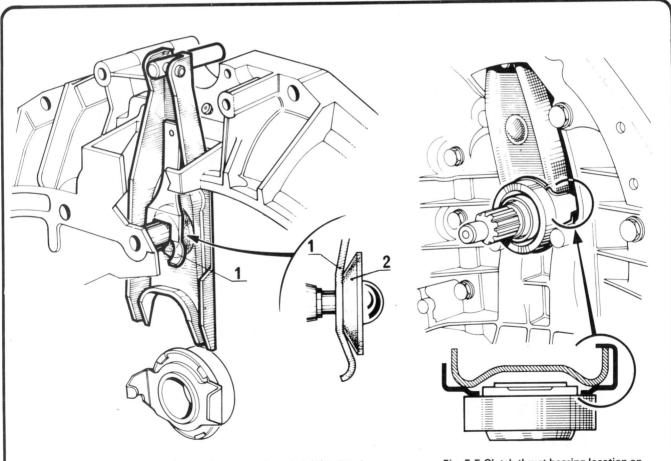

Fig. 5.4 Clutch withdrawal mechanism – note how fork (1) is fitted behind the seal (2) (Sec 4)

Fig. 5.5 Clutch thrust bearing location on withdrawal arm (Sec 4)

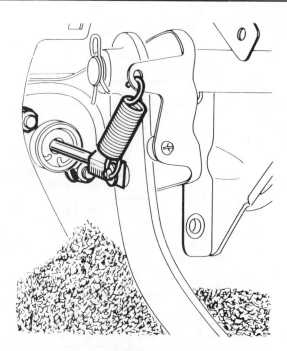

**Fig. 5.6 Clutch master cylinder pushrod to pedal attachment
(Sec 5)**

hydraulic system during this and subsequent operations on the
hydraulic components.
2   Detach the master cylinder reservoir to clutch master cylinder
hydraulic pipe.
3   Working within the car, disconnect the cylinder pushrod at the
clutch pedal, then carefully withdraw it from the master cylinder whilst
tilting it downwards about 40°.
4   Unscrew and remove the master cylinder retaining bolts and then
remove the cylinder.
5   Refitting is a reversal of the removal procedure. The master
cylinder to scuttle joint should be smeared with a strip of suitable
sealant prior to fitting.
6   When the master cylinder is refitted and the pushrod connected,
top up the master cylinder reservoir and bleed the circuit as given in
Section 8, then check the amount of slave cylinder travel as shown in
Fig. 5.7.

6   Clutch slave cylinder – removal and refitting

1   Remove the master cylinder reservoir cap and syphon off some of
the fluid so that its level is just below the line of the clutch master
cylinder hydraulic feed pipe connection on the side of the reservoir.
2   Disconnect the hydraulic pipe to the slave cylinder (at the slave
cylinder end). Plug the pipe to prevent the ingress of dirt.
3   Unscrew the two slave cylinder retaining bolts and withdraw the
cylinder.
4   Refitting is the reversal of the removal procedure. Top up the
master cylinder reservoir fluid level on completion and then check the
slave cylinder travel. This is shown in Fig. 5.7.
5   To bleed the clutch hydraulic system refer to Section 8.

7   Clutch master and slave cylinders – overhaul

1   Although Renault do not give any overhaul details for these
cylinders, they can be disconnected and renovated in a similar manner
to a normal hydraulic cylinder.
2   Check before dismantling to ensure that an overhaul kit for the
cylinder in question is available.
3   Particular care must be taken not to allow dirt to enter any part of
the hydraulic system, and therefore a clean work area must be
prepared prior to dismantling.

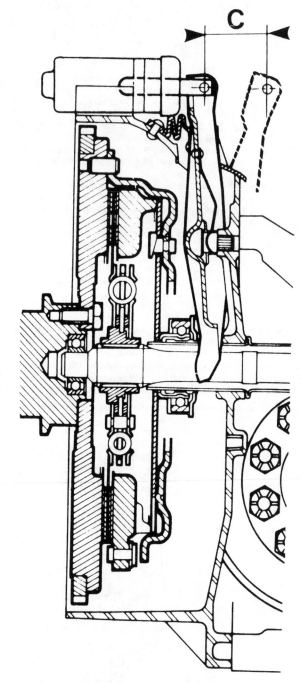

**Fig. 5.7 Clutch slave cylinder operating travel 'C' should be 0.47 in
(12 mm) minimum (Sec 5)**

4   Prise free the dust cover from the end of the slave cylinder. On the
master cylinder, the internal retaining clip must be extracted.
5   Apply a limited amount of air pressure into the hydraulic hose
connection aperture. Hold a cloth over the exposed end of the cylinder
in which to catch the piston assembly and spring when they exit.
6   With the piston and spring removed, wash the respective components in methylated spirit and wipe dry with a non-fluffy cloth. The seal
and dust cover should always be renewed when removed. If the piston
and/or cylinder bore are damaged, scored or excessively worn, the
complete cylinder must be renewed.
7   Before reassembly, smear the piston seal and cylinder bore with
hydraulic fluid. Locate the new seal on the piston and note that the
wider spring coils are located at the opposite end to the piston. Insert
them into the cylinder, taking care not to damage the seal lips. Locate
the dust cover and circlip as applicable.

8 Bleeding the clutch hydraulic circuit

Bleeding following work on the clutch hydraulic system
1   If the reason for bleeding is that the clutch hydraulic system has been disconnected, eg for new components to be fitted, bleeding is carried out as described for the brake hydraulic system. Refer to Chapter 9, Section 9, for a description of the various methods.

Bleeding following work on the brake hydraulic system
2   If the reason for bleeding is simply to remove air from the line between the fluid reservoir and the clutch master cylinder – eg after removing and refitting the brake master cylinder – there is no need to bleed this air all the way through the clutch system. Instead, proceed as follows.
3   You will need approximately 1 metre of transparent plastic hose, the end of which will fit snugly over the clutch slave cylinder bleed nipple. Fill the hose with hydraulic fluid and fit one end to the bleed nipple. Hold the hose vertically.
4   Slacken the clutch slave cylinder bleed nipple, observing the fluid level in the hose. Tighten the nipple before the fluid level in the hose falls to the same level as the reservoir.
5   Remove the hose and check for correct clutch operation.
6   If the above method is not successful, the system will have to be bled in the usual way.

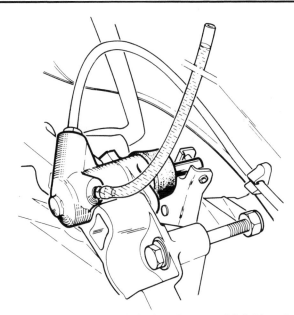

Fig. 5.8 Attach pipe to bleed nipple and top up with fluid as shown (Sec 8)

9 Fault diagnosis – clutch

Symptom	Reason(s)
Judder when taking up drive	Loose engine/gearbox mountings or over-flexible mountings Badly worn friction surfaces, or friction plate contaminated Worn splines in the friction plate hub or on the gearbox input shaft
Clutch spin (failure to disengage) so that gears cannot be meshed	Clutch friction disc sticking because of rust on splines (usually apparent after standing idle for some length of time) Damaged or misaligned pressure plate assembly Incorrect release bearing fitted Air in hydraulic circuit
Clutch slip (increase in engine speed does not result in increase in car speed – especially on hills)	Clutch friction surfaces worn beyond minimum limit, or oil soaked
Squealing noise when clutch pedal depressed	Release bearing worn

Chapter 6 Manual gearbox and final drive

Contents

Specifications

General

Gearbox type	Four-speed (R1273/1275) or five-speed (R1278); synchromesh on all forward gears
Renault type number:	
Four-speed	367
Five-speed	369

Gear ratios (:1)

	Four-speed	Five-speed
1st	3.36	3.36
2nd	2.06	2.06
3rd	1.32	1.38
4th	0.93	1.06
5th	–	0.82
Reverse	3.18	2.09

Final drive ratio

Final drive ratio	4.125 or 3.8 : 1 according to model

Lubrication

Oil type	Castrol Hypoy B EP80 or equivalent
Oil capacity:	
4-speed, up to 1978	7.0 Imp pints (4.0 litres)
4-speed, from 1979	5.6 Imp pints (3.2 litres)
5-speed (all models)	6.0 Imp pints (3.4 litres)

Overhaul data

Differential bearings preload (see text):	
Re-used bearings	Free turning, no endfloat
New bearings	2 to 7 lbf (1 to 3 kgf)
Primary shaft endfloat	0.001 to 0.005 in (0.02 to 0.12 mm)

Torque wrench settings

	lbf ft	Nm
Gearcase half housing bolts:		
8 mm	23	30
10 mm	34 to 41	46 to 55
Rear cover bolts:		
8 mm	15 to 23	20 to 30
10 mm	34 to 41	46 to 55
Clutch housing bolts	34 to 41	46 to 55
Reverse gear selector bolt	23 to 30	30 to 40
Crownwheel bolts	90 to 105	120 to 140
Secondary shaft nut	90 to 113	120 to 150
Bearing plate bolts	34 to 41	45 to 55
Primary shaft nut	90 to 113	120 to 150

1 General description

Depending on the vehicle model, either a four-speed (type 367) or five-speed (type 369) gearbox will be fitted. On both gearbox types the layout is similar. The aluminium gearcasing comprises four sections, being the clutch housing, the right- and left-hand housings, (housing the main gear assemblies also the differential unit), and the rear cover unit (containing the selector control shaft and selector finger). On the 369 gearbox, the rear cover also houses the fifth gear and its synchromesh assembly.

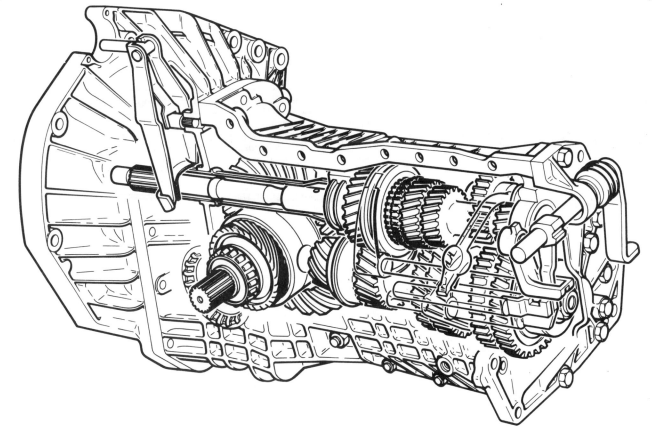

Fig. 6.1 Gearbox and differential unit – type 367 (4-speed) (Sec 1)

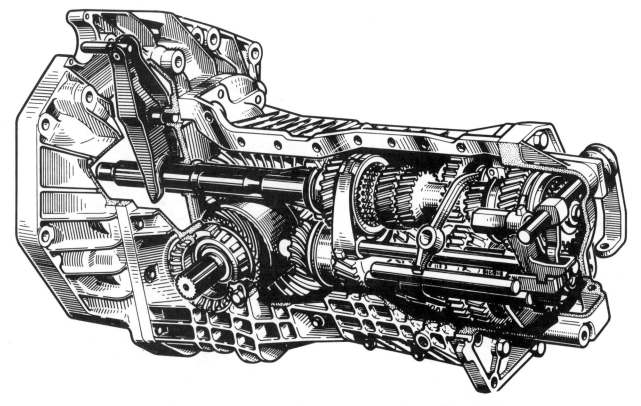

Fig. 6.2 Gearbox and differential unit – type 369 (5-speed) (Sec 1)

All forward gears on both gearbox types are fitted with synchromesh. Drive to the gears from the flywheel and clutch unit is via the clutch shaft, which is engaged with the primary shaft splines. The clutch shaft passes through the differential compartment. The primary shaft transmits motion via the respective gears to the pinion (secondary) shaft. The reverse idler gear is located on a separate shaft in the rear of the main casing.

Motion is transmitted when a particular gear is engaged, transferring the drive from the primary to the secondary shaft, which in turn drives the differential unit and consequently the driveshafts.

The gear selector forks and shafts are located in the side of the gear casing and are actuated by the selector rod shift mechanism located in the rear casing. The selector forks are in constant engagement with the synchro sliding hubs which move to and fro accordingly to engage the gear selected.

The speedometer drivegear is attached to the differtial unit and this in turn drives the drive gear unit to which the drive cable is attached. Both the speedometer cable and driven gear unit can be removed with the gearbox in place. Removal of the drivegear, however, necessitates removal of the gearbox.

Inspection of the gear assemblies and the differential unit can only be made with the gearbox removed from the vehicle and the respective casing sections separated. Only the rear cover can be removed with the gearbox in the vehicle. On the 369 type gearbox this means that the fifth gear can be inspected/refitted with the gearbox in place.

Although the transmission unit is basically simple in operation, certain dismantling, adjustment and reassembly operations require the use of specialised tools. Therefore, if you are contemplating overhauling the gearbox it is essential that you read through the relevant sections before starting any work.

Another point to consider is the availability of necessary parts. You will not really know what you require until the casing sections are separated. It is at this stage that an assessment should be made on the extent of work required and any parts that will be needed. Do check with your Renault dealer before proceeding further. In some instances, certain items are only supplied as complete assemblies, and in many cases the simplest course of action is to reassemble the casings and get an exchange unit – usually the most satisfactory and economical solution.

2   Gearbox – removal and refitting

1   Although the gearbox is located behind the engine in the conventional manner, it is a relatively bulky unit and removing it rearwards and downwards, whilst possible, can prove difficult. The main problem with removal in this manner is that the upper and lower body crossmembers, situated immediately to the rear of the clutch housing, must not be removed. They therefore tend to restrict movement of the gearbox. Removal in this manner necessitates the aid of a couple of fit assistants to work underneath the vehicle and help in manoeuvring the gearbox free. As the gearbox also contains the differential assembly it is quite a heavy unit.

2   In view of these factors, it is probably better to remove the engine first as given in Chapter 1. The gearbox can then easily be disconnected and withdrawn through the engine compartment.

3   Drain the transmission oil. Raise and support the front of the vehicle, and remove the front roadwheels.

4   A spacer leg must now be located between the suspension lower arm pivot and the lower shock absorber on each side. Renault dealers use special tool No T Av 603 as shown in Fig. 6.3. However, you may decide to fabricate your own spacers. Make sure they are securely located.

5   If removing the gearbox with the engine in position, unbolt and detach the clutch slave cylinder and withdraw it from the operating rod, but do not disconnect the hydraulic hose. The cylinder can be positioned out of the way, but support it to prevent the hose being stretched.

6   Referring to Chapter 8, disconnect the driveshafts from the differential. When disconnected each side, pivot the stub axle carrier units downwards to withdraw each driveshaft.

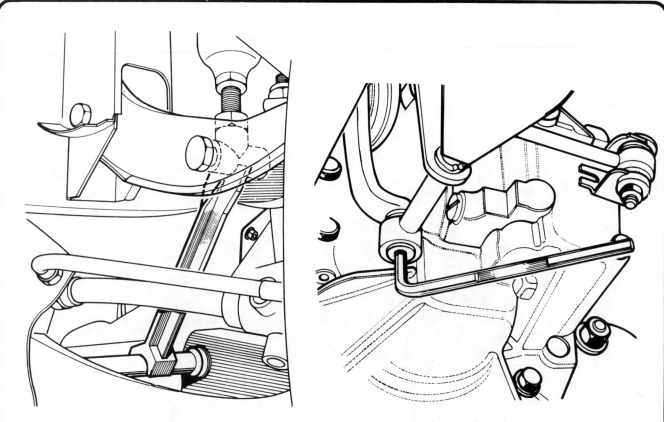

Fig. 6.3 Spacer T Av 603 in position (Sec 2)   Fig. 6.4 Disconnect the gear lever control linkage (Sec 2)

7 Referring to Section 7, disconnect the gear lever control linkage.
8 Detach the speedometer cable by withdrawing the retaining clip and extracting the cable from its location housing.
9 Detach the reversing light wire spade connector from the switch.
10 Position a jack (preferably a trolley type) under the gearbox and raise it to support – not lift – the gearbox.
11 If not already done, disconnect the TDC sensor unit with its bracket.
12 Unscrew and remove the upper and lower engine-to-gearbox retaining bolts.
13 Unscrew the gearbox side mounting bolts, ensuring that the jack is securely supporting the gearbox. Removal may be easier if the mountings are removed completely (if possible).
14 Before removal, check that all gearbox attachments are free, then with the aid of an assistant, manoeuvre it forwards into the engine compartment and lift it clear.
15 If removing the gearbox rearwards from underneath, attach a lifting sling and hoist to the engine in such a manner that it can be raised and tilted upwards at the front end sufficiently to enable the gearbox to be withdrawn from underneath. As previously mentioned, for this method a couple of assistants will probably be required at this stage.
16 Whichever removal method is employed, be sure not to allow the weight of the gearbox to rest on the input shaft during removal (or refitting).
17 Once clear of the car, the gearbox should be cleaned externally and then removed to the work area for inspection and overhaul.
18 Refitting is a reversal of the removal process, but note the following points.
19 Smear the clutch shaft splines with a small amount of molybdenum grease prior to assembly. Ensure that the clutch fork is securely located, and secure it in position as the gearbox is fitted to prevent the withdrawal pad becoming detached.
20 As the gearbox is lowered into position, reconnect it to the mountings and connect the removed mountings to the chassis. The gearbox and mountings can then be slid back in the slotted adjuster holes in the chassis to the original position.
21 When the selector lever linkage is reconnected, check its adjustment as given in Section 7.
22 Note that when reconnecting the driveshafts the roll pin holes are slightly offset. If the roll pin is difficult to drive through, disconnect the shaft and rotate it 180°, then relocate it to align the holes. Always use new roll pins.
23 On completion, top up the gearbox oil level.

3 Gearbox – dismantling

1 The types 367 and 369 gearbox are similar in construction, the principal difference being the 5th gear assembly in the type 369 gearbox. The gear and differential assemblies are housed in the gearcase, which consists of four sections: the clutch housing at the front, the rear cover and the right- and left-hand casing halves. All casings must be separated for access to the gears and differential unit. Proceed as follows.
2 First remove the clutch housing, but before removing the retaining bolts, punch-mark or scribe an identification mark on the two 'dowel bolt' positions (these have recessed bolt heads). This will ensure correct reassembly. Next, unscrew and remove the twelve bolts retaining the housing.
3 Carefully, tap the housing free from the rear using a soft-headed mallet or a piece of wood and remove the gasket (photo).
4 Detach the gearbox mountings on each side at the rear (if not already done).
5 On the type 369 gearbox, unscrew and remove the 5th gear screw spring and interlock ball from the selector shaft.
6 Unscrew the rear housing retaining bolts, taking note of their respective lengths/positions. Do not forget the bolt in front of the control lever.
7 Lightly tap the rear housing free, using a soft-headed hammer, and manoeuvre the gear control lever free from the selector rods and remove the cover.
8 Before separating the gearcase halves, consideration should be given as to whether or not the primary and secondary shaft assemblies are likely to require attention. If it is decided they will require attention, on late type 367 gearboxes and all type 369 gearboxes, the respective primary and secondary shaft rear locknuts must be loosened. This is best done at this stage as the shafts can be prevented from turning by tapping the selector rods to 'in gear' positions to lock the shafts.
9 Once the shafts are locked, relieve the nut staking from the secondary and primary shafts (photo). Get an assistant to steady the gearbox whilst you loosen off the primary and secondary shaft locknuts. You will need 36 mm and 30 mm box spanners respectively.
10 On the type 369 gearbox, remove the nuts from each shaft and then withdraw the washer; also remove the 5th gear dog clutch and synchro ring from the primary shaft. Before removing the hub from the sliding pinion, their relative positions must be marked (if not so already) for correct reassembly positions. Remove the slider pinion with fork arm and shaft. Withdraw the 5th gear and retain the half-needle roller bearings. Remove the spacer links and double ball-bearing support washer. From the secondary shaft, withdraw the washer and 5th driven gear. Remove the 'tilting lock' and the biconical bearing plate.
11 On all gearboxes, remove the speedometer drive pinion unit.
12 Unscrew and remove the two half casing central retaining bolts (photo). Position the gearbox on its side, with the crownwheel teeth facing upwards. Unscrew the sixteen outer flange bolts and nuts from the casing halves and, as each is removed, note its length and location. When the bolts are removed invert the gearbox, (crownwheel teeth downwards) and carefully tap the housings apart using a soft-headed

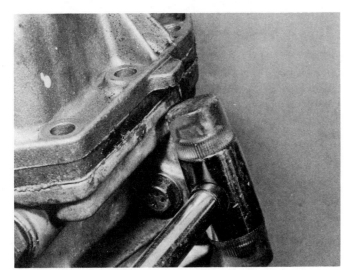

3.3 Tap protruding flanges to separate housing joints

3.9 Prise the nut staking from the shaft flat face (arrowed) to release

3.12 Remove the central retaining bolts

3.13A Primary and secondary shaft assembled in position in the gearcase half housing (the clutch shaft has been separated)

3.13B Note location of seals and washer as they are removed for access to the bearing and 4th gear

mallet or piece of wood against the protruding flange sections. Once the seal is broken, the housings can be separated from the location dowel and the right-hand side case lifted clear.

13 The differential unit and gear assemblies can now be lifted out of the half casing (photos)

14 The respective assemblies are now ready for cleaning, inspection and further dismantling/overhaul as necessary.

Primary shaft dismantling

15 To separate the primary shaft from the input (clutch) shaft, withdraw the sleeve and drive out the roll pin that locates the two shafts then slide them apart.

16 On the early type 367 gearbox, withdraw the bearing at the differential end of the shaft. A suitable puller is essential here – Renault suggest the use of special puller number Mot 49 and adaptor

Rou 407. On later type 367 and the 369 type gearbox, extract the circlip and remove the needle roller bearing unit cages.

17 Withdraw the 4th gear and synchromesh ring. Keep the needle roller bearings in a safe place.

18 Before removing the 3rd/4th sliding gear, mark its position relative to the synchro hub as shown in Fig. 6.6. Remove the sliding gear and retain the three balls with it.

19 Remove the 3rd gear synchromesh hub retaining circlip.

20 Next, support the assembly in a soft-jawed vice so that the rear end face of the large gear section rests on top of the vice. If available, use the special Renault tool T Ar 65 as shown in Fig. 6.7. Press or drive the shaft assembly through and remove the synchromesh hub, and synchro ring and 3rd gear. Retain the needle roller half bearings in a safe place.

21 Remove the taper bearing or ball-bearing (as applicable) in a similar manner using tool T Ar 65 if available.

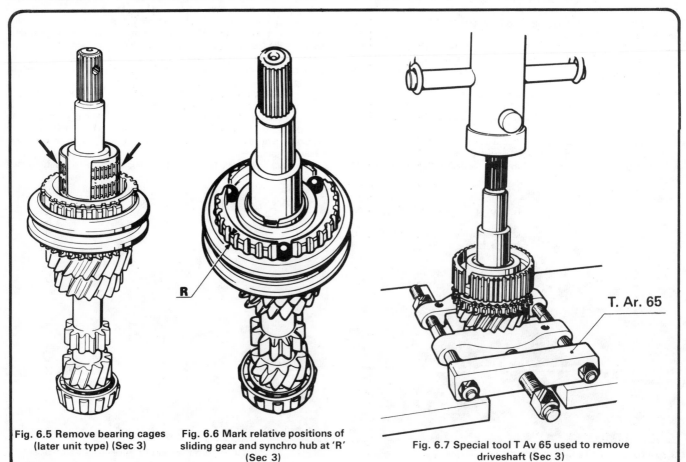

Fig. 6.5 Remove bearing cages (later unit type) (Sec 3)

Fig. 6.6 Mark relative positions of sliding gear and synchro hub at 'R' (Sec 3)

Fig. 6.7 Special tool T Av 65 used to remove driveshaft (Sec 3)

3.22 The double track ball-bearing fitted to later type 367 gearboxes

3.28 The secondary shaft dismantled as far as is possible

22 On later type 367 gearboxes the rear bearing of the primary shaft was modified and a locknut and tab washer fitted to the end of the shaft. When the nut and tab washer are removed, extract the inner rear ball-race of the biconical bearing unit (photo), then withdraw the bearing using a puller, (noting which way round it is fitted).

Secondary shaft dismantling

23 First, remove the nut from the rear end of the shaft. If not already loosened off as suggested earlier, fit the gear train in a soft jaw vice and grip the 3rd/4th gear cluster. Unscrew the nut and remove it with the washer.

24 Withdraw the bearing assembly. On type 367 gearboxes, the double taper roller bearing, rear cone and outer race are removed first. Then withdraw the inner bearing race and spacer using a suitable puller. As the bearing is a flush fit, there is little room in which to engage the puller legs. Therefore hold the assembly in the hand and tap the end of the shaft downwards onto a wooden block (bearing end down). This shock treatment should ease the bearing down the shaft sufficiently to allow the puller legs to engage fully behind the bearing to draw it off. Take care not to damage the bearing and check that the balls of the synchro unit are not allowed to fall out.

25 The 1st speed gear and needle roller bearings can now be withdrawn – keep them together. Remove the synchro ring.

26 Mark the position of the 1st/2nd sliding gear relative to the hub and remove it.

27 Remove the synchro hub retaining circlip from its groove. Use a puller and remove the synchro hub and ring followed by the synchro ring and 2nd gear. Keep the needle roller half bearings with the 2nd gear.

28 This is as far as the shaft can be dismantled. No attempt should be made to remove the 3rd and 4th gear cluster (photo).

Gear control and reverse idler dismantling

29 Centralise the respective shafts, then drive out the fork arm retaining pins from the 1st/2nd and 3rd/4th forks.

30 Withdraw each shaft in turn (1st/2nd then 3rd/4th) and keep each with its selector fork and interlock balls and springs.

31 To remove the reverse selector, unscrew the retaining screw and withdraw the selector and shaft.

32 To remove the reverse idler gear on the early type 367 gearbox, press out the lockpin and withdraw the shaft, pinion and the friction washers. Retain the spring pin and locking spring.

33 On later type 367 gearbox and also the type 369, pull the shaft to the rear to remove, and keep the pinion with its friction washers.

Rear casing dismantling

34 On the early type 367 gearbox, extract the circlip and drive out the control finger retaining pins. If the outer breather is removed, the pins can be punched out through the breather hole. Withdraw the shaft and

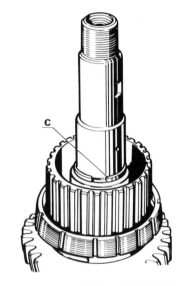

Fig. 6.8 Synchro hub retaining clip (C) (369 gearbox) (Sec 3)

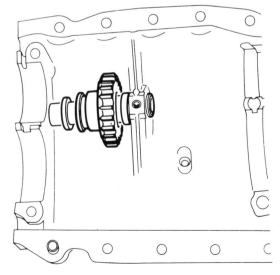

Fig. 6.9 Reverse idler gear on the later type 367 and the 369 type gearboxes (Sec 3)

keep with the selector finger, spring and bellows. The seals and rings can now be removed from the casing.
35 On later type 367 gearboxes and also the type 369, a forked spring compressing tool will be needed to relieve the spring tension and enable the four half shells to be extracted (see Fig. 6.10). Drive out the retaining pins and remove the rear casing cap. Remove the control finger, the spring and lipped seal.

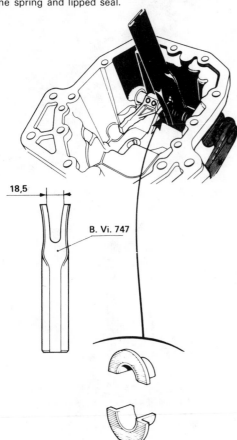

Fig. 6.10 Use special forked spring compressor to relieve spring tension in the 369 gearbox cover (Sec 3)

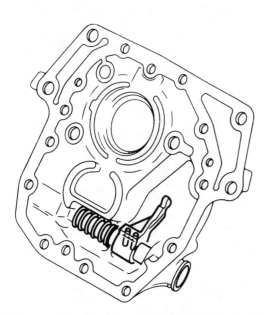

Fig. 6.11 The 367 rear cover and selector shaft/finger showing roll pin positions (Sec 3)

4 Inspection for wear of transmission components

Once the gearbox has been dismantled into its major sub-assemblies, it can be cleaned and inspected. Clean the respective components in petrol or other suitable cleaning solvent, then wipe dry, ready for inspection.
1   Check the casing for cracks or damage, particularly near the bearing housings and on the mating surfaces. Casings are only available in matched pairs so both will have to be renewed.
2   Check all the gears for chips and possible cracks and renew where necessary (photo). You should be able to tell whether this should be so from the initial diagnosis before dismantling.
3   Check all the shafts and splines for wear and flat spots and renew if necessary. The gears through which the shafts pass should be a good sliding fit and not rock about.
4   Inspect the synchromesh units for signs of damage or excessive wear (photo). Once the gearbox is fully dismantled, it is always advisable to renew the synchro rings as a matter of course, since their relative cost is quite low.
5   Inspect the differential unit and its bearings for signs of wear and/or damage. Although the outer bearings may be renewed by the home mechanic, he may well have difficulty in setting up the final drive in the casing afterwards.

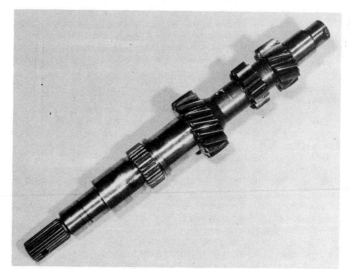

4.2 Check the gears and splines for damage

4.4 Inspect the synchromesh units and sliding gears for wear

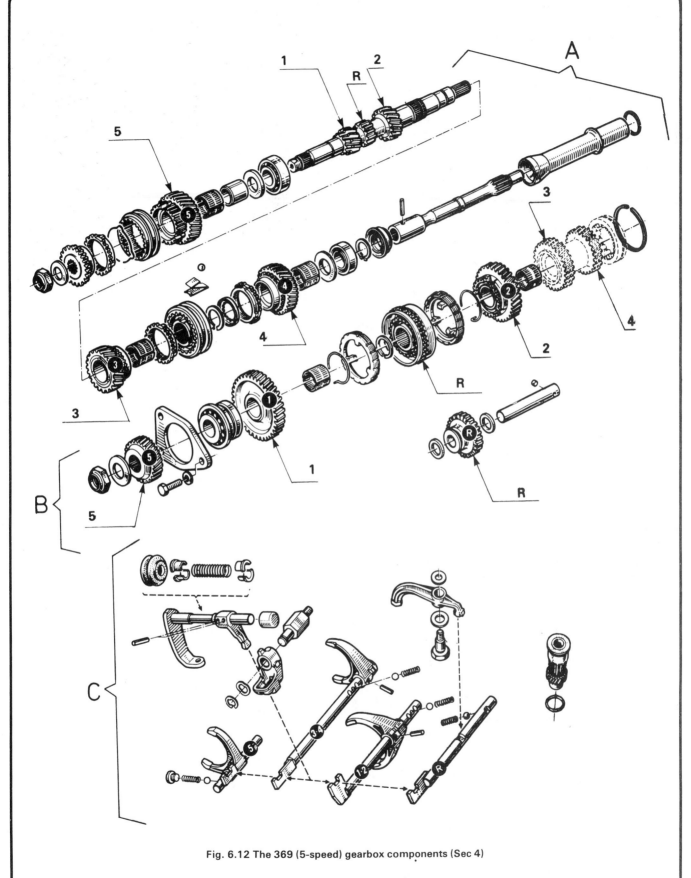

Fig. 6.12 The 369 (5-speed) gearbox components (Sec 4)

A	Primary clutch shaft assembly	assembly	2 2nd gear components	5 5th gear components
		C Selectors	3 3rd gear components	R Reverse gear components
B	Secondary (pinion) shaft	1 1st gear components	4 4th gear components	

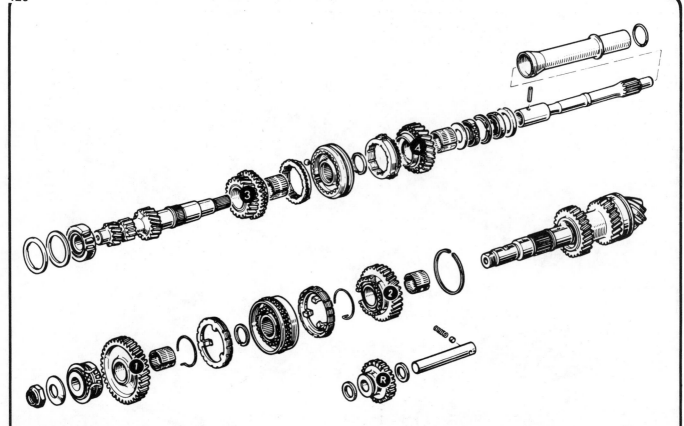

Fig. 6.13 The general layout of the clutch shaft, primary shaft and secondary shaft components in the 367 type gearbox. The respective gears are marked accordingly and the primary shaft shown is only fitted to the early models (Sec 4)

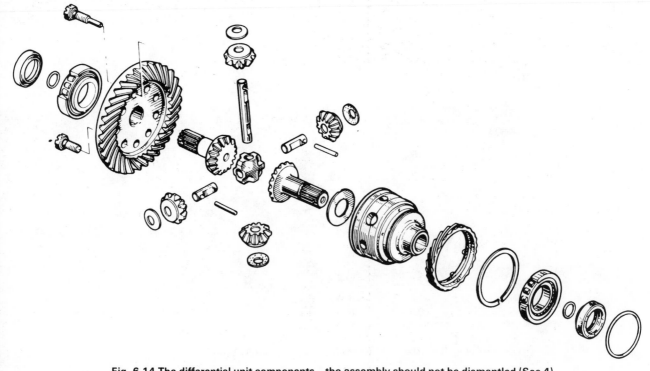

Fig. 6.14 The differential unit components – the assembly should not be dismantled (Sec 4)

6   Any failure within the final drive unit will necessitate renewal of the complete assembly, with the possible exception of the outer bearings and of course the speedo drivegear (photos). We did not dismantle the crownwheel and pinion because it is not a task which can be undertaken, at least at the reassembly stage, by the home mechanic. The cost of purchasing a new crownwheel without a new pinion, madness anyway, is again approximately half that of a new exchange transmission unit. Purchasing the two together, crownwheel assembly and pinion assembly, to enable them to mesh and set-up correctly is approximately the cost of the exchange transmission and you will not get the guarantee.

7   Check that the speedometer pinion is in good condition and running easily in its bush.

8   Check the selector forks for wear. Measure them with a pair of calipers and compare their ends with the thickest point; if in doubt renew them. They should only be fractionally worn.

9   Check the gearshift mechanism. The tongue which slots into the selectors may have worn considerably, in which case this too must be renewed. Failure to do so will promote difficulty in gear changing caused by a sloppy action.

10   Inspect the casings for signs of damage and cracks. Always renew the seals and gaskets as a matter of course when reassembling and do not forget to check the transmission unit mountings. Renew them if the rubber is perished or oil impregnated.

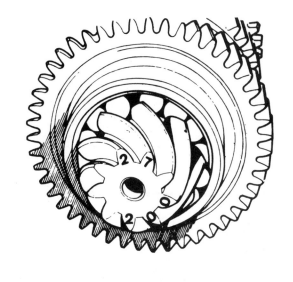

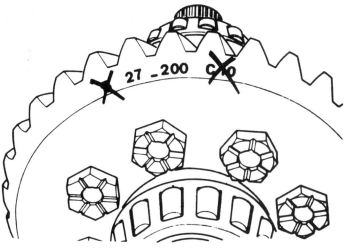

Fig. 6.15 The crownwheel and pinion are a matched pair and are marked accordingly (Sec 4)

4.6A The speedometer drivegear (A) is retained by the large C-clip arrowed (B)

4.6B Check the differential bearing cones for wear or damage ...

4.6C ... also the bearing cups in the half housings

5 Gearbox – reassembly

1   Before starting to reassemble the gearbox it pays to spend some time in preparing plenty of clean space. If your work bench is rough, cover it with hardboard or paper for a good non-gritty surface. Do not start until you have all the necessary parts and gaskets assembled and make sure that all the ones you have obtained are going to fit. Gasket sets often contain items covering other models so you will not need them all – this is why it helps to keep the old gaskets you take off until the job is eventually finished. All parts must be kept meticulously clean during assembly, and as each component/sub-assembly is refitted, lubricate it with clean gearbox oil. The gear clusters must be assembled before they are refitted. The assembly of each cluster is time consuming and requires patience and accuracy; do not try to rush things! Start by reassembling the secondary shaft.

Secondary shaft assembly

2   Grease and assemble the two halves of the roller bearing cage to the shaft (photo).
3   Slide the 2nd gear into position and locate the synchro spring as shown (photo) with the hooked spring located into the hole in the shouldered segment of the gear.
4   Locate the synchro ring (photo) to the 2nd gear, but take care not to confuse the 1st speed gear ring with that of the 2nd, as the two differ dimensionally as shown in Fig. 6.16.
5   The synchro hub is now fitted with its offset shoulder facing towards the 3rd gear. When fitting the hub, Renault recommend it be preheated to a temperature of 250°C (482°F). A domestic oven can be used to heat up the hub accordingly, then press it into position on the shaft. Not having a cooker at hand we pressed our hub on cold using a suitable tube drift, but extra care must be taken when 'cold fitting' to avoid damage. Once in position, check that the hub abuts the stop shoulder, with the lugs below the shoulder level (photo).
6   Locate the new retaining circlip (photo).
7   The 1st/2nd sliding gear is now fitted with the gear section offset to the rear (photo) and the alignment markings corresponding.
8   Fit the synchro ring (photo).
9   Smear the half cage needle roller bearings with grease and locate together with the 1st gear (photo) and synchro ring.
10   Fit the double taper roller bearing inner cone and spacer (photo).
11   Next, fit the double taper roller bearing cup and outer bearing cone (photo).
12   The dished washer is now fitted onto the shaft with its concave face towards the bearing.
13   Screw a new locknut into position on the end of the shaft. The nut can either be tightened at this stage, by holding the gear assembly firm in a soft-jawed vice and tightening the nut to the specified torque, or it can be left until the gearbox is reassembled so that the gears can be locked in position and the nut tightened (prior to refitting the rear cover) (photo).

5.2 Locate the needle roller bearing

5.3 Fit 2nd gear and locate the synchro spring

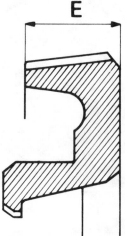
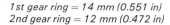

Fig. 6.16 The 1st and 2nd synchromesh rings differ dimensionally
– measure across Section E to identify (Sec 5)

1st gear ring = 14 mm (0.551 in)
2nd gear ring = 12 mm (0.472 in)

5.4 Locate the synchro ring followed by ...

5.5 ... the synchro hub with offset shoulder to 3rd gear

5.6 Fit the retaining clip (arrowed)

5.7 Locate 1st/2nd sliding gear ...

5.8 ... and synchro ring

5.9 Assemble the needle roller halves to the shaft and slide 1st gear into position

5.10 Fit the taper bearing cone ...

5.11 ... followed by its outer cone and cup assembly

5.13 The fully assembled secondary shaft unit

5.15 Fit the twin roller bearing, washer and locknut onto the primary shaft (later 367 models)

Primary shaft assembly

14 On the early type 367 gearbox, support the shaft and press or drive the taper roller bearing cone into position on the rear of the shaft.

15 On the later type 367 gearbox, relocate the special ball-bearing onto the shaft, pressing the main section of the bearing into position with a suitable tube drift. Locate the bearing half track, the washer and locknut (photo). To tighten at this stage, grip the 3rd/4th gear cluster in a soft-jawed vice and tighten the nut to the specified torque.

16 On the type 369 gearbox, relocate the bearing so that it butts against the 1st gear. Slide the washer down and fit flush to the bearing.

17 To the front end of the shaft, assemble the 3rd gear needle roller bearing half casings (smear with grease) (photo).

18 Slide the 3rd speed gear into position and locate its synchro ring (photo).

19 On the early type 367 gearbox, heat up the synchro hub to about 250°C before fitting if possible. Where a new hub is being used, it can be fitted either way round. If employing the old hub however, fit it so that it is located as when removed, this being shown by the alignment mark which should be towards the 3rd speed gear. The notches of the hub must of course align with the synchro ring bosses when fitted (photo). When the hub is pressed into position, allow it to cool naturally before continuing. Refit the hub locating circlips.

20 On later type 367 gearboxes and also the type 369, the hub must be fitted so that the alignment marks correspond. Where a new hub is to be used, locate it so that the large recess is to the 4th gear and be sure to align the hub notches with the synchroniser ring bosses. Refit the circlip to retain the hub.

21 Refit the 3rd/4th sliding gear carefully into position and, smearing grease into the hub spring and ball locations, insert the balls and springs. As the hub is fitted ensure that the relative markings are in alignment if the original gear and hub are being used. Compress the balls and springs with a screwdriver to ease assembly (photos). During the subsequent operations be careful not to allow the springs and balls

5.17 Assemble 3rd gear needle roller bearings and fit the 3rd gear

5.18 Locate the synchro ring followed by ...

5.19 ... the synchromesh hub

5.21A Insert the spring and ball ...

5.21B ... and locate the sliding gear

5.22 Locate the circlip (arrowed)

5.23 Fit the synchromesh ring

5.24 Locate the needle bearings

5.25 Slide 4th gear into position

5.26 Locate the thrust washer

5.27 Fit the bearing and secure with circlip

5.29 Reverse idler gear in position

to eject from their locations, should the sliding gear be dislodged.

22 Locate the circlip into position between the hub and the sliding gear (photo).

23 Fit the 4th speed synchro ring (photo).

24 Smear the needle roller half bearings with grease and locate them onto the shaft (photo).

25 Slide the 4th gear into position over the bearings (photo).

26 Locate the thrust washer with its flat face flush to the gear (photo). Drive it into position using a suitable drift.

27 Drive the roller bearing into position in a similar manner and make secure by fitting the retaining circlip (photo). The primary and secondary shafts are now ready for fitting into the gearbox.

Reverse idler gear

28 On the early type 367 gearbox the shaft is inserted into position and engages the 3mm friction washer, the idler gear, the pinion and the 5mm friction washer. Locate the spring and pin through the shaft recess and casing to secure as shown in Fig. 6.17.

29 On the later type 367 and all type 369 gearboxes, recess the pin into the shaft leaving 8mm (0.314 in) proud, then insert the shaft locating the 3 mm thick friction washer, the idler gear and the 5 mm friction washer (photo).

Gear selectors

30 Slide the reverse gear selector shaft into position and locate the reverse gear selector arm, engaging with the slot in the shaft. Screw in the retaining bolt with special washers and tighten to the specified torque (photo).

31 Fit the 3rd/4th selector shaft interlock ball and spring, then slide the shaft into position and locate the selector fork. Align the fork and shaft roll pin hole and drive in a new roll pin with its slot facing rearwards (photos).

32 Fit the 1st/2nd speed selector interlock ball and spring. Slide the shaft into position, locating the fork as it is fitted. Align the fork and shaft roll pin hole and drive a new pin into position with its slotted face to the rear (photo).

33 Prior to refitting the reversing light switch on the outside of the cover, insert the reverse gear selector shaft interlock ball and spring (photo). Then fit the switch to retain the ball and spring, (photo).

Rear cover

34 Insert the rings and seals into the end case, then locate the bellows onto the control shaft. Fit the shaft and engage with the spring and selector finger. Using new roll pins, drive them through the finger and shaft to secure the two (photo). To fit the half-shells, compress the spring sufficiently enough to insert them. Earlier 367 gearboxes differ in that the selector finger assembly is secured by a circlip.

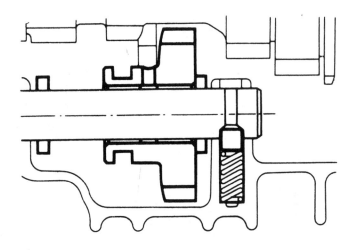

Fig. 6.17 The reverse idler gear interlock spring and ball position – early type 367 gearbox (Sec 5)

5.30 Reverse gear selector arm and shaft in position

5.31A Insert 3rd/4th selector shaft interlock ball and spring and press down as shown to allow shaft to pass through

5.31B Then locate the selector fork

5.32 The assembled selector rods and forks

5.33A Insert reverse gear selector shaft interlock ball and spring and ...

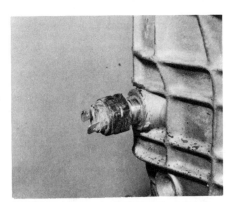

5.33B ... make secure by fitting the reversing light switch

5.34 Relocate the selector control shaft assembly

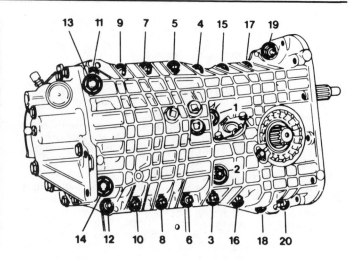

Fig. 6.18 Tighten casing bolts in the sequence shown (Sec 6)

6   Gearbox — final reassembly

1   Whenever the gearbox is being reassembled, irrespective of what work has been undertaken, it is important that the differential unit bearing preload is checked and adjusted as necessary.
2   First check that the two half-casings are perfectly clean and the bearing cups of the differential taper bearings are seated fully in their housings. The right-hand housing cup should be fitted so that it is slightly below the casing inner face.
3   Locate the differential unit into the left-hand half housing, carefully lower the right-hand casing into position and then insert and tighten the retaining bolts to the torque specified and in the sequence shown in Fig. 6.18.
4   Smear the adjustment nut thread with CAF33 or equivalent solution then locate the nut into the half-housing so that it butts against the bearing cup. Adjustment is made by the right-hand nut.
5   Screw the nut in, to the point where the differential unit can be rotated with a slightly stiff motion where new bearings have been fitted. If the old bearings are being reused, simply screw in the nut to the point where the differential can be rotated without any slack.
6   The differential preload must now be checked. To do this you will need a spring balance and some cord. Tie the cord to the balance and wind the cord round the differential case as shown in Fig. 6.19. Pull the spring balance until the differential starts to rotate and note the loading of the balance. The loading is correct when the balance reads within the range given in the Specifications. If required, screw the nut in or out accordingly to achieve the correct bearing preload.
7   Once the preload is set, unscrew and remove the bolts retaining the right-hand casing in position and separate the two half housings.
8   Fit the seals and the location washer (with lug) onto the front of the primary gear shaft, then slide the clutch shaft into position, aligning the roll pin holes. Drive a new roll pin into position to secure the two shafts, then fit the guide tube.
9   Into the right-hand housing fit the pinion shaft and the primary shaft assembly. When in position, ensure that the guide tube drain hole points downwards. Refit the differential unit (photos).
10 Smear the mating surfaces of each half housing with a suitable sealant, then carefully assemble the two. As they are assembled, check that the locating lug of the washer on the front end of the primary shaft is engaged in its location hole in the half housing. Also ensure that the location pin protruding from the rear of the left-hand housing is aligned with the corresponding location slot in the periphery of the secondary shaft rear bearing (photo).
11 Insert the respective housing bolts to secure, but on earlier 367 models, do not fully tighten the bolts yet, as the primary gear endfloat must be checked. To do this refer to Fig. 6.20. Relocate any adjustment shims removed during dismantling, together with the distance washer. Lightly tap the washer to seat the bearings, then locate the rear cover gasket. You will need a dial indicator gauge to

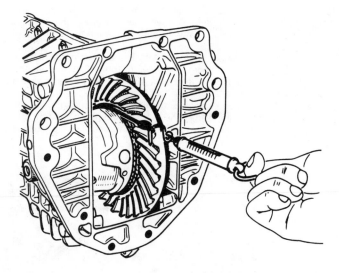

Fig. 6.19 Method of checking bearing preload adjustment (Sec 6)

6.9A Locate the primary shaft into the gearcase

6.9B Engage the clutch shaft and sleeve and drive in a new roll pin to secure

6.9C Fit the clutch pad guide sleeve with oil hole (arrowed) downwards

6.9D Relocate the differential unit

6.10 Align the bearing slot and location pin for engagement

6.13A Tighten the primary (where applicable) and secondary shaft nuts ...

6.13B ... and peen over the flanges to secure (arrowed)

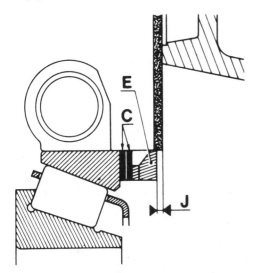

Fig. 6.20 Check the primary shaft endfloat (early 367 models). Clearance at J must be as specified (Sec 6)

E   Distance piece   C   Shims

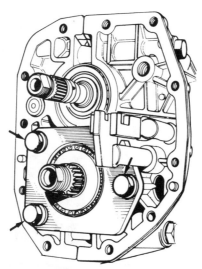

Fig. 6.21 Relocate the bearing stop plate onto the rear face of the 369 gearbox (Sec 6)

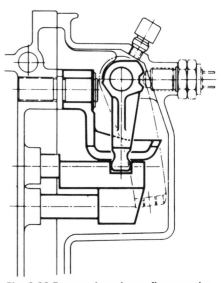

Fig. 6.22 Engage the selector finger as the cover is fitted (Sec 6)

check the endfloat, which should be within the specified limits. If the clearance is incorrect, add or subtract shims as applicable.

12 Tighten the half housing retaining bolts to the specified torque and in the sequence shown in Fig. 6.18.

13 On the later type 367 gearboxes, the primary and secondary shaft tail nuts can now be tightened. Engage two gears to lock them in position for tightening to the specified torque. When the nuts are tightened, peen over the end flange of each nut to lock it in position (photos). Unlock the gears and check that the gears rotate freely.

14 On the type 369 gearbox, relocate the bearing stop plate and its three retaining bolts as shown in Fig. 6.21. Tighten the bolts and then

fit the 5th gear, flat washer and retaining nut onto the secondary shaft. Assemble the flat washer, spacer collar, half needle roller bearings (smeared with grease) and the 5th gear, together with the synchromesh unit onto the primary shaft. Refit the flat washer and the special retaining nut, tighten the nut to the specified torque and peen over the end flange to lock it in position. The secondary shaft assembly tail nut can also be tightened and peened over to lock in position. Lock the two shafts by engaging two gears at once. This prevents the shafts turning when tightening the nuts. Once tightened, engage neutral and check the shafts for freedom of rotation.

15 The rear cover for both types of gearbox can now be refitted.

6.15 Fit the rear cover

6.19A Insert speedometer drive pinion ...

6.19B ... and secure with lockplate and bolts

6.20 Fit the O-ring seal onto the clutch pad
sleeve

6.21A Refit the clutch housing

6.21B Special dowel bolt (arrowed)

Smear the faces of the gearbox rear end and the rear cover with sealant and locate the gasket. Ensure that the selectors are in neutral end engage the selector control finger as the cover is fitted (photo).
16 Insert the rear cover retaining bolts and at the same time refit the right- and left-hand rear mountings (if removed).
17 Tighten the cover bolts to the specified torque.
18 On the type 369 gearbox, relocate the interlock ball and spring for 5th gear, apply some sealant to the retaining bolt thread and insert it to secure.
19 Fit the speedometer driven gear unit into the gearbox housing and retain in position with the plate and bolts (photos).
20 Locate the new O-ring seal onto the clutch pad guide sleeve flush to the flange (photo).
21 Smear the front face of the gearcase with sealant, also the mating face of the clutch housing. Locate the gasket onto the face of the gearcase and carefully refit the clutch housing (photo). Check that the clutch shaft guide sleeve drain hole is still facing downwards, then insert and tighten the retaining bolts, not forgetting that the special dowel bolts must be inserted into their original locations. You may recall that these two bolts are recognisable by their recessed heads (photo). Once bolt is located at the top right side (in a row of three bolts) and the other on the bottom left-hand corner (in a row of four bolts).
22 The gearbox should now be ready for refitting, apart from fitting the clutch withdrawal lever, as described in Chapter 5. If the reversing light switch is still to be fitted do not forget to also fit the reverse gear selector interlock ball and spring at the same time. Refit the drain plug and tighten to secure.

7 Gear lever and control rod – removal, refitting and adjustment

1 Working inside the car, unscrew and remove the lever bellows retaining screws.
2 Unscrew the four floor frame plate bolts and the two bolts retaining the lever housing.

3 As removal now continues underneath the vehicle, it must be raised and supported securely on chassis stands.
4 Unscrew and remove the four undertray retaining screws. Detach the undertray.
5 Unscrew the lever housing bolts, then disconnect the control rod from its linkage at the gearbox end and withdraw it (photo).
6 Reassembly is a reversal of the removal procedure.
7 To adjust the linkage control, select neutral and on early models loosen the clamp arm nut to allow the control rod to rotate freely (Fig. 6.23). On later models, slacken the nut indicated in Fig. 6.24.

7.5 The adjuster clamp (A) and control rod (B)

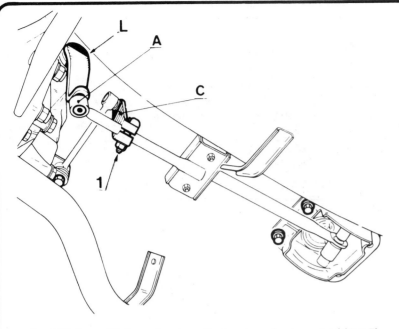

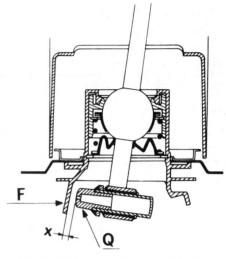

Fig. 6.23 Control linkage showing adjuster clamp (early models) (Sec 7)

1 Clamp nut   A Joint
C Clamp   L Lever (gearbox)

Fig. 6.26 The control lever position for adjustment (Sec 7)

F Housing face   X 2 mm (Type 367)
Q End fitting   or 13 mm (Type 369)

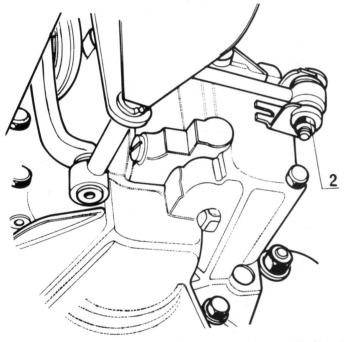

Fig. 6.24 Slacken nut (2) to adjust control linkage on later models (Sec 7)

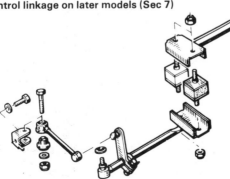

Fig. 6.25 The gear lever and control rod assembly components (Sec 7)

8   On the type 367 gearbox the dimension X must equal 2 mm. For the type 369 gearbox it must equal 13 mm. A feeler gauge or spacer of the appropriate thickness is inserted between faces F and Q as indicated (Fig. 6.26) and the locknut tightened to set the clearance.

8   Differential unit − removal and refitting

1   Access to the differential unit is only available after removal and separation of the gearbox casings, as described previously in this Chapter.

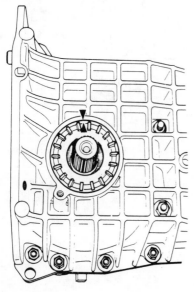

Fig. 6.27 Ring nut and casing alignment mark (Sec 8)

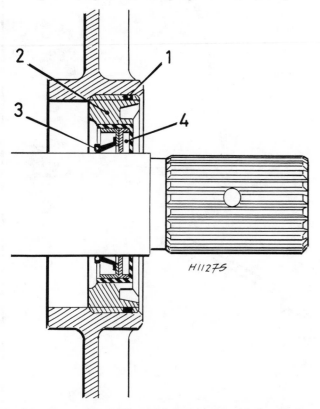

Fig. 6.28 The modified differential ring nut assembly fitted to later 367 type gearbox models (Sec 8)

1   O-ring   3   Lip seal
2   Ring nut   4   Felt suction

2   Once the gearbox has been removed and the right- and left-hand half casings separated the differential unit can be lifted clear for inspection.
3   The differential unit can now be cleaned and inspected for signs of excessive wear and/or damage. Where this is readily apparent, it is recommended that the unit be repaired or exchanged by your Renault dealer, as overhaul is not a task for the DIY mechanic. Further inspection notes on this are given in Section 4.
4   Items that can be removed and renewed include the taper roller bearings (using a suitable puller) and the speedometer drivegear which is secured by a large circlip. Extract the circlip and prise the nylon gear free for renewal.
5   If renewing the taper roller bearings, the respective cups (outer races) must also be removed from the gearcase half housings. This necessitates removal of the adjuster rings and seals from the outside in order to drive the cups out of their housings. Mark the positions of the adjuster ring in relation to the gearcase halves as an approximate guide to adjustment on reassembly (Fig. 6.27).
6   New taper roller bearings must be pressed carefully into position. Always use new seals on reassembly. On later models also fit new O-rings to the adjuster ring as shown in Fig. 6.28.
7   If the speedometer drivegear is badly worn or damaged also check the driven gear; it too will probably be in need of renewal.
8   When refitting the differential unit, check the bearing preload adjustment as given in Section 6.
9   Final gearbox reassembly is described in Section 6, whilst gearbox refitting is dealt with in Section 2.

9   Driveshaft oil seals − renewal

1   Partially drain the oil in the final drive housing to lower the level and thus prevent spillage through the seal housing.
2   The driveshaft on the side concerned must now be disconnected as described in Chapter 8.
3   If the oil seal only is being renewed, then it is not necessary to disturb the ring nut. Should it be necessary to remove the ring nut for any reason, mark its position relative to the casing before unscrewing it. It should be noted that on later models the ring nuts differ from the earlier type in that the O-ring seal is fitted to the outer edge and a deflector is fitted (see Fig. 6.29). The later nut type is not inter-changeable with that of the earlier type.
4   The offending oil seal can now be hooked and prised out of its location within the ring adjuster nut (photo).

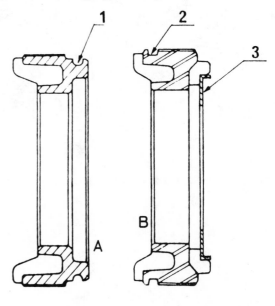

Fig. 6.29 Sectional views of the early (A) and late (B) ring nuts (Sec 9)

1   O-ring location on inside edge − early type
2   O-ring location on outside edge − later type
3   Deflector fitted for seal lubrication − later type

9.4 Differential housing seal shown with ring nut removed

5   Clean the inside diameter on the ring adjuster nut before inserting the new seal. Lubricate the new seal with oil to assist refitting.

6   Use a tube drift of suitable diameter and drive the new seal into position, cavity side inwards so that when fully fitted, the outer face of the seal is flush with the ring nut seal housing edge.

7   Where the ring nut has been removed it is advisable to renew its O-ring seal. Lubricate the O-rings before fitting and screw in the adjuster the same number of turns to the position marked and refit the lockplate.

8   Relocate and attach the driveshaft, then top up the final drive housing oil level.

10 Speedometer cable – renewal

1   The speedometer cable is a conventional inner/outer driven cable. It is fixed at the gearbox by a clamp or retaining spring clip, and at the speedometer head by a knurled nut on the outer cable. It is easily renewed. The whole cable must be renewed; 'inners' and 'outers' are not available separately. Make sure it passes through its original passage. Fluttering and whining is quite common, and a sign of impending cable failure.

2   When refitting a cable, make sure that it is located in the same manner as the original, with no sharp bends, and ensure that the clip or clamp is securely located.

11 Fault diagnosis – manual gearbox

1   Faults can be sharply divided into two main groups: some definite failure with the transmission not working, and noises implying some component worn, damaged, or out of place.

2   If there is a definite fault within the transmission then it has to be removed and dismantled to repair it, so further diagnosis can wait till the parts can be examined.

3   If the problem is a strange noise, the decision must be taken whether in the first place it is abnormal, and if so whether it warrants action.

4   Noises can be traced to a certain extent by doing the test sequence as follows.

5   Find the speed and type of driving that makes the noise. If the noise occurs with engine running, car stationary, clutch disengaged, gear engaged, the noise is not the transmission. If it goes after the clutch is engaged in neutral, halted, it is the clutch.

6   If the noise can be heard faintly in neutral, clutch engaged, it is in the gearbox. It will presumably get worse on the move, especially in some particular gear.

7   Final drive noises are only heard on the move. They will only vary with speed and load, whatever gear is engaged.

8   Noise when pulling is likely to be either the adjustment of preload of the differential bearings, or the crownwheel and pinion backlash.

9   Gear noise when free-wheeling is likely to be the relative positions of crownwheel and pinion.

10   Noise on corners implies excessive tightness or excessive play of the bevel side gears or idler pinions in the differential.

11   In general, whining is gear teeth at the incorrect distance apart. Roaring or rushing or moaning is bearings. Thumping or grating noise suggests a broken gear tooth.

12   If subdued whining comes on gradually, there is a good chance the transmission will last a long time to come, but check the transmission oil level.

13   Whining or moaning appearing suddenly, or becoming loud, should be examined quickly.

14   If thumping or grating noise appear, stop at once. If bits of metal are loose inside, the whole transmission, including the casing, could quickly be wrecked.

15   Synchromesh wear is obvious. When changing gear quickly crashing occurs.

16   Difficulty in engaging gears can be caused by an incorrectly adjusted selector control mechanism, so check this before assuming the problem is within the gearbox.

Chapter 7 Automatic transmission

Contents

Specifications

General

Transmission type	Fully automatic with manual override provision
Renault type number	4141-00
Number of speeds	3 forward, 1 reverse

Gear ratios

1st	2.31 : 1
2nd	1.42 : 1
3rd	0.96 : 1
Reverse	3.88 : 1

Lubricant (gearbox)

Type	Elf Renaultmatic D2, Castrol TQ Dexron® II, or equivalent
Capacity:	
From dry	10.5 Imp pints (6.1 litres)
Drain and refill	5.3 Imp pints (3.0 litres) approx

Lubricant (final drive)

Type	Castrol Hypoy B EP80 or equivalent
Capacity	3 Imp pints (1.6 litres)

Torque wrench settings

	lbf ft	Nm
Converter casing bolts	30 to 33	40 to 45
Final drive case-to-gearcase bolts	13.5 to 16.5	18 to 22
Sump bolts (gearcase)	2.25 to 3.0	3 to 4
Converter driveplate-to-crankshaft bolts (must be renewed after dismantling)	49 to 52	66 to 71

1 General description

Fully automatic gearchanging is provided without the use of a clutch, but override selection is still available to the driver.

The automatic transmission consists of three main assemblies; the torque converter, the final drive and the gearbox. A cutaway view of the transmission unit with the three main assemblies sub-divided is shown in Fig. 7.1.

The converter takes the place of the conventional clutch and transmits the drive automatically from the engine to the gearbox, providing increased torque when starting off.

The converter receives its lubricant from the pump mounted on the rear of the gearcase, and is driven directly by the engine. This pump also distributes fluid to the respective gears, clutch and brake assemblies within the gearbox.

The gearbox comprises an epicyclic gear train giving three forward and one reverse gear, selection of which is dependent on the hydraulic pressure supplied to the respective clutches and brakes. The hydraulic

pressure is regulated by the hydraulic distributor, and gear selection is determined by two solenoid valves. These are actuated by the electrically operated governor/computer. The exact hydraulic pressure is regulated by a vacuum capsule and pilot valve operating according to engine loading.

The clutches (E1 and E2) and brakes (F1 and F2) are multi-disc oil bath type and, according to the hydraulic loading, engage or release the epicyclic gear train components.

The governor is in effect a low output alternator which provides variable current to the computer. It is driven by a worm gear on the final drive pinion and its output depends on the vehicle speed and engine loading.

The computer acts upon the variation of current from the governor combined with the selected lever position to open or close the solenoid valves accordingly. In addition it acts as a safety device to prevent the 1st gear 'hold' position being selected at a speed in excess of 22 mph (35 kph) at light throttle.

The system also incorporates a kickdown switch, operated by pressing the throttle pedal to its fully open position, at which point under certain engine loading and speeds, the computer will be activated and a lower gear automatically selected.

The drive selected in the gearbox is transferred to the differential unit via stepdown gears, which compensate for the diffference in levels between the main gear assemblies in the gearbox and the level of the crownwheel and pinion in the differential housing.

The selector lever is centrally situated within the car and has six positional alternatives, as follows:

P (Park): With the lever in this position, the transmission is neutralised and the drive wheels are locked
R (Reverse): Reverse gear position, which when selected also actuates the reversing light switch
N (Neutral): The transmission is in neutral.
1 (1st gear): 1st gear hold position
2 (2nd gear): Automatic operation between 1st and 2nd gears
A (Automatic) or D (Drive): Gears engage automatically according to engine loading and car speed

In addition to the above, the kickdown switch causes a lower speed to be selected at a higher speed than normal when the throttle pedal is suddenly pressed fully down. This device is designed to give sudden acceleration when required, such as for overtaking.

Because of the obvious hazards of starting the car when in gear, a starter inhibitor switch is fitted and only allows the starter to be operated when the selector is in Park or Neutral position. The inhibitor switch is fitted below the transmission governor/computer units. Its removal necessitates withdrawal of the oil sump plate – not a DIY mechanic job. Another safety feature built into this transmission on models from 1977, is the design of the selector lever handle which must be compressed by hand before Park, Reverse or 1st gear can be selected. This locking device prevents accidental selection of those positions when the engine is running.

The automatic transmission is a relatively complex unit and therefore should problems occur, it is recommended that the fault be discussed with your Renault dealer, who should be able to advise you on the best course of action to be taken. Items that can be attempted by the home mechanic are given in the following Sections in this Chapter. To obtain trouble-free operation and maximum life expectancy from your automatic transmission, it must be serviced as described and not be subjected to abuse.

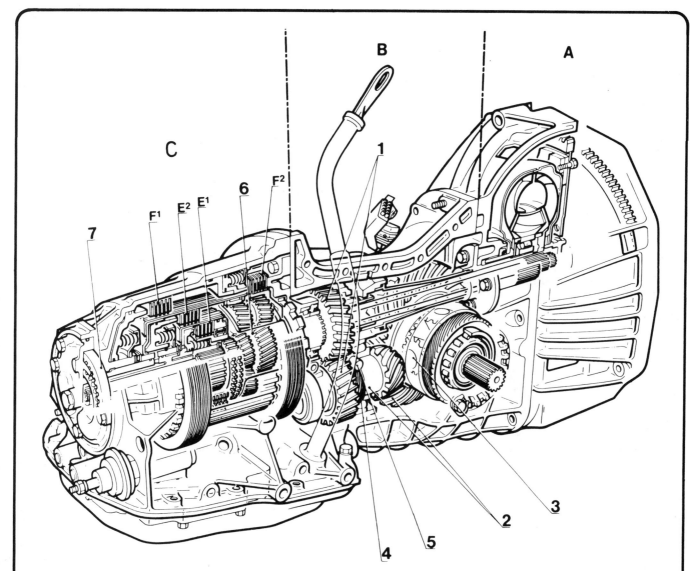

Fig. 7.1 Cutaway view of the Renault 4141-00 type automatic transmission showing the converter housing (A), final drive (B) and gearbox (C) (Sec 1)

1	Step down gears	4	Worm gear	7	Oil pump	F1 Brake discs
2	Crownwheel and pinion	5	Governor	E1	Multi-disc clutch	F2 Brake discs
3	Differential	6	Epicyclic gear train	E2	Multi-disc clutch	

2 Automatic transmission vehicles – towing

1   Should your car need to be towed (due to a breakdown in the automatic transmission or otherwise) it is important that the front wheels be raised clear of the ground. This is necessary because the oil pump within the transmission unit is actuated by drive from the engine and it would therefore be non-operational in the event of a breakdown.

2   If circumstances do not allow the car to be towed in this fashion, or only a limited mileage is to be covered, the car can be towed in the normal manner but only providing that the following precautions are taked:

(a) *The mileage to be covered must not exceed a distance of 30 miles (50 km)*
(b) *An additional quantity of 2 Imp qts (2 litres) of the recommended transmission oil (see Specifications) must be added to the transmission*
(c) *The maximum permissible towing speed under these conditions is 18mph (30 km/h)*

3   On arrival at the towing destination, do not forget to drain off the surplus lubricant.

3.7 Topping up the automatic transmission fluid level

3 Maintenance – transmission and differential

Transmission
1   The automatic transmission fluid level must be checked regularly at 1200 to 3000 mile (2000 to 5000 km) intervals.
2   When checking oil level, position the vehicle on flat ground and place the hand control in 'P'. Start the engine and run it for two minutes to allow the converter to fill up.
3   Allow the engine to tick over and, with the lever still in 'P', check the oil level on the dipstick, as shown in Fig. 7.2.
4   Dependent on whether the car has just finished a run and the engine/gearbox is thoroughly hot or whether it has just been started from cold, use the hot or cold markings on the dipstick accordingly. Do not allow the oil level to drop below the minimum mark and never overfill as this may cause overheating.
5   The transmission fluid must be drained and renewed at regular intervals of 20 000 miles (32 000 km). If the vehicle is used for towing, the change should be at more frequent intervals.
6   The transmission fluid must be drained whilst hot but with the engine stopped. When draining, do not confuse the transmission and differential drain plugs, both of which are shown in an illustration in

the Routine Maintenance section at the start of the manual. Remove the plug and drain the fluid into a suitable container for disposal. Allow the fluid to drain for at least five minutes, then refit the drain plug, making certain that it is secure.
7   Insert a suitable funnel into the dipstick tube and top up the fluid level. Although the capacity is about 10½ pints (6 litres), the normal topping-up requirement after draining is only about 5½ pints (3 litres). Top up using only the lubricant type specified for the transmission (not the differential) and take care not to overfill (photo). Observe scrupulous cleanliness at all times.

Differential (final drive unit)
8   The differential unit has a combined level check and filler plug on the side of the casing.
9   The plug should be removed and the level checked every 5000 miles (8000 km). The oil level should be maintained to the bottom of the filler plug hole.
10   Every 20 000 miles (32 000 km), remove the differential drain plug and drain the old lubricant into a suitable container. Refit the

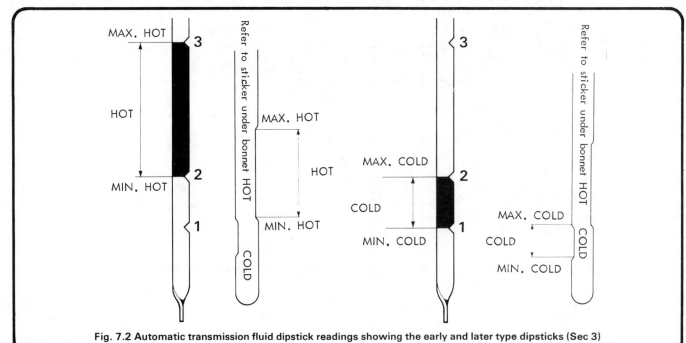

Fig. 7.2 Automatic transmission fluid dipstick readings showing the early and later type dipsticks (Sec 3)

drain plug, remove the level plug and refill with new oil of the specified grade to the level required. Then refit the level plug. The differential case should take 3 pints (1.6 litres) when being refilled.

---

4   Selector control – removal, refitting and adjustment

1   Two types of selector control have been fitted and these are known respectively as the horizontal selector gate type and the vertical selector gate type. The component parts of each are shown in Figs. 7.3 and 7.4.

2   Disconnect the battery earth lead before beginning work.
3   Remove the radio console panel as given in Chapter 10.
4   Remove the selector lever knob, which is secured by a screw.
5   Remove the two rear selector panel retaining screws, which are under the base covering within the storage space directly beneath the handbrake.
6   Prise free the plastic control panel and withdraw it.
7   Working underneath the vehicle, remove the retaining nut from the lever-to-linkage pivot to detach the lever.
8   Working inside the car again, remove the control unit retaining screws or nuts as applicable and withdraw it. Detach the wiring connectors underneath for full removal (photo).

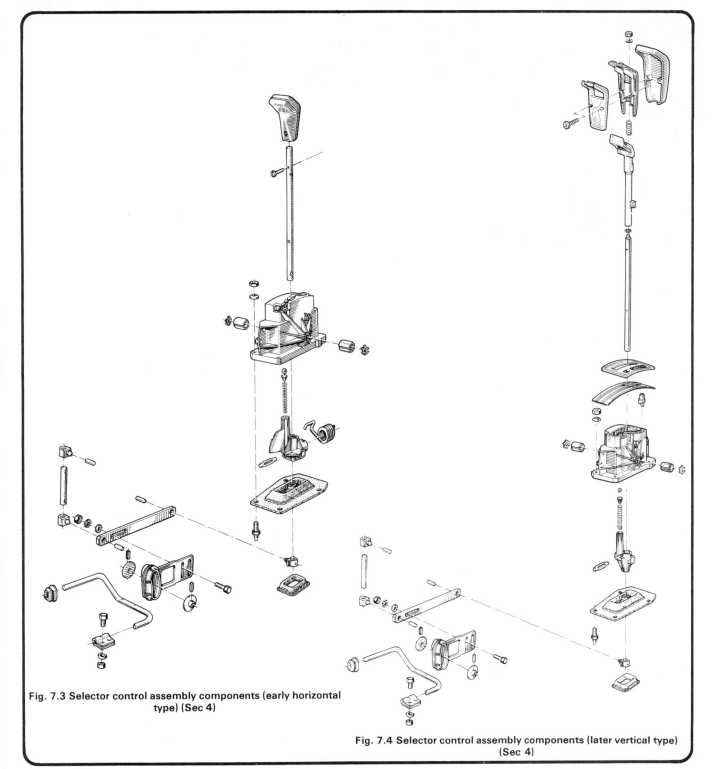

Fig. 7.3 Selector control assembly components (early horizontal type) (Sec 4)

Fig. 7.4 Selector control assembly components (later vertical type) (Sec 4)

4.8 Selector control shown with console and selector panel removed

9   On the horizontal selector gate type, slide it out of its location having removed the console and console bridge.

10   To remove the linkage assembly, detach the cover and unscrew the rod clamp nuts. Detach the rod connections to the lever and frame.

11   Reassembly is a reversal of the removal procedure, but ensure that the control shaft and linkage abut to each other and adjust the selector mechanism as follows.

12   Position the selector lever in the 2nd gear 'hold' location. Push the control shaft fully inwards (to the 2nd gear 'hold'' position), then extract it by one notch. Slacken off the adjuster bolts as shown in Fig. 7.5 and have an assistant check that the selector lever is still engaged in the 2nd gear 'hold' position. Retighten the two retaining bolts, then road test the car to ensure correct selection adjustment has been achieved.

5   Governor control cable – renewal and adjustment

1   To remove the governor control cable, unhook it from the quadrant location at the governor and unscrew the outer cable retaining nuts (Fig. 7.6).

2   From the engine end of the cable, unhook the inner cable from the throttle connecting quadrant cam near the carburettor as shown in Fig. 7.7. Detach the outer cable from the bracket.

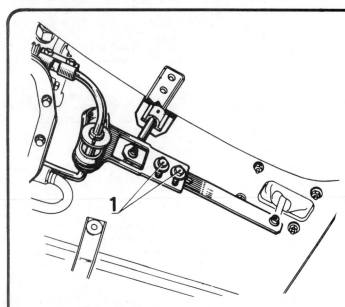

Fig. 7.5 The selector control shaft showing the adjuster bolts (1) (Sec 4)

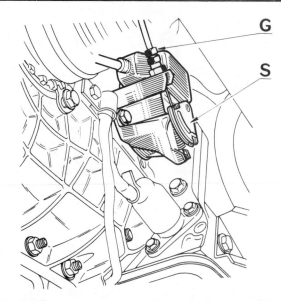

Fig. 7.6 The governor showing the cable sleeve stop (G) and control quadrant (S) (Sec 5)

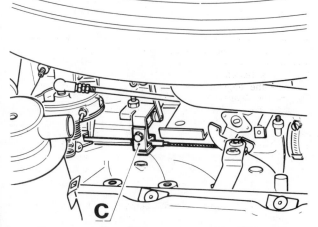

Fig. 7.7 Governor cable at carburettor end showing the sleeve stop (C) (Sec 5)

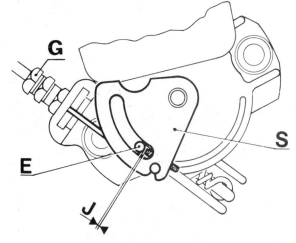

Fig. 7.8 Clearance point (J) between stop peg (E) and quadrant (S). For clearance see text (Sec 5)

3   Refitting is a reversal of the removal procedure, but the cable must be adjusted.
4   Turn the outer cable adjuster at the governor end to allow the maximum cable extension and locate the control cable into the quadrant. At the other end, locate the cable to the carburettor connecting quadrant.
5   To adjust the cable get an assistant to press the throttle pedal down fully whilst you retension the cable at the carburettor end. Adjust the cable at its location bracket so that the quadrant is fully opened.
6   At the governor end of the cable, loosen the outer cable location nuts, then adjust the cable to give a clearance of 0.3 to 0.5 mm (0.012 to 0.020 in) between the quadrant and the stop peg as indicated in Fig. 7.8. Tighten the locknut to secure the cable.
7   Check the adjustment of the throttle cable – see next Section.

6   Kickdown switch/throttle cable – checking, renewal and adjustment

1   To check the kickdown switch for operation, connect a test light and lead between the switch and battery. When the throttle pedal is pressed hard down the test light should glow; if it does not the switch is faulty.
2   Renewal of the switch necessitates renewal of the throttle cable also, as the two are combined.
3   Disconnect the cable at the carburettor end and also at the throttle pedal end (see Chapter 3) and remove with the switch.
4   Refit in the reverse order but ensure the throttle cable has sufficient free play to allow 3 to 4 mm ($\frac{1}{8}$ to $\frac{5}{32}$ in) movement of the stop sleeve (as shown in Fig. 7.9) as the throttle is fully pressed.
5   Check the adjustment of the governor cable as described in the previous Section.

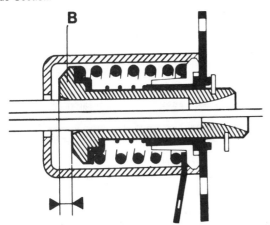

Fig. 7.9 Check the throttle cable free play adjustment at stop sleeve (B) with accelerator pedal fully down. For clearance see text (Sec 6)

7   Automatic transmission – removal and refitting

1   Experience has shown that the best method of removing the automatic transmission unit is forward and up through the engine compartment, but not attached to the engine. Renault specify that the lower body crossmember must not be removed, and it is this that limits the manoeuvrability of the transmission unit when removing.
2   Although Renault suggest that the transmission can be withdrawn rearwards and from underneath, this should not be attempted unless a vehicle lifting hoist or work pit are available to provide sufficient working area beneath the vehicle for the awkward manoeuvring procedures involved.
3   Although not a method to be recommended, if your lifting tackle is adequate, the engine and gearbox can be removed as a combined unit as described in Chapter 1, Section 6.
4   To remove the units separately, first refer to Section 5 in Chapter 1 and remove the engine, then proceed as follows.
5   Drain the oil from the final drive casing, and the fluid from the transmission casing, by removing the respective drain plugs.

7.6 Detach the speedometer cable

6   Remove the retaining clip and disconnect the speedometer cable at its transmission connection (photo).
7   Referring to Chapter 1, Section 6, proceed as given in paragraphs 4 to 10 inclusive and 14 to 17 inclusive, to disconnect the transmission ready for removal.
8   Before withdrawing the transmission unit, check that its respective fittings and attachments are free and will not interfere with its removal. Also ensure that the torque converter is secured in position with a clamp plate of some description – see photo 5.21 in Chapter 1.
9   The transmission should now be ready for removal. You will require an assistant to help guide it forward whilst supporting it and then help lift it from the engine compartment.
10   Refitting is a reversal of the removal procedure. Lubricate the converter location aperture in the rear end of the crankshaft with molybdenum grease or similar prior to refitment; at the transmission end of the converter, lubricate the oil seal bearing surface and white metal bush with automatic transmission fluid.
11   When refitting the engine, align the driveplate correctly so that the three converter attachment bolts can be fitted and secured before fully tightening the engine-to-transmission retaining bolts.
12   With the engine and transmission refitted, reconnect and adjust the governor cable, the throttle cable and the selector control linkage. Do not forget to top up the transmission fluid level and also the final drive oil.

8   Differential unit driveshaft oil seal – renewal

Refer to Chapter 6, Section 9.

9   Converter driveplate – removal and refitting

1   This is bolted to the rear end of the engine crankshaft and therefore the engine must be removed from the car first. This is described in Chapter 1.
2   Normally, there are only two reasons for removing the converter driveplate; to inspect and renew due to worn starter ring teeth, or to inspect and check the run-out of the plate.
3   To check the run-out, clamp a dial gauge to a fixed location on the cylinder block. Turn the driveplate, take readings at each converter bolt hole in turn and note any variation. The maximum run-out permissible is 0.3 mm (0.012 in) as shown in Fig. 7.10 (if exceeded renew the driveplate).
4   To remove the converter driveplate, support or jam it to prevent rotation and unscrew the seven retaining bolts. Withdraw the plate from the crankshaft.
5   Refitting is a reversal of the removal procedure, but note that new driveplate retaining bolts must be used. Do not forget to locate the

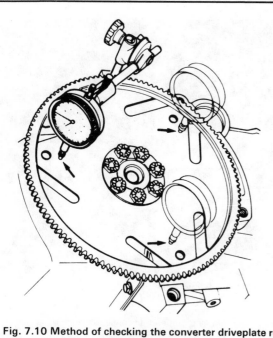

Fig. 7.10 Method of checking the converter driveplate runout using a dial gauge. Note respective check positions (arrowed) (Sec 9)

special spacer washer on each side of the driveplate during assembly, and tighten the retaining bolts to the specified torque. The bolt threads must be smeared with Loctite Frenetanch or similar.

10 Converter oil seal – renewal

1   Refer to Chapter 1 and remove the engine.
2   Extract the converter from its housing for access to the seal. Using a suitable tool, prise the seal from its housing, taking care not to damage the location aperture. Clean out the oil seal and converter housings.
3   Smear the new oil seal lightly with transmission fluid and locate it into the chamfered aperture. Use a tube drift of suitable diameter and drift it fully into position.
4   Carefully refit the converter into position and then refit the engine.

11 Oil cooler pipes – general

1   The oil cooler is integral with the radiator. The hose connections to and from the automatic transmission are connected to it on the left-hand side.
2   The cooler and its hoses give very little in the way of problems, but a check should be made occasionally to ensure that the hoses and connections are in good condition and secure.
3   If at any time the hoses are removed, renewed or simply disconnected, ensure when reconnecting that the respective pipe location clamps and clips are correctly relocated and securely retained. Check that the pipes are not chafing on surrounding fittings.

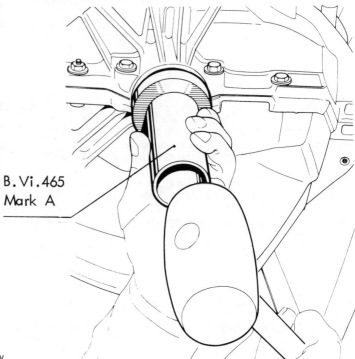

B.Vi.465
Mark A

Fig. 7.11 Drive the oil seal into position – use Renault special tool B Vi 465 Mark A if available (Sec 10)

4   When pipes are disconnected, watch out for a certain amount of oil spillage – especially if the oil is hot!

12 Fault diagnosis – automatic transmission

1   Automatic transmission faults are almost always the result of low fluid level or incorrect adjustment of the selector linkage or governor control cable.
2   If these items are checked and found to be in order, the fault is probably internal ahd should be diagnosed by your Renault dealer who is specially equipped to pinpoint the problem and effect any necessary repairs.
3   Do not allow any defect in the operation of the automatic transmission to go unchecked – it could prove expensive!
4   If the starter fails to function at any time, it is possible that the starter inhibitor switch is at fault but first check that, (a) the selector control lever adjustment is correct, and (b) the transmission wiring harness plugs and socket connections are secure. Check the starter circuit wiring for continuity to the switch plug. The inhibitor switch is situated beneath the transmission governor/computer unit and within the hydraulic section of the unit. The sump plate would have to be removed to gain access to the switch and this is therefore best entrusted to your Renault dealer.

Chapter 8 Driveshafts, wheels and tyres

Contents

Specifications

Driveshafts
Outer joint .... Lobro – 6-ball coupling
Inner joint .... GI 82 coupling
Note: *The driveshaft on manual transmission models is longer than that for automatic transmission models*

Driveshaft lubricant
GI 82 coupling .... 160 grams of Elf S747
Lobro coupling .... 140 grams of Elf S747

Wheels
Size .... 5.50J x 14
Maximum permissible rim run-out .... 1.2 mm (0.046 in)
Maximum permissible rim ovality .... 1.2 mm (0.046 in)

Tyres
Size .... 175 x 14
Inflation pressures:
    Front .... 26 lbf/in^2 (1.9 bar)
    Rear .... 29 lbf/in^2 (2.0 bar)
Note: *On automatic transmission models, add 1.5 lbf/in^2 (0.1 bar) to the front tyre pressures. For fully laden and/or motorways usage, add 3 lbf/in^2 (0.2 bar) to front and rear tyres (all models)*

Torque wrench settings

	lbf ft	Nm
Wheel nuts	45 to 60	60 to 80
Stub axle nut	158	210
Steering arm balljoint	26	35
Top balljoint nut	75	100

---

1 General information

The driveshafts transmit the motion from the transmission unit to the front roadwheels. The driveshaft to each front wheel is fitted with a constant velocity joint at each end to allow for the variations of movement between the transmission and the roadwheels due to steering and suspension movement.

The shaft is located by splines to both the transmission and front wheel hub. At the transmission end, the driveshaft is retained in position by a roll pin, whilst on the outer end the wheel hub bearing nut and special washer secure it in position.

Each joint assembly is covered by a rubber bellows to protect it from the ingress of dirt, which would cause rapid wear of the joint unit.

Whenever the driveshafts are renewed, take the old one along for exchange and compare the old and new units to ensure correct replacement. The automatic tramsmission models are fitted with shorter driveshaft units compared with their manual transmission counterparts.

The driveshafts do not require servicing, being pre-lubricated during assembly. No repairs to the joint units are possible by the home mechanic; removal and refitting only. Regular inspection of the rubber bellows should be made, since if splits or cracks are remedied promptly, the joint itself may not be damaged.

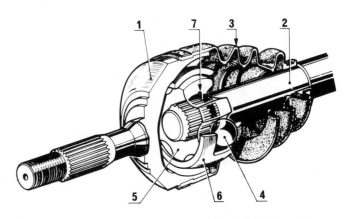

Fig. 8.1 Cutaway view showing the driveshaft ball coupling components (Sec 1)

1 Stub axle	*5 Ball hub*
2 Driveshaft	*6 Ball cage*
3 Rubber bellows	*7 Retaining ring*
4 Balls	

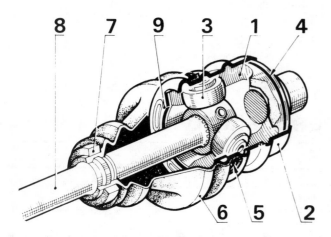

Fig. 8.2 Cutaway section of the inner joint coupling of the driveshaft (Sec 1)

1	Yoke	6	Rubber bellows
2	Cover	7	Retaining ring
3	Spider	8	Driveshaft
4	Seal	9	Anti-separation plate
5	Retaining clip		

2.8 Withdraw the driveshaft from the transmission

2　Driveshaft – removal

1　To support the suspension during removal and refitting of the driveshaft, you will need to fabricate a spacer leg to locate between the lower suspension arm pivot pin and the upper arm-to-anti-roll bar connecting link (as shown in Fig. 8.3) to hold the front axle compressed. Renault dealers use special tool number T Av 603. Refer to Chapter 11 for details.

2　Having borrowed or fabricated the spacer leg, compress the suspension at the front and locate the leg securely into the position described above.

3　Raise the front of the vehicle and make secure on axle stands, then remove the roadwheel.

4　The driveshaft inner coupling (to transmission) roll pin must now be extracted. Rotate the shaft to a suitable position, and from underneath, drive the roll pin out using a suitable punch drift as shown in Fig. 8.4.

5　Locate a lever between two wheel nut studs on the hub to prevent it turning, unscrew the stub axle nut and remove it with the washer.

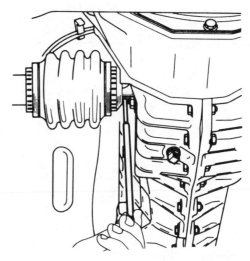

Fig. 8.4 Roll pin removal using a drift (Sec 2)

6　Referring to Chapter 9, remove the brake caliper unit but do not disconnect the hydraulic hose. Support the caliper by suspending it with a suitable length of wire, or place it on blocks, so that the weight of the caliper is not taken by the hose.

7　Unscrew the upper suspension arm and steering arm balljoint retaining nuts and, using a balljoint separator or wedges, detach the joints.

8　The driveshaft can now be withdrawn from the transmission shaft, tilting the hub unit back to suit (photo).

9　Temporarily relocate the steering arm balljoint.

10　Use a soft drift of suitable diameter and drive the driveshaft inwards through the hub. Once the shaft is clear of the hub, the steering arm balljoint can again be detached and the hub manoeuvred to allow the driveshaft to be removed completely.

3　Driveshaft joints – general inspection

1　As mentioned in Section 1, very little in the way of maintenance or repair can be done by the average home mechanic.

2　Although easily dismantled for inspection, there is no repair possible if the joint assembly is worn or defective and it must therefore be renewed as a unit. All components are match fitted during production, thus preventing ready renewal of an individual component.

3　Even renewal of the rubber bellows, if damaged or defective, is beyond the scope of the home mechanic unless the special fitting cage

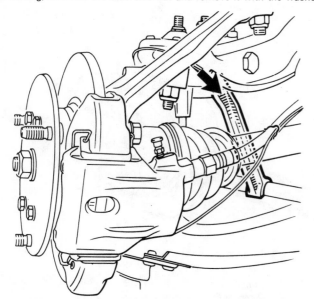

Fig. 8.3 Locate the spacer leg (arrowed) as shown (Sec 2)

is purchased. If on removal the joint is obviously worn or defective, take it for renewal or any possible repairs to your Renault dealer, who will have the necessary tools and equipment required to undertake any servicing operations that may be possible.

4 Driveshaft – refitting

1 Clean the driveshaft splines thoroughly, then smear then with Molykote BR2 grease or equivalent.
2 Align the roll pin location holes between the driveshaft and transmission intake splines and slide the shaft into position. When the respective holes for the roll pin are level, check that they are in exact alignment, as the shaft only fits in one position. If the holes are not in exact alignment the shaft is 180° out and must be extracted and repositioned.
3 Always use new roll pins and drive them carefully into position using a suitable drift. Seal each end of the roll pin with a suitable sealant (Fig. 8.5).
4 Relocate the driveshaft outer end into the stub axle carrier unit. As the shaft is fitted, take care not to damage the inner hub bearing oil seal. The driveshaft to stub axle assembly will be eased with the aid of the special tool shown in Fig. 8.6. If you are not able to fabricate this tool, use Renault tool T Av 602 (for 20 mm driveshaft nuts) or equivalent.
5 With the shaft in position in the hub, relocate the suspension and steering arm balljoints. Tighten the balljoint retaining nuts to the specified torque settings.

6 The stub axle nut and washer can now be refitted. Tighten the nut to the specified torque and check that the hub is free to rotate without binding.
7 Refit the brake caliper unit and press the brake pedal a few times to centralize the disc pads.
8 Refit the roadwheel, lower the car and compress the suspension to remove the spacer leg.
9 Recheck the balljoint nut for tightness. Also check the transmission oil level and top up if necessary.

5 Wheels – general information

Because of the design of the suspension of the car the strength and the trueness of the roadwheels is critical, particularly at the front. A great deal of excessively fast wear on the wheel bearings and universal joints can be attributed to buckled and deformed wheels. Check every 3000 miles, or when there is a sudden difference of feeling at the steering wheel, that the wheels are not buckled or dented. Check also that the front wheels are balanced. If any deformity is noticed the wheel concerned should be renewed. Do not attempt to 'repair'.

6 Tyres – general information

1 In the same way that the condition and suitability of the wheels fitted is critical so it is with the tyres. It is always wise to fit radial ply

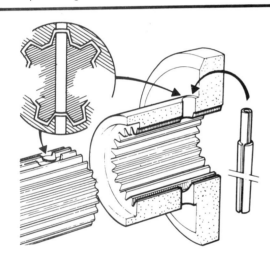

Fig. 8.5 The inner and outer roll pins and their location (Sec 4)

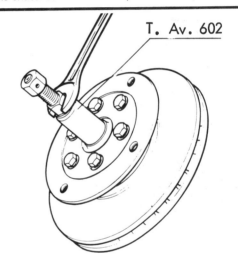

Fig. 8.7 Driveshaft-to-stub axle fitting tool T Av 602 (Sec 4)

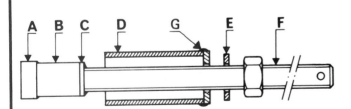

Fig. 8.6 Driveshaft-to-stub axle refitting tool (Sec 4)

A   18 mm* driveshaft nut (150 pitch ground on o/d)
B   Sleeve (21 mm o/d x 15 mm i/d x 30 mm long)
C   Washer (20 mm o/d x 7 mm i/d x 2.5 mm thick)
D   Tube (34 mm dia x 60 mm long)
E   Washer (30 mm o/d x 16 mm i/d x 3 mm thick)
F   Threaded rod (M16 x 210 mm long)
G   Washer (34 mm o/d x 16 mm i/d x 4 mm thick)
* 20 mm driveshaft nut on some models

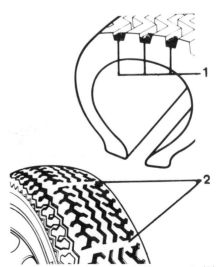

Fig. 8.8 Tyre tread minimum depth indicator strip (2), showing position in tread grooves (1) (Sec 6)

tyres on all wheels of these cars. Tyre wear is not great under any circumstances but the front tyres will wear faster than the rear. Do not fit oversize tyres. The wheel rims are not able to take a larger section tyre. Tyre pressures are critical too.

2 Where tyres are wearing unevenly, it is indicative of either incorrect pressures or a misalignment of the front or rear suspension/steering (as applicable). It is essential, for obvious reasons, that this should not be allowed to continue unchecked.

3 Apart from the increased cost caused by rapid tyre wear, the general handling and safety of the car may well be affected if the suspension geometry or tyre inflation pressures are incorrect.

4 Many tyres now produced have minimum allowable tread wear indicators moulded into the tread base, as shown in Fig. 8.8. When the tyres have worn down to the indicated level thay are due for renewal. Wherever possible, renew the tyre(s) with the same make and type as fitted elsewhere on the car.

5 If it is wished to interchange the positions of the tyres to even out wear, this should only be done from front to rear and vice versa on the same side of the car. Do not interchange radial tyres from side to side of the vehicle.

Chapter 9 Braking system

Contents

Specifications

General
System type .... Disc brakes at front and rear. Cable-operated handbrake to rear wheels. Servo-assisted, hydraulic brake actuation with pressure limiter on rear wheels

Hydraulic fluid specification .... SAE J1703F

Front brakes
Type .... Bendix III B
Disc diameter .... 9.921 in (252 mm)
Disc thickness (new) .... 0.945 in (24 mm)
Disc thickness (minimum) .... 0.866 in (22 mm)
Maximum allowable disc run-out .... 0.004 in (0.1 mm)
Pad thickness (with backing) – new .... 0.728 in (18.5 mm)
Pad thickness (with backing) – minimum .... 0.354 in (9 mm)

Rear brakes
Type .... Bendix III ACG
Disc thickness (new) .... 0.472 in (12 mm)
Disc thickness (minimum) .... 0.435 in (11 mm)
Maximum allowable disc run-out .... 0.004 in (0.1 mm)
Pad thickness (with backing) – new .... 0.551 in (14 mm)
Pad thickness (with backing) – minimum .... 0.225 in (7 mm)

Master cylinder stroke .... 1.339 in (34 mm)

Brake servo
Diameter:
    Early models (R 1273 and 1275 up to No 300) .... 9 in (228 mm)
    Later models (and all R 1278) .... 8 in (203 mm)
Pushrod adjustments:
    Servo to master cylinder .... 0.354 in (9 mm)
    Pedal to servo – early models (as above) .... 4.921 in (125 mm)
    Pedal to servo – later models (as above) .... 5.0 in (127 mm)

Brake limiter setting values
Fuel tank full .... 544 lbf/in² (37.5 bar)
Fuel tank half full .... 493 lbf/in² (34 bar)
Fuel tank empty .... 442 lbf/in² (30.5 bar)

Torque wrench settings

	lbf ft	Nm
Bleed screw	4 to 5	5 to 7
Hydraulic hose to caliper union	15	20
Master cylinder unions:		
Primary circuit (2 outlets)	15	20
Secondary circuit to bypass	20	25
Secondary circuit to compensator	15	20
Brake limiter valve inlet	20	25
Limiter and bypass outlet	15	20
Caliper bracket bolts	41 to 58	55 to 75
Stub axle nut:		
Front	158	210
Rear	See text (Section 8)	See text (Section 8)

1 General description

The braking system is of four-wheel hydraulic type, with disc brakes on all wheels.

A mechanically operated handbrake operates on the rear wheels only.

Actuation of the braking system is by means of a foot-operated pedal working through a master cylinder and combined fluid reservoir.

A brake pressure limiter valve is fitted in the system to prevent locking of the wheels and to adjust the braking effort between the front and rear wheels in conjunction with the weight and suspension characteristics of the vehicle.

The brakes are servo-assisted, the servo unit receiving its vacuum from the inlet manifold.

The tandem type master cylinder also incorporates a pressure drop indicator switch, to give early warning should a fault occur within the hydraulic circuit.

An additional circuit from the master cylinder on certain models provides extra pressure to the rear brakes should a fault occur in the front brake circuit. When operated, this additional circuit overrides the brake limiter valve.

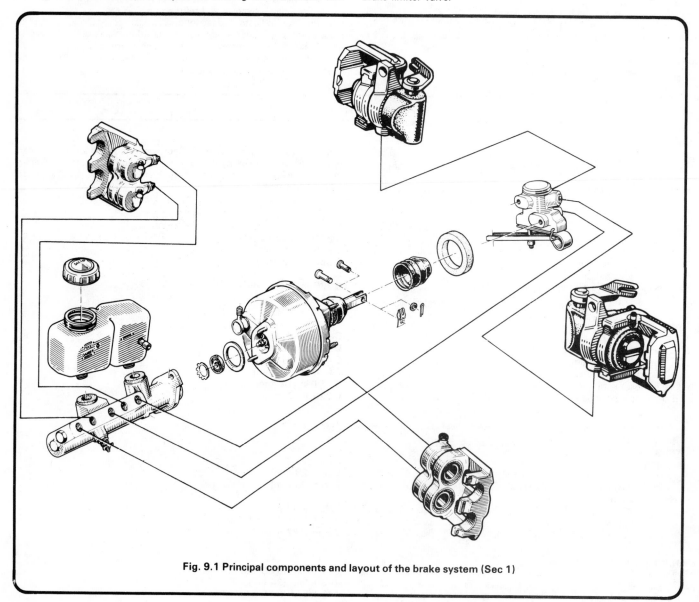

Fig. 9.1 Principal components and layout of the brake system (Sec 1)

2 Front brake disc pads – removal, inspection and refitting

Inspection does not necessitate the removal of the disc pads themselves. The pads abut the disc surface at all times, Therefore it is possible to put the end of a steel rule (the measure must start at the end of the rule) on the disc at a right-angle to the caliper as shown in Fig. 9.2. The total pad thickness (with backing plate) must not be less than that specified. If the pads have worn down beyond this, they must be renewed as a set.

1   Before dismantling any parts of the brakes they should be thoroughly cleaned. The best cleaning agent is hot water and a mild detergent. Do not use petrol, paraffin or any other solvents which could cause deterioration of the friction pads or piston seals.

2   Jack up the car and remove the wheel. Support the car on safety stands.

3   Extract the key retaining clips (on the inside) as shown (photo).

4   Use a suitable punch to drive out and withdraw the keys (photo).

5   Push down on the caliper unit and pull it away from the brake unit whilst supporting it (photo).

6   Lever the pads away from the discs, and withdraw them. The springs under the pads can be left in position or withdrawn as required (photos).

7   Do not apply pressure to the brake pedal whilst the caliper section and pads are detached. Support the caliper whilst removed, to prevent straining the flexible hose.

8   Measure the pad thicknesses and compare them with the minimum allowable thickness given in the Specifications.

9   The caliper piston dust covers can be detached from their housing and the end of each piston cleaned with methylated spirit. The piston skirt can be treated with a suitable brake grease. Clean the dust covers and refit them, then push back the piston with a block of wood or similar.

10 Relocate the pad springs and insert the new pads. If fitting the original pads, refit them to their original locations. Always renew pads as a complete axle set – not individually.

11 Check that the pads slide freely in their locations when fitted.

12 Relocate the caliper, inserting one end of it between the key bearing surface and the spring clip. Compress both springs and fully locate the caliper whilst levering it downwards (Fig. 9.3).

13 Slide one key into position and then prising the second key slot open with a screwdriver insert the second key. Check that both keys are fully located and then insert the retaining clips to secure.

14 Press the brake pedal a few times to set the pistons against the pads.

15 Repeat the operations on the other side of the car, if necessary.

16 Refit the roadwheel(s) and lower the car to the ground

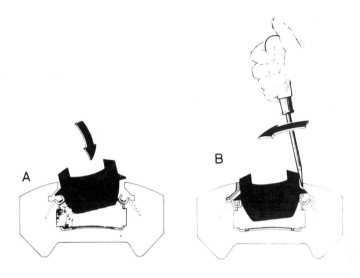

Fig. 9.3 Caliper location method (Sec 2)

A   *Initial fitting*   B   *Prise as shown for full location*

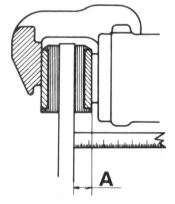

Fig. 9.2 Check the disc pad thickness (A) as shown (Sec 2)

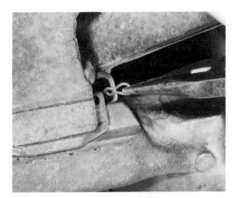

2.3 Extract the key retaining clips

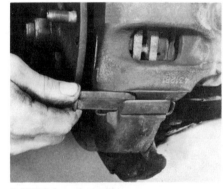

2.4 Withdraw the keys

2.5 Remove the caliper

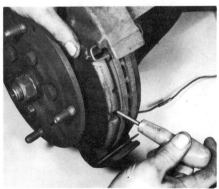

2.6A Lever the pads free from the discs

2.6B Remove the spring if wished

3 Front disc brake caliper bracket – removal and refitting

1   Refitting to the previous Section, follow paragraphs 1 to 7 and detach the pads and caliper unit. Do not disconnect the flexible hydraulic hose.
2   Unscrew and remove the caliper bracket retaining bolts on the inside of the stub axle, as shown in Fig. 9.4. Remove the bracket.
3   Refit the bracket and caliper unit/pads in the reverse order, but ensure the caliper and pads are cleaned prior to fitting.
4   Tighten the bracket bolts, the threads of which should be smeared with Loctite Frenbloc or equivalent, to the specified torque.

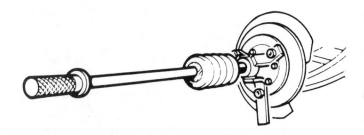

Fig. 9.5 The special Renault hub removal tools, Nos T Av 601 and MS 580 (Sec 4)

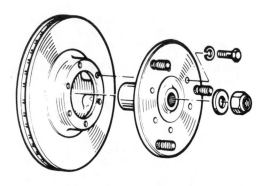

Fig. 9.6 The wheel hub and disc (Sec 4)

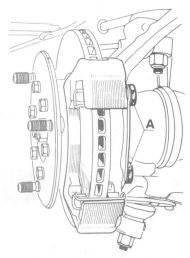

Fig. 9.4 The caliper bracket retaining bolts (A) – front (Sec 3)

4 Front brake discs – removal and refitting

1   Referring to Sections 2 and 3, remove the disc caliper and caliper bracket.
2   Locate a bar between two of the wheel studs, to prevent the hub from turning, and loosen the wheel hub nut (photo). Remove the nut and washer.
3   It should now be possible to withdraw the hub/disc unit by light leverage or tapping from the rear with a soft-headed mallet. Failing this it will be necessary to use a suitable puller or slide hammer. The official Renault tool for this purpose is tool number T Av 601 used with attachment MS 580 as shown in Fig. 9.5.

4.2 Method used to prevent the hub turning when removing or fitting the hub nut

4   The disc is held to the hub by retaining bolts with spring washers.
5   The disc cannot be resurfaced, and if badly grooved, damaged or worn beyond the specified limits, must be renewed.
6   Refitting is a reversal of the removal procedure. All parts must be cleaned before fitting and the respective fastenings tightened to the specified torque settings, where given. Clean and grease the hub bearings before fitting. On completion, apply pressure to the brake pedal a few times to reseat the caliper pistons.
7   If difficulty is experienced in mating the hub/disc and stub axle, refer to Chapter 8.

5 Front disc brake calipers – removal, servicing and refitting

1   Refer to Section 2 and withdraw the caliper unit from its bracket.
2   Detach the brake pad wear warning wire and the hydraulic hoses. Clamp or plug the hoses to prevent leakage of fluid and the ingress of dirt.
3   Clean thoroughly the exterior of the caliper with methylated spirit prior to dismantling.
4   Detach the rubber dust cover from the piston to be removed. If both pistons are to be removed, attend to them individually so that they are kept with their respective bores.
5   To extract the piston, apply a regulated amount of air pressure into the hydraulic hose connection in the caliper, but position a piece of wood or rubber to cushion the piston as it emerges, to prevent damaging its end face.
6   Carefully extract the caliper seal. Avoid scoring the piston surface and caliper bore in any way. Use a new seal on reassembly.
7   Clean the piston thoroughly in methylated spirit. Then inspect it for any signs of excessive wear, scoring or possible corrosive pittings. Renew the piston if defective. Similarly clean and inspect the caliper bore.
8   Smear the new seal in clean brake fluid and insert it into position in the caliper groove, using only the fingers for manipulating it to avoid scoring the groove or caliper bore.
9   Assemble the piston, pushing it carefully into position in the cylinder bore (which must also be lubricated with clean hydraulic fluid). Smear the end of the piston with suitable brake grease.
10 Fit the new dust cover to the caliper, then repeat the operations on the other piston.
11 Inject some clean brake fluid into the flexible hose locating holes.

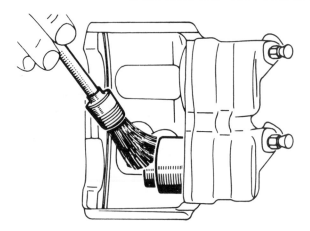

Fig. 9.7 Clean the caliper prior to dismantling (Sec 5)

The bleed screw should be removed during this operation and, as the cylinder is fitted, tilt the caliper to and fro to extract the air. Refit the bleed screw when full. This action will greatly assist bleeding the brakes later.

12 Reattach the hydraulic flexible hoses (having first removed the plugs) and use new copper seal washers.

13 Refit the caliper unit and pads.

14 Refit the roadwheel and bleed the brakes as described in Section 9 to complete.

---

6 Rear brake disc pads – removal, inspection and refitting

1 Jack up the car at the rear and support it with safety stands, then remove the wheels. Chock the front wheels and engage reverse gear (manual transmission) or 'P' (automatic transmission).

2 Release the handbrake.

3 Before dismantling any parts of the brakes they should be thoroughly cleaned externally. The best cleaning agent is hot water and a mild detergent. Do not use petrol, paraffin or any other solvent which could cause deterioration of the friction pads or hydraulic seals.

4 Before dismantling it should be noted thae the inner and outer pads are of differing grades. The outer pad is marked 'EXT' for identification.

5 Disconnect the handbrake cable from its clevis connection in the actuating lever (photo).

6 The brake pads can now be removed in a similar manner to that described for the front disc brake pads (Section 2). Remove the key retaining clips (photo), prise the caliper downwards with a screwdriver and withdraw the keys (photos). With the keys removed, withdraw the caliper and extract the pads and springs (photo). Support the caliper to prevent distortion of the hydraulic hose.

7 Do not apply pressure to the brake pedal whilst the caliper is removed.

8 Measure the pad thicknesses and compare them with the minimum allowable thickness given in the Specifications. Renew the pads only as a complete set if any one is worn down to, or possibly beyond, the specified minimum thickness. Similarly, renew all the pads if any contamination has occurred.

9 Refitting is basically a reversal of the removal process, but note the following.

10 Enter the piston into the caliper, turning it clockwise until it is at its limit, whilst still able to rotate. Locate the piston so that the 'R' line (Fig. 9.8) is positioned as shown in the caliper. This ensures that the caliper will bleed correctly and that the pad engages in the piston slot when assembled.

11 Ensure that the handbrake cable is fully located in its slot.

12 Press the footbrake pedal several times on completion to position the pistons against the pads. Check the handbrake for correct operation and adjustment.

6.5 Disconnect the handbrake cable

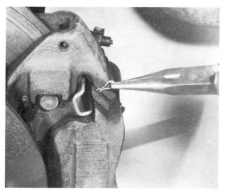

6.6A Remove the key retaining clips ...

6.6B ... withdraw the upper key ...

6.6C ... the lower key ...

6.6D ... and the pads and springs

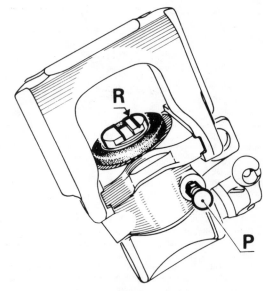

Fig. 9.8 Position piston as shown in caliper, with line 'R' aligned with bleeder screw 'P' (Sec 6)

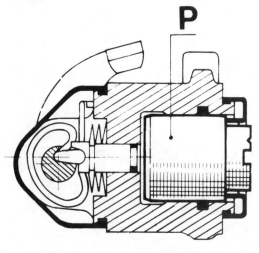

Fig. 9.9 Sectional view of piston (P) and cylinder (Sec 7)

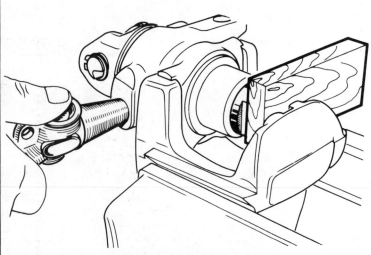

Fig. 9.10 Piston removal using compressed air. Note wooden block (Sec 7)

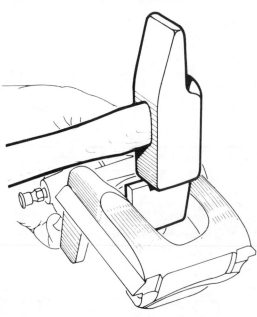

Fig. 9.11 Spread bracket flanges with a wedge (Sec 7)

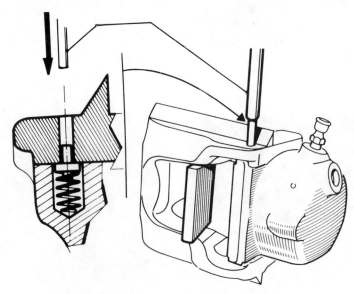

Fig. 9.12 Press retaining peg in to allow cylinder to be removed (Sec 7)

7 Rear brake calipers – removal, servicing and refitting

1   Refer to Section 6 and remove the caliper as given in paragraphs 1 to 7 inclusive. Detach the hydraulic hose from the caliper on removal and plug or clamp the hose to prevent fluid leakage and the ingress of dirt.
2   Support the caliper in a vice with soft jaws and then prise free the rubber dust covers.
3   Unscrew and remove the piston; once removed, it must **not** be dismantled. If difficulty is experienced, apply some compressed air into the cylinder through the fluid line aperture to fully eject the piston. Position a rag or block of wood over the end to catch the piston should it eject suddenly (Fig. 9.10).
4   Extract the seal from its groove using a suitable implement which will not score or damage the bore.
5   Clean all parts in methylated spirit and blow dry with an air line (front pump will do). If the cylinder or piston are scored or damaged in any way they must be renewed. Renew the seal in any case.
6   To separate the cylinder from its bracket, spread the bracket flanges using a wedge just far enough to allow the cylinder to be slid free. The retaining peg must be pressed into the cylinder body to allow it to be slid free (Fig. 9.12).
7   Insert a new cylinder whilst wedging open the bracket. Ensure that the piston location peg is fully engaged in the bracket on completion.
8   If you wish to remove the handbrake mechanism components, refer to Fig. 9.13 and withdraw the dust cover. Remove the operating pin circlip, compress the spring washers and remove the handbrake operating pin (pulling the lever), the plunger, spring and adjuster screw. Keep the single washer and flat washers. Remove the O-ring seal from the adjuster screw.

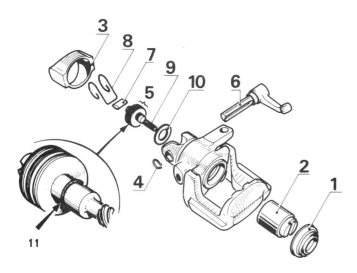

Fig. 9.13 Rear caliper components

1	Dust cover	7	Plunger
2	Piston	8	Spring
3	Dust cover (handbrake)	9	Adjusting screw
4	Circlip	10	Washer
5	Spring washers	11	O-ring
6	Operating pin (handbrake) and lever		

9   Reassembly of the handbrake mechanism is a reversal of the dismantling process. Renew any worn or damaged parts. When refitted check that the spring washers are as shown in Fig. 9.14 enabling the handbrake lever to take an 'off' position.
10 To reassemble a dismantled piston/cylinder unit, lubricate the piston and seal with hydraulic fluid and then insert the piston into its bore, taking care not to damage or distort the seal.
11 With the piston initially fitted, screw it further in until fully positioned and check that it can be rotated. Position it as shown in Fig. 9.8 with the 'R' line aligned with the bleed screw.
12 Fit a new dust cover and refit the pads and caliper (Section 6).
13 To complete, bleed the brakes, referring to Section 9.

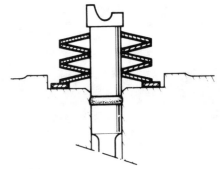

Fig. 9.14 Stack spring washers as shown (Sec 7)

8 Rear brake discs – removal and refitting

1   Referring to Section 6, follow paragraphs 1 to 7 and remove the pads and caliper unit, but do not disconnect the flexible hydraulic hose. Support the caliper unit on removal to prevent distortion of the hydraulic hose.
2   Prise free the wheel hub grease cap (trying not to distort it too much), then clean the grease from the hub nut.
3   Extract the split pin (photo), withdraw the nut lock (photo) and then unscrew and remove the nut. Withdraw the thrust washer.

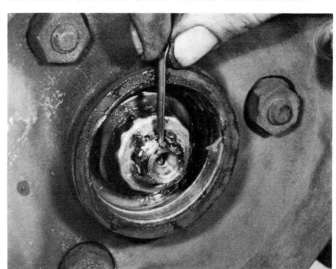

8.3A Withdraw the split pin ...

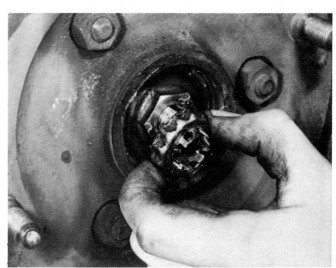

8.3B ... and remove the locknut

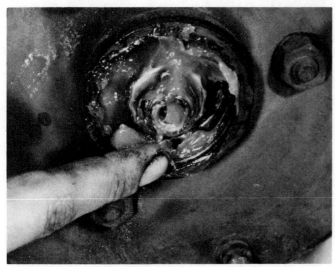

8.8A Lubricate the hub bearing ...

8.8B ... and grease cap

4   The hub/disc unit can now be withdrawn complete with the bearings.

5   The hub and disc can be separated by removing the retaining nuts and washers. To renew the bearings, see Chapter 11.

6   The disc cannot be resurfaced and if badly grooved, damaged or worn beyond the specified limits, it must be renewed.

7   Reassembly is a reversal of the removal procedure, but the following items bear particular attention.

8   Smear some wheel bearing grease onto the hub bearings before refitting the hub/disc unit (photo). Refit the thrust washer and tighten the stub axle nut to a torque of 22.5 lbf ft (30 Nm) whilst simultaneously rotating the hub/disc unit. Then loosen the nut a quarter of a turn and check the hub/bearing endplay, using a dial gauge if available. The endplay should be from 0.004 to 0.012 in (0.01 to 0.03 mm). If a dial gauge is not available, this corresponds to barely

perceptible endplay. Further adjust the hub nut to achieve this endplay if necessary, then fill the grease cap $\frac{3}{4}$ full of bearing grease, refit the nut lock and secure with a new split pin. Tap the grease cap into position (photo).

9   Refit the caliper and pads as described in Section 6.

9   Bleeding the hydraulic system

1   If any of the hydraulic components in the braking system have been removed or disconnected, or if the fluid level in the master cylinder has been allowed to fall appreciably, it is inevitable that air will have been introduced into the system. The removal of all this air from the hydraulic system is essential if the brakes are to function correctly, and the proceess of removing it is known as bleeding.

2   There are a number of one-man do-it-yourself brake bleeding kits currently available from motor accessory shops. It is recommended that one of these kits should be used wherever possible as they greatly simplify the bleeding operation and also reduce the risk of expelled air or fluid being drawn back into the system.

3   If one of these kits is not available then it will be necessary to gather together a clean jar and a suitable length of clear plastic tubing which is a tight fit over the bleed screw, and also engage the help of an assistant.

4   Before commencing the bleeding operation check that all rigid pipes and flexible hoses are in good condition and that all hydraulic unions are tight. Take care not to allow hydraulic fluid to come into contact with the vehicle paintwork, otherwise the finish will be seriously damaged. Wash off any spilled fluid immediately with cold water.

5   If hydraulic fluid has been lost from the master cylinder, due to a leak in the system, ensure that the cause is traced and rectified before proceeding further or a serious malfunction of the braking system may occur.

6   To bleed the system, clean the area around the bleed screw at the wheel cylinder to be bled. Note that each front brake caliper has two bleed nipples. Bleed nipples may also be fitted to the pressure drop indicator and brake limiter. If the hydraulic system has only been partially disconnected and suitable precautions were taken to prevent further loss of fluid, it should only be necessary to bleed that part of the system. However, if the entire system is to be bled, start at the right-hand rear caliper. The order for full bleeding is as follows:

(a) Right-hand rear
(b) Left-hand rear
(c) Brake limiter valve
(d) Right-hand front upper
(e) Left-hand front upper
(f) Right-hand front lower
(g) Left-hand front lower
(h) Master cylinder/pressure drop indicator (as applicable)

Fig. 9.15 Check the hub endplay. Dial gauge mounting arrowed
(Sec 8)

7   Remove the master cylinder filler cap and top up the reservoir. Periodically check the fluid level during the bleeding operation and top up as necessary.

8   If a one-man bleeding kit is being used, connect the outlet tube to the bleed screw and then open the screw half a turn. If possible position the unit so that it can be viewed from the car, then depress the brake pedal to the floor and slowly release it. The one-way valve in the kit will prevent dispelled air from returning to the system at the end of each stroke. Repeat this operation until clean hydraulic fluid, free from air bubbles, can be seen coming through the tube. Now tighten the bleed screw and remove the outlet tube (photos).

9   If a one-man brake bleeding kit is not available, connect one end of the plastic tubing to the bleed screw and immerse the outer end in a jar containing sufficient clean hydraulic fluid to keep the end of the tube submerged. Open the bleed screw half a turn and have your assistant depress the brake pedal to the floor and then slowly release it. Tighten the bleed screw at the end of each downstroke to prevent expelled air and fluid from being drawn back into the system. Repeat this operation until clean hydraulic fluid, free from air bubbles, can be seen coming through the tube. Tighten the bleed screw at the end of a downstroke and remove the plastic tube.

10   If the engine system is being bled the procedures described above should now be repeated at each wheel, finishing at the wheel nearest

to the master cylinder. Do not forget to recheck the fluid level in the master cylinder at regular intervals and top up as necessary.

11   When completed, recheck the fluid level in the master cylinder, top up if necessary and refit the cap. Check the 'feel' of the brake pedal which should be firm and free from any 'sponginess' which would indicate air still present in the system.

12   Discard any expelled hydraulic fluid as it is likely to be contaminated with moisture, air and dirt which makes it unsuitable for further use.

10   Hydraulic pipes and hoses – inspection, removal and refitting

1   Periodically, and certainly well in advance of the MOT Test, all brakes pipes, connections and unions should be completely and carefully examined.

2   Examine first all the unions for signs of leaks. Then look at the flexible hoses for signs of fraying and chafing (as well as for leaks) (photo). This is only a preliminary inspection of the flexible hoses, as exterior condition does not necessarily indicate interior condition which will be considered later.

3   The steel pipes must be examined equally carefully. They must be thoroughly cleaned and examined for signs of dents or other percussive damage, rust and corrosion. Rust and corrosion should be scraped off, and, if the depth of pitting in the pipes is significant, they will require renewal. This is most likely in those areas underneath the chassis and along the rear suspension arms where the pipes are exposed to the full force of road and weather conditions.

4   If any section of pipe is to be removed, first take off the fluid reservoir cap, line it with a piece of polythene film to make it airtight and screw it back on. This will minimise the amount of fluid dripping out of the system when the pipes are removed.

5   Rigid pipe removal is usually quite straightforward. The unions at each end are undone and the pipe drawn out of the connection. The clips which may hold it to the car body are bent back and it is then removed. Underneath the car the exposed union can be particularly stubborn, defying the efforts of an open-ended spanner. As few people will have the special split ring spanner required, a self-gripping wrench is the only answer. If the pipe is being renewed, new unions will be provided. If not, then one will have to put up with the possibility of burring over the flats on the unions and of using a self-gripping wrench for refitting also.

6   Flexible hoses are always fitted to a rigid support bracket where they join a rigid pipe, the bracket being fixed to the chassis or rear suspension arm (photo). The rigid pipe unions must first be removed from the flexible union. Then the locknut securing the flexible pipe to the bracket must be unscrewed, releasing the end of the pipe from the bracket. As these connections are usually exposed they are, more often than not, rusted up and a penetrating fluid is virtually essential to aid

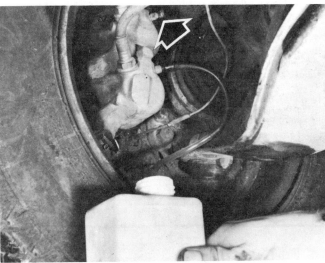

9.8A Using a one-man bleeder kit on the front brakes. Note second bleed nipple (arrowed) which must also be bled

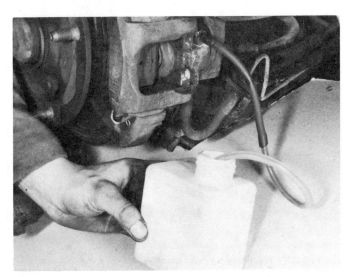

9.8B Rear brake caliper bleeding (one nipple per caliper)

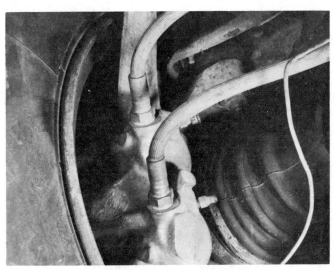

10.2 Twin flexible hose connections to front brake caliper

10.6 Flexible hose support bracket and rigid pipe connections

removal. When undoing them, both halves must be supported as the bracket is not strong enough to support the torque required to undo the nut and can be snapped off easily.

7 Once the flexible hose is removed, examine the internal bore. If clear of fluid it should be possible to see through it. Any specks of rubber which come out, or signs of restriction in the bore, mean that the inner lining is breaking up and the hose must be renewed.

8 Rigid pipes which need renewing can usually be purchased at your local garage where they have the pipe, unions and special tools to make them up. All that they need to know is the pipe length required and the type of flare used at the ends of the pipe. These may be different at each end of the same pipe. If possible, it is a good idea to take the old pipe along as a pattern.

9 Refitting of pipes is a straightforward reversal of the removal procedure. It is best to get all the sets (bends) made prior to fitting. Also, any acute bends should be put in by the garage on a bending machine otherwise there is the possibility of kinking them, and

restricting the bore area and thus, fluid flow.

10 With the pipes refitted, remove the polythene from the reservoir cap and bleed the system as described in the previous Section.

11 Rigid brake pipes made of copper or copper alloy may be available from specialist suppliers. Such pipes are obviously immune from rusting, but they may be prone to failure through vibration. Extract support clips may be required; follow the manufacturer's instructions carefully.

11 Brake pressure limiter valve – inspection, adjustment, removal and refitting

1 Correct adjustment of the brake pressure limiter valve is essential for safe and efficient braking. Before checking can be carried out, the vehicle must be placed on a level surface with a full fuel tank and a person sitting in the driver's seat.

2 A pressure gauge is essential (400 – 600 lbf/in^2 range) and it must incorporate a bleed valve.

3 Connect the pressure gauge in place of one of the rear brake caliper bleed nipples.

4 Bleed the system through the gauge bleed valve in a manner similar to that described previously, but it will not be necessary to bleed other than from the gauge nipple.

5 Apply the footbrake pedal several times in succession and check the reading on the pressure gauge. Where necessary, loosen the nut and adjust the position of the link until the pressure reading on subsequent pedal applications lies within the range specified.

6 On R 1278 models the brake limiter differs as shown in Fig. 9.17. If adjustment is necessary, loosen the locknut and rotate the adjuster rod accordingly to set the pressure. Check the cut-off pressure from a caliper at the rear.

7 On all models remove the gauge, refit the original bleed nipple, bleed the brakes (Section 9), and top up the master cylinder reservoir.

8 The brake pressure limiter valve cannot be serviced. In the event of failure or leakage, renew the complete unit.

9 To remove the limiter valve, detach the respective pipeline connections (photos) and plug them to prevent leakage and the ingress of dirt.

10 Unscrew and remove the retaining bracket bolts and detach the limiter valve.

11 Refit in the reverse order, bleed the system and then adjust the cut-off pressure as described above.

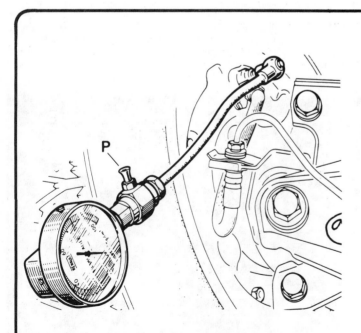

Fig. 9.16 Method of checking the brake limiter valve pressure – 'P' is the gauge unit bleed nipple (Sec 11)

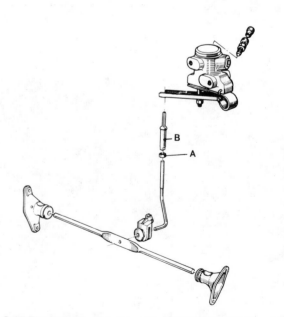

Fig. 9.17 The brake limiter assembly – R1278 models (Sec 11)

A   Locknut   B   Adjuster rod

11.9A The limiter valve lower linkage layout (R1273 and R1275 models)

11.9B Limiter valve location showing respective hydraulic pipes (R1273 and R1275 models shown)

12 Master cylinder – removal and refitting

1   Renault specify that the brake master cylinder cannot be repaired, and therfore if this unit is known to have failed it must be renewed.
2   To remove the master cylinder, first fit a suitable clamp over the feed pipe from the brake master cylinder to the clutch master cylinder, but take care not to damage the pipe.
3   Ideally, before removal of the master cylinder, the brake fluid should be drained from the reservoir. The fluid may be syphoned out or one of the unions disconnected and the foot brake pedal depressed until the fluid is expelled from the master cylinder and the reservoir.
4   Disconnect all the fluid pipe unions from the master cylinder, shown in Fig. 9.18.
5   Detach the pressure drop indicator switch wire.
6   Remove the fluid reservoir from the cylinder, but leave the feed pipe to the clutch master cylinder attached.
7   Unscrew and remove the master cylinder-to-servo unit retaining bolts and remove the master cylinder.
8   Plug the ends of the respective brake lines to prevent leakage and the ingress of dirt.
9   To refit the master cylinder, engage the operating rod with the piston assembly, and bolt the master cylinder into its location. If necessary, make the adjustments in paragraphs 11 to 14 inclusive, before fitting the cylinder.
10   Reconnect the unions and the pressure drop indicator wire, refill the reservoir and bleed the brake hydraulic system as described in Section 9. If necessary, also bleed the clutch circuit (having removed the clamp). To do this refer to Chapter 5, Section 8.
11   Check the master cylinder operating clearance. Adjustment may be necessary at one of two places – at the pushrod and master cylinder endface, or at the operating rod-to-pedal clevis at the rear of the servo unit.
12   The adjustment points are shown in Fig. 9.19. The respective clearances for your model are given in the Specifications.

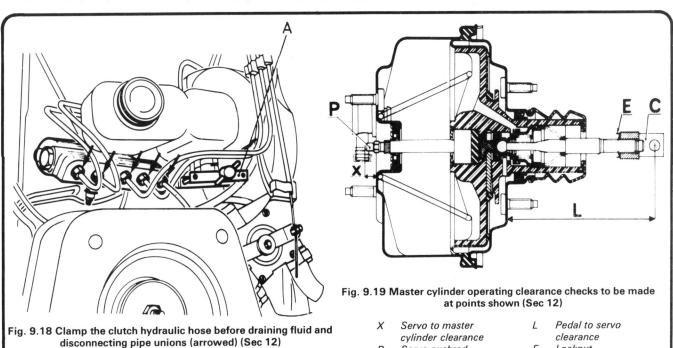

Fig. 9.18 Clamp the clutch hydraulic hose before draining fluid and disconnecting pipe unions (arrowed) (Sec 12)

A   Clamp

Fig. 9.19 Master cylinder operating clearance checks to be made at points shown (Sec 12)

X	Servo to master cylinder clearance	L	Pedal to servo clearance
P	Servo pushrod	E	Locknut
		C	Clevis

13 To adjust clearance X, turn pushrod nut P accordingly.
14 To adjust clearance L, disconnect the brake pedal (Section 18), unscrew the clevis locknut E and turn the clevis C in the desired direction, then retighten the locknut to secure.

13 Pressure drop indicator – description

1 This component is fitted integrally with the master cylinder to indicate any difference in hydraulic pressure between the two independent braking circuits.
2 A sectional view of a typical pressure drop indicator is shown in Fig. 9.20.
3 The operating principle is that where the two circuit hydraulic pressures are equal, then the pistons (3) are in balance. Any variation in pressure between one circuit and the other will cause the pistons to move and complete an electrical circuit to give a warning through an indicator lamp on the facia panel.
4 The warning lamp will illuminate for one of the following reasons; system requires bleeding, leakage (externally) from some part of the hydraulic system, operating fault within the tandem master cylinder.
5 Fault diagnosis should be made and the fault rectified immediately.
6 On certain models, when the failure is in the front brake circuit an additional circuit to the rear brakes becomes operational. This additional circuit is only used when there has been a failure in the front brake circuit, whereby the hydraulic pistons will move to the rear of the cylinder (direction of arrow in Fig. 9.20) and the additional circuit to the rear brakes becomes operational. Whilst the additional circuit is operational, the brake limiter becomes non-operational, thereby allowing additional pressure to the rear brakes.

then normal hydraulic braking will still be available by foot pressure, though greater effort will be required.
2 Leaks in, or failure of, the servo unit may be detected by a sudden increase in the brake pedal pressure required to restart or stop the vehicle. Uneven running or stalling of the engine may also indicate leaks in the servo system.
3 If problems do occur, check that the vacuum hose and connection from the manifold is in good condition and secure (including the one-way valve, see Fig. 9.21).
4 If the problem appears to be in the servo unit, there is very little you can do apart from exchanging it for a new one.
5 It might, however, be an idea to have your Renault dealer give the unit a vacuum pressure check to be absolutely sure before removing it.
6 The only servicing the servo unit requires is to renew the air filter periodically. To do this, disconnect the brake pedal, unscrew the locknut on the operating rod clevis (near the pedal) and then remove the clevis (fig. 9.22).
7 Free the rubber dust boot from the rear of the unit, prise the filter retaining spring clip free and hook out the filter.
8 Insert the new filter and retain with spring clip. Check the operating clearance as described in Section 12, then reconnect the brake pedal.
9 To change the one-way valve, detach the vacuum inlet pipe to the servo unit, then pull whilst turning the one-way valve simultaneously and remove it. If in poor condition or known to be defective, renew it. Refit in the reverse procedure to removal.
10 To remove the servo unit, disconnect the battery earth lead, then remove the master cylinder unit as described in Section 12.

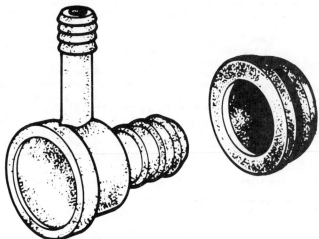

Fig. 9.21 The servo one-way valve (Sec 15)

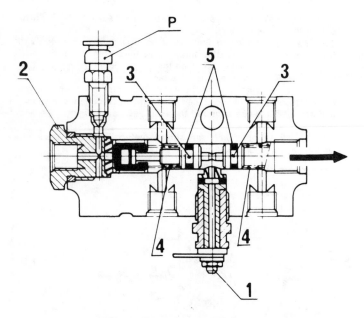

Fig. 9.20 The pressure drop indicator (Sec 13)

1	Terminal	4	Springs
2	End plug	5	Seals
3	Pistons	P	Bleed nipple

14 Pressure drop indicator – removal and refitting

The pressure drop indicator is integral with the master cylinder, and no attempt should be made to separate the two. In the event of malfunction, renewal is the only solution.

15 Brake servo unit – servicing, removal and refitting

1 The brake servo unit operates from vacuum supplied from the engine manifold. It is emphasised that in the event of the unit failing

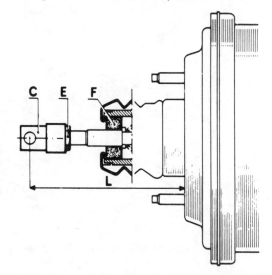

Fig. 9.22 The servo unit filter location (F) showing clevis (C) and locknut (E) – 'L' is operating clearance (Sec 15)

11 Loosen the vacuum hose clip at the servo unit end and detach the hose.
12 Working inside the vehicle, extract the brake pedal-to-operating rod clevis pin which is retained by a split pin.
13 The servo unit retaining nuts to the bulkhead can now be unscrewed, enabling the servo unit to be removed.
14 As mentioned earlier, the servo cannot be repaired or adjusted in any way and must therefore be renewed if defective.
15 Refit in the reverse order, but ensure that the operating clearance is correct and in accordance with Section 12.

16 Handbrake – adjustment

1 Adjustment of the handbrake should not be required unless the cable has stretched or components of the rear braking assembly have been dismantled or reassembled.
2 Jack up the rear of the vehicle and release the handbrake fully. Additionally support with axle stands. Chock the front wheels.
3 Loosen the nuts and turn the adjuster sleeve to give a minimum travel of 12 notches on the handbrake lever (photo), locking the rear wheels when fully applied. Fully release the handbrake and check that the rear wheels are free to rotate. A slight drag is permissible where the pads rub very slightly against the discs initially after application of the brakes.
4 When adjustment is satisfactory, retighten the locknuts to maintain the setting.

17 Handbrake mechanism – removal and refitting

Handbrake lever
1 With the vehicle parked on level ground, place it in gear (or 'P' – automatic transmission) and put chocks under the wheels.

16.3 Handbrake primary rod adjuster and locking nut

2 From inside the car, release the handbrake and remove any trim from the base of the handbrake (as applicable). Unscrew and remove the two handbrake lever retaining bolts.
3 Lift the lever and detach the primary rod clevis pin to release it.
4 Refitting is a reversal of the removal procedure.

Primary rod
5 Raise and support the vehicle with axle stands and chock the wheels.

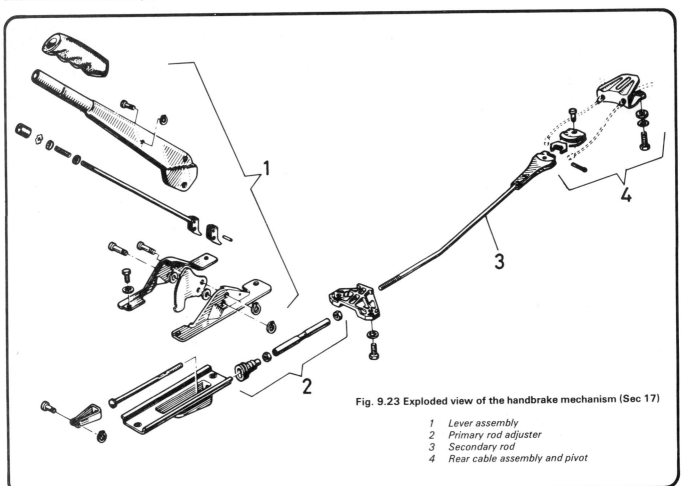

Fig. 9.23 Exploded view of the handbrake mechanism (Sec 17)

1   Lever assembly
2   Primary rod adjuster
3   Secondary rod
4   Rear cable assembly and pivot

6   Working underneath, unscrew the primary rod adjuster nuts and detach the sleeve.
7   Remove the handbrake lever (see above) and extract the clevis pin to release the rod.
8   Refitting is a reversal of the removal sequence but if necessary, adjust the handbrake as given in the previous Section.

Rear linkage
9   Unscrew the adjuster nuts and detach the sleeve. Extract the swivel lever pivot pin which is retained by a split pin.
10   Refit in the reverse order and adjust the handbrake as necessary.

Rear cable renewal
11   Working underneath, extract the swivel lever hinge pin and withdraw the pin (photo).
12   Release the cable from its holder and tap the sleeve from its location.
13   Detach the cable at the caliper ends and remove it.
14   Refitting is a reversal of the removal procedure. Use new split pins; grease the swivel pin. On completion, press the brake pedal a few times to take up the adjustment. If necessary, readjust the handbrake as given in Section 16.

17.11 The handbrake cable pivot

18 Brake and clutch pedals – removal and refitting

1   Remove the spring clip and free the spring from the clutch pedal.
2   Remove the split pin and clevis pin from the brake master cylinder operating rod to pedal connection.
3   Withdraw the cltuch pedal from the pedal cross-shaft, then use a soft drift to remove the cross-shaft to the right sufficiently far so that the brake pedal can be removed.
4   Refitting is a reversal of removal, but smear the cross-shaft with grease and adjust the clutch and brake pedal clearances if necessary as described in Chapter 5 and Section 12 of this Chapter respectively.

19 Brake light switch – general

1   The brake light switch is mechanically rather than hydraulically operated. It is attached to the steering column support bracket just above the brake pedal and is affixed by a nut. As the pedal is depressed, the contacts close in the brake light switch.
2   If the switch fails, it must be renewed. Disconnect the feed wires and withdraw the unit. Refitting is a simple reversal of this procedure.

20 Disc pad wear warning system – general

1   Depending on operating territory and production date, some models are equipped with a disc pad wear warning system. A warning light illuminates when the brakes are applied if the front pads are in need of attention.
2   The system operates by means of an electrical contact on each inner front brake pad. When either pad is worn to the point where the contact touches the disc during braking, the circuit is completed and the warning light illuminates.
3   The existence of this system should not be regarded as an excuse to neglect regular visual inspection of the front brake pads. If wear is allowed to proceed to the point where the warning light comes on, the pads must be inspected without delay.
4   To check the operation of the system, earth each of the pad wear sensor wires in turn whilst an assistant observes the warning light (ignition on). The light should illuminate when either wire is earthed.
5   Periodically check the system wires for security and good condition.

21 Fault diagnosis – braking system

Symptom	Reason(s)
Pedal travels a long way before the brakes operate	Leak in one hydraulic circuit Disc pads excessively worn
Stopping ability poor, even though pedal pressure is firm	Pads or discs badly worn or scored One or more caliper pistons seized Brake pads contaminated with oil Wrong type of pads fitted (too hard) Brake pads incorrectly assembled Servo unit not functioning
Car veers to one side when brakes are applied	Brake pads on one side are contaminated with oil Hydraulic pistons in calipers are partially or wholly seized on one side A mixture of pad materials used between sides Unequal wear between sides caused by partially seized hydraulic pistons in brake calipers Tyre pressures uneven
Pedal feels spongy when the brakes are applied	Air is present in the hydraulic system Master cylinder brake caliper mounting bolts loose

Symptom	Reason(s)
Pedal travels right down with little or no resistance and brakes are virtually non-operative	Leak in hydraulic system resulting in lack of pressure for operation of wheel cylinders If no signs of leakage are apparent the master cylinder internal seals are failing to sustain pressure
Binding, juddering, overheating	One, or a combination of causes given in the foregoing sections Reservoir air vent blocked
Rear wheels lock in heavy braking	Pressure regulator valve defective or maladjusted

Chapter 10 Electrical system, heating and air conditioning

Contents

Specifications

System type .... 12 volt, negative earth

Battery
Type .... Lead acid
Capacity (typical) .... 50 Ah

Alternator
Make and type:
    Ducellier 7580
    Paris-Rhone .... A13 R 166, 167, 189 or 212
    SEV-Marchal 712 304 12, 712 307 12, 712 311 12, 712 314 12, 716 504 12
Maximum output .... 52 amps at 14 volts and 8000 alternator rpm
Regulated voltage .... 13.5 to 15.0 volts

Starter motor
Type .... Pre-engaged
Maker .... Paris-Rhone
Maker's designation .... D8E 132 or D10E 59

Fuses (typical)

Fuse No	Circuit protected	Rating (amps)
1	Flasher unit/stop-light switch	8
2	LH side and tail lights	5
3	LH headlight dipped beam	5
4	RH side and tail lights	5
5	RH headlight dipped beam	5
6	Interior lights/cigar lighter/clock/load area light	8
7	LH headlight main beam	5
8	Windscreen wiper and washer	8
9	RH headlight main beam	5
10	Spare	–
11	LH front door window winder	16
12	Spare	–
13	RH front door window winder	16
14	Automatic transmission	5
15	Reversing lights/heated rear window	16
16	Instrument panel/wiper time delay	5
17	Heater fan motor/air conditioning (if fitted)	16
18	Spare	–

1 General description

The electrical system is of 12 volt type and comprises a battery (negative earth), an alternator and voltage regulator to keep the battery charged and supply the electrical requirements of the vehicle.

The alternator is driven by a V-belt from the crankshaft pulley. The same belt drives the coolant pump.

Electrical ancillary components are of conventional type and include a starter motor, distributor and ignition accessories and all necessary wiring harness.

On specified models, the sunroof, the windows, the screen washers and the heated rear window are all electrically operated and are described in later Sections of this Chapter.

2 Battery – removal and refitting

1   The battery is positioned within the engine compartment on a tray directly in front of the bulkhead.
2   Disconnect the earthed negative lead and then the positive lead by slackening the retaining nuts and bolts, or by unscrewing the retaining screws if these are fitted.
3   Remove the battery clamp and carefully lift the battery off its tray. Hold the battery vertical to ensure that no electrolyte is spilled.
4   Refitting is a direct reversal of this procedure. Refit the positive lead and the earth (negative) lead, smearing the terminals with petroleum jelly to prevent corrosion. NEVER use an ordinary grease as applied to other parts of the car.

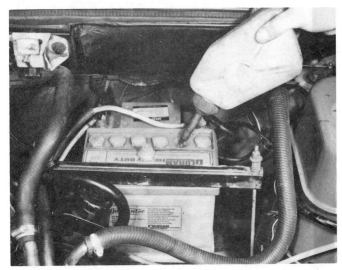

3.2 Topping up the battery electrolyte level

3 Battery – maintenance and inspection

1   The modern battery seldom requires topping up but nevertheless the electrolyte level should be inspected weekly as a means of providing the first indication that the alternator is overcharging or that the battery casing has developed a leak.
2   When topping up is required, use only distilled water or melted ice from a refrigerator (frosting not ice cubes) (photo).
3   Acid should never by required if the battery has been correctly filled from new, unless spillage has occurred.
4   Inspect the batttery terminals and mounting tray for corrosion. This is the white fluffy deposit which grows at these areas. If evident, clean it away and neutralise it with ammonia or baking soda. Apply petroleum jelly to the terminals and paint the battery tray with anti-corrosive paint.
5   An indication of the state of charge of a battery can be obtained by checking the electrolyte in each cell using a hydrometer. The specific gravity of the electrolyte for fully charged and fully discharged conditions at the electrolyte temperature indicated, is listed below.

Fully discharged	Electrolyte temperature	Fully charged
1.098	38°C (100°F)	1.268
1.102	32°C (90°F)	1.272
1.106	27°C (80°F)	1.276
1.110	21°C (70°F)	1.280
1.114	16°C (60°F)	1.284
1.118	10°C (50°F)	1.288
1.122	4°C (40°F)	1.292
1.126	-1.5°C (30°F)	1.296

6   There should be very little variation in the readings between the different cells, but if a difference is found in excess of 0.025 then it will probably be due to an internal fault indicating impending battery failure. This assumes that electrolyte has not been spilled at some time and the deficiency made up with water only.
7   Keep the top surface of the battery casing dry.

4 Battery – charging

1   With normal motoring, the battery should be kept in a good state of charge by the alternator and never need charging from a mains charger.
2   However, as the battery ages, it may not be able to hold its charge and some supplementary charging may be needed. Before connecting the charger, disconnect the battery terminals or better still, remove the battery from the vehicle.
3   Specially rapid 'boost' charges which are claimed to restore the power of the battery in 1 to 2 hours are most harmful as they can cause serious damage to the battery plates by overheating.
4   Note the precautions to be observed in order to prevent damage to the alternator – these are listed in Section 5.

5   Alternator – description and precautions

The alternator generates alternating current (AC) which is rectified by diodes to DC and is the current needed for battery storage.

The regulator is a transistorized unit which is permanently sealed and requires no attention. It will last indefinitely provided no mistakes are made in wiring connections.

Apart from the renewal of the rotor slip ring brushes and rotor shaft bearings, there are no other parts which need periodic inspection. All other items are sealed assemblies and must be renewed if indications are that they are faulty.

If there are indications that the charging system is malfunctioning in any way, care must be taken to diagnose faults properly, otherwise damage of a serious and expensive nature may occur to parts which are in fact quite serviceable. Fault diagnosis generally requires sophisticated test equipment, and should be entrusted to an auto-electrician.

The following basic requirements must be observed at all times, therefore, if damage is to be prevented:

1   ALL alternator systems use a NEGATIVE earth. Even the simple mistake of connecting a battery the wrong way round could burn out the alternator diodes in a few seconds.

2   Before disconnecting any wires in the system the engine and ignition circuits should be switched off. This will minimise accidental short-circuits.

3   The alternator must NEVER be run with the output wire disconnected.

4   Always disconnect the battery from the car's electrical system if an outside charging source is being used.

5   Do not use test wire connections that could move accidentally and short-circuit against nearby terminals. Short-circuits will not blow fuses – they will blow diodes or transistors.

6   Always disconnect the battery cables and alternator output wires before any electric welding work is done on the car body.

7   Never lever on the alternator body when adjusting the belt drive. The casing is easily fractured.

8   No lubrication is required as the bearings are grease sealed.

9   The drivebelt tension must be maintained at all times. The adjustment procedure is given in Section 9 of Chapter 2.

6   Alternator – removal and refitting

1   Disconnect the battery earth cable from its terminal.

2   Unscrew and remove the alternator mounting bolt and adjuster strap bolt (photo).

3   Detach the drivebelt from the alternator pulley and remove the alternator from its mounting position. If the alternator is to be removed completely, take a note of the respective cables and their locations and detach them from their connecting points on the rear face of the alternator, before lifting it clear. If the alternator is being removed solely to gain access to the air conditioning compressor or other associated fittings, it can be left attached to the wiring and laid aside in the nearside wing panel recess.

4   Refit in the reverse order to removal, but do not fully retighten the retaining bolts until after the drivebelt tension has been adjusted. This is described in Chapter 2, Section 9.

5   Ensure that the wiring connections are secure before reattaching the battery earth lead (photo).

7   Alternator diode carrier and brush assembly – removal and refitting

Diode carrier

1   Remove the rear cover from the alternator, then on the Paris-Rhone model, undo the diode carrier retaining nuts and strut and withdraw the diode carrier.

2   On the Ducellier alternator you will have to carefully unsolder the three diode carrier wires (noting which is which) before the diode carrier can be withdrawn. **Do not** dismantle the diode bridge under any circumstances!

3   On the SEV-Marchal model 716 504 12 alternator, the diode carrier can be removed by unclipping the plastic cover, removing the three carrier retaining nuts and then unsoldering the winding wires (noting connections).

4   On other SEV alternators, remove the stator and the four nuts with star washers and insulating washers retaining the carrier then separate the stator and diode carrier from the rear bearing.

5   If it is known to be defective, renew the diode carrier complete and reassemble in the reverse order to removal. Check that the wires are routed correctly and not touching the rotor.

Brushes

6   The location of the brushes on each type of alternator is shown in the accompanying diagrams (Figs. 10.5, 10.6 and 10.7). It can be seen that they are retained in position by setscrews or bolts, and can be easily removed for checking and possible replacement if they are well worn down (photo).

7   Refit in the reverse order to removal.

8   Exploded views of the alternator types used are shown in Figs. 10.8, 10.9 and 10.10.

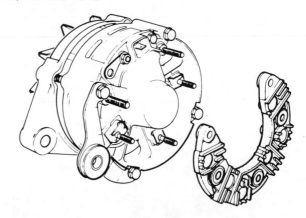

Fig. 10.1 The diode carrier – Paris-Rhone alternator (Sec 7)

6.2 The alternator mounting/adjustment strap

6.5 Alternator wiring connections

7.6 Checking the brushes on the SEV-Marchal alternator

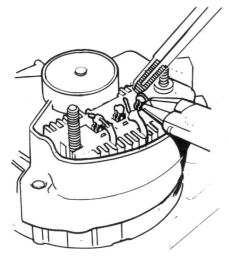

Fig. 10.2 Unsolder the three diode wires –
Ducellier alternator (Sec 7)

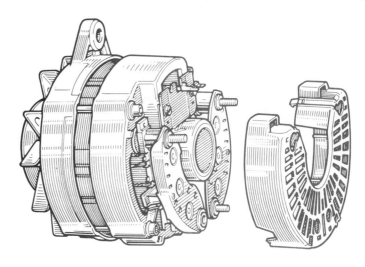

Fig. 10.3 One type of SEV alternator (Sec 7)

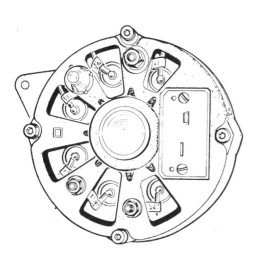

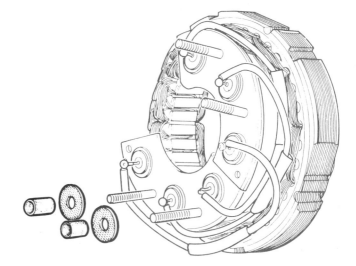

Fig. 10.4 An alternative SEV alternator fitted to some models (Sec 7)

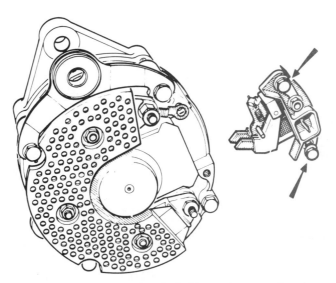

Fig. 10.5 Brush holder unit – Paris-Rhone alternator. Securing
screws arrowed (Sec 7)

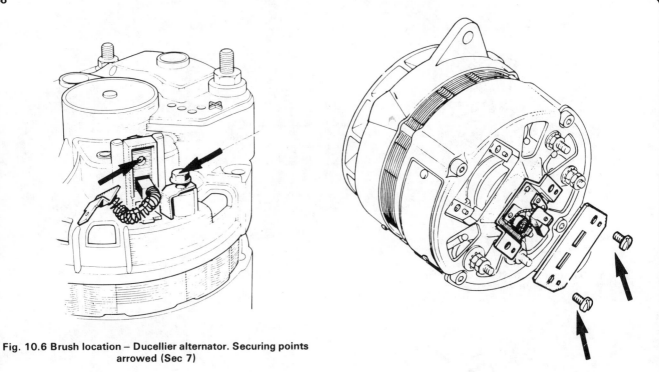

Fig. 10.6 Brush location – Ducellier alternator. Securing points
arrowed (Sec 7)

Fig. 10.7 Brush holder location – SEV alternator. Securing screws
arrowed (Sec 7)

Fig. 10.8 Exploded view of the Paris-Rhone alternator (Sec 7)

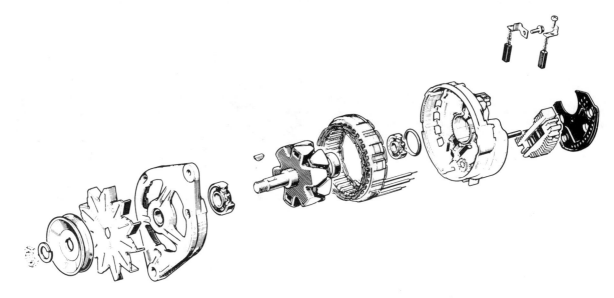

Fig. 10.9 Exploded view of the Ducellier alternator (Sec 7)

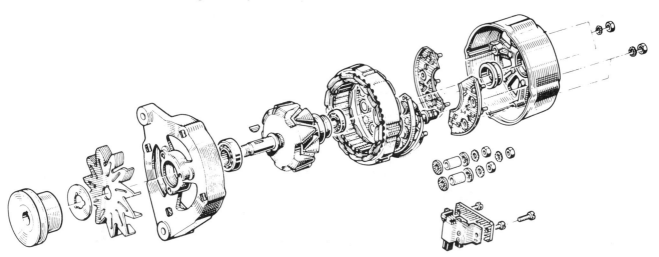

Fig. 10.10 Exploded view of the SEV alternator (Sec 7)

8 Starter motor – description and testing

1   A pre-engaged type starter motor is fitted to all models. Refer to Fig. 10.11 for the starter circuit diagram.

2   The starter motor solenoid is actuated through movement of the key in the ignition/starter switch.

3   Access to the starter motor is not good. For general inspection you will need to raise and support the car at the front and remove the engine undertray. Make some preliminary checks first to ensure that the problem is not something basic.

4   Check the state of charge of the battery and the security of the bad connections to it.

5   In the case of automatic vehicles, check that the gear selection lever is in P or N. If so and the starter does not operate, check that the lever and cable adjustment is correct (see Chapter 7).

6   If the above mentioned items are in order then you will need to check the security of the starter motor and solenoid electrical leads. As previously mentioned, access is from underneath, so raise and support the vehicle at the front with safety stands (or run onto ramps if available) and remove the engine undertray. You will need a lead light when under the vehicle, and as the starter motor is fairly close to the nearside exhaust pipe, allow the engine to cool off before attempting any inspection or removal procedures.

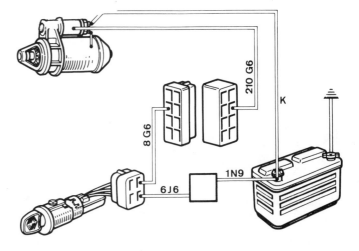

Fig. 10.11 Starter motor circuit diagram (Sec 8)

7   As the starter motor is of the pre-engaged type, any failure of the drivegear will mean that the pinion and screwed armature shaft must be cleaned as described in Section 10 and any defective parts renewed.
8   Disconnect the lead from the distributor LT terminal in order to prevent the engine from firing, and then connect a 0-20V voltmeter between the main starter terminal and earth. Operate the starter switch to crank the engine and note the voltmeter reading. A minimum reading of 7 volts indicates satisfactory cable and switch connections. Very slow cranking at this voltage suggests a fault in the starter motor.
9   To remove the starter motor, proceed as given in the following Section.

9   Starter motor – removal and refitting

1   Disconnect the battery earth lead from its terminal.
2   Raise and support the car at the front end and remove the engine undertray.
3   Position a container under the oil filter and then remove it, taking care not to get an armful of oil, especially if it's still hot! You may need a strap wrench to remove the filter (see Chapter 1).
4   Clean the respective wires to the starter motor, note their positions and then disconnect them (photo).
5   Remove the three starter motor retaining bolts, then tilt and withdraw the starter motor.
6   Refitting is a reversal of the removal procedure, but take care when engaging the starter drive teeth with the flywheel ring gear. If the teeth are worn, chipped or otherwise defective, the pinion and/or the ring gear must be renewed.
7   Refit the oil filter as given in Chapter 1, then lower the car so that it is standing level. Top up the engine oil level and run the engine to check for any signs of leaks from around the oil filter, then refit the engine undertray.

10   Starter motor – dismantling and reassembly

1   Such is the inherent reliability and strength of the starter motor fitted that it is very unlikely that a motor will ever need dismantling

9.4 Starter motor wiring connections

until it is totally worn out and in need of renewal. It is not a task for the home mechanic. Although the dismantling is reasonably easy to undertake, the reassembly and adjustment before refitting is beyond his scope because of the need of specialist equipment. It would under all circumstances be realistic for the work to be undertaken by a specialist auto-electrician. It is possible to renew solenoids and brushes on starter motors.
2   The starter motor components are shown in Fig. 10.12.
3   First remove the solenoid unit, by unscrewing the holding nuts and detaching the solenoid plunger from the operating lever. Mark the relative positions of the solenoid body to pinion housing (photo).
4   Unscrew and remove the end cover retaining nuts and remove the cover, through-bolts and brush holder plate. The brushes will have to be extracted from their holders to remove the end plate completely, therefore hook back each brush retaining spring carefully in turn and

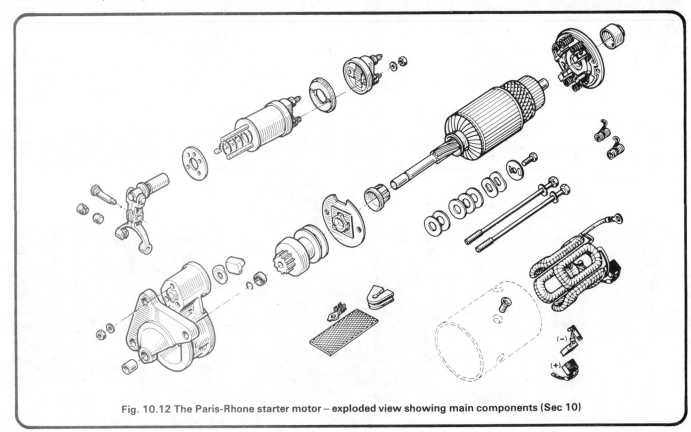
Fig. 10.12 The Paris-Rhone starter motor – exploded view showing main components (Sec 10)

withdraw the brushes. Note the plate to housing location and make an alignment mark to ensure correct reassembly.

Note: *The through-bolts may be tight to remove due to being treated with a thread-locking compound when assembled.*

5   The pinion housing and armature arm can now be withdrawn from the main body.

6   To dismantle and inspect the pinion/starter gear unit the special lever pivot pin must be tapped out.

7   To withdraw the pinion from the armature, tap back the special collar washer and extract the snap-ring from the groove in the shaft. The pinion assembly can then be slid from the shaft.

8   With the starter motor dismantled the various components can be cleaned and inspected for general wear and/or signs of damage. The principal components likely to need attention will be the brushes, the solenoid or possibly the drive pinion unit.

9   The brushes can be removed by unsoldering the connecting wires from the holder and the field coil unit. Take care not to damage the latter during removal and refitting of the brushes.

10 If the starter motor has shown a tendency to jam or a possible reluctance to disengage then the starter pinion is almost certainly the culprit. Dirt around the pinion and shaft could cause this. When cleaned, check that the pinion can move freely along the shaft. If the pinion tends to bind or is defective in any way renew it.

11 Undercut the separators of the commutator using an old hacksaw blade as shown (photo), to a depth of about 0.5 to 0.8 mm (0.02 to 0.03 in). The commutator may be further surface cleaned using a strip of very fine glass paper. **Do not** use emery cloth for this purpose as the carborundum particles will become embedded in the copper surfaces.

12 Testing of the armature is best left to an auto-electrician, but if an ohmmeter is available it can be done by placing one probe on the armature shaft and the other on each of the commutator segments in turn. If there is a reading indicated at any time during the test, then the armature is defective and must be renewed.

13 The field coil can also be tested using an ohmmeter. Connect one probe to the field coil positive terminal and the other to the positive brush holder. If there is no indication of a reading then the field coil circuit has a break in it.

14 Connect one lead of the meter to the field coil positive lead and the other one to the yoke. If there is a low resistance then the field coil is earthed due to a breakdown in the insulation. If this proves to be the case the field coils must be renewed. As field coil renewal requires special tools and equipment it is a job that should be entrusted to your auto-electrician. In fact it will probable prove more economical and beneficial to exchange the starter motor for a reconditioned unit.

15 Reassembly of the rest of the starter motor is a direct reversal of the removal procedure, but note the following:

(a)   *The snap-ring and collar can be difficult to relocate. Use a valve compressor as shown (photo)*
(b)   *Reassemble the correct number of thrust washers (photo)*
(c)   *Check that the brushes slide freely in their holders*
(d)   *Lubricate the commutator shaft sparingly, using a medium grease*
(e)   *Do not forget to install the separator and washer (photo)*
(f)   *Realign the brush holder and body notches (photo)*
(g)   *Realign the marks made on dismantling when assembling the solenoid, and fit the coil spring and washer*

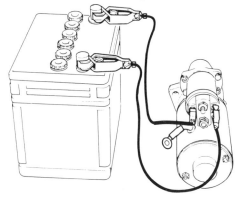

Fig. 10.13 Starter motor testing and drive pinion-to-stop clearance check method (Sec 10)

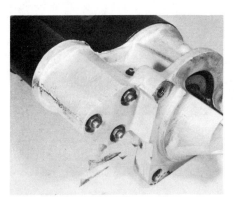

10.3 Solenoid retaining nuts

10.11 Method of undercutting the commutator segments using an old hacksaw blade shaped to suit

10.15A Using a valve spring compressor to assemble the snap-ring and collar

10.15B Relocate any thrust washers onto the shaft

10.15C Fit the separator and special washer as shown

10.15D Align the body and cover notches/markings on assembly

10.16 Drive pinion-to-stop clearance adjuster

11.2 Check the drive pinion condition

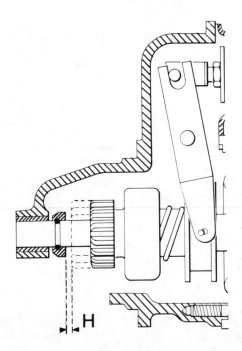

Fig. 10.14 Drive pinion-to-stop clearance (H) (Sec 10)

16 Before fitting the starter motor to the car, connect leads from a battery to the starter motor as shown (Fig. 10.13) and with the starter motor activated, check that the drive pinion-to-stop clearance is 0.059 in (1.5 mm), see Fig. 10.14. If adjustment is necessary, turn the actuating fork pivot pin accordingly (photo) to set at this clearance.

11 Starter motor drive pinion – inspection and repair

1 Persistent jamming or reluctance to disengage may mean that the starter pinion assembly needs attention. The starter motor should be removed first of all for inspection.
2 With the starter motor removed, thoroughly remove all grime and grease with a petrol soaked rag, taking care to stop any liquid running into the motor itself. If there is a lot of dirt this could be the trouble and all will now be well. The pinion should move freely in a spiral movement along the shaft against the light spring and return easily on being released. To do this the spiral splines should be completely clean

12.3 The fuses with cover removed

and free of oil. (Oil merely collects dust and grime and gums up the splines). The spring should be intact (photo).
3 Check the pinion-to-stop clearance as given in paragraph 16 of the previous Section, and adjust if necessary.
4 If the preceding cleaning and check does not remove the fault, the starter motor will need to be stripped down to its component parts and a further check made. This has been explained in the preceding Section.

12 Fuses and accessories plate – general

1 The various electrical circuits are fused. Therefore, should a fault occur within any particular circuit, check the fuse first. It may be that it is simply loose or badly connected, but if blown, a fault has occurred within the circuit concerned and must be found and rectified.
2 Check the circuit wiring and connections before assuming it is the component which is at fault.
3 The fuse box is located under the dashpanel and the cover simply unclips (photo).
4 Whenever a fuse is being renewed, refit one of the correct type and rating. If using one of the two spare fuses supplied in the fuse box, do not forget to obtain a replacement at the earliest opportunity.
5 Refer to the Specifications for typical fuse applications.

12.7A Remove the thumb screw to release fuse box

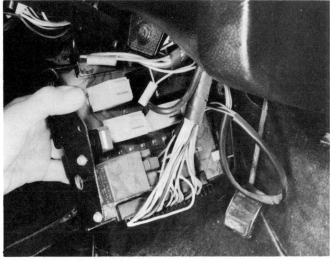

12.7B Accessories plate on rear face of fuse box

6   The accessories plate is located behind the fuse box. It retains the flasher unit, various circuit relays and components. Refer to Fig. 10.16 for component identification.

7   Accessibility to the rear of the fuse box is gained by removing the thumb screw and pulling the box away from the dashpanel lower face (photos).

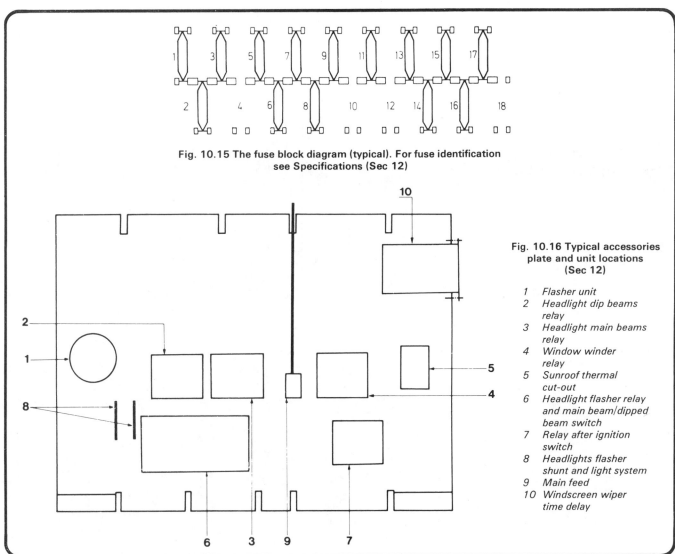

Fig. 10.15 The fuse block diagram (typical). For fuse identification see Specifications (Sec 12)

Fig. 10.16 Typical accessories plate and unit locations (Sec 12)

1   Flasher unit
2   Headlight dip beams relay
3   Headlight main beams relay
4   Window winder relay
5   Sunroof thermal cut-out
6   Headlight flasher relay and main beam/dipped beam switch
7   Relay after ignition switch
8   Headlights flasher shunt and light system
9   Main feed
10   Windscreen wiper time delay

13 Headlights and bulbs – adjustment, removal and refitting

Adjustment

1   Apart from the vertical beam adjustment control (from the knob on the steering column control within the car), the lights are individually adjustable for vertical and horizontal plane from within the engine compartment.

2   Adjustments other than from the column control should not normally be made unless in an emergency, as special optical beam setting equipment is needed for accurate adjustment.

3   Separate adjuster screws are provided in the rear of each unit (photo). When making adjustment, the vehicle must be unladen and the beam height adjuster knob must be rotated fully anti-clockwise.

4   Whenever an adjustment has been made, have it checked by your Renault dealer or local garage, using optical beam setting equipment for fine adjustments to be made.

Bulb renewal

5   The headlight bulbs can easily be removed for renewal. Raise and support the bonnet, then detach the connector from the rear of the headlight unit.

6   Unclip and pivot the bulb holder spring clips open, then extract the bulb (photo). Remove the seal washer.

7   Take care not to touch the bulb glass with your fingers. If the glass is accidentally touched, clean it at once with methylated spirit. The grease from your fingers will blacken the bulb and may cause early failure.

8   When fitting the new bulb, locate the seal washer and check that the boss on the holder ensures the correct fitting.

14 Headlight unit – removal and refitting

1   Disconnect the battery earth lead.

2   Remove the front grille panel, retained in position by two screws, and the headlight surround panel which is secured by two screws also, one at the top (photo) and one at the front.

3   Pulling the headlight unit forward, unclip the spring. To prevent the spring retracting through the headlight support frame, leave the pliers in position through the spring eye (photos).

4   Detach the wiring connectors and withdraw the headlight unit.

5   Refit in the reverse sequence to removal. Check and if necessary adjust the headlight beam alignment (see Section 13) on completion.

15 Headlight remote control adjuster unit – removal and refitting

1   The headlight remote control adjuster is hydraulic in operation working on a similar principle to that of the brake circuit. As the control knob is turned, hydraulic fluid displacement in the sealed circuit pushes the setting screw plate on the headlight.

2   If a fault occurs in the circuit, it must be renewed as a unit – it cannot be repaired. When removing or fitting a system never *dismantle the pipe sleeves shown in Fig. 10.17*. Remove the system as follows.

3   Pull the adjuster control knob free from its shaft.

4   Unscrew and detach the upper and lower steering column half casings.

5   Remove the retaining screws from the pedal assembly bracket.

6   Unclip and remove the adjuster knob shaft retaining clip and unscrew the shaft.

7   Detach the plunger unit and then unclip the control chamber(s).

8   Unclip the receiving chamber from its location at the headlight unit and carefully remove the circuit concerned.

9   Refitting is a reversal of the removal procedure. Check the headlight adjustment on completion.

16 Front combination light – bulb and unit removal and refitting

1   To check or renew the bulb, remove the two lens retaining screws and detach the lens (photo). The bulbs are removed in the normal way by pressing and twisting.

2   Refitting is a reversal of the removal procedure. Check the light operation on completion.

3   To remove the unit, unscrew the three retaining screws (two on

13.3 Headlight adjusters (arrowed)

13.6 Removing a headlight bulb

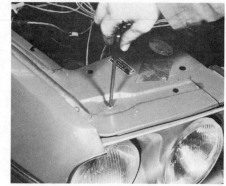
14.2 Headlight cover screw removal

14.3A Detach the spring ...

14.3B ... and retain it by leaving plier nose in coil eye

16.1 Remove lens to change front combination light bulbs

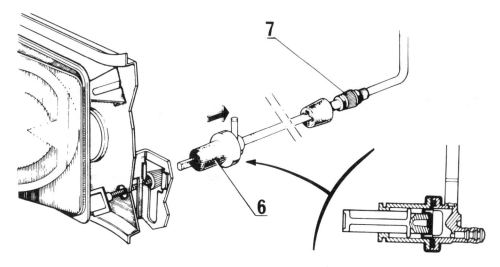

Fig. 10.17 Never detach the pipe sleeves (7) — receiving chamber (6) shown inset (Sec 15)

17.1A Remove rear combination light lens ...

17.1B ... for bulb replacement

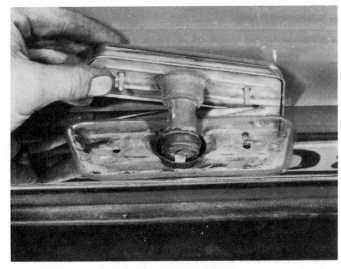

18.1 Withdraw the number plate from the bumper

top and one underneath the main body) and withdraw it. Detach the wires.

4   Refitting is a reversal of the removal procedure.

17 Rear combination light – bulb and unit removal and refitting

1   Unscrew and remove the five lens retaining screws and detach the lens. Press and twist the bulbs to remove (photos).
2   Refit the bulb(s) in the reverse manner.
3   To remove the light unit, disconnect the unit wires from their connectors in the corner of the luggage area.
4   Insert a suitable socket with extension through the rear panel apertures to remove the unit retaining nuts, then withdraw the unit.
5   Refitting is a direct reversal of the removal procedure, but check the operation of all rear lights on completion.

18 Number plate light – bulb renewal

1   Remove the two retaining nuts from the bumper underside and pull the light unit through its aperture in the bumper (photo).
2   Remove the cover/lens and then remove the bulb from its holder (photo).
3   Refit in the reverse order to removal, and check operation.

18.2 Remove the lens to renew the bulb

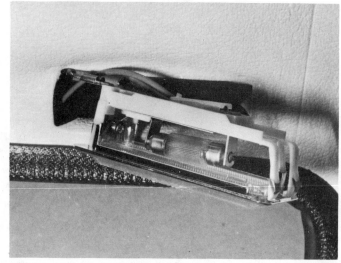

19.2 Interior light prised free from location for bulb renewal

19 Interior lights – bulb renewal, unit removal and refitting

1   Both the roof mounted interior lights simply clip into position and can be prised free using a small screwdriver. Take care not to damage the headlining however.
2   With the unit removed, the bulb can readily be renewed if necessary (photo).
3   To remove the unit completely, disconnect the battery earth cable, then detach the wires from the light unit concerned.
4   Refitting is the reverse of the removal procedure.

20 Horns – removal and refitting

The horns are fitted one below each headlight unit within the front panel. If either should fail, it cannot be repaired, but before renewing check the earthing, and also that it is receiving current when the horn button is pushed. If these are in order, unbolt and remove the horn(s) for renewal.

21 Column control switches – removal and refitting

1   All column controlled switches (windscreen wiper/washer switch, lights/dipper/horn switch. headlight beam adjuster and indicator switch) are located in a similar manner on the upper steering column. To remove any or all of these switches proceed as follows.
2   Disconnect the battery earth lead.
3   Unscrew and remove the steering column upper and lower covers,

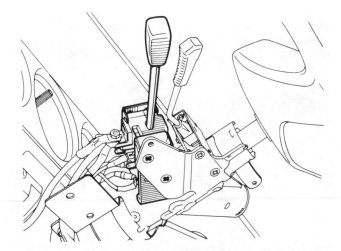

Fig. 10.18 Direction indicator switch and retaining screws (Sec 21)

the retaining screws being accessible from underneath. Note the respective screw lengths and positions for reassembly (photo).
4   Detach the switch wiring concerned at the main loom connector.
5   Remove the switch retaining screws and withdraw the switch. The switches are not repairable and if defective, must therefore be renewed (photos).
6   Refitting is a reversal of the removal procedure. Check the switch operation on completion.

21.3 Removing the steering column lower cover

21.5A Headlight adjuster unit (remote control) retaining screws

21.5B Windscreen wiper/washer switch retaining screws in column cover

22 Control panel switches and heater controls – removal and refitting

Switches

1   Pull the heater control knobs free from the controls. The knobs on our car were a tight fit, so a firm, straight pull was required (photo).
2   The panel can now be prised free to gain access to the switches and heater controls (photo).
3   The switches are easily removed by pushing them through the panel. Detach the earth wire to the battery first however, then detach the switch wire (photo).
4   The switches are not repairable and if defective must therefore be renewed.

Heater fan control knob

5   To change the heater fan control knob, detach the knob spindle clip as shown in Fig. 10.19. Then rotate the knob 180° to position the contact straps at right angles to the panel front (facing out). Remove the knob.
6   Refit in the reverse order.

23 Instrument panel and heater control panel – removal and refitting

1   Disconnect the battery earth cable.
2   Unscrew and remove the steering column lower cover, the retaining screws being accessible from underneath.
3   Unscrew the fuse box retaining thumb screw and partially remove the box.
4   Detach the speedometer cable by pulling it free.
5   Prise the blanking plugs free from each endface of the dash surround and, using a socket and extension, unscrew the panel retaining bolts (photo).

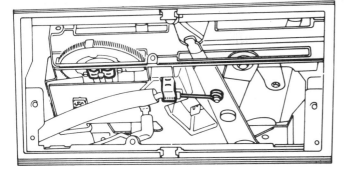

Fig. 10.19 Detach the heater fan knob spindle clip (Sec 22)

22.1 Remove the heater control knobs

22.2 Prise free the panel

22.3 Switch removal from panel

23.5 Remove the instrument panel side retaining bolts

6 Detach the three heater control knobs, pulling them free.
7 Detach the heater control panel.
8 Disconnect the junction blocks at the rear of the control panel.
9 Remove the three heater control panel retaining screws and the single central retaining bolt within the heater control panel aperture, position 'X' in Fig. 10.20.
10 Unbolt and remove the four central console panel retaining bolts and screws from the positions shown in Fig. 10.20. Withdraw the panel from the instrument panel.

11 Lift and support the dashpanel to gain access to the rear.
12 Detach the respective connectors at the rear of the instrument panel, noting their locations. Pivot the panel, allowing the dashboard to be removed.
13 A typical instrument panel layout is shown in the accompanying illustration. Little can be done in the way of overhaul, renewal being the normal procedure.
14 Refitting is a direct reversal of the removal provedure. Ensure that the electrical connections are refitted correctly and securely.

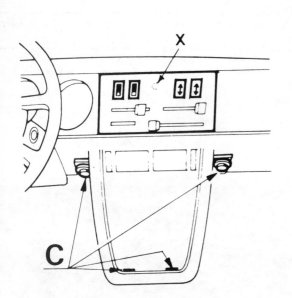

Fig. 10.20 Centre console retaining screws/bolt positions (C). X is panel centre retaining bolt (Sec 23)

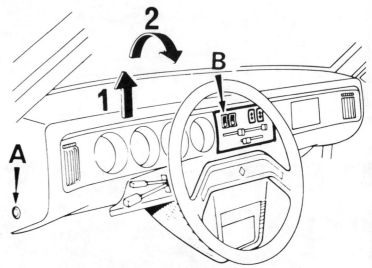

Fig. 10.21 Instrument panel removal. Lift (1) and tilt (2), having removed side bolts (A) and heater control panel (B) (Sec 23)

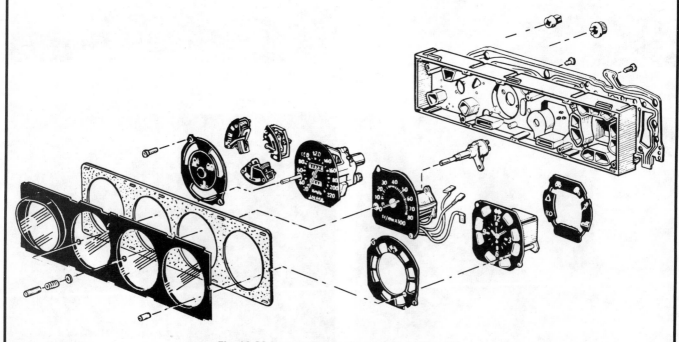

Fig. 10.22 Instrument panel components (Sec 23)

24 Central console, floor-mounted control panel, armrest and switches – removal and refitting

1   To remove the floor-mounted switches from the central control panel (forward of the gear lever), simply prise them free and lift them from the panel (photo). If disconnecting the switch wires, note their connections before detaching them. The battery earth lead must also be disconnected as a safety precaution.

2   To remove the panel, first disconnect the battery earth lead, then remove the radio console panel. This is secured by a bolt each side at the top and by two screws located under the base aperture covering (photo). If this panel is to be completely removed you will have to detach the radio wiring, the aerial lead connection and the cigarette lighter wiring connections.

3   Remove the gear selector lever knob. (Unscrew the knob on manual transmission models, or remove the retaining screw on automatic transmission models, as applicable).

4   To remove the selector cover on automatic transmission models, prise it free and lift it clear (photo).

5   Remove the two central floor panel retaining screws located under the carpet in the storage compartment directly beneath the handbrake.

6   Remove the two retaining screws from within the control unit and then lift the panel unit clear, disconnecting the switch wires (note their locations) (photos).

24.1 Floor panel switch removal

24.2 Radio console lower retaining screws removal

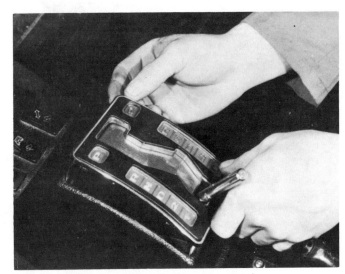

24.4 Automatic transmission selector cover removal

24.6A Remove the panel retaining screws from the automatic transmission selector unit

24.6B Lift the panel clear

7   To remove the armrest, remove its two retaining screws at the rear, then lift it forwards and upwards to release from the handbrake and seat belts. Detach the cigarette lighter lead from underneath (at the rear). To remove the lighter unit prise it free from the armrest (photos).

8   Refitting of the various panels and switches is a reversal of the removal procedure. Ensure that all electrical lead connections are correctly and securely made and check their respective operations on completion.

25 Radio and speakers – removal and refitting

1   Disconnect the battery earth lead.

Radio
2   Detach and remove the radio console panel as given in Section 24.

3   Pull the aerial free from its socket connection in the rear of the radio. Also detach the speaker wires and main feed wire.

4   Pull free the radio control knobs and remove the bezel panel, then withdraw the radio through its aperture in the console.

5   Refitting is a reversal of the removal procedure.

Speakers
6   If a mono speaker is fitted into the dashpanel, unscrew the three grille retaining nuts. Remove the speaker and grille cardboard and then separate the two. Disconnect the speaker wire.

7   If the car is fitted with dual speakers, one in each door panel at the front, prise free the speaker grille on the side concerned (photo), then

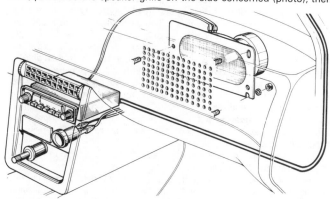

Fig. 10.23 Radio installation with mono speaker (Sec 25)

24.7A Armrest removal

24.7B Rear compartment cigarette lighter removal

25.7A Prise free the speaker grille (door mounting) ...

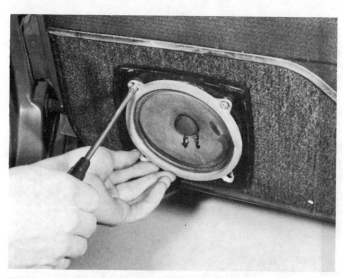

25.7B ... and remove the speaker retaining screws

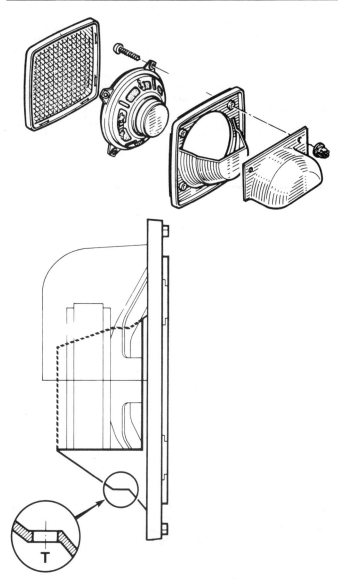

Fig. 10.24 Door mounted speaker components. Inset 'T' shows drain hole location in case (Sec 25)

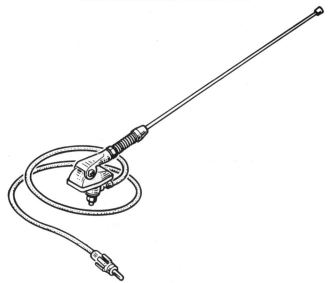

Fig. 10.25 Roof mounted aerial (Sec 26)

remove the speaker retaining screws (photo). Withdraw the speaker and detach its wires for full removal.

8   Refitting of the speakers, whichever type, is a reversal of the removal process.

26 Radio aerial – removal and refitting

Roof mounted aerial
1   A roof aerial is the standard fitting for use with car radios fitted to the Renault 30. This is preferred to prevent distortion at high speeds.
2   If a problem exists with the radio (poor reception or possibly none at all) and the aerial is suspected, first check the aerial lead connection at the back of the radio. Removal of the radio is covered in Section 25.
3   If the roof aerial is to be removed, it is generally recommended that it be entrusted to your Renault dealer, since it involves partial removal of the interior headlining. This is a specialised task requiring great care or damage can easily result.
4   A simple check can be made to see if the problem is caused by the aerial by taking the car to a good reception area and connecting up an alternative aerial such as that fitted to a door window. If the aerial is proved to be working satisfactorily, check the radio, its speakers and the suppressors in the system.
5   Most radios are fitted with a fine tuner adjustment screw. This should also be checked for proper adjustment before assuming that the aerial is at fault.

Wing mounted aerial
6   Refer to the remarks above if you wish to check the aerial.
7   Disconnect the aerial lead from the radio.
8   From under the front wing, undo and remove the retaining nut. Carefully ease the aerial lead through the body and lift the aerial clear, together with its mounting cups.
9   Refitting is the reversal of the removal process. Ensure that the aerial is securely mounted and properly earthed.

27 Radio suppressors and filters – general

1   Where a radio was fitted as standard, suppressors and filters will have been fitted to the ignition coil, the distributor, the alternator and regulator units.
2   Other items that may need suppression include the windscreen wiper motor and door window electric motors.
3   Additional suppression may also be necessary through the chassis components likely to cause static interference such as the disc brakes when applied or the flexing of the exhaust system (photo).
4   It is most important if they are to function efficiently, that the

27.3 Earth braid from chassis to exhaust system

suppressors, filters and their wires and braid connections be secure and good earth connections made.

5   Should it be necessary to renew a condenser, one of the correct capacity must be used. Your Renault dealer will be able to advise you on this accordingly.

28 Electro-magnetic door locking system – general

1   This system enables all four doors to be simultaneously locked or unlocked with a door key on the outside or by a switch on the inside. On certain models the device also locks and unlocks the tailgate and fuel filler cap.

2   An inertia switch and thermal cut-out are incorporated into the electrical circuit of the system, and these act as safety devices which unlock all the doors automatically in the event of a collision at a speed in excess of 9 mph (15 km/h). This safety margin is necessary to safeguard against the doors being unlocked accidentally by a light impact, for example by another vehicle when parking.

3   Should an electrical fault occur, the doors can still be locked and unlocked in the normal manner, using the door lock key provided.

4   A general circuit layout is shown in Fig. 10.30. The wiring diagram is shown in Fig. 10.31.

5   The mechanical door locks comprise three main interconnected components: the barrel, the changeover switch and the electro-magnetic actioner.

6   The front doors are each fitted with a barrel. The inner opening control lever is pivoted eccentrically on a pin.

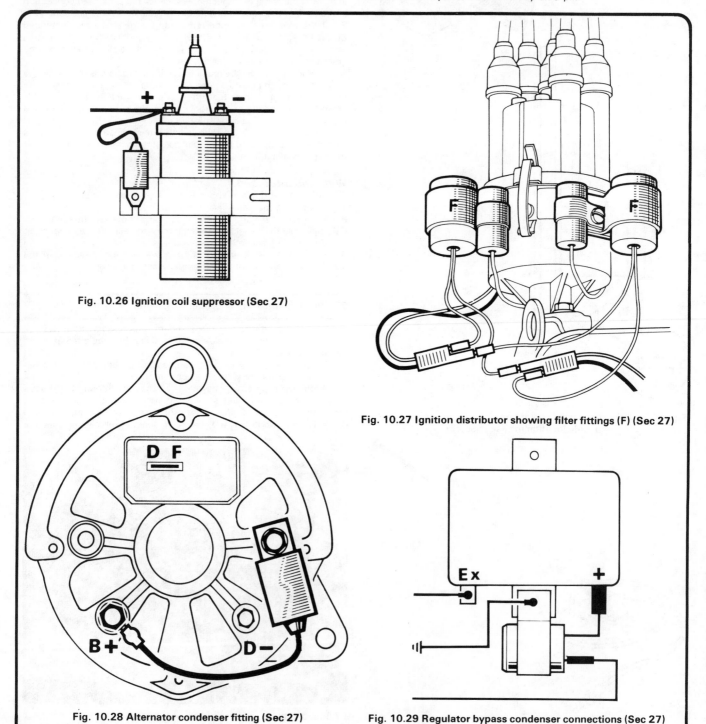

Fig. 10.26 Ignition coil suppressor (Sec 27)

Fig. 10.27 Ignition distributor showing filter fittings (F) (Sec 27)

Fig. 10.28 Alternator condenser fitting (Sec 27)

Fig. 10.29 Regulator bypass condenser connections (Sec 27)

183

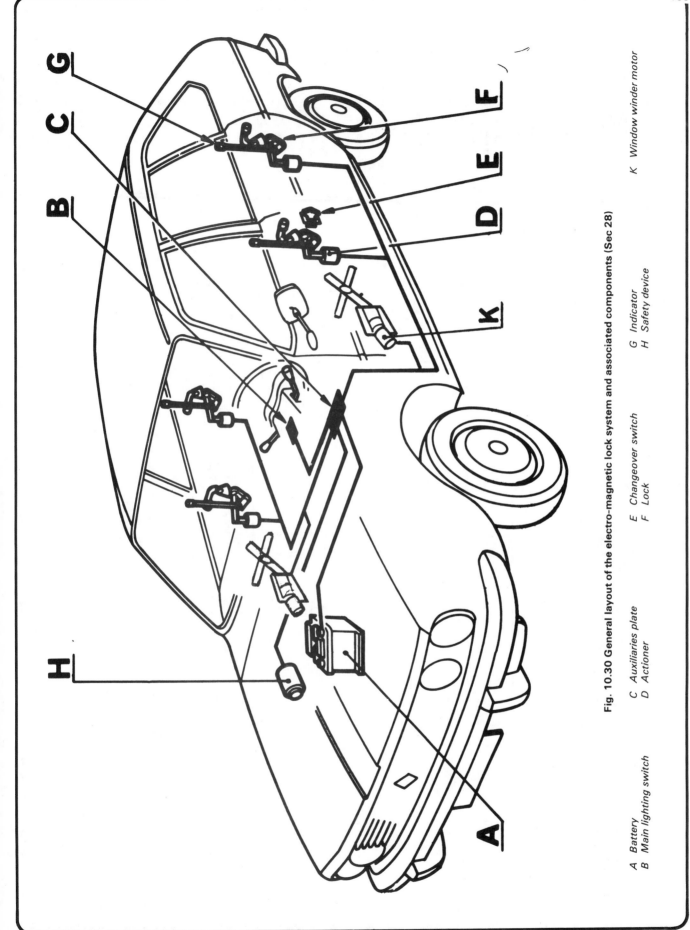

Fig. 10.30 General layout of the electro-magnetic lock system and associated components (Sec 28)

A Battery
B Main lighting switch
C Auxiliaries plate
D Actioner
E Changeover switch
F Lock
G Indicator
H Safety device
K Window winder motor

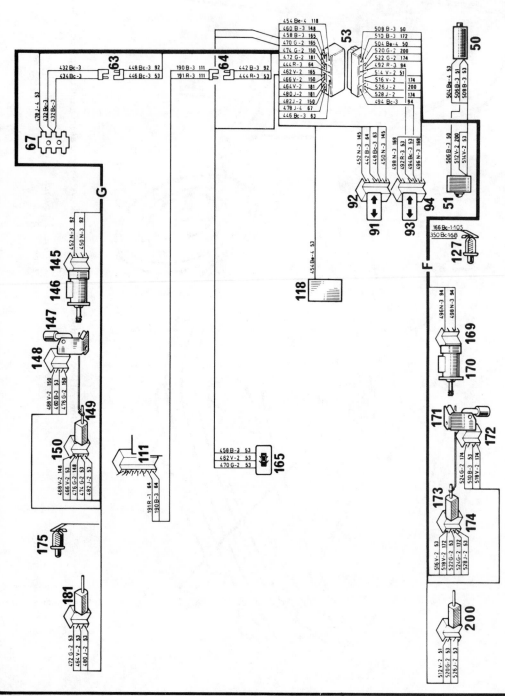

111 Junction block (front harness to auxiliaries plate)
118 Junction plate (before switch)
127 RH front door pillar switch
145 Junction block (electro-magnetic door locks harness to LH front door electric window winder motor)
146 LH window winder motor
147 LH front door electro-magnetic lock changeover switch
148 Junction block (electro-magnetic locks harness to changeover switch)
149 LH front door servo-lock
150 Junction block (electro-magnetic door locks harness to servo-lock)
165 Electro-magnetic door locks switch
169 Junction block (electro-magnetic door locks harness to RH front door electric window winder motor)
170 RH window winder motor
171 RH front door electro-magnetic lock changeover switch
172 Junction block (electro-magnetic door locks harness to changeover switch)
173 RH front door servo-lock
174 Junction block (electro-magnetic door locks harness to servo-lock)
175 LH rear door pillar switch
181 LH rear door servo-lock
200 RH rear door servo-lock

Wire colour code

Be Beige
Bc White
B   Blue
C   Clear
G   Grey
J   Yellow
N   Black
S   Pink
R   Red
V   Green
M   Maroon
Vi Violet
Or Orange

Key to wire code

Example S16V-2 53

S16 Wire code number
V   Wire colour
2   Wire gauge
53   Destination of wire

50 Inertia switch
51 Thermal cut-out
53 Electro-magnetic locks junction block
63 Earth plug and socket (LH and RH front changeover switch)
64 Plug and socket (LH and RH front door window winders)
67 Junction plate (earth)

91 LH front door window winder switch
92 Junction block (electro-magnetic locks harness to LH front door window winder switch)
93 RH front door window winder switch
94 Junction block (electro-magnetic locks harness to RH front door window winder switch)

Fig. 10.31 The electro-magnetic door locking system wiring diagram (Sec 28)

28.12 The inertia switch unit and reset button

28.16 The thermal cut-out and reset button (arrowed)

7   The swing lever for locking/unlocking is interconnected to the actioner by a rod. This is actuated by the front door lock barrels or the electro-magnetic actioner.

8   The changeover switch is a two-position type and one is fitted to each front door.

9   The electro-magnetic actioner (fitted to all doors) is regulated by the changeover switch location, dependent on the key position. Turn the key $\frac{1}{4}$ turn to the left to lock the doors and $\frac{1}{4}$ turn to the right to unlock them.

10   Each door contains a small lock position indicator capsule. When the doors are locked the red indicator should pop up into the capsule. On unlocking the doors it will drop below the capsule.

11   The electro-magnetic actioner in each door comprises two coils, between which is located a ferrite disc which slides up or down accordingly to each coil. When a coil is activated (by an electrical impulse from the switch) it causes the ferrite disc to thrust against the opposing coil. When it is against the upper coil, the system is locked. When it drops to the lower coil the system is unlocked. The control knob in each front door panel will also activate the system when rotated accordingly.

12   The inertia and thermal cut-out are located in front of the glovebox on the inside face of the bulkhead (photo).

13   In the event of an accident, the inertia switch is activated and automatically causes the doors to be unlocked.

14   The thermal cut-out is fitted to deactivate the electrical circuit after a given period (10 to 60 seconds) should the inertia switch be activated when the doors are locked. The circuit is thus turned off automatically.

15   Reset buttons are provided on top of the switches to reset them should they be activated accidentally.

16   Normally, the system is trouble free and requires no special maintenance. The following observations should be made to ensure correct usage, however:

   (a) Ensure that the doors are fully closed before locking. Slamming the door may unlock it
   (b) Check that all of the red indicators are visible in each door when locked. Should one doorlock indicator fail to appear, check that the door is closed properly.
   (c) If the system should fail to operate at any time and the above cautional items have been adhered to, check the inertia switch reset button and the cut-out switch button (photo) and if necessary, reset them

17   Better access to the inertia switch can be obtained by emptying out the glovebox and then detaching its rubber stay strap, allowing it to be fully lowered as shown in photo 28.12.

18   For improved access to the thermal cut-out switch, remove the front side panel trim by detaching the retainer strip and folding back the trim.

19   If the system fails to operate correctly, after checking the doors for full closure and resetting the appropriate switches, it is advisable to have the system checked by your Renault dealer. Should you suspect the door locks of being defective, they can be inspected and removed if necessary, as described in Chapter 12.

20   The internal door lock switch is clipped into the top face of the centre console and is easily removed by prising it free and disconnecting the wiring plug. Refitting is a reversal of the removal procedure, but check door lock operation on completion.

29 Windscreen wiper motor and mechanism – removal and refitting

1   Disconnect the battery earth lead.

2   Referring to Chapter 12, remove the scuttle panel.

3   Detach the wire connector to the wiper motor.

4   Unscrew and remove the three motor and mechanism plate mounting screws, and lift the assembly clear.

5   To detach the motor from the link mechanism, unscrew and remove the link retaining nut.

6   Little can be done to effect repairs on the wiper motor or linkage,

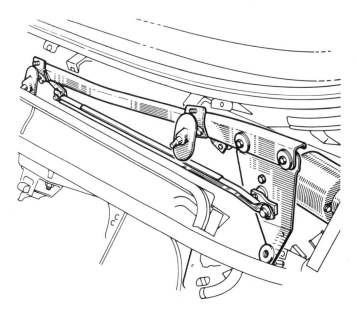

Fig. 10.32 Windscreen wiper linkage and motor location (Sec 29)

renewal being the normal procedure. A competent auto-electrician may, however, be able to repair the motor. But check any repair costs against new replacements first – it may be more expensive (due to labour costs).

7   Refitting is a reversal of the removal procedure. Make sure the motor is securely retained and the respective linkage washers fitted. Lubricate the linkage pivot points during assembly.

30 Windscreen wiper arms and blades – removal and refitting

1   To remove the windscreen wiper blade, hinge the arm away from the screen, pivot the blade, and push the arm through, as shown (photos) to detach.
2   The arm and blade assembly can be removed complete, by hinging back the nut cover and unscrewing the nut (photo).
3   Pull the arm from the wiper pivot shaft.
4   Refitting of the arm and blade is a reversal of the removal

procedure. Fit the arm to its original position on the pivot shaft so it gives the required amount of arc over the screen when operated, and stops in the correct position when cancelled.

31 Tailgate wiper assembly – removal and refitting

1   The wiper blade can easily be removed by unscrewing the retaining screw (photo).
2   The wiper arm is secured by an Allen screw which when loosened with a key (photo) will allow its removal from the pivot shaft.
3   If it is necessary to remove the tailgate wiper motor, first detach the battery earth lead, then raise and support the tailgate.
4   Remove the wiper arm and blade.
5   Pull the motor wiring harness from its cavity in the tailgate (photo) and disconnect the wiring snap connector, but tape the wires left in the cavity of the body to the tailgate to prevent them dropping down. This will save you from having to fish for them later.

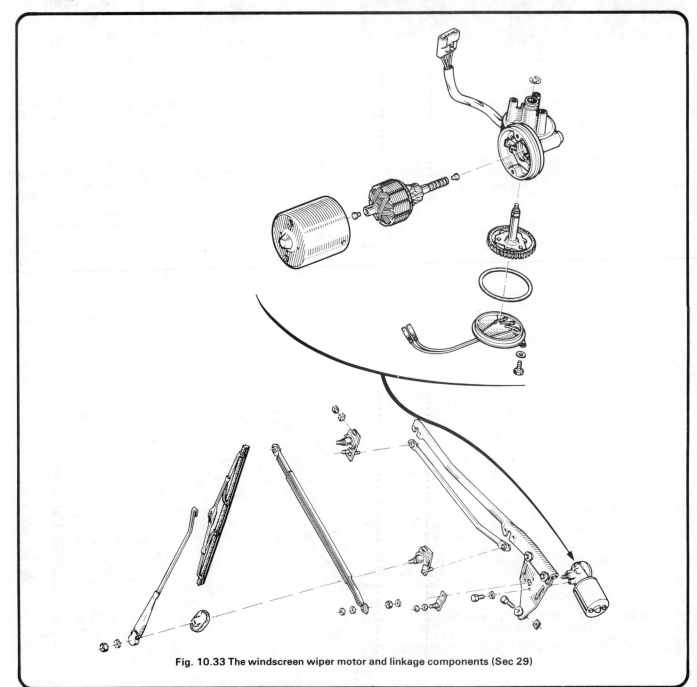

Fig. 10.33 The windscreen wiper motor and linkage components (Sec 29)

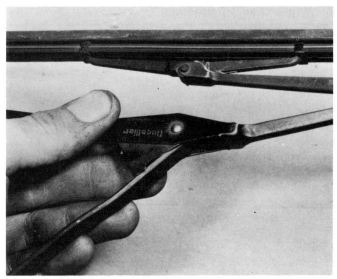

30.1A Hinge wiper arm from screen and ...

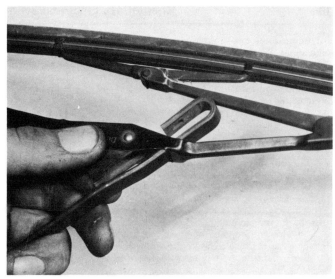

30.1B ... push blade down arm to release

30.2 Wiper arm nut exposed for removal

31.1 Tailgate wiper blade retaining screw removal

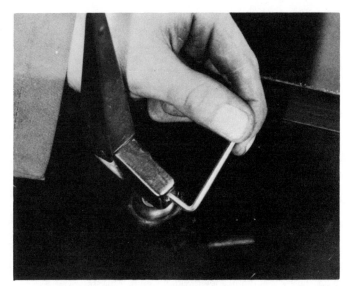

31.2 Tailgate wiper arm retaining screw removal

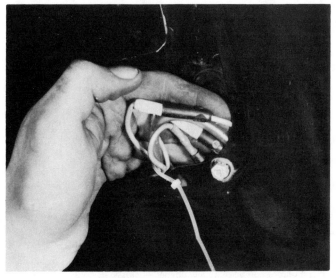

31.5 Rear wiper motor wire connections – pull up from tailgate cavity

6   Remove the three motor unit retaining bolts and detach the earth wire screw. The motor can now be withdrawn (photo).

7   As with the front windscreen wiper motor, there is little that can be achieved in the way of repairs to the motor. It should therefore be entrusted to an auto electrician for testing and any repairs that may be possible, or renewed as a unit.

8   Refitting is a direct reversal of the removal procedure. Check the wiper operation on completion.

32 Sunroof electric motor – removal and refitting

1   Should the sunroof motor fail to operate, the roof can be opened or closed by removing the blanking plug from the point indicated in Fig. 10.34. This will expose the motor drive spindle. The spindle can then be turned as required, using a screwdriver (photo).

2   To remove the motor, open the roof slightly to gain access to the retaining screws inside the front edge.

3   Disconnect the battery earth cable.

4   Unscrew and remove the motor embellisher retaining screws, move the motor to the rear and disconnect the wires at the connectors (photo).

5   Unscrew and remove the guide bearing screws, and pull them rearwards.

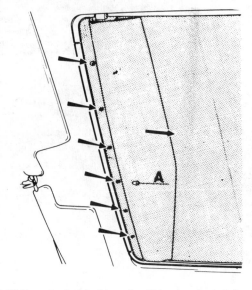

Fig. 10.34 Detach the blanking plug 'A' to hand wind the sunroof. Embellisher screws indicated along front edge (Sec 32)

31.6 The tailgate wiper motor and retaining screws (arrowed)

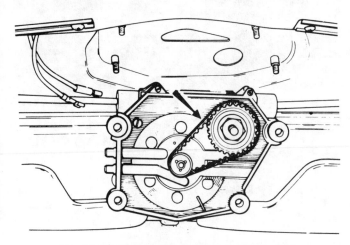

Fig. 10.35 Sunroof drivebelt (arrowed) (Sec 32)

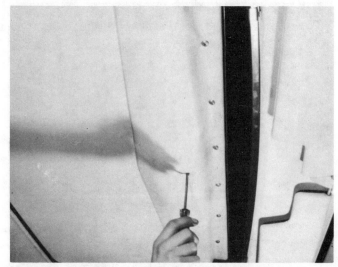

32.1 Sunroof can be manually opened or closed using a screwdriver through hole shown when plug is removed

32.4 The sunroof motor shown with the embellisher removed

6   Remove the motor retaining screws, lift the roof and withdraw the motor.

7   The motor driveshaft can be detached by driving out the retaining pin, using a suitable punch.

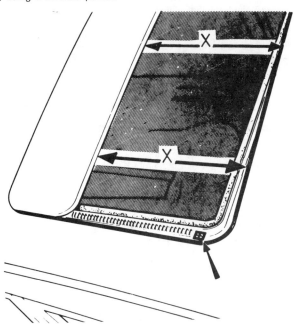

Fig. 10.36 Check distances X and adjust racks to equalise if necessary. RH rack securing screw arrowed (Sec 32)

8   If the motor is known to be defective, renew it, as it cannot be repaired. The drivebelt *can* be renewed, however. This is on the back of the motor as shown in Fig. 10.35.

9   Refitting is a reversal of the removal procedure, but ensure that the sunroof is located squarely with the front edge at an equal distance from the front of the aperture on each side as shown in Fig. 10.36. Move the racks accordingly to adjust.

33 Heated rear window – general

The heating element of the rear tailgate window is integral with the glass, and as such should it become defective, cannot be repaired. Check the wiring circuit to the window for any faults using a circuit tester. If the circuit is operational, take the car to your Renault dealer or auto-electrician and have the element tested. They will be able to advise you regarding removal and renewal/refitting.

Proprietary conductive paints are now available at motor accessory shops; one of these may be suitable for repairing breaks in the heating element. Follow the directions supplied with the respective paint.

34 Heater motor – removal and refitting

1   Detach the battery earth lead.

2   Referring to Chapter 12, remove the scuttle panel.

3   Detach the feed wires to the fan motor.

4   Unscrew and remove the fan motor unit retaining screws and withdraw the unit.

5   Remove the clips and unseal the unit base to detach the upper and lower housing.

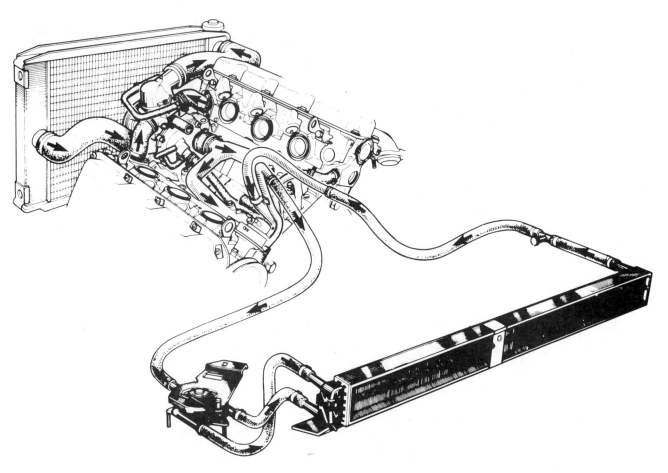

Fig. 10.37 The heater circuit (Sec 34)

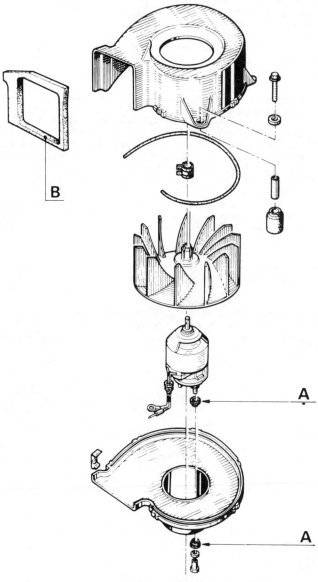

Fig. 10.38 Heater motor main components, showing the rubber cushion washer locations (A) – do not forget to seal B on reassembly (Sec 34)

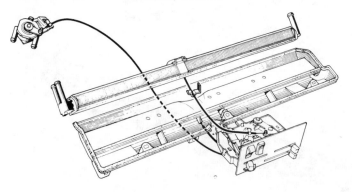

Fig. 10.39 Heater control cable assembly (Sec 35)

6   Remove the turbine retaining clip and pull the turbine from the spindle. See Fig. 10.38.
7   Unscrew and remove the motor retaining screws and extract the motor unit.

8   If defective, renew the motor and any other items in need of renewal.
9   Refitting is a reversal of the removal procedure, but be sure to locate the rubber cushion washers round the correct way and restick the aperture seal into the housing.

35 Heater control cable – removal and refitting

1   Detach the battery earth lead.
2   Remove the control panel fillet and unscrew the panel retaining screws on the dashboard.
3   Lift the panel assembly clear and detach the cable from it.
4   Loosen off the cable outer sleeve retaining clips at the panel and then at the valve end (against the bulkhead).
5   Disconnect the cable from the valve and withdraw the cable. See Fig. 10.39.
6   Refitting is a reversal of the removal procedure, but the cable must be set so that when the valve is shut, the adjuster knob at the panel is not quite at the end of the slide – see Fig. 10.41.

36 Heater valve – removal and refitting

1   To avoid draining the cooling and heater system, you will need some suitable clamps with which to compress the heater hoses as close as possible to the valve unit (photo).

36.1 The heater valve unit showing the hose and cable connections

2   When the hoses are suitably clamped they can be detached from the valve unit, but allow for a small amount of spillage and wipe any antifreeze solution from the surrounding paintwork.
3   Detach the control cable.
4   Compress the valve unit retaining lugs and remove it from the bulkhead crossmember, as shown in Fig. 10.40.
5   Fit in the reverse sequence. When fitted, the cable should allow the control knob a small clearance from the end of the slide as shown in Fig. 10.41. When the hoses are reconnected and the clamps released, top up the cooling system and bleed it as given in Chapter 1. Then check for any signs of leaks.

37 Heater matrix – removal and refitting

1   Referring to Chapter 12, remove the scuttle panel.
2   Close the heater hot water valve and fit suitable clamps to compress the heater return hose after the bleed screw, the matrix inlet hose and the outlet hose. When the clamps are securely in position and the hoses compressed, disconnect the respective hoses from the matrix.
3   Remove the matrix bulkhead. Take care when unsticking the seals.

4   Detach the air flap control cable.

5   Unscrew the retaining bolts and withdraw the matrix.

6   Refitting is a reversal of the removal procedure, but when reconnecting the cable, adjust it so that the travel of the flap and control knob are equal.

7   Top up and bleed the cooling system as given in Chapter 2. Check for leaks around the disturbed hoses.

38 Heater ventilators – removal and refitting

Side ventilators

1   Referring to Section 23, remove the dashboard. Unscrew the ventilator retaining nuts and remove it.

2   Refitting is a reverse of the removal procedure.

Centre ventilators

3   Remove the dashboard (see Section 23). Unscrew and remove the ventilator retaining nuts to remove the ventilator.

4   Refit in the reverse sequence.

39 Heater air entry flap cable – removal and refitting

1   Disconnect the battery earth lead.

2   Referring to Chapter 12, remove the scuttle panel.

3   Carefully, free the heater matrix bulkhead, taking care when unsticking the seals.

4   Loosen the air flap block cable lock screw, then partially withdraw the heater matrix, but do not disconnect the hoses.

5   Withdraw the control panel fillet and remove the panel plastic cover.

6   Detach the cable at the control end as shown in Fig. 10.42. Unclip the outer sleeve retainers from the panel and scuttle upper crossmember, and remove the cable with sleeve.

7   Fit in the reverse order. Adjust the control lever in the closed position, but with a gap of 2 mm ($\frac{5}{64}$ in) relative to the slide. In this position, close the gap and tighten the cable retaining screw.

40 Air conditioning system – description and precautions

1   When an air conditioning system is fitted, it is necessary to observe special precautions whenever dealing with any part of the system, its associated components and any items within the engine and heating compartment that necessitate disconnection of the system.

2   The refrigeration circuit contains a liquid gas (Freon) and it is therefore dangerous to disconnect any part of the system without specialised knowledge and equipment. If for any reason the system must be disconnected (engine removal for example), entrust this task to your Renault dealer or a refrigeration engineer.

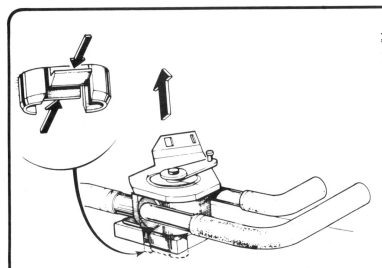

Fig. 10.40 Compress the lugs to remove the unit (Sec 36)

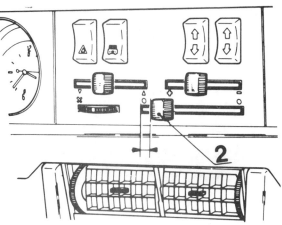

Fig. 10.41 Check when valve is shut that clearance exists between end of slide panel and knob (2) (Sec 36)

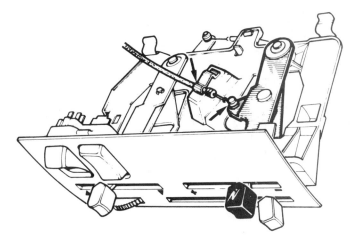

Fig. 10.42 Cable to control rod connection (Sec 39)

3   Fig. 10.43 shows the layout and principal components of the system.

4   Whenever working on the car in the vicinity of the air conditioning components the following special precautions must be adhered to:

(a) *Do not smoke, use a naked flame, or heat up any components in the vicinity of the system components*

(b) *Should any part of the system malfunction and cause a leakage of the liquid or gas, do not breathe in the refrigerant fumes. Should the fluid get in the eyes it can cause permanent blindness and a doctor should be consulted without delay! To reduce the effects of fluid contact with the eyes or skin, a few drops of mineral oil can be applied, then wash clean with a weak boric acid solution*

(c) *In the event of a sudden leak in the system switch off the engine (if running) and disconnect the compressor drivebelt. Get the system fault repaired without delay*

5   The following air conditioning system components can be removed and refitted without the need to disconnect the Freon pipes:

(a) Thermostat
(b) Rheostat
(c) Diodes
(d) Blower motor

These are dealt with in the following Sections.

41 Thermostat (air conditioning system) – removal and refitting

1   Disconnect the battery earth lead.
2   Remove the console as given in Section 24.
3   Remove the glovebox and its retaining bracket.
4   Remove the combination light switch half shroud (Section 21).
5   Detach and remove the air cooling hose from each side of the evaporator unit (Fig. 10.44).

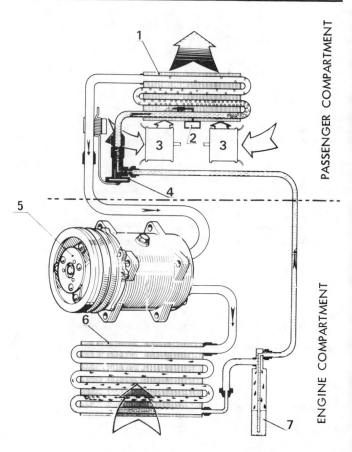

Fig. 10.43 Air conditioning system components and layout
(Sec 40)

1 Evaporator	5 Compressor
2 Thermostat	6 Condenser
3 Fans	7 Dehydrator
4 Reducing valve	

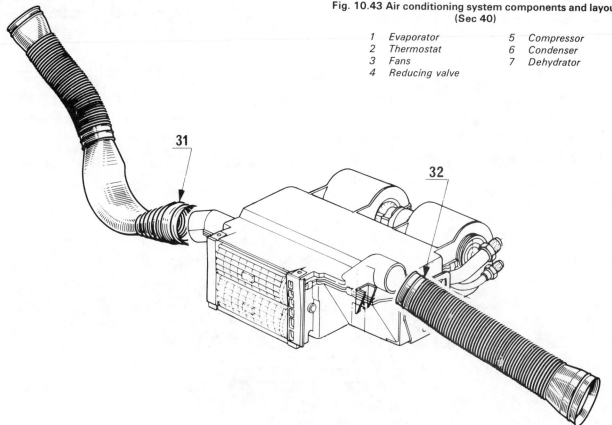

Fig. 10.44 Detach cooling hoses (31 and 32) (Sec 41)

6   Disconnect the wiring junction blocks and the lower hose connection, and unscrew the bracket bolt (refer to Fig. 10.45).
7   Unscrew and remove the three bolts shown in Figs. 10.45 and 10.46, then manoeuvre the blower unit to the right. Remove its top cover, having unclipped it and unscrewed its central securing bolt.
8   Detach the two vent grilles.
9   Disconnect the rheostat and thermostat wires and then unbolt and remove the thermostat unit (Fig. 10.47).
10   Rotate the control knob to align the white line with the 'O' mark, then turn the thermostat rod to its fullest extent in the direction of the arrow.
11   Locate the knob onto the thermostat spindle, then refit the combined thermostat/rheostat unit and reconnect their respective wires.
12   Referring to Fig. 10.48, insert the capillary tube as shown into the evaporator fins by $1\frac{3}{16}$ in (3 cm).
13   The remainder of the refitting procedures are the reverse of removal.

42 Rheostat (air conditioning system) – removal and refitting

The rheostat is combined with the thermostat unit and the removal and refitting details are therefore identical (refer to previous Section for details).

43 Air conditioner diodes – removal and refitting

1   On the earlier models you will need to proceed as given in paragraphs 1 to 7 of Section 41 to open the cool air blower unit. The diode wires can then be detached (Fig. 10.49).
2   On later models the diodes are more accessible and can be disconnected on removal of the glovebox. The diodes on later models are integrated into the cables (44 and 45 in Fig. 10.49).
3   Refitting is a reversal of the removal procedure.

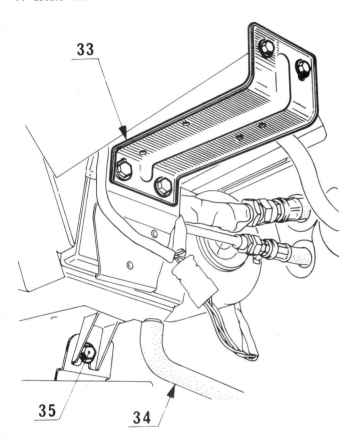

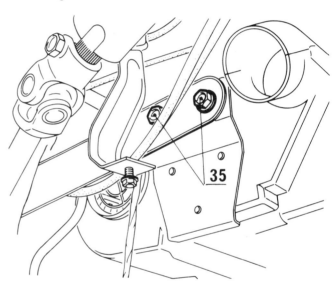

Fig. 10.45 Detach hose (34), remove bracket (33) and retaining bolt (35) (Sec 41)

Fig. 10.46 Remove bolts indicated (35) (Sec 41)

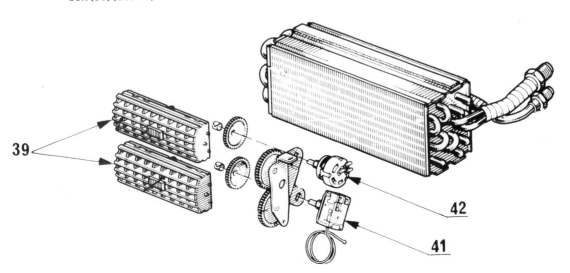

Fig. 10.47 The vent grilles (39), thermostat (41) and rheostat (42) (Sec 41)

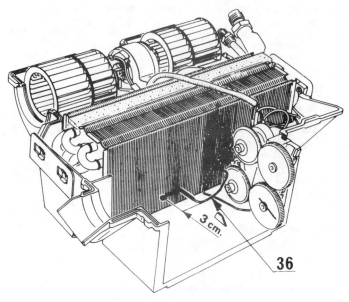

Fig. 10.48 Insert capillary tube (36) into evaporation fins by amount shown (3 cm) (Sec 41)

44 Air conditioner blower motor – removal and refitting

1   Proceed as given in Section 41, paragraphs 1 to 7, removing the support bracket shown in Fig. 10.45.
2   Detach the two wires from the motor unit and then remove the blower motor.
3   Refitting is a reversal of the removal procedure.

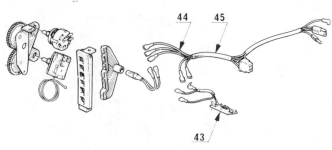

Fig. 10.49 Air conditioning system diode locations (Sec 43)

43 Early models   45 Later models (in table 44)

45 Fault diagnosis – electrical system

Symptom	Reason(s)
Starter fails to turn engine	Battery discharged Battery defective internally Battery terminal leads loose or earth lead not securely attached to body Loose or broken connections in starter motor circuit Starter motor solenoid faulty Starter brushes badly worn, sticking, or brush wires loose Commutator dirty, worn or burnt Starter motor armature faulty Field coils earthed Gear selector lever not engaged in 'P' or 'N' (automatic transmission)
Starter turns engine very slowly	Battery in discharged condition Starter brushes badly worn, sticking or brush wires loose Loose wires in starter motor circuit
Starter spins but does not turn engine	Starter motor pinion fork sticking Pinion or flywheel gear teeth broken or worn
Starter motor noisy or excessively rough engagement	Pinion or flywheel gear teeth broken or worn Starter motor retaining bolts loose
Battery will not hold charge for more than a few days	Battery defective internally Electrolyte level too low or electrolyte too weak due to leakage Plate separators no longer fully effective Battery plates severely sulphated Alternator drivebelt slipping Battery terminal connections loose or corroded Alternator not charging Short circuit causing continual battery drain Regulator unit not working correctly
Ignition light fails to go out, battery runs flat in a few days	Drivebelt loose and slipping or broken Alternator brushes worn, sticking, broken or dirty Alternator brush springs weak or broken Internal fault in alternator
Horn operates all the time	Horn push either earthed or stuck down Horn cable to horn push earthed
Horn fails to operate	Cable or cable connection loose, broken or disconnected Horn has an internal fault

Symptom	Reason(s)
Horn emits intermittent or unsatisfactory noise	Cable connections loose
Lights do not come on	If engine not running, battery discharged Wire connections loose, disconnected or broken Light switch shorting or otherwise faulty
Lights come on but fade out	If engine not running battery discharged Light bulb filament burnt out or bulbs broken Wire connections loose, disconnected or broken Light switch shorting or otherwise faulty
Lights work erratically – flashing on and off, especially over bumps	Battery terminals or earth connection loose Lights not earthing properly Contacts in light switch faulty
Wiper motor fails to work	Blown fuse Wire connections loose, disconnected or broken Brushes badly worn Armature worn or faulty Field coils faulty
Wiper motor works very slowly and takes excessive current	Commutator dirty, greasy or burnt Armature bearings dirty or unaligned Armature badly worn or faulty
Wiper motor works slowly and takes little current	Brushes badly worn Commutator dirty, greasy or burnt Armature badly worn or faulty
Wiper motor works but wiper blades remain static	Wiper motor gearbox parts badly worn Faulty linkage
Central door locking system fails to operate	Inertia switch and/or thermal cut-out tripped and not reset Inertia switch and/or thermal cut-out defective Fuse blown

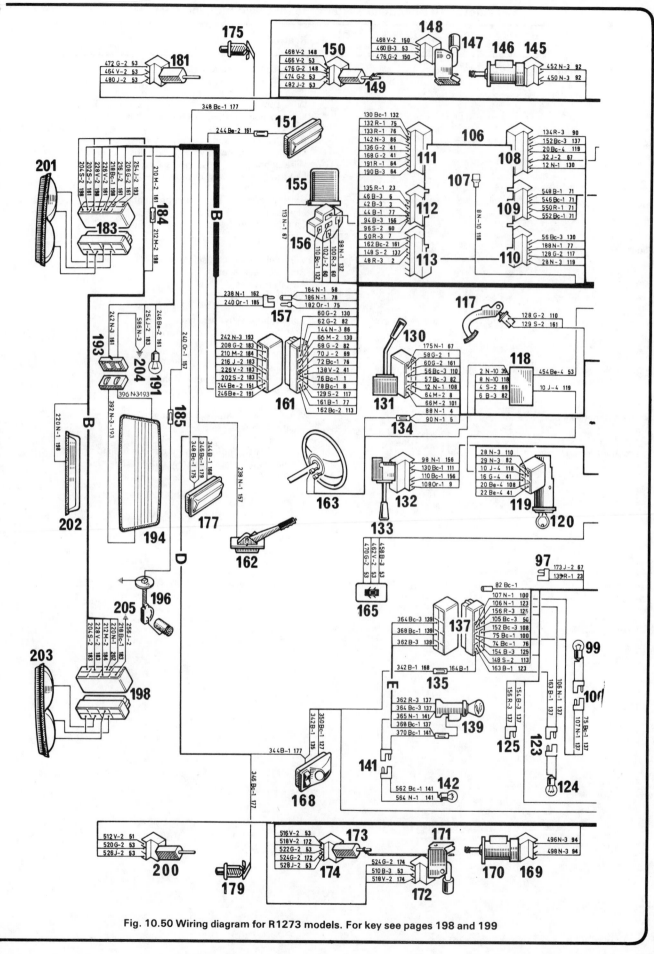

Fig. 10.50 Wiring diagram for R1273 models. For key see pages 198 and 199

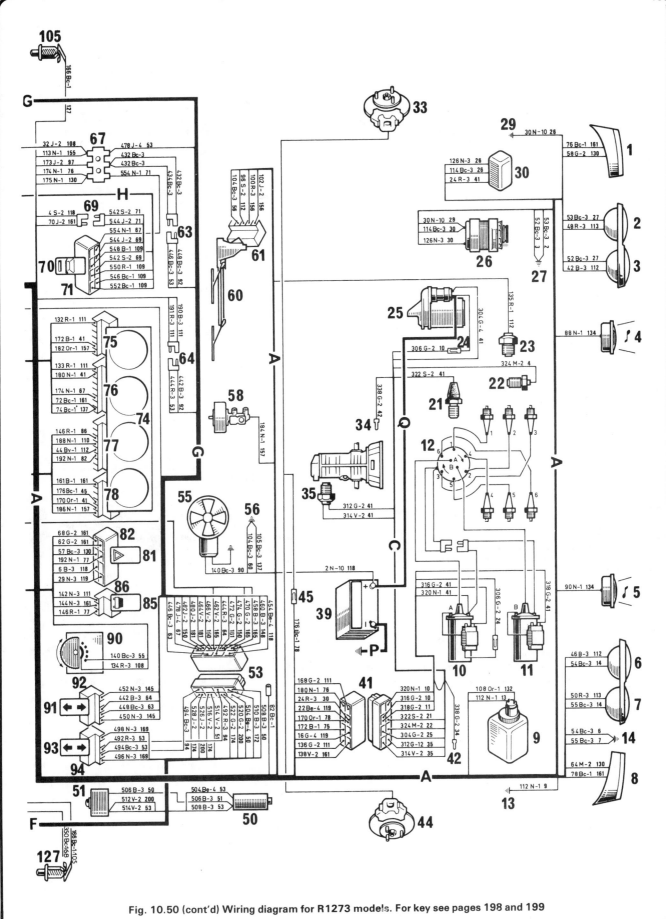

Fig. 10.50 (cont'd) Wiring diagram for R1273 models. For key see pages 198 and 199

Key to Fig. 10.50

1	Side light and LH front direction indicator	70	Lighting switch
2	LH outer headlight	71	Junction block – dashboard lighting switch harness to combination lighting switch
3	LH inner headlight	74	Instrument panel
4	LH horn	75	Instrument panel – connector 1
5	RH horn	76	Instrument panel – connector 2
6	RH inner headlight	77	Instrument panel – connector 3
7	RH outer headlight	78	Instrument panel – connector 4
8	Side light and RH front indicator	81	Hazard warning lights system switch
9	Windscreen washer electric pump	82	Junction block – front harness to Hazard warning lights switch
10	Group A ignition coil	85	Heated rear screen switch
11	Group B ignition coil	86	Junction block – front harness to heated rear screen switch
12	Distributor	90	Heater fan rheostat
13	Windscreen washer pump earth (ground)	91	LF front door window winder switch
14	RH headlights earth (ground)	92	Junction block – electro-magnetic locks harness to LH front door window winder switch
21	Oil pressure switch	93	RH front door window winder switch
22	Water temperature switch	94	Junction block – electro-magnetic locks harness to RH front door window winder switch
23	Thermal switch on radiator	99	Heater fan rheostat illumination
24	Plug and socket – ignition coil A to starter relay	100	Plug and socket for heater fan rheostat illumination
25	Starter	105	LH front door pillar switch
26	Alternator	106	Auxiliaries plate
27	Earth (ground)	107	Feed to auxiliaries plate
29	Alternator earth (ground)	108	Junction block – front harness to auxiliaries plate
30	Regulator	109	Junction block – lighting switch to auxiliaries plate
33	LH front brake	110	Junction block – front harness to auxiliaries plate
34	Plug and socket for air conditioning magnetic clutch	111	Junction block – front harness to auxiliaries plate
35	Reversing lights switch	112	Junction block – front harness to auxiliaries plate
39	Battery	113	Junction block – front harness to auxiliaries plate
41	Junction block – front harness to engine harness	117	Stop-light switch
42	Plug and socket for air conditioning magnetic clutch	118	Junction plate before ignition switch
44	RH front brake	119	Junction block – front harness to ignition-starter switch
50	Inertia switch	120	Ignition-starter switch
51	Thermal cut-out	123	Plug and socket for glove compartment illumination
53	Junction block – electro-magnetic lock harnesses	124	Glove compartment illumination
55	Heater fan motor	125	Plug and socket for sunroof
56	Windscreen wiper motor earth and cigar lighter	127	RH front door pillar switch
58	Brake pressure drop indicator	130	Junction block – front harness to direction indicators switch
60	Windscreen wiper plate	131	Direction indicators switch
61	Junction block – engine front harness to windscreen wiper	132	Junction block – front harness to windscreen wiper switch
63	Changeover switch earth (ground) plug and socket for LH and RH front doors	133	Windscreen wiper switch
64	Plug and socket for LH and RH front door window winder	134	Plug and socket for horn push in steering wheel
67	Earth (ground) junction plate		
69	Plug and socket for lighting switch		

Key to Fig 10.50 (cont'd)

135 Plug and socket for interior light
137 Junction block – front harness to bridge harness
138 Plug and socket for rear interior light
139 Cigar lighter
141 Plug and socket for ashtray illumination
142 Ashtray illumination
145 Junction block – electro-magnetic door lock harness to LH front door electric window winder
146 LH window winder motor
147 LH front door electro-magnetic door lock changeover switch
148 Junction block – electro-magnetic lock harness to changeover switch
149 LH front door servo lock
150 Junction block – electro-magnetic door lock harness to servo lock
151 LH interior light
155 Windscreen wiper temperature time switch
156 Junction block – front harness to temperature time switch
157 Plug and socket – fuel gauge tank unit to brake pressure drop indicator
161 Junction block – front harness to rear harness
162 Handbrake
163 Horn push in steering wheel
165 Electro-magnetic door locks switch
168 Map reading light
169 Junction block – electro-magnetic door lock harness to RH door window winder motor
170 RH window winder motor
171 RH front door electro-magnetic lock changeover switch
172 Junction block – electro-magnetic lock harness to changeover switch
173 RH front door servo lock
174 Junction block – electro-magnetic door lock harness to servo lock

175 LH rear door pillar switch
177 Rear interior light
179 RH rear door pillar switch
181 LH rear door servo lock
183 Junction block – rear harness to LH rear lights
184 Plug and socket for RH rear direction indicator
185 Plug and socket for fuel gauge tank unit
191 Luggage compartment illumination
192 Earth (ground)
193 Heated rear screen switch
194 Heated rear screen
196 Fuel gauge tank unit
198 Junction block – rear harness to RH rear lights
200 RH rear door servo lock
201 LH rear lights
202 Licence plate light
203 RH rear lights
204 LH rear lights earth (ground)
205 RH rear lights earth (ground)

Harness identification

A Engine front
B Rear
C Engine (manual shift gearbox)
D Rear interior light
E Bridge
F Electro-magnetic lock
G Electro-magnetic lock
H Lighting switch
Q Starter positive
P Starter negative (earth)

Wire colour code

Be	Beige	G	Grey	S	Pink	M	Maroon
Bc	White	J	Yellow	R	Red	Vi	Violet
B	Blue	N	Black	V	Green	Or	Orange
C	Clear						

Key to wire code

Example S16V-2 53
S16 Wire code number
V Wire colour
2 Wire gauge
53 Destination of wire

Wire gauge code

No	1	2	3	4	5	6	7	8	9
Wire diameter (mm)	0.7	0.9	1.0	1.2	1.6	2.0	2.5	3.0	4.5

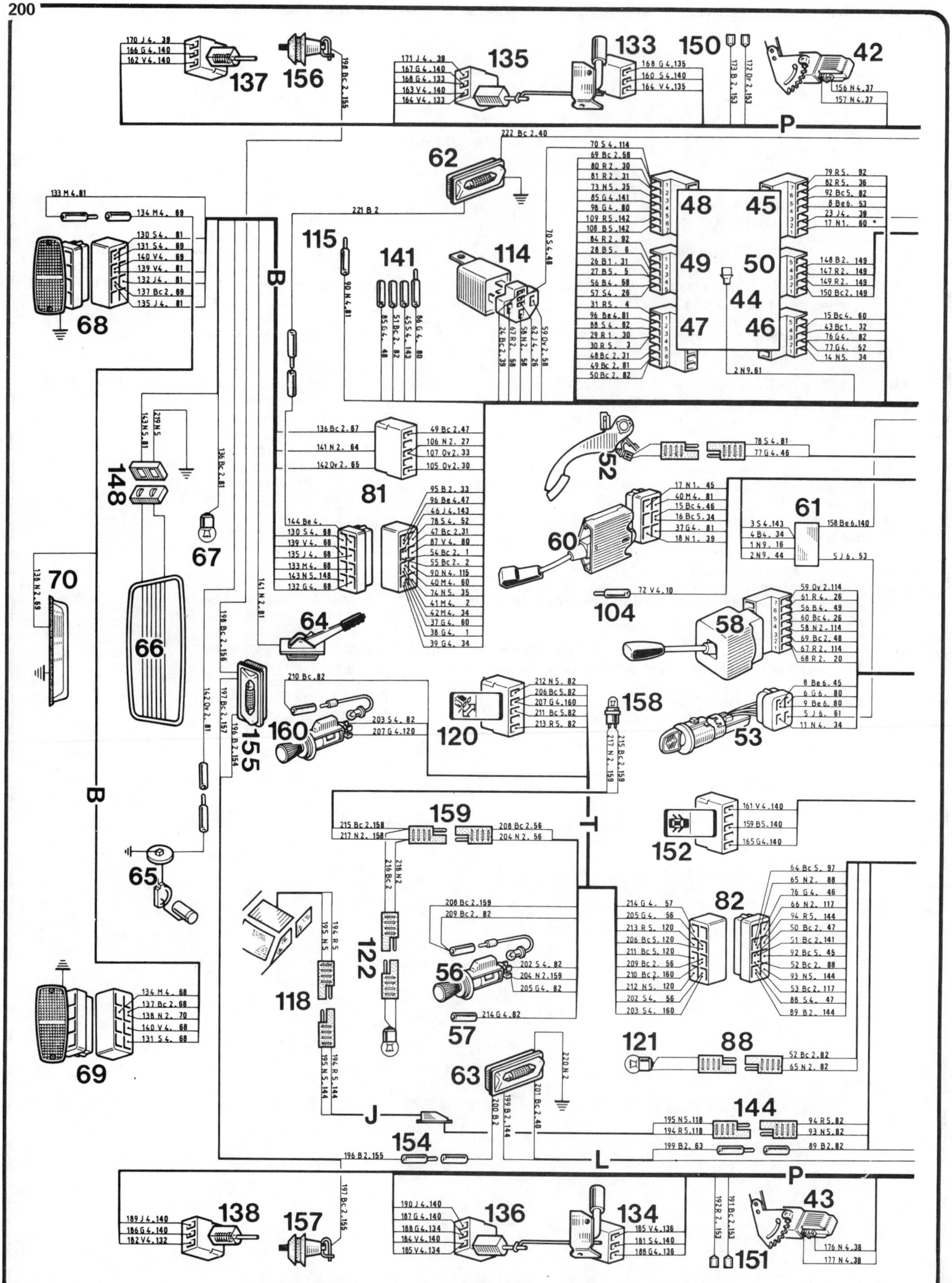

170 J 4 . 38
166 G 4 . 140
162 V 4 . 140

137 **156**

198 Bc 2 . 155

171 J 4 . 38
167 G 4 . 140
168 G 4 . 140
163 V 4 . 140
164 V 4 . 133

135

133 **150**

173 B 2 . 153
172 Ov 2 . 153

168 G 4 . 135
160 S 4 . 140
164 . V 4 . 135

42

156 N 4 . 37
157 N 4 . 37

P

222 Bc 2 . 40

62

221 B 2

70 S 4 . 114
69 Bc 2 . 58
80 R 2 . 30
81 R 2 . 31
73 N 5 . 35
85 G 4 . 141
94 G 4 . 80
109 R 5 . 142
108 B 5 . 142
84 R 2 . 92
28 B 5 . 6
26 B 1 . 31
27 B 5 . 5
56 B 4 . 68
57 S 4 . 28
31 R 5 . 4
96 Be 4 . 81
88 S 4 . 82
29 R 1 . 30
30 R 5 . 3
48 Bc 2 . 31
49 Bc 2 . 81
50 Bc 2 . 82

70 S 4 . 48
59 Ov 2 . 58
62 J 4 . 26
26 Bc 2 . 39
58 N 2 . 58
67 R 2 . 58

79 R 5 . 92
82 R 5 . 36
92 Bc 5 . 82
8 Be 6 . 53
23 J 4 . 38
17 N 1 . 60

148 B 2 . 149
147 R 2 . 81
149 R 2 . 149
150 Bc 2 . 149

15 Bc 4 . 60
43 Bc 1 . 32
76 G 4 . 82
77 G 4 . 82
14 N 5 . 34

2 N 9 . 61

48 **45**

49 **50**

44

47 **46**

115 **141** **114**

133 M 4 . 81

134 M 4 . 69
130 S 4 . 81
131 S 4 . 69
140 V 4 . 69
139 V 4 . 81
132 J 4 . 81
137 Bc 2 . 69
135 J 4 . 81

68

B

90 M 4 . 81

85 G 4 . 48
51 Bc 2 . 82
67 R 2 . 143

86 G 4 . 80

52

78 S 4 . 81
77 G 4 . 46

136 Bc 2 . 87
141 N 2 . 64
142 Ov 2 . 65

49 Bc 2 . 47
106 N 2 . 27
107 Ov 2 . 33
105 Ov 2 . 30

81

143 N 5 . 81
219 N 5
136 Bc 2 . 81

148

67

144 Be 4 .
130 S 4 . 68
139 V 4 . 68
135 J 4 . 68
133 M 4 . 68
143 N 5 . 148
132 G 4 . 68

95 B 2 . 33
96 Be 4 . 47
46 J 4 . 143
78 S 4 . 52
47 Bc 2 . 31
87 V 4 . 80
54 Bc 2 . 1
55 Bc 2 . 2
90 N 4 . 115
40 M 4 . 60
74 N 5 . 35
41 M 4 . 2
42 M 4 . 34
37 G 4 . 60
38 G 4 . 1
39 G 4 . 34

60

104

17 N 1 . 45
40 M 4 . 81
15 Bc 4 . 46
16 Bc 5 . 34
37 G 4 . 81
18 N 1 . 39

3 S 4 . 143
4 B 4 . 34
1 N 9 . 16
2 N 9 . 44

158 Be 6 . 140

61

5 J 6 . 53

72 V 4 . 10

59 Ov 2 . 114
61 R 4 . 26
56 B 4 . 49
60 Bc 4 . 26
58 N 2 . 114
69 Bc 2 . 48
67 R 2 . 114
68 R 2 . 20

58

8 Be 6 . 45
6 G 6 . 80
9 Be 6 . 80
5 J 6 . 61
11 N 4 . 34

53

70

132 N 2 . 69

66

138 Bc 2 . 81

141 N 2 . 81

198 Bc 2 . 156

197 Bc 2 . 157
196 B 2 . 154

142 Ov 2 . 81

64

210 Bc . 82

203 S 4 . 82
207 G 4 . 120

160 **155**

212 N 5 . 82
206 Bc 5 . 82
207 G 4 . 160
211 Bc 5 . 82
213 R 5 . 82

120

215 Bc 2 . 159
217 N 2 . 159

158

161 V 4 . 140
159 B 5 . 140
165 G 4 . 140

152

B

65

215 Bc 2 . 158
217 N 2 . 158

216 Bc 2
218 N 2
216 Bc 2

208 Bc 2 . 56
204 N 2 . 56

159

193 N 5

194 R 5
195 N 5

122

208 Bc 2 . 159
209 Bc 2 . 82

202 S 4 . 82
204 N 2 . 159
205 G 4 . 82

214 G 4 . 82

56

57

214 G 4 . 57
205 G 4 . 56
213 R 5 . 120
206 Bc 5 . 120
211 Bc 5 . 120
209 Bc 2 . 56
210 Bc 2 . 160
212 N 5 . 120
202 S 4 . 56
203 S 4 . 160

82

64 Bc 5 . 97
65 N 2 . 88
76 G 4 . 46
66 N 2 . 117
94 R 5 . 144
50 Bc 2 . 47
51 Bc 2 . 141
92 Bc 5 . 45
52 Bc 2 . 88
93 N 5 . 144
53 Bc 2 . 117
88 S 4 . 47
89 B 2 . 144

194 R 5 . 144
195 N 5 . 144

118

134 M 4 . 68
137 Bc 2 . 68
138 N 2 . 70
140 V 4 . 68
131 S 4 . 68

69

121 **88**

52 Bc 2 . 82
65 N 2 . 82

63

220 N 2

201 B 2 . 40
200 B 2
199 B 2 . 144

J

195 N 5 . 118
194 R 5 . 118
199 B 2 . 63

144

94 R 5 . 82
93 N 5 . 82
89 B 2 . 82

154

196 B 2 . 155

L

P

197 Bc 2 . 155

189 J 4 . 140
186 G 4 . 140
182 V 4 . 132

138 **157**

190 J 4 . 140
187 G 4 . 140
188 G 4 . 140
184 V 4 . 140
185 V 4 . 134

136 **134**

185 V 4 . 136
181 S 4 . 140
188 G 4 . 136

192 R 2 . 153
191 Bc 2 . 153

43

176 N 4 . 38
177 N 4 . 38

151

Fig. 10.51 Wiring diagram for R1275 models. For key see page 202

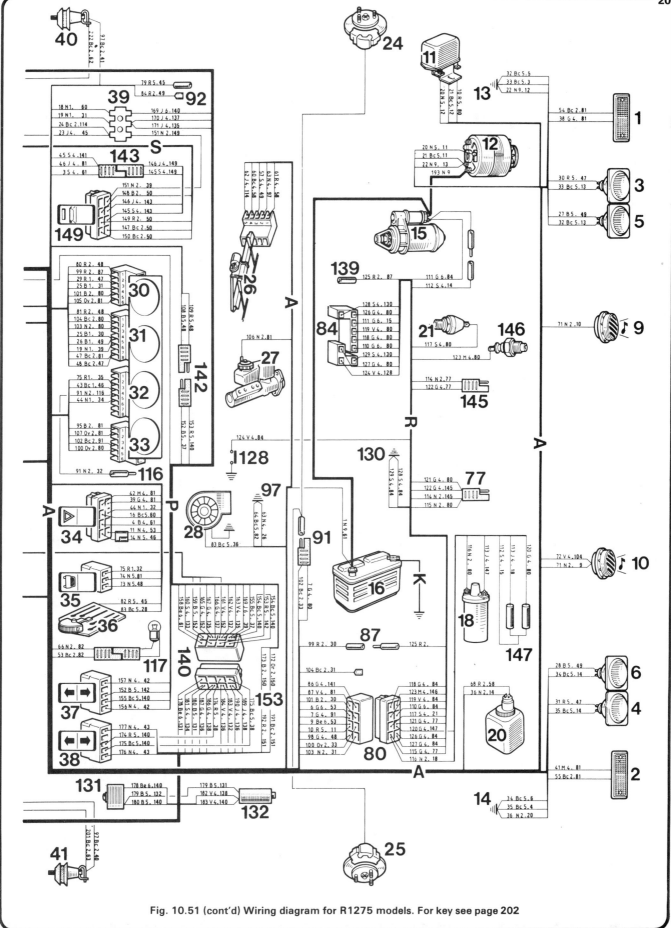

Fig. 10.51 (cont'd) Wiring diagram for R1275 models. For key see page 202

Key to Figs. 10.51 and 10.52

1 LH front sidelight and direction indicator
2 RH front sidelight and direction indicator
3 LH dipped beam headlight
4 RH dipped beam headlight
5 LH main beam headlight
6 RH main beam headlight
7 LH headlight unit
8 RH headlight unit
9 LH horn
10 RH horn
11 Regulator
12 Alternator
13 LH side earth
14 RH side earth
15 Starter
16 Battery
17 Engine cooling fan motor
18 Ignition coil
19 Distributor
20 Windscreen washer pump
21 Oil pressure switch
22 Thermal switch on radiator
24 LH front brake
25 RH front brake
26 Windscreen wiper plate
27 Brake master cylinder
28 Heating-ventilating fan motor
30 Instrument panel - No 1 connector
31 Instrument panel - No 2 connector
32 Instrument panel - No 3 connector
34 Hazard warning light switch
35 Rear screen demister switch
36 Heating-ventilating fan motor rheostat
37 LH window winder switch
38 RH window winder switch
40 LH door pillar switch
41 RH door pillar switch
42 LH window winder
43 RH window winder
44 Accessories plate (fusebox)
45 Junction block - front harness to accessories plate
46 Junction block - front harness to accessories plate
47 Junction block - front harness to accessories plate
48 Junction block - front harness to accessories plate
49 Junction block - front harness to accessories plate
50 Junction block - front harness to accessories plate
52 Stop-lights switch
53 Ignition-starter switch
54 Heating-ventilating control panel illumination
55 Glove compartment light
56 Cigar lighter
58 Windscreen wiper-washer switch
59 Lighting switch
60 Direction indicators switch
61 + Feed connection before ignition switch
62 LH side interior light
63 RH side interior light
64 Handbrake
65 Fuel gauge tank unit
66 Rear screen demister
67 Luggage compartment light
68 LH rear light assembly
69 RH rear light assembly
70 Licence plate light

72 Reversing lights switch
77 Diagnostic socket junction
80 Junction block - front harness to engine harness
81 Junction block - front harness to rear harness
82 Junction block - front harness to console bridge harness
86 Junction block - time switch relay harness
91 Wire junction - brake pad wear warning light
92 Wire junction - optional air conditioning
97 Body earth
99 Dashboard earth
100 LH scuttle panel earth
101 Fuel tank mounting earth
104 Wire junction - steering wheel horn push
106 Rear foglight switch
110 Engine cooling fan motor relay
114 Windscreen wiper time switch
116 Wire junction - rear foglight harness
131 Electro-magnetic locks cut-out
132 Electro-magnetic locks inertia switch
133 LH front door lock switch
134 RH front door lock switch
135 LH front door lock solenoid
136 RH front door lock solenoid
137 LH rear door lock solenoid
138 RH rear door lock solenoid
140 Junction block - electro-magnetic door locks harness
142 Wire junction - window winder harness
143 Wire junction - main lighting switch harness
144 Wire junction - interior lights harness
145 Wire junction - transistorized ignition
146 Thermal switch
147 Ignition coil resistance
148 Tailgate fixed contact
149 Lighting switch
150 LH front door loudspeaker
151 RH front door loudspeaker
152 Electro-magnetic door locks switch
153 Radio loudspeaker wire
154 Wire junction - rear interior light harness
155 Rear interior light
156 LH rear door pillar switch
157 RH rear door pillar switch
158 Automatic transmission selector illumination
160 Rear passengers cigar lighter
164 Fuel pump
165 Wire junction - fuel injection harness
182 Tailgate RH counterbalance
186 Wire junction - fuel pump harness
187 Speedometer relay
188 Pump switch relay
189 Fuel filler lock solenoid
190 Fuel priming pump (tp)
191 Tailgate lock solenoid
192 Tailgate earth
193 Tailgate opening switch
194 Junction block - engine cooling fan motor harness
195 Idle cut-out

Harness identification
A Engine front
B Rear
K Starter
L Interior light - door pillar switches
P Electro-magnetic locks
R Engine
T Console bridge

Colour code

Be	Beige	G	Grey	S	Pink	M	Maroon
Bc	White	J	Yellow	R	Red	Vi	Violet
B	Blue	N	Black	V	Green	Or	Orange
C	Clear						

Key to wire code

Example S16V-2 53
S16 Wire colour number
V Wire colour
2 Wire gauge
53 Destination of wire

Wire gauge code

| No | 1 | 2 | 3 | 4 | 5 | 6 | 7 | 8 | 9 |
| Wire dia. (mm) | 0.7 | 0.9 | 1.0 | 1.2 | 1.6 | 2.0 | 2.5 | 3.0 | 4.5 |

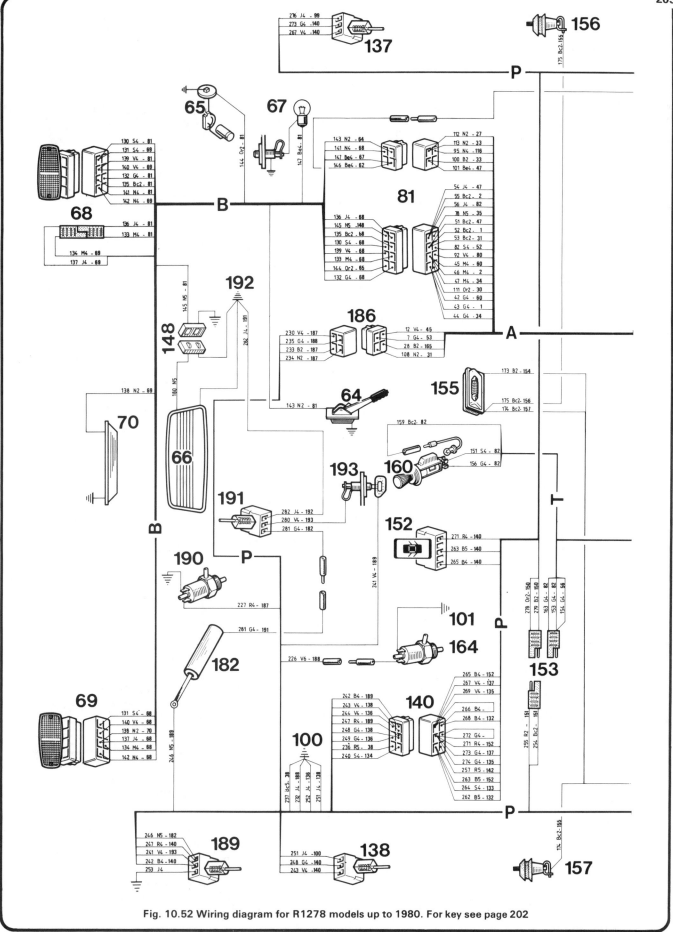

Fig. 10.52 Wiring diagram for R1278 models up to 1980. For key see page 202

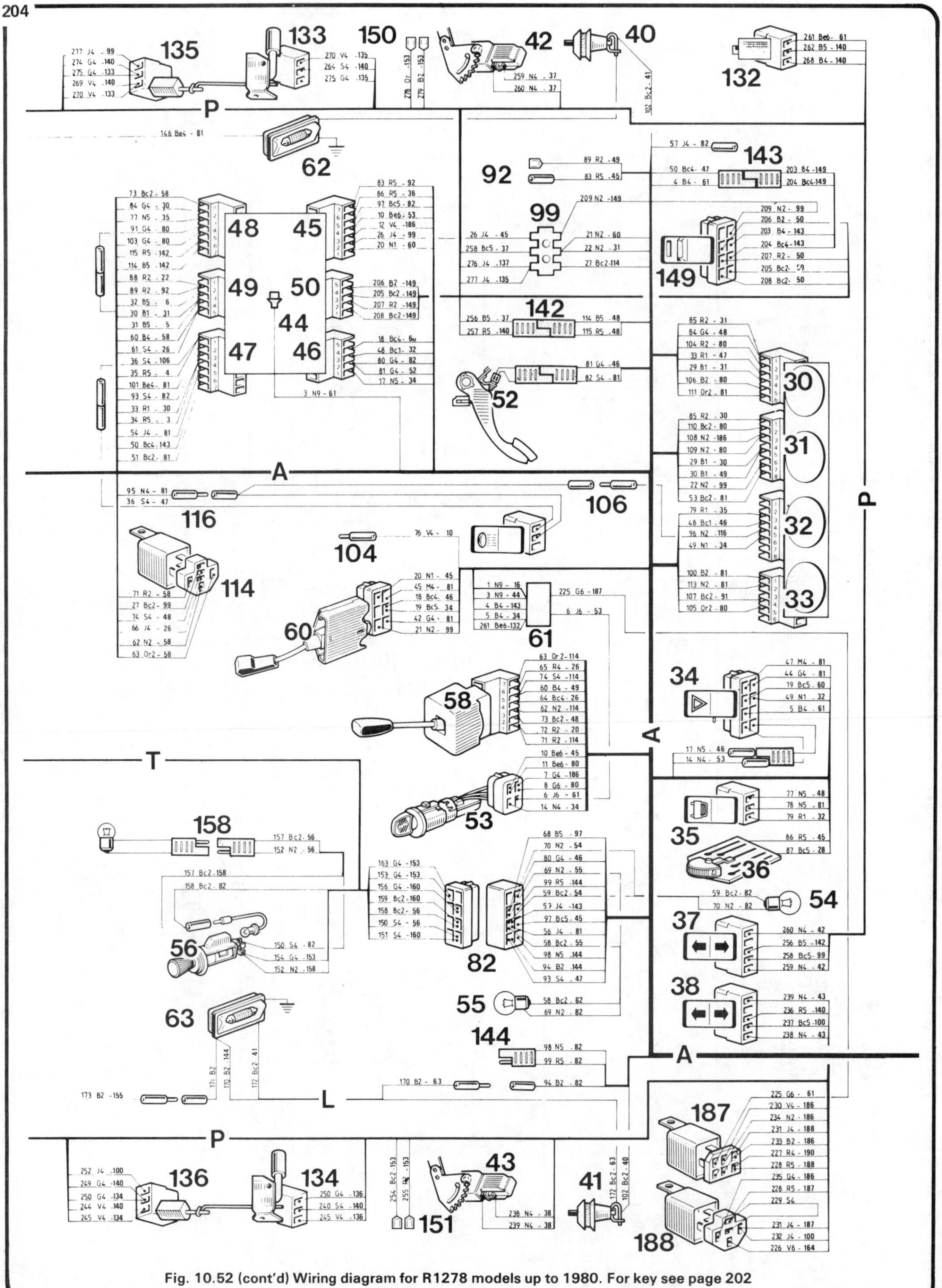

135
277 J4 - 99
274 G4 - 140
275 G4 - 133
269 V4 - 140
270 V4 - 133

133
150
270 V4 - 135
266 S4 - 140
275 G4 - 135
278 Or - 153
279 B2 - 153

42
259 N4 - 37
260 N4 - 37

40
102 Bc2 - 41

132
261 Be6 - 61
262 B5 - 140
268 B4 - 140

146 Be4 - 81

62

92
89 R2 - 49
83 R5 - 45

143
57 J4 - 82
50 Bc4 - 47
4 B4 - 61
203 B4 -149
204 Bc4-149

209 N2 -149

99
26 J4 - 45
258 Bc5 - 37
276 J4 - 137
277 J4 - 135
21 N2 - 60
22 N2 - 31
27 Bc2-114

149
209 N2 - 99
206 B2 - 50
203 B4 - 143
204 Bc4-143
207 R2 - 50
205 Bc2- 50
208 Bc2- 50

73 Bc2 - 58
84 G4 - 30
77 N5 - 35
91 G4 - 80
103 G4 - 80
115 R5 -142
114 B5 -142

48 **45**
83 R5 - 92
86 R5 - 36
97 Bc5 - 82
10 Be6 - 53
12 V4 -186
26 J4 - 99
20 N1 - 60

88 R2 - 22
89 R2 - 92
32 B5 - 6
30 B1 - 31
31 B5 - 5

49 **50**
44
206 B2 -149
205 Bc2 -149
207 R2 -149
208 Bc2-149

60 B4 - 58
61 S4 - 26
36 S4 -106
35 R5 - 4
101 Be4 - 81
93 S4 - 82
33 R1 - 30
34 R5 - 3
54 J4 - 81
50 Bc4-143
51 Bc2 - 81

47 **46**
18 Bc4- 6u
48 Bc1- 32
80 G4 - 82
81 G4 - 52
17 N5 - 34

3 N9 - 61

142
256 B5 - 37
257 R5 -140
114 B5 - 48
115 R5 - 48

52
81 G4 - 46
82 S4 - 81

85 R2 - 31
84 G4 - 48
104 R2 - 80
33 R1 - 47
29 B1 - 31
106 B2 - 80
111 Or2 - 81

30

85 R2 - 30
110 Bc2 - 80
108 N2 -186
109 N2 - 80
29 B1 - 30
30 B1 - 49
22 N2 - 99
53 Bc2 - 31

31

79 R1 - 35
48 Bc1 - 46
96 N2 - 116
49 N1 - 34

32

100 B2 - 81
113 N2 - 81
107 Bc2 - 91
105 Or2 - 80

33

A

95 N4 - 81
36 S4 - 47

106

116

104
76 V4 - 10

71 R2 - 58
27 Bc2 - 99
74 S4 - 48
66 J4 - 26
62 N2 - 58
63 Or2 - 58

114

60
20 N1 - 45
45 M4 - 81
18 Bc4- 46
19 Bc5 - 34
42 G4 - 81
21 N2 - 99

1 N9 - 16
3 N9 - 44
4 B4 - 143
5 B4 - 34
261 Be6-132

61
225 G6 - 187
6 J6 - 53

34
47 M4 - 81
44 G4 - 81
19 Bc5 - 60
49 N1 - 32
5 B4 - 61

A

63 Or2 -114
65 R4 - 26
74 S4 -114
60 B4 - 49
64 Bc4 - 26
62 N2 -114
73 Bc2 - 48
72 R2 - 20
71 R2 -114

58

10 Be6 - 45
11 Be6 - 80
7 G4 -186
8 G6 - 80
6 J6 - 53
14 N4 - 34

17 N5 - 46
14 N4 - 53

35
77 N5 - 48
78 N5 - 81
79 R1 - 32

T

53

36
86 R5 - 45
87 Bc5 - 28

158
157 Bc2 - 56
152 N2 - 56

157 Bc2 -158
158 Bc2 - 82

82
68 B5 - 97
70 N2 - 54
80 G4 - 46
69 N2 - 55
99 R5 -144
59 Bc2 - 54
57 J4 -143
97 Bc5 - 45
56 J4 - 81
58 Bc2 - 55
98 N5 -144
94 B2 -144
93 S4 - 47

163 G4 -153
153 G4 -153
156 G4 -160
159 Bc2 -160
158 Bc2 - 82
150 S4 - 56
151 S4 -160

54
59 Bc2 - 82
70 N2 - 82

37
260 N4 - 42
256 B5 -142
258 Bc5-99
259 N4 - 42

56
150 S4 - 82
154 G4 -153
152 N2 -158

55
58 Bc2 - 62
69 N2 - 82

38
239 N4 - 43
236 R5 -140
237 Bc5-100
238 N4 - 43

63

144
98 N5 - 82
99 R5 - 82

173 B2 -155
171 B2
170 B2 -144
172 Bc2 - 41

170 B2 - 63
94 B2 - 82

A

L

187
225 G6 - 61
230 V4 -186
234 N2 -186
231 J4 -188
233 B2 -186
227 R4 -190
228 R5 -188
235 G4 -186
228 R5 -187
229 S4

P

136
252 J4 -100
249 G4 -140
250 B4 -134
244 V4 -140
245 V4 -134

134
250 G4 -136
240 S4 -140
245 V4 -136

151
254 Bc2 -153
255 R5 -153

43
238 N4 - 38
239 N4 - 38

41
172 Bc2 - 63
102 Bc2- 40

188
231 J4 -187
232 J4 -100
226 V6 -164

P

Fig. 10.52 (cont'd) Wiring diagram for R1278 models up to 1980. For key see page 202

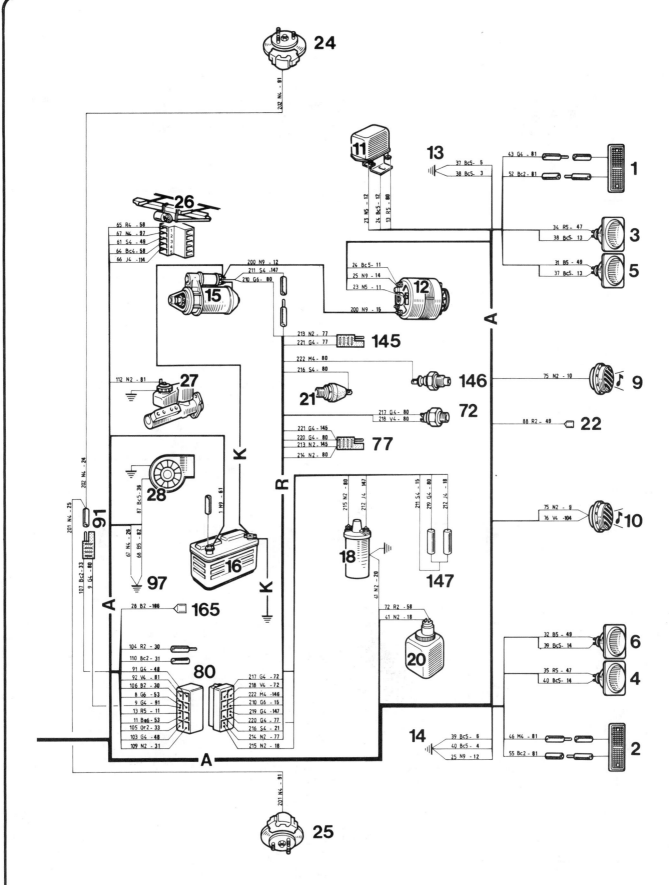

Fig. 10.52 (cont'd) wiring diagram for R1278 models up to 1980. For Key see page 202

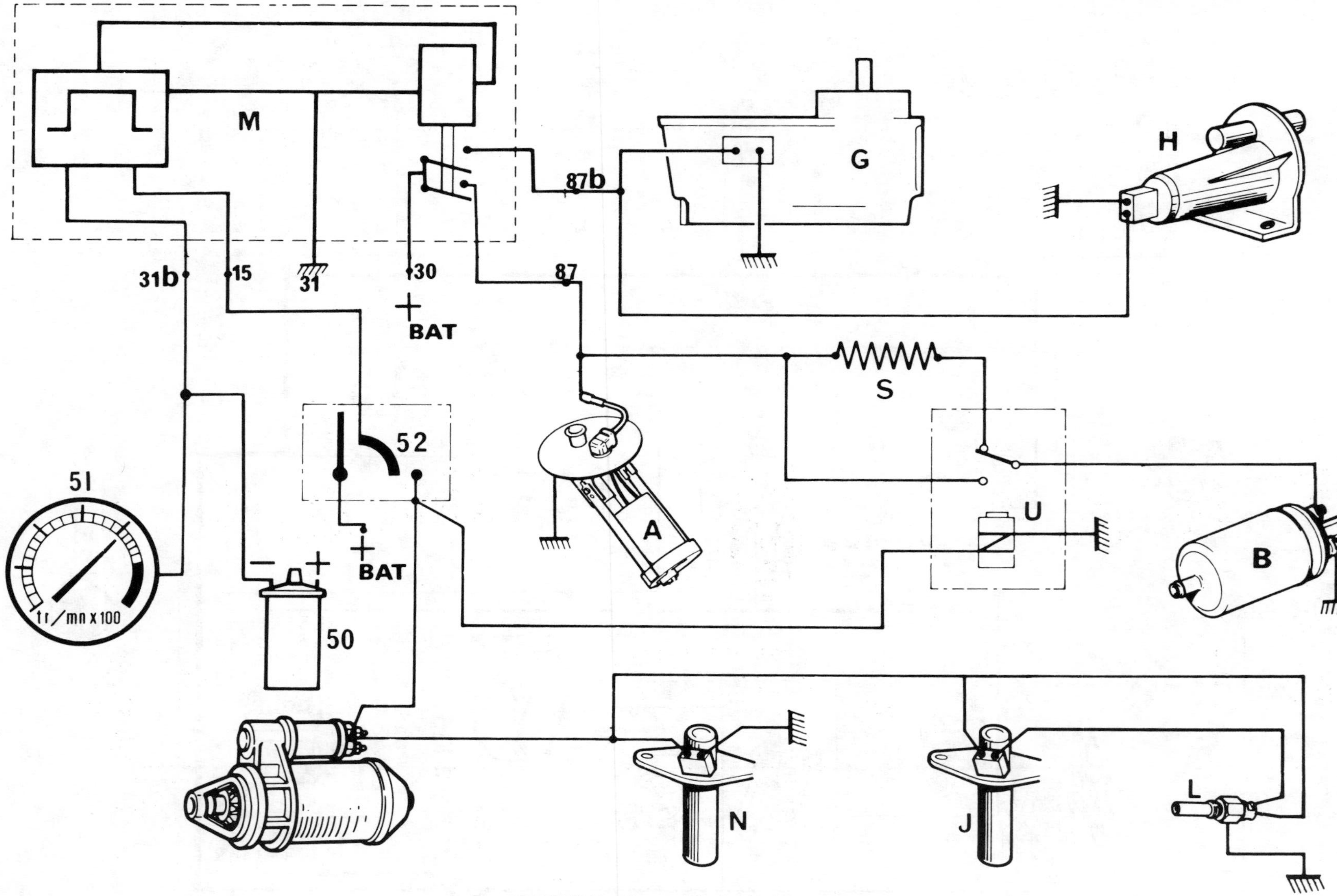

Fig. 10.53 Wiring diagram for fuel injection system

Key to Fig. 10.53

A Immersed fuel priming pump
B Main fuel pump
G Compensating pressure regulator
H Auxiliary air device

J Cold start injector
L Thermo-line switch
M RPM relay

N Electro-magnetic valve
S Resistance wire
U Inversing relay

50 Ignition coil
51 Tachometer
52 Starter switch

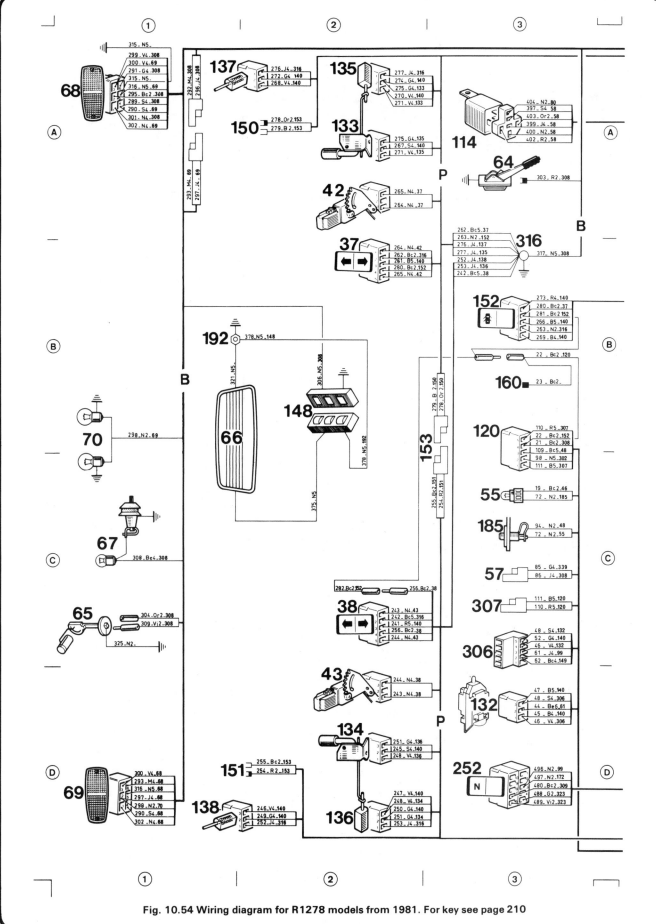

Fig. 10.54 Wiring diagram for R1278 models from 1981. For key see page 210

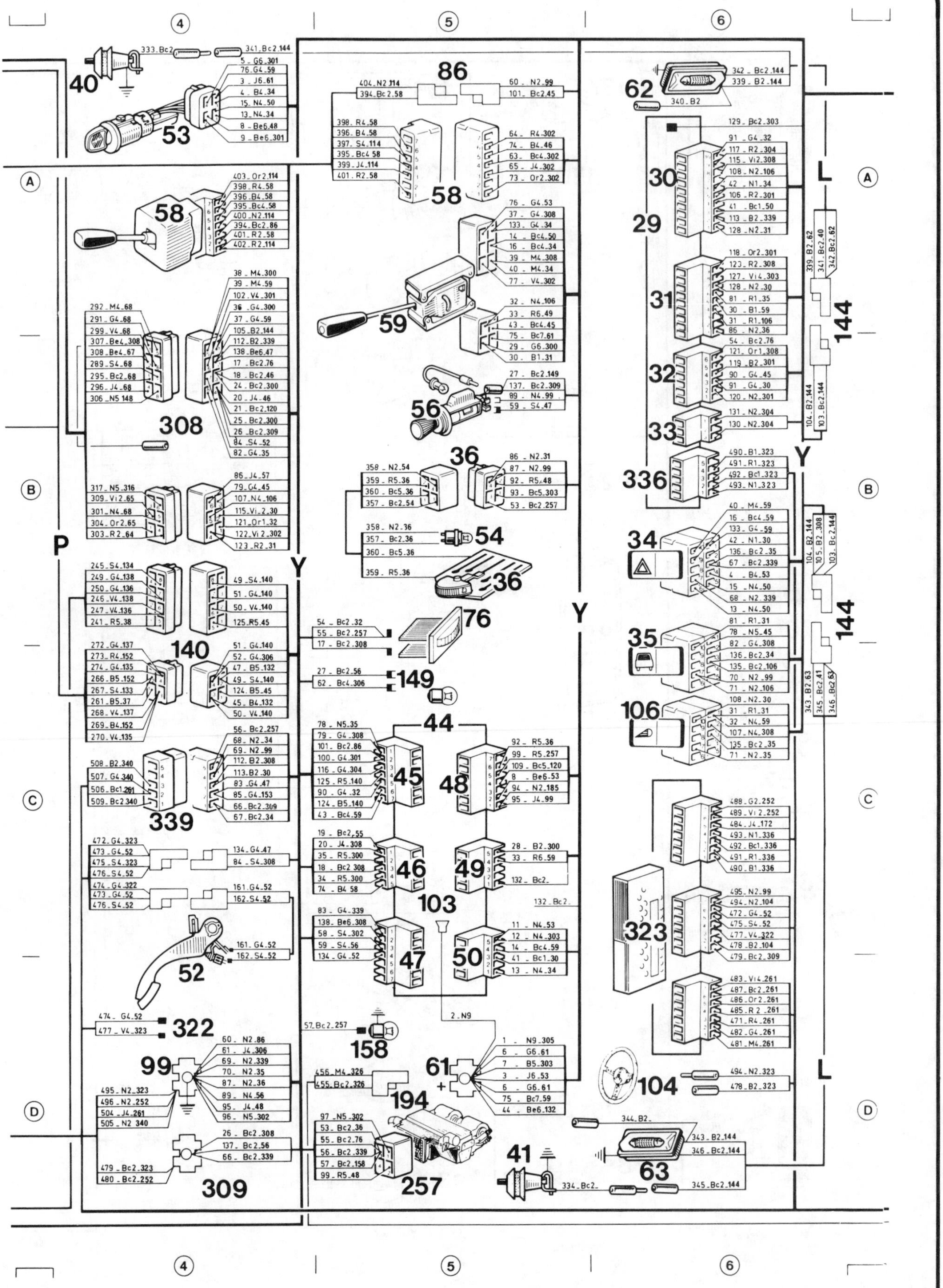

Fig. 10.54 (cont'd) Wiring diagram for R1278 models from 1981. For key see page 210

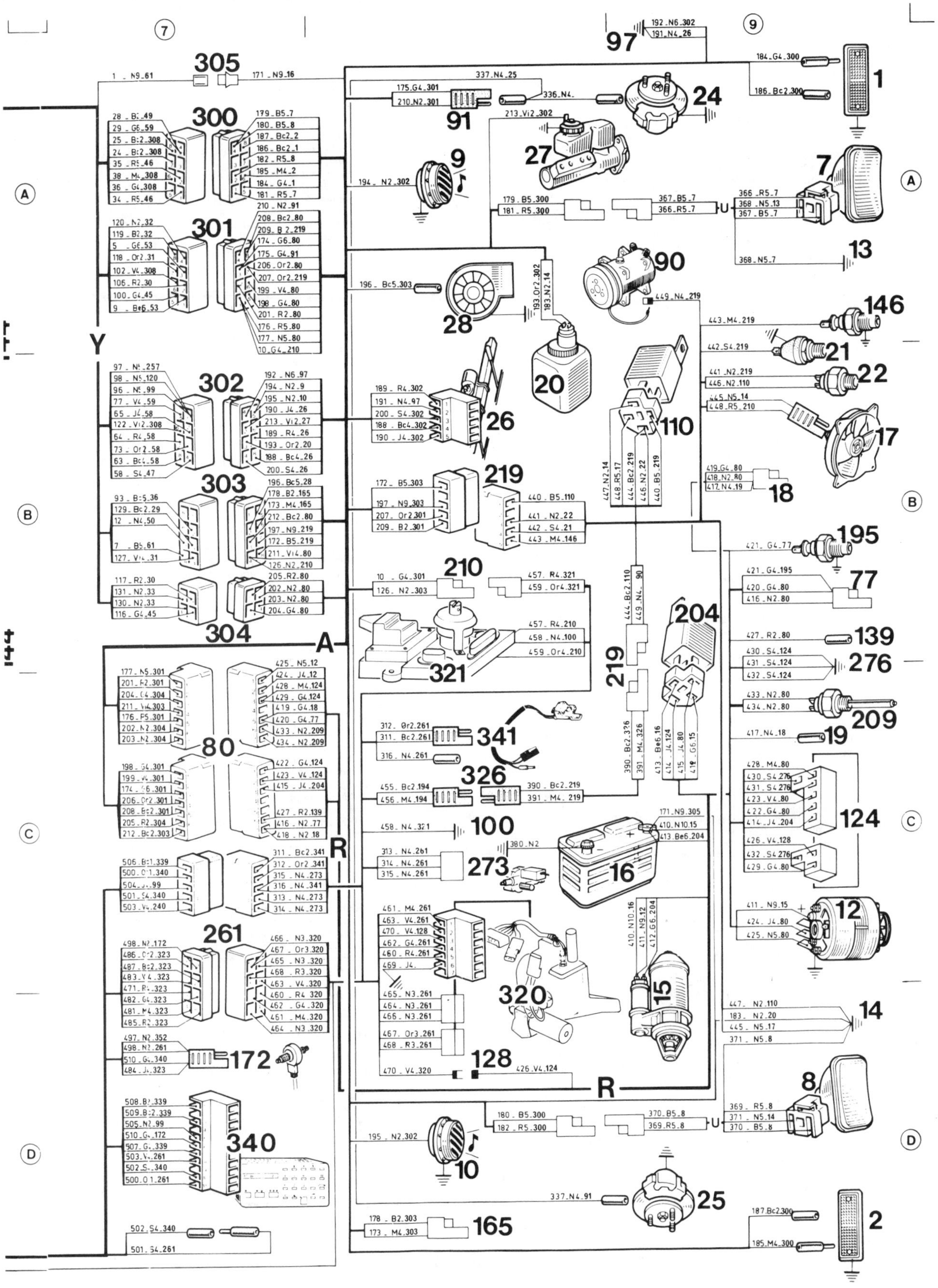

Fig. 10.54 (cont'd) wiring diagram for R1278 models from 1981. For key see page 210

Key to Fig. 10.54. Note all items are fitted to all models

Item		Location
1	LH sidelight and direction indicator	A–9
2	RH sidelight and direction indicator	D–9
7	LH headlight	A–9
8	RH headlight	D–9
9	LH horn	A–8
10	RH horn	D–8
12	Alternator	C–9
13	LH earth	A–9
14	RH earth	D–9
15	Starter	D–9
16	Battery	C–9
17	Engine cooling fan motor	B–9
18	Ignition coil	B–9
20	Windscreen washer pump	B–8
21	Oil pressure switch	B–9
22	Thermal switch on radiator	B–9
24	LH front brake	A–9
25	RH front brake	D–9
26	Windscreen wiper plate	B–8
27	Master cylinder	A–8
28	Heating – ventilating fan motor	A–8
29	Instrument panel	A–6
30	Connector No 1 – Instrument panel	A–6
31	Connector No 2 – Instrument panel	A–6
32	Connector No 3 – Instrument panel	B–6
33	Connector No 4 – Instrument panel	B–6
34	Hazard warning light switch	B–6
35	Rear screen demister switch	C–6
36	Heating – ventilating fan resistance	B–5
37	LH front door window switch	B–2
38	RH front door window switch	C–2
40	LH front door pillar switch	A–4
41	RH front door pillar switch	D–5
42	LH window winder	A–2
43	RH window winder	D–2
44	Accessories plate	C–5
45	Junction block – front harness and accessories plate	C–5
46	Junction block – front harness and accessories plate	C–5
47	Junction block – front harness and accessories plate	D–5
48	Junction block – front harness and accessories plate	C–5
49	Junction block – front harness and accessories plate	C–5
50	Junction block – front harness and accessories plate	D–5
52	Stoplights switch	D–4
53	Ignition – starter switch	A–4
54	Heater controls illumination	B–5
55	Glove compartment light	C–3
56	Cigar lighter	B–5
57	Feed to car radio	C–3
58	Windscreen wiper-washer switch	A–5 & A–4
59	Lighting switch	B–5
61	Junction – + feed before ignition	D–5
62	LH interior light	A–6
63	RH interior light	D–6
64	Handbrake On Warning light switch	A–3
65	Fuel gauge tank unit	C–1
66	Rear screen demister	B–1
67	Luggage compartment light	C–1
68	LH rear light assembly	A–1
69	RH rear light assembly	D–1
70	Number plate light	B–1
76	Instrument panel lighting rheostat	B–5
77	Wire junction – diagnostic socket	B–9
80	Junction block – front and engine harnesses	C–7
86	Junction block – time switch relay harness	A–5
90	Wire junction – air conditioning electro-magnetic clutch	A–9
91	Wire junction – brake pad wear warning light	A–8
97	Bodyshell earth	A–9
99	Dashboard earth	D–4
100	Scuttle panel gusset earth	C–8
103	Feed to accessories plate	C–5
104	Wire junction – steering wheel switch	D–6
106	Rear foglight switch	C–6
110	Engine cooling fan motor relay	B–9
114	Windscreen wiper time switch	A–3

Item		Location
120	Sunroof switch	D–3
138	Kickdown switch	D–8
132	Inertia switch	D–3
133	LH front door lock switch	A–2
134	RH front door lock switch	D–2
135	LH front door electro-magnetic switch	A–2
136	RH front door electro-magnetic switch	D–2
137	LH rear door electro-magnetic switch	A–1
138	RH rear door electro-magnetic switch	D–1
139	Automatic transmission oil temperature switch	B–9
140	Junction block – lock harness	B–4
146	Thermal switch	A–9
148	Tailgate fixed contact	B–2
149	Headlight switch illumination	C–5
150	LH front door loudspeaker	A–2
151	RH front door loudspeaker	D–1
152	Electro-magnetic door locks switch	B–3
153	Car radio loudspeaker wires	B–2
158	Auto-transmission selector	D–5
158	Auto-transmission selector illumination	D–5
160	Rear cigar lighter	B–3
165	Wire junction – fuel injection harness	D–8
172	Impulse generator	D–7
185	Glove compartment switch	C–3
192	Tailgate earth	B–1
194	Junction block – engine cooling fan motor	D–5
195	Idle cut-out	B–9
204	Starter relay	B–9
209	Engine oil level indicator sensor	C–9
210	Junction block – engine front harness to integral electronic ignition harness	B–8
219	Junction block – engine cooling fan feed relay	B–8
252	NORMALUR Cruise Control switch	D–3
257	Cool air fan motor	D–5
261	Wire junction – rpm control	C–7
273	Flowmeter	C–8
300	Junction block No 1 – dashboard and engine front harnesses	A–7
301	Junction block No 1 – dashboard and engine front harnesses	A–7
302	Junction block No 3 – dashboard and engine front harnesses	B–7
303	Junction block No 4 – dashboard and engine front harnesses	B–7
304	Junction block No 5 – dashboard and engine front harnesses	B–7
305	Junction block No 6 – dashboard and engine front harnesses	A–7
306	Remote unlocking control	C–3
307	Wire junction – sunroof motor	C–3
308	Wire junction – dashboard and rear harnesses	B–4
309	Junction plate – sidelights	D–4
316	Console earth	B–3
320	NORMALUR servo motor	D–8
321	Junction – electronic ignition module	C–8
322	Clutch pedal switch	D–4
323	NORMALUR electronic box	C–6
326	Junction – NORMALUR with air conditioning	C–8
336	Connector No5 – instrument panel	B–6
339	Junction with driving aid harness	C–4
340	Driving aid control box	D–7
341	Temperature sensor	C–8

Harness identification

A	Engine front
B	Rear
L	Interior lights – door pillar switches
R	Electro-magnetic door locks
R	Engine
U	Headlights
Y	Dashboard

Colour code

Be	Beige	C	Clear	S	Pink	M	Maroon
Bc	White	J	Yellow	R	Red	Vi	Violet
B	Blue	N	Black	V	Green	Or	Orange

Key to wire code

Example   S16-V2 53
S16   Wire code number
V   Wire colour
2   Wire gauge
53   Destination of wire

Chapter 11 Suspension and steering

Contents

Specifications

Suspension type
Front .... Independent, double wishbones with coil springs and telescopic shock absorbers. Anti-roll bar fitted

Rear .... Independent, wishbones and articulated bars. Coil springs, telescopic shock absorbers, anti roll bar

Steering type .... Rack-and-pinion with power assistance

Front axle and steering geometry
Camber angle (unladen) .... 30' ± 30' (non-adjustable)
Kingpin inclination (unladen) .... Equal to within 1° between each side (non-adjustable)
Toe-out .... 0 to 0.125 in (0 to 3 mm)

Anti-roll bar diameter
Front .... 0.885 in (22.5 mm)
Rear .... 0.748 in (19 mm)

Rear suspension
Camber angle .... 0° ± 1° (non-adjustable)
Parallelism – rear wheels .... 0 ± 1 mm (0 ± 0.039 in)

Lubricants
Power steering oil type .... Mobil ATF 220, Elf Renaultmatic DR, or equivalent
Capacity .... 1.25 Imp pints (0.7 litres)

Torque wrench settings

	lbf ft	Nm
Steering knuckle upper balljoint nut	75	100
Steering knuckle lower balljoint nut	45	60
Front hub nut	158	210
Lower balljoint retaining nut	11	15
Upper suspension arm pivot bolt	71	95
Upper balljoint retaining nut	75	100
Lower suspension arm pivot bolt	98	130
Front shock absorber upper retaining nut	11	15
Front shock absorber lower retaining nut	45	60
Front shock absorber lower eye bolt	60	80
Steering wheel nut	33	45
Steering rack/ram eye bolt	37	50
Hydraulic ram-to-eye nut	26	35
Hydraulic ram retaining bolt (steering box end)	55	75
Tie-rod balljoint nut	26	35
Tie-rod end fitting locknut	26	35
Axial balljoint (tie-rod to steering rack)	30	40
Steering box retaining bolts	38	50
Lower column universal joint bolts	23	30

	lbf ft	Nm
Flexible coupling bolts	11	15
Rack end fitting locknuts	30	40
Steering arm fork end pin	38	50
Castor tie-rod nut	75	100
Caliper bracket retaining bolts	50	65
Roadwheel nuts	45 to 60	60 to 80
Front anti-roll bar-to-half axle nuts	15	20
Link to front anti-roll bar retaining nuts	11	15
Side-member clamp nuts	11	15
Lateral arm self-locking nuts	26	35
Rear shock absorber bottom mounting pin	75	100
Rear shock absorber top mounting nut	53	70
Rear anti-roll bar fastening	15	20

1   General description and maintenance

The suspension system on all four wheels is independent, having double wishbones at the front with coil springs and a 'three element' type layout at the rear. This comprises one transverse and one lateral swing arm to each side, together with a vertical coil spring and shock absorber.

An anti-roll bar is fitted front and rear; the shock absorbers are of the telescopic double-acting type.

Rack-and-pinion steering gear is employed and is located at the rear of the engine above the transmission housing. In this position it is unlikely to sustain any damage in the event of front end collision (although should you be unlucky enough to be so involved it should be checked before using the car).

A jointed type of steering column is used and an anti-theft steering lock incorporated into the ignition switch. Power assisted steering is fitted and this consists of three main components: the hydraulic pump (belt driven from the camshaft), the rotary valve unit (attached to the steering box at the lower end of the column) and the double-acting ram, mounted in line with the box.

Some steering and suspension tasks require the use of special tools and it is therefore suggested that you read through the relevant Section concerned, prior to undertaking any jobs. For the same reason, steering and suspension adjustments should be entrusted to your Renault dealer who has the specialised tools and knowledge required to achieve the necessary accuracy.

For maximum safety combined with vehicle efficiency, the steering and suspension systems should be checked regularly during the normal maintenance procedures. Although there are no grease nipples to the steering and suspension joints, it does not mean they can be completely ignored. The following items should be checked occasionally, and definitely prior to the annual government vehicle test.

Inspect the outside of the shock absorbers for leakage and check their operation by pressing down the front end of the car and releasing it. It should return to its normal position without any repeated 'bouncing' action.

With the car parked on level ground, check that it sits level from side to side, and does not appear to be drooping at one end, particularly down at the back.

Examine all the rubber bushes of the suspension arms. The rubber should be firm, not softened by oil or cracked by weathering. The pin which pivots in the bush should be held centrally, and not able to make metal-to-metal contact.

Check the outside of the springs. If rusting, they should be sprayed with oil.

Check the tightness of all nuts, particularly those holding the front suspension balljoints and the shock absorbers to their fixings.

Grip the top of each wheel in turn and rock vigorously. Any looseness in the bearings or the suspension can be felt, as can failed rubber bushes giving metal-to-metal contact sound.

Freewheel slowly with the engine switched off, and listen for unusual noises.

The rubber boots of the balljoints that exclude dirt and water should be inspected to ensure they are properly in position and not torn (photo). If dirt or water gets into such a joint, it is ruined within a few hundred miles. The joint should be removed and a new boot fitted without delay.

Check the steering for wear. An assistant should wiggle the steering to and fro, just hard enough to make the front wheels move. Watch the balljoints. There should be no visible free movement. Then grasp a front wheel with the hands at three and nine o'clock on the wheel. Work at the wheel hard to twist it. The rocking should shift the steering wheel but no lost motion should be felt.

Check the power assisted steering hoses and associated fittings for any signs of leakage. Check that the hoses are not chafing against surrounding components.

Check that the steering rack to tie-rod gaiters are in good condition and securely located.

Check the condition of the anti-roll bar and bushes (photo).

1.0A Check condition of rubber boots

1.0B Check the anti-roll bar location bushes for signs of wear, severe cracking and decay

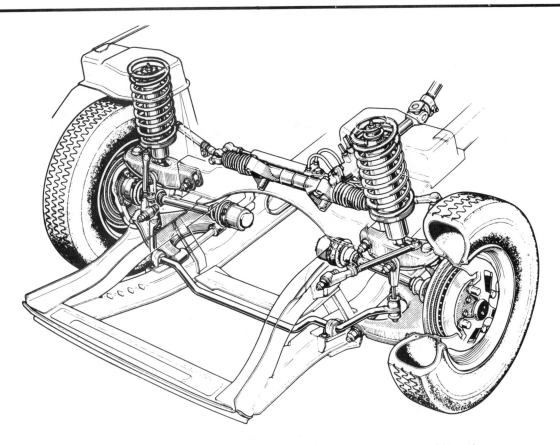

Fig. 11.1 The front suspension and steering layout (left-hand drive shown) (Sec 1)

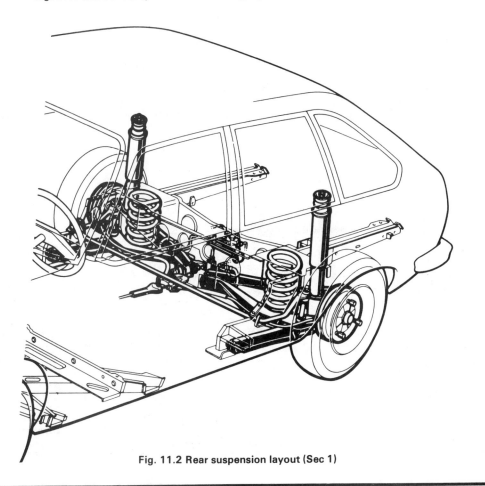

Fig. 11.2 Rear suspension layout (Sec 1)

2 Front shock absorbers and coil springs – removal and refitting

1   Raise the front of the vehicle and support with axle stands or blocks. Remove the front roadwheel(s).
2   You will now need a suitable coil spring compressor similar to that shown in Fig. 11.3. The tool shown is the official Renault tool number Sus 596, which should be used if available. **Do not** use makeshift methods – serious injury could result.
3   Compress the spring sufficiently to permit the spring to be lifted clear of the shock absorber cup.
4   Detach the shock absorber at its top mounting position in the engine compartment inner wing panel (photo). Loosen and remove the top locking nut and then the retaining nut; see Fig. 11.4.
5   At the bottom of the shock absorber, hold firm with a suitable wrench and unscrew and remove the lower retaining nut.
6   Unscrew the shock absorber to detach it complete with the compressed spring assembly.
7   Unscrew the spring compressor bolts in a cautious and progressive manner so the spring is not allowed suddenly to become

2.4 Front shock absorber top mounting

released when under compression. **Take care** – the spring is under considerable pressure.
8   It may be possible to have a defective production type shock absorber overhauled by having a new cartridge fitted but this should be entrusted to your Renault dealer.
9   If renewing a shock absorber or coil spring, the replacement should be of the same setting type as that removed. The shock absorber must be pumped whilst holding it vertically to prime it prior to fitting.
10   Refitting is a reversal of the removal procedure. When inserting the spring into position, locate its upper end into the top thrust plate and ensure that the cups are fitted in the correct manner as shown in Fig. 11.5.
11   When the shock absorber and spring assembly are reinstalled, tighten the locknut to the specified torque whilst retaining the shock absorber with a wrench at the bottom.

3 Front suspension upper arm – removal and refitting

1   Raise the front of the vehicle so that both front wheels are clear of the ground and support with axle stands or blocks to make secure. Remove the roadwheel from the side to be worked on.
2   Loosen the shock absorber lower mounting locknut.
3   Remove the castor tie-rod retaining nut from the suspension upper arm and detach the rod.
4   Unscrew and remove the shock absorber lower mounting pivot bolt.
5   Unscrew and remove the upper arm balljoint retaining nut and use a balljoint separator to detach the joint.
6   Unscrew and remove the suspension arm pivot bolt, lifting it sufficiently clear to allow the shock absorber lower mounting to be unscrewed and detached (Fig. 11.7).
7   Remove the suspension arm. Refer to Section 6 for bush renewal.
8   Refitting is a reversal of the removal procedure, but do not tighten the respective retaining nuts and bolts fully until the fitting is complete. Then lower the car and tighten the respective fastenings to their specified torque settings.

4 Suspension balljoints – removal and refitting

1   The suspension balljoints are sealed for life and therefore need renewal rather than servicing if defective. However, it may be possible to purchase a new rubber bellows kit if one should fail as long as the

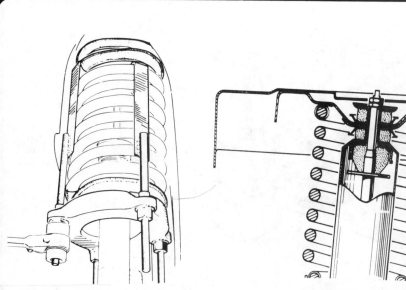

Fig. 11.3 Coil spring compressor (typical) in position (Sec 2)

Fig. 11.4 Front shock absorber upper mounting (Sec 2)

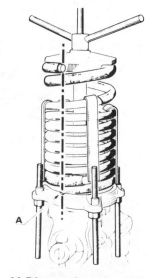

Fig. 11.5 Locate the spring with small diameter in cup and align end of top coil with the notch in the cup (A) (Sec 2)

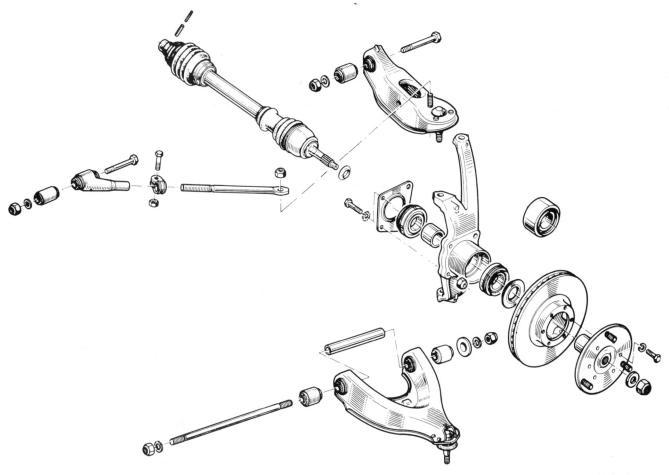

Fig. 11.6 Exploded view of the front stub axle, driveshaft and upper/lower suspension arm assembly components (Sec 3)

joint remains in good condition. Follow the procedure for balljoint removal but go only so far as to enable the old bellows to be cut off and the new one fitted. Repack the balljoint with high melting-point grease and take care fitting the circlip.

2 *Top balljoints:* Jack up the car and place on axle stands. Fit the spacer leg described in Section 7. Turn the steering to left lock when working on a right-hand balljoint and vice versa. Unscrew the balljoint nut.

3 Using a balljoint separator, split the top balljoint (photo). If necessary, to free the balljoint from the upright finally, obtain a small wowoden wedge. With a tyre lever or strong screwdriver, lever on the

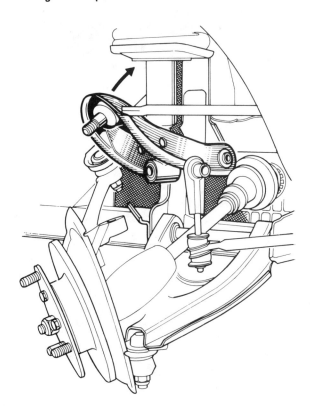

Fig. 11.7 Front suspension upper arm removal (Sec 3)

4.3 Balljoint separator

wedge under the upper suspension arm on top of the driveshaft outer joint. The balljoint should then be free.

4   The original balljoints are riveted onto the wishbones, as shown in Fig. 11.8. These rivets will have to be drilled out. Clean up the rivet heads with a wire brush and file a good flat onto their heads. Use an electric drill if possible. Be patient and very careful. It is not a 'rush' job. Do not attempt to drill from below and try not to drill into the wishbone itself. If done carefully it is not necessary to remove the wishbone from the vehicle.

5   When purchasing new balljoints make sure that the correct fixing setscrews and nuts, to replace the rivets, are supplied. This is important.

6   Fit the new balljoint into its correct seating and place the setscrews from below up through the balljoint and then through the wishbone. Tighten the nyloc nuts firmly.

7   Refit all the parts in an opposite procedure to their removal. Be sure that the balljoints are finally tight onto the upright when the car is resting on all four wheels.

8   It is advisable to have the front wheel alignment checked if a balljoint is refitted. Have this done by a Renault agent.

9   *Lower balljoints:* The suspension arm must be removed for renewal. This is described in Section 5. The balljoint refitting procedure is otherwise the same as that for the upper joint as described in paragraphs 4 to 7.

5   Front suspension lower arm – removal and refitting

1   Before proceeding to remove either or both of the front suspension lower arms, the following should be noted:

   (a) *The right-hand arm differs from that of the left and should therefore be kept separate if both are removed (Fig. 11.9)*
   (b) *Do not remove the chassis crossmember located between the front side-members*

2   Raise the front of the vehicle and make secure with axle stands or blocks. Remove the roadwheel on the side concerned.

3   Unscrew the suspension arm lower balljoint retaining nut and detach the joint using a suitable separator.

4   Unscrew and remove the lower arm pivot bolt (photo) and remove the lower suspension arm as shown in Fig. 11.10. Refer to Section 6 for bush renwal.

5   Refit in reverse order and ensure that the castor shim is correctly relocated at the rear as shown (Fig. 11.11). Locate the balljoint and hand tighten the nut initially.

6   Smear the pivot bolt with grease and reassemble. Do not tighten fully at this stage.

7   Lower the vehicle, then tighten the pivot bolt and balljoint nut to their specified torque wrench settings.

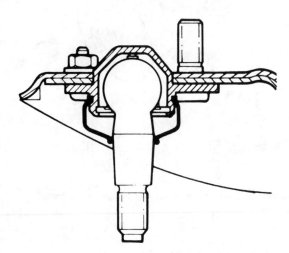

Fig. 11.8 The balljoint location showing rivet and retaining nut positions (Sec 4)

5.4 Front suspension lever arm pivot bolt and nut

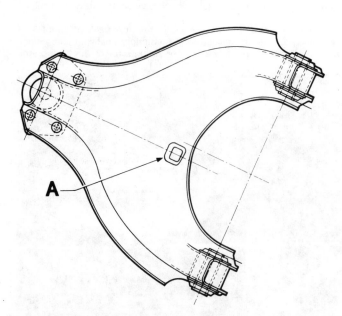

Fig. 11.9 Front suspension lower arm – the left-hand arm is dished at 'A' (Sec 5)

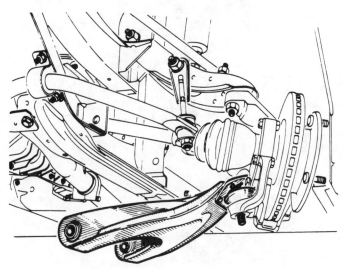

Fig. 11.10 Lower suspension arm removal (Sec 5)

6 Front suspension arm bushes – renewal

1 The removal and refitting of the suspension arm bushes necessitates removal of the upper and/or lower wishbone arm as applicable (refer to Section 3 or 5 accordingly).

The resilient (rebound) bush – lower wishbone

2 With the arm removed, each bush must be removed and a new one fitted, one at a time. This is necessary to enable the symmetrical bush spacing and alignment with the pivot pin to be kept.

3 To press a bush out you should support the arm in a vice.

4 Using a piece of suitable tube with an outside diameter of 40 mm (1.575 in) press or drive the old bush out of its housing. Where the old bush is difficult to remove, use a hacksaw blade and cut through the old bush to section it. Take care not to cut beyond the bush!

5 Clean out the housing and press the new bush into position. When fitted, check that the distance between the bushes is as shown in Fig. 11.13.

6 Repeat the procedure with the opposing bush and recheck the clearance.

Flexible bush – upper wishbone

7 The flexible suspension bushes are removed in a similar manner to that described above except that the press tube diameter differs. See Fig. 11.14. It should also be noted that the flexible bushes are centralised as shown and this must be taken into account when fitting.

7 Front stub axle and hub bearings – removal and refitting

1 Raise the side of the car to be worked on and support with axle stands or blocks to secure. Remove the roadwheel.

2 A spacer leg will have to be positioned between the lower mounting pin of the shock absorber and the suspension lower arm hinge pin as shown in Fig. 11.15. Spacer legs can be manufactured quite easily, using some 1 in square section tubing out to length. The end sections must have an inverted 'V' shape to locate on the hinge

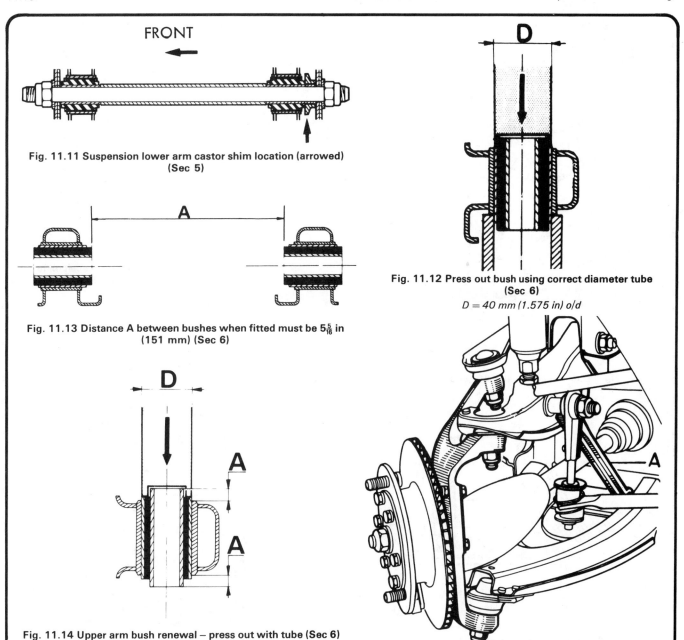

Fig. 11.11 Suspension lower arm castor shim location (arrowed) (Sec 5)

Fig. 11.13 Distance A between bushes when fitted must be 5⁵⁄₁₆ in (151 mm) (Sec 6)

Fig. 11.12 Press out bush using correct diameter tube (Sec 6)
D = 40 mm (1.575 in) o/d

Fig. 11.14 Upper arm bush renewal – press out with tube (Sec 6)
A = A
D = 31.5 mm (1.240 in) o/d

Fig. 11.15 Locate spacer leg 'A' as shown (Sec 7)

pin and mounting pin. The official Renault spacer legs are designated tool number T Av 603. It is worth making up or obtaining a pair of these spacer legs as several operations require the use of them.

3   With a spacer leg firmly in position as described, refer to Chapter 9 and remove the disc caliper unit from the front axle. Do not detach the hydraulic pipe, nor allow the caliper unit to hang suspended by the pipe – support its weight.

4   Remove the front hub and disc assembly (see Chapter 9).

5   Unscrew and remove the respective balljoint retaining nuts, using a balljoint separator to detach each joint in turn (Fig. 11.16).

6   Carefully withdraw and remove the stub axle unit, disengaging it from the driveshaft.

7   Remove the hub-to-disc retaining bolts to separate the two.

8   To remove the inner track ring you will require Renault special tool No T. Ar 65 with bolts or screws from Renault clamp B Tr 02 as shown

in Fig. 11.17. Alternatively, fabricate or obtain a similar split extractor. On removal of the inner track ring, retain the thrust washer.

9   The bearing closure plate and distance piece must now be removed, and the outer bearing track ring pressed out. Use one of the inner track rings to achieve this. The bearing ball cage and seals are left in position (Fig. 11.18).

10 Before fitting the new bearings, remove the plastic cover from each side (Fig. 11.20).

11 To press the new bearing into position you will need a length of tube with an 83 mm (3.268 in) outside diameter and 76 mm (2.992 in) inside diameter, the loading to be taken on the outer bearing. Press the bearing into position in its stub axle carrier with the plastic retainer securing the inner track rings.

12 Insert the thrust washer, locating it against the outer track ring, then fit the closure plate which must be smeared with sealant.

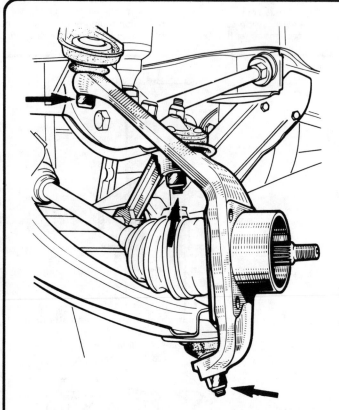

Fig. 11.16 Stub axle balljoints (arrowed) (Sec 7)

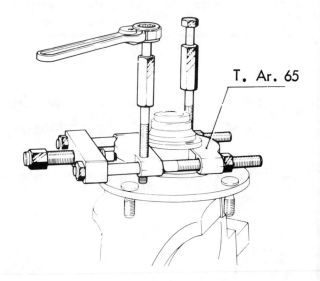

Fig. 11.17 Renault special tool T Av 65 in position for removal of track ring (Sec 7)

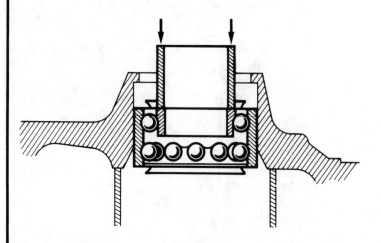

Fig. 11.18 Press out the outer track ring with an inner track ring located as shown (Sec 7)

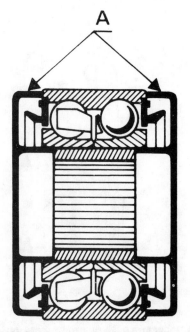

Fig. 11.19 Remove new bearing plastic covers (A) (Sec 7)

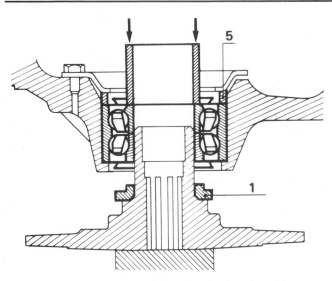

Fig. 11.20 Hub-to-disc refitting showing location of thrust washers (1 and 5) (Sec 7)

13   Fit and tighten the closure plate retaining bolts. Apply some multi-purpose bearing grease onto each seal lip.
14   Locate the hub thrust washer (Fig. 11.20) and press the hub/disc unit into position using a suitable piece of tube (53 mm (2.087 in) outside diameter, 43 mm (1.693 in) inside diameter), pressing on the bearing inner track ring.
15   The stub axle and driveshaft can now be refitted. Refer to Chapter 8, Section 4 for details.
16   If the stub axle unit has been renewed, the front axle geometry must be checked and adjusted accordingly. This task is best entrusted to your Renault dealer.

8   Anti-roll bar (front and rear) – removal and refitting

1   The anti-roll bar is normally only removed to renew its rubber bushings, if damaged (due to an accident), or possibly to give access to surrounding components. Whatever the reason, always check the condition of the bushes and renew them if they are suspect. If the bar is defective, renew it.
2   It is easiest if the vehicle is over a pit when removing the anti-roll bar. Otherwise, make sure the vehicle is properly secure on stands (if available) or on the ground with the handbrake on. It is not always necessary to remove the front wheels.

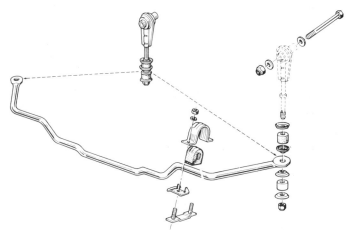

Fig. 11.21 Front anti-roll bar assembly components (Sec 8)

Front anti-roll bar
3   Unbolt and remove the engine undertray.
4   Unscrew and remove the roll bar-to-connecting link retaining nut on each side (photo).
5   Unscrew and remove the roll bar-to-chassis mounting nuts and remove the bar complete with bushes and clamps (photo).
6   To remove the connecting link, unscrew the retaining nut from the suspension arm pivot and withdraw it forwards.
7   Refit in the reverse sequence, ensuring the bushes and cups are correctly located. See Fig. 11.21.

Rear anti-roll bar
8   The rear anti-roll bar is attached at each end to the respective transverse arm at each end and centrally on the body underside by two rubber cushioned brackets.
9   To remove the bar, unscrew and withdraw the retaining bolt on each side, removing simultaneously the respective cup washers, rubber bushes and distance piece, keeping them in order.
10   Unscrew and remove the two retaining bracket nuts and brackets, rubber distance pieces and anti-roll bar.
11   Check the bar for alignment and renew if necessary. Inspect the various rubber distance pieces and bushes and renew any that have perished or are badly worn.
12   Refitting is a reversal of the removal procedure. Do not tighten the fastenings until the reassembly is complete. Ensure that the respective bushes, cup washers and distance pieces are correctly located as shown in Fig. 11.22.

8.4 Anti-roll bar connecting link showing bushes and washers

8.5 Anti-roll bar chassis mounting

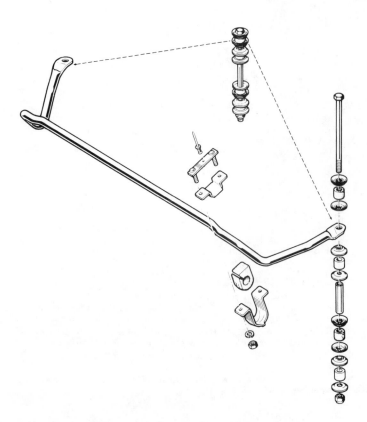

Fig. 11.22 Rear anti-roll bar assembly components (Sec 8)

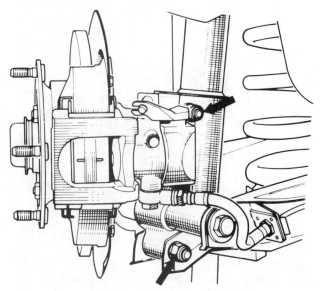

Fig. 11.23 Rear shock absorber mounting bolt positions (Sec 9)

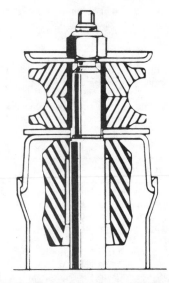

Fig. 11.24 Rear shock absorber upper mounting – sectional view showing bush and cup locations (Sec 9)

9 Rear shock absorber – removal and refitting

1   Raise the vehicle at the rear and make secure on axle stands or blocks. Remove the wheel(s).
2   Position a pillar jack under the suspension arm on the side to be worked on and raise it to just support the arm.
3   From inside the vehicle, unfasten and remove the rear shelf to gain access to the upper mounting of the shock absorber which is covered by rubber. Prise the cover free and unscrew the retaining nut (photo).
4   Unscrew and remove the shock absorber lower mounting bolts as shown in Fig. 11.23.
5   Compress the shock absorber downwards to detach it from its upper location and when clear, tilt it outwards and remove it.
6   Refer to Section 2, paragraphs 8 and 9, regarding shock absorber repair and renewal.
7   Refitting is a reversal of the removal process. Grease the bottom mounting bolts before fitting and tighten them to the specified torque.
8   To relocate the upper threaded portion of the unit into its location, align it and raise the upper section into position sufficiently to enable the retaining nut to be fitted. You will probably require an assistant to achieve this unless you fabricate a suitable tool with which to draw the threaded section upwards into position from within the car. Ensure that the bushes and cups are correctly located before tightening the nut to the specified torque, as shown in Fig. 11.24.

10 Rear suspension coil spring – removal and refitting

1   Remove the rear shock absorber on the side concerned as described in the previous Section.
2   You will need a suitable coil spring compressor, which when located onto the spring should be progressively tightened sufficiently to enable the spring to be removed rearward from its location. **Take great care** during this operation as the spring will be under considerable tension. Make sure that the spring compressor is of a suitable type and is fully located.
3   Unwind the spring compressor in a progressive manner.

9.3 Remove rubber cap for access to rear shock absorber upper mounting nut

4   Refitting is a reversal of the removal procedure, but note the following:

(a) *The spring must be fitted with its small diameter end located in the lower dish retainer and with the colour code marking at the end of the second coil from the bottom*

(b) *When the spring is relocated, unwind the compressor carefully, ensuring the spring is seated correctly into the top and bottom location cups*

(c) *Once the spring is in position and the compressor removed, refit the shock absorber as described in the previous Section and tighten the fastenings to the specified torque*

11 Lateral arm – removal and refitting

1   Raise the rear of the vehicle and support on axle stands or blocks to secure.
2   Unscrew the pivot bolt retaining nuts and extract the bolts (Fig. 11.26).
3   Pull the transverse arm rearward and remove the lateral arm.
4   Refitting is a reversal of the removal procedure. Smear the pivot pins with grease prior to fitting and use new self-locking nuts when assembling. Tighten the nuts to the specified torque only when the vehicle is lowered to its free standing position.

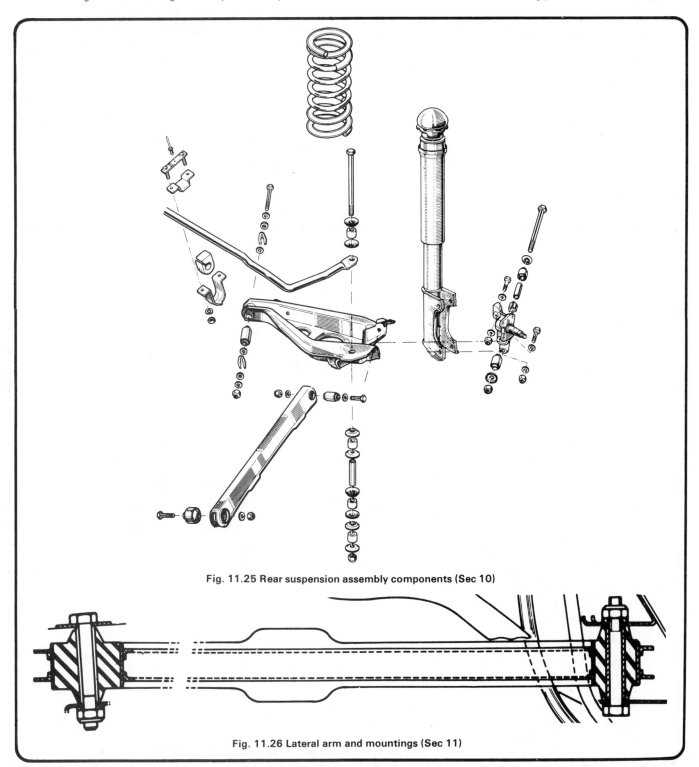

Fig. 11.25 Rear suspension assembly components (Sec 10)

Fig. 11.26 Lateral arm and mountings (Sec 11)

12 Transverse arm – removal and refitting

1   Raise the car at the rear and support on axle stands or blocks to make secure. Remove the wheel at the rear from the side to be worked on.
2   Referring to Sections 9 and 10, remove the rear shock absorber and suspension coil spring. Disconnect the anti-roll bar link.
3   Unscrew the lateral arm pivot bolt retaining nut and remove the bolt.
4   Referring to Chapter 9, disconnect the brake hoses and limiter control unit from the arm.
5   Detach the handbrake cable from its retaining clip.
6   Unscrew the inner pivot bolt retaining nut and extract the bolt.
7   Make a note of the adjuster shim positions and remove them. Keep them safe for correct reassembly when the time comes.
8   The transverse arm can now be removed.
9   Refitting of the transverse arm is a direct reversal of the removal process, but note the following:

   (a) *Be sure to refit the exact number of shims to their relative locations*
   (b) *Use new self-locking nuts to retain the pivot pin bolts and tighten to the specified torque once the vehicle is fully reassembled and free standing*
   (c) *Referring to Chapter 9, reconnect the brake lines and limiter unit. Bleed the brakes and, if necessary, adjust the limiter*
   (d) *If the shims have been renewed (and even if they have not) have the rear wheel alignment checked by your Renault dealer*

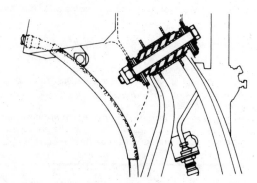

Fig. 11.27 Transverse arm pivot location – note shims each side (Sec 12)

13 Rear wheel bearings – removal and refitting

1   Raise the car at the rear on the side concerned and support with axle stands or blocks to make secure. Remove the roadwheel.
2   Referring to Chapter 9, remove the brake disc.
3   Place the outer bearing inner track ring to one side and extract the seal from the brake disc.
4   Withdraw the bearing outer tracks from the disc, either using a suitable puller or by driving out using a soft drift.
5   The inner bearing track ring can be removed from the hub using a suitable puller.

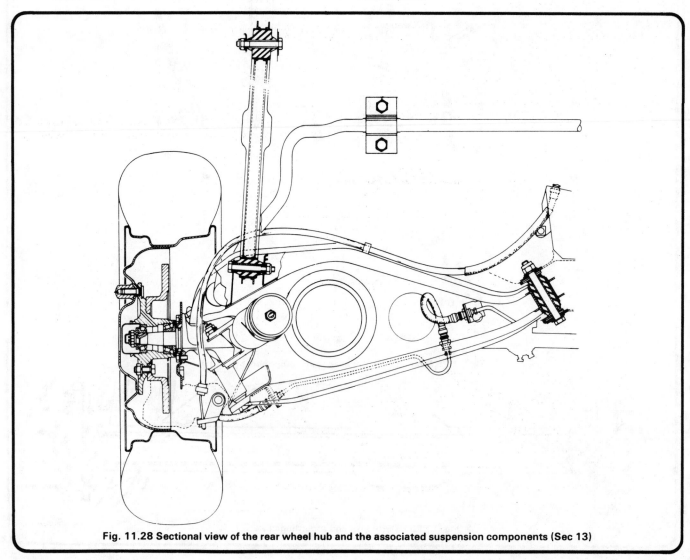

Fig. 11.28 Sectional view of the rear wheel hub and the associated suspension components (Sec 13)

6   Clean and inspect the respective bearing assemblies and also the stub axle. Where signs of damage or excessive wear are apparent, renew the defective components concerned. Where the bearings are being renewed, it is important that the new bearing inner and outer tracks and rings are renewed as a pair. Do not fit a new bearing cone (inner track) to a used bearing cup (outer track).
7   If a new stub axle thrust washer is being fitted, it can be heated to ease assembly or drifted into location together with the bearing using a suitable tube drift.
8   Smear the bearings and tracks with grease prior to fitting.
9   Carefully, press or drift the new bearing outer tracks (cups) into position in the brake disc using a tube drift of suitable diameter.
10 Fit a new oil seal using a suitable tube drift.
11 Smear about 20 g (0.75 oz) of wheel bearing grease between the bearings in the disc and relocate the disc to the stub axle.
12 Locate the outer bearing inner track (cone) and retain the disc assembly with the thrust washer and nut.
13 Tighten the nut to adjust the wheel bearings as given in Chapter 9, Section 8.

14 Rear axle geometry and body height – checking and adjustment

1   The rear axle assembly settings and body height will rarely need adjustment; only after an accident or possibly when new rear suspension components are fitted.
2   It is generally recommended that any checking and adjustments of the rear suspension and body height be entrusted to your Renault dealer who is equipped to tackle this task.
3   Before assuming that the suspension is in need of adjustment, first check that the following points are correct as there are several basic factors that contribute towards the accuracy of the rear axle geometry:

(a) *Tyre inflation pressures*
(b) *Shock absorbers must be in good condition*
(c) *The suspension pivot points must be in good order and their fastenings correctly tightened*
(d) *The wheel bearing/hub endplay must be correct*
(e) *The roadwheel run-out and balance must be correct*

4   If these items are known to be in order, arrange for your Renault dealer to make further checks and adjustments (if required).

15 Steering assembly – general information

1   The rack-and-pinion steering system fitted to all models is a maintenance-free design, although an occasional check should be made to ensure that it is securely located and the steering arm protective bellows are in good condition.
2   The steering rack unit is located directly to the rear of the engine above the clutch housing, and mounted to the body crossmember.
3   The steering column shaft is interconnected with the steering box by a universal joint.
4   The column shaft is connected via a rotary valve unit which regulates the direction of flow to the double acting ram unit, attached to the steering gear, and actuates the steering arm accordingly. A belt-driven pump provides the hydraulic pressure.
5   The maintenance procedures for the power steering unit are given in Section 16.
6   Apart from removing and refitting the steering gear and/or power steering component units, there is little that a home mechanic can do to repair or overhaul them; specialised tools and fitting techniques are

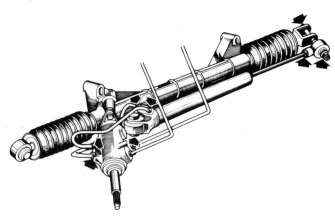

Fig. 11.29 Steering rack, hydraulic ram and rotary valve unit assembly (left-hand drive shown). Ram disconnection points arrowed (Sec 15)

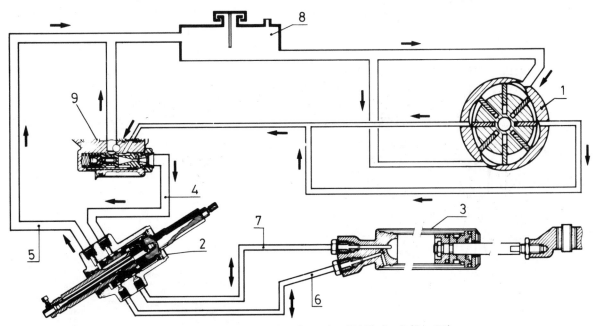

Fig. 11.30 The power assisted steering (PAS) circuit (Sec 15)

1 *Pump*	4 *Feed from regulator to rotary valve*	6 *Valve to ram connection*	9 *Regulator valve (integral with pump)*
2 *Rotary valve*	5 *Return from rotary valve to reservoir*	7 *Valve to ram connection*	
3 *Hydraulic ram*		8 *Fluid reservoir (integral with pump)*	

required. Therefore if damage or excessive wear exist in any of the major units of the steering system, remove the offending item and let your Renault dealer effect any repairs that are possible.

16 Power steering – servicing and problem diagnosis

Oil level – check and top-up
1   Where power steering is fitted it is essential that the oil level in the system is kept to the correct level and also that the specified grade of oil is used.
2   Check the level every 5000 miles (8000 km).
3   Check the level using the dipstick incorporated in the reservoir filler cap (photo). Note that there are different markings for use depending on whether the oil is hot or cold; read the dipstick accordingly.
4   A continuous need to top up indicates a leak in the system and a check should be made around the pump and the interconnecting hoses to the ram on the steering box for obvious signs of leakage. It may be that a hose joint simply needs tightening, but if it is otherwise defective, renew it.

Pump drivebelt – tension adjustment and renewal
5   The power steering drivebelt must be in good condition and correctly adjusted or the pump will not function effectively.
6   The belt tension is correct when there is a deflection of $\frac{3}{32}$ to $\frac{1}{8}$ in (2.5 to 3 mm) in the middle of its run between the camshaft and pump pulleys. To adjust the tension, slacken the pump mounting and adjustment strap bolts just sufficiently to allow the pump to be pivoted accordingly for the correct tension. Do not overtension the belt or the pump drive bearings will suffer.
7   If the belt is in need of renewal loosen the mounting bolts right off, pivot the pump fully inward and remove the old belt. Fit and retension the new belt, run the engine for about ten minutes then recheck the tension. New belts tend to stretch a fraction initially and will probably require further slight adjustment.

16.3 Check the power steering reservoir fluid level

Power steering – problem diagnosis
8   Should the steering develop problems or become abnormally stiff in action, do not assume that it is necessarily the power steering system which is at fault.
9   Make some initial checks of the steering and front suspension components as described in Section 1. If these are in order, check that the oil level in the steering hydraulic circuit is up to normal level and that the pump drivebelt is tensioned correctly as described earlier.
10   Check that the power steering pump unit and ram unit on the steering box are secure.

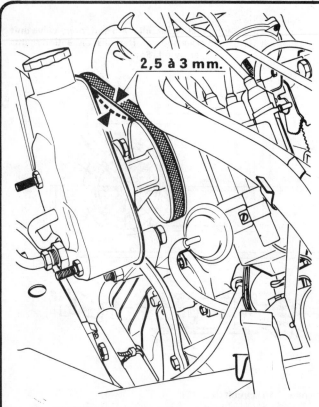

Fig. 11.31 Power steering pump showing the drivebelt tension checking point and amount of deflection required (Sec 16)

2,5 à 3 mm.

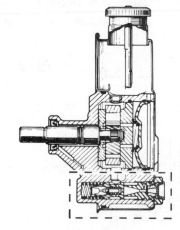

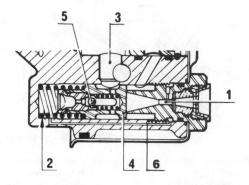

Fig. 11.32 The pump unit regulator components (Sec 16)

1   Pressure release bore
2   Plunger spring
3   Bypass hole
4   Flow regulator plunger
5   Ball valve (pressure release)
6   Regulator pressure channel

11 If these items are in order, the problem can be diagnosed according to its symptoms. If the steering is stiff and heavier than normal, the problem is most likely to be within the steering pump or hydraulic ram on the steering box. If the steering requires normal pressure at the steering wheel but is defective in other aspects, the problem is unlikely to be associated with the power steering. Where power assistance is felt to be intermittent in action, a check can be made to ensure that the regulator valve in the pump unit is in order by removing the valve assembly and checking that the ball and seat are perfectly clean. The regulator valve unit is located in the base of the pump unit, the components of which are shown in Fig. 11.32. If the above checks do not solve the problem, get your Renault dealer to inspect the system. In particular, he will be able to conduct a pressure check of the hydraulic circuit in the power steering system. It is essential to diagnose this whether the problem is within the pump or ram unit.

12 Both the power steering pump and hydraulic ram unit are easily removed, but repairs should be entrusted to your Renault dealer.

17 Power steering pump – removal and refitting

1 Disconnect the battery earth lead.
2 Remove the pump reservoir cap and syringe out the fluid.
3 Detach the pipes from their rotary valve connections. As the pipes are loosened and detached, allow for a certain amount of fluid leakage, as there will almost certainly be some left remaining in the system.
4 Unscrew and remove the pump unit retaining bolt and nut from their clutch housing fixings, then disconnect the drivebelt from the pump pulley and lift the pump clear.
5 Refitting is a reversal of the removal procedure. When in position, reconnect and retension the drivebelt (photo). Ensure that the hoses are securely connected and top up the system as necessary (see Section 16).

18 Power steering hydraulic ram – removal and refitting

1 Disconnect the battery earth and positive cables from the terminals. Remove the battery retaining clamps, lift the battery from its tray and place safely out of the way.
2 Disconnect and remove the battery support tray (photo).
3 To minimise oil spillage, clamp the hydraulic supply and return pipes as close as possible to their connections to the hydraulic ram.
4 Detach the steering arm connecting pin bolt from the rack unit (photo).
5 Note the respective hydraulic pipe connections and detach them carefully from the unions to the ram unit.
6 Unscrew and remove the ram pivot bolt (photo).
7 Withdraw the ram unit.

17.5 Tensioning the power steering pump drivebelt

18.2 Remove battery support tray for access to steering components

18.4 Steering arm to rack and hydraulic ram piston arm connection

18.6 Hydraulic ram feed pipe connections (arrowed) and pivot belt

8   Refitting is a reversal of the removal procedure, but note the following:

(a) The car must be free standing when tightening the flexible bushes and steering arm pin. Tighten to the specified torque (where given)

(b) Ram adjustment is possible once it is fitted into position (if necessary). Turn the steering to full lock position, enabling the rack to be extended fully on the non-pinion side. In this position, the rack end fitting nut should be in contact with the steering box at the pinion end. If it is not adjust as follows

(c) Referring to Fig. 11.33 loosen the locknut (1) and unscrew the piston rod a few revolutions to adjust so the rack end fitting nut is in contact with the steering box. With the steering held in this position, the ram piston is then screwed back until it contacts its bearing, at which point unscrew it about $\frac{3}{4}$ turn to give a clearance of 1 mm (0.040 in) between the piston and its bearing. Tighten the locknut in this position

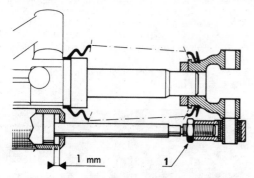

Fig. 11.33 Loosen locknut (1) and adjust ram to give 1 mm (0.040 in) clearance as indicated (Sec 18)

19 Steering box – removal and refitting

1   Disconnect the battery earth and positive leads, remove the battery retaining clamp and lift the battery clear.
2   Remove the battery support tray.
3   Clamp the hydraulic hoses at the steering box end to minimize oil loss when disconnected.
4   Unscrew and remove the steering shaft lower universal joint connecting bolt, then lift the steering tube as much as possible to disconnect the universal joint.
5   Unscrew the steering arm balljoint nuts and, using a balljoint separator, disconnect the arms.
6   Note their relative positions, then disconnect the hoses to the rotary valve unit at the base of the column.
7   Unscrew and remove the steering box retaining bolts and carefully withdraw the steering box unit.
8   Refitting is a reversal of the removal procedure, but note the following.
9   The steering arm balljoint stems must be smeared with a general purpose grease prior to assembly.
10 Whenever the steering rack or steering box unit is renewed, the steering rack travel must be readjusted as follows:

(a) Position the rack against the pinion end stop, screw in the end nut (Fig. 11.34) and fork end at the opposite end to the pinion so that the 'Y' dimension shown is equal to $5\frac{9}{16}$ in (141 mm). This is the provisional setting for the fork ends, the final adjustment is made after the steering box is refitted

(b) The pinion locknuts vary according to type, as shown in Fig. 11.35

(c) To adjust the rack travel, screw in the end fitting, and locate the pinion end locknut $1\frac{17}{32}$ in (39 mm) from the centre eye of the end fitting as shown in Fig. 11.36. Now screw in the locknut until it just touches the rack, but don't tighten yet

(d) Move the rack along to the pinion end stop and screw in the opposing end nut and end fitting so that dimension 'Y' in Fig. 11.37 is equal to $6\frac{31}{32}$ in (177 mm)

(e) Steering geometry and tie-rod adjustment checks should be made on completion

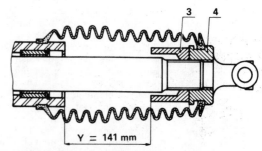

Fig. 11.34 Position nut (3) and fork end (4) as shown to set dimension 'Y' to amount given (Sec 19)

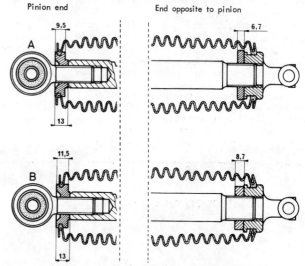

Fig. 11.35 Locknut fitting positions and identifications (Sec 19)

A Early models with manual transmission
B Late models with manual transmission, and all automatic transmission models

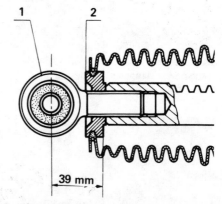

Fig. 11.36 End fitting (1) to locknut (2) distance to be set as shown (Sec 19)

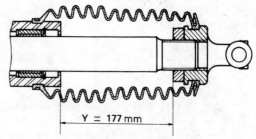

Fig. 11.37 Pinion end fitting and nut to be set to give dimension specified between points 'Y' (Sec 19)

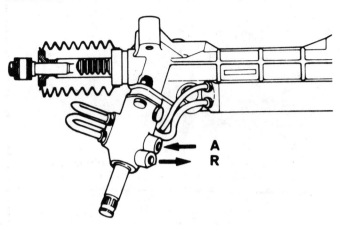

Fig. 11.38 Rotary valve showing inlet (A) and return to reservoir (R) pipe positions (Sec 19)

11 In reconnecting the hydraulic pipes, locate them beneath the rotary valve as shown in Fig. 11.38 and locate the hose in its clip underneath the engine mounting.
12 The tie-rod balljoint and pin bolts must be tightened to the specified torque only with the car free standing.

13 Reconnect the steering column and universal joint with the steering wheel spokes horizontal.
14 Top up the power steering circuit as given in Section 16 and check for leaks around the pipe joints.
15 Arrange to have the steering box height and parallelism checked by your Renault dealer at the earliest opportunity.

20 Steering tie-rods – removal, refitting and adjustment

1 Removal of either or both of the steering tie-rods (track rods) does not necessitate rack removal. The unit is not repairable although the end fittings can be renewed when necessary.
2 Use a suitable balljoint separator to detach the outer joint at the stub axle connection.
3 Remove the inner connecting bolt from the steering arm connection and withdraw the rod assembly.
4 As can be seen by the accompanying illustrations, the right and left-hand steering tie-rods differ. The right-hand tie-rod of the early R1273 model differs from that of the later types.
5 The right-hand tie-rod of the early R1273 model is not adjustable. If adjustment is required it is necessary to detach it at the steering rack end. The rack end fitting locknut can then be loosened and the end fitting turned accordingly for any adjustment necessary (a complete turn equalling $\frac{1}{8}$ in (3 mm) of toe-in/out as applicable). With this type the tie-rod and balljoint complete must be renewed if worn or damaged.

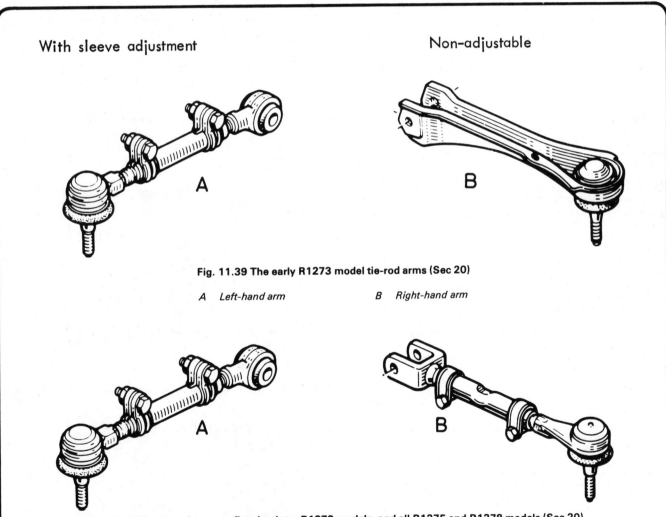

Fig. 11.39 The early R1273 model tie-rod arms (Sec 20)

A Left-hand arm   B Right-hand arm

Fig. 11.40 The tie rod arms as fitted to later R1273 models, and all R1275 and R1278 models (Sec 20)

A Left-hand arm   B Right-hand arm

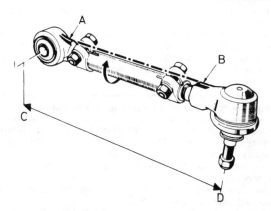

Fig. 11.41 Note relative settings (A and B) of end pieces before removal, also distance C to D (Sec 20)

20.13 Check that steering arm pivot bolt (arrowed) has clearance to pass power steering and brake hydraulic hoses

6　On the adjustable type rods, they too must be renewed if worn or damaged, but the balljoint, rod and rack end fitting can be renewed individually as required.

7　To renew either of the end pieces, clean any dirt from the threads using a wire brush. Referring to Fig. 11.41, measure between points C and D and make a note of the distance. Also note the relative set angles of each end piece.

8　Loosen the clamp bolt, grip the rod and unscrew the end piece.

9　Refit in the reverse order but check the end piece is positioned to give the original distance measured (point C to point D), then tighten the clamp bolt. This will provide a guide for the track setting.

10　Grease the connecting pin before refitting to the steering arm. The car must be free-standing when tightening the respective fastenings to the specified torque settings.

11　Arrange to have your Renault dealer check the track and steering angles after renewal as they are most important to the general handling and safety of the car.

12　If you have an accurate means of checking the toe-out, then the respective rods can be adjusted when in place by loosening the clamp bolts and rotating the rod sleeve using suitable grips. Set the steering in the straight-ahead position when checking and adjusting the track setting. A complete rotation of a sleeve is equal to $\frac{11}{32}$ in (9 mm) difference in toe-in/out as applicable. On the steering tie-rod fitted with the axial balljoint, loosen off the locknuts and screw the balljoint in or out as required to adjust. A complete rotation in this instance equals $\frac{1}{8}$ in (3 mm) of toe-in/out as applicable.

13　When an adjustment has been made, check on completion that the steering arm connecting bolt has sufficient clearance to pass the power steering hydraulic pipes. Cut or grind down the end of the bolt if necessary to give sufficient clearance (photo).

21　Steering column – removal and refitting

1　Disconnect the battery earth lead from its terminal.

2　Unscrew and remove the lower column housing retaining screws. Unclip the housing from the top half to remove, then detach the upper half to expose the switches.

3　Disconnect the bonnet release catch lever from the column.

4　Unscrew and release the respective switches from their column locations or take a note of their respective positions and detach the various switch wires-to-harness connectors.

5　To remove the steering wheel, prise the central embellisher free and mark the relative alignment positions of the steering wheel and shaft (photo). Unscrew the retaining nut and withdraw the wheel. A special steering wheel puller may be required here to avoid damaging the wheel, should it prove tight to withdraw from the shaft.

6　Disconnect the clutch and brake pedal pushrods from the pedals, then unscrew and withdraw the lower shaft universal joint through-bolt (photo).

7　Pull the plastic retaining bungs from the carpet surround section around the clutch and brake pedal support bracket, where it is mounted to the bulkhead. Pull the carpet away and then unscrew the four bracket retaining bolts.

8　Disconnect the brake light switch wire.

21.5 Prise free the steering wheel embellisher for access to the retaining nut

21.6 Brake pedal/pushrod clevis (A) and steering column lower joint (B)

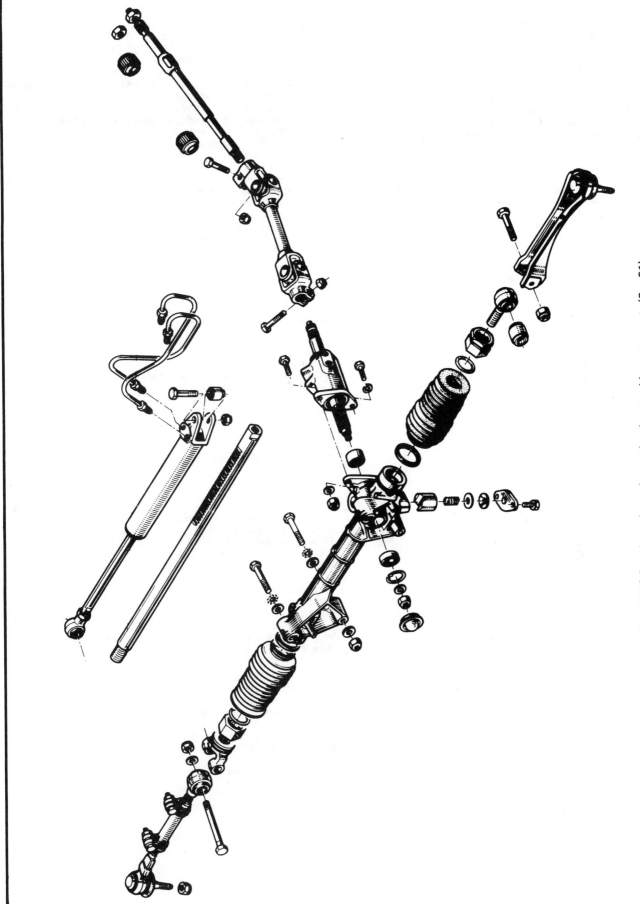

Fig. 11.42 Steering column, box and rack assembly components (Sec 21)

9   Unscrew the retaining bolt and disconnect the column from its mounting to the upper bulkhead at the point just to the right of the speedometer (viewed from the driving position).

10 Check that all column connections and fittings are disconnected, then withdraw the column assembly from the car through the interior.

11 Refitting the column is a reversal of the removal procedure but the following points must be observed:

  (a) *Do not tighten the respective column and bracket bolts fully until the assembly is complete*
  (b) *Tighten the bolts to the specified torque settings*
  (c) *When assembly is complete, check the clutch and brake pedal free play and adjust if necessary. Also check the various switch circuit operations when the battery is reconnected*

22 Steering column bushes – renewal

1   Where play in the steering column shaft is evident, the problem is almost certainly caused by worn upper and lower column bushes, and they must therefore be renewed.

2   To do this, first remove the steering column as described in the previous Section.

3   To extract the lower bush, tap the splined end of the shaft at the top (steering wheel end). Protect the end of the shaft against hammer blows with a plastic or hardwood block.

4   The lower bush should be ejected with its split collar.

5   Before withdrawing the shaft downward, turn the ignition key to unlock the column anti-theft lock.

6   At the top end, remove the retaining circlip from the sleeve and then drive the top bush out using a length of suitable tubing, inserted from the lower end of the column.

7   Refitting of the new bushes is a reversal of the removal procedure, but note the following:

  (a) *Ensure that the upper bush is hard up against the depression in the column when fitted*
  (b) *Locate the bottom bush onto the shaft and also the collar halves. Drive them carefully into position, using a suitable angled drift working evenly round until fully fitted. Apply grease to the bushes (upper and lower) before fitting*

23 Fault diagnosis – suspension and steering

Symptom	Reason(s)
Front suspension and steering	
Heavy steering	Tyre pressures incorrect
	Corroded or seized balljoints
	Incorrect suspension geometry and track
	Power steering unit defective
Lost motion (steering)	Worn flexible coupling bolt holes
	Worn steering column universal joint
	Loose steering wheel
	Worn balljoints
	Worn rack and pinion mechanism
Wheel wobble and vibration	Worn hub bearings
	Loose wheel bolts
	Worn suspension arm bushes
	Driveshafts bent or out of balance
	Driveshafts couplings worn
	Front roadwheels out of balance
	Wear in rack and pinion and balljoints
	Incorrect steering geometry
Poor roadholding and cornering	Tyre pressures incorrect
	Dampers unserviceable
	Weak coil springs
Sensitive to road camber	Wear in upper or lower suspension arm balljoints
	Wear in hub bearings
Rear suspension	
Wheel wobble and vibration	Damper (shock absorber) rubber bushes worn
	Loose damper mounting
	Suspension arm bushes worn
Uneven tyre wear	Rear stub axles twisted or out of alignment
	Hubs incorrectly adjusted for endfloat
Poor roadholding and cornering	Tyre pressures incorrect
	Dampers unserviceable

Chapter 12 Bodywork and fittings

Contents

1 General description

The bodywork is of all-steel monocoque construction, the integral components being spot welded together. In addition to the normal hinged body panels, the front wings are removable, being bolted into position.

Apart from the normal cleaning, maintenance and minor body repairs, there is little that the DIY owner can do in the event of structural defects caused by collision damage or possibly rust. This Chapter is therefore devoted to the normal maintenance, removal and refitting of those parts of the vehicle body and associate components that are readily dismantled.

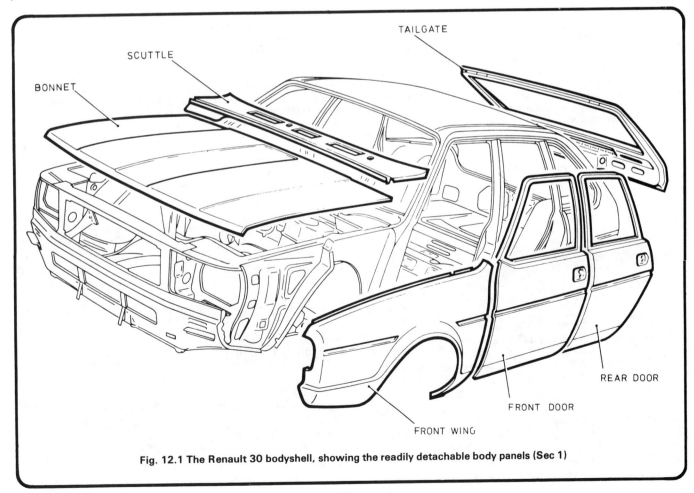

Fig. 12.1 The Renault 30 bodyshell, showing the readily detachable body panels (Sec 1)

Although the underbody is given a protective coating when new, it is still unlikely to suffer from corrosion in certain exposed areas or where road dirt deposits can congeal. Light corrosion can be treated as described in Section 4, but severe rusting of a structural area in the underbody must be repaired by your Renault dealer or competent vehicle body repair shop.

2 Maintenance – bodywork and underframe

1 The general condition of a vehicle's bodywork is the one thing that significantly affects its value. Maintenance is easy but needs to be regular. Neglect, particularly after minor damage, can lead quickly to further deterioration and costly repair bills. It is important also to keep watch on those parts of the vehicle not immediately visible, for instance the underside, inside all the wheel arches and the lower part of the engine compartment.

2 The basic maintenance routine for the bodywork is washing – preferably with a lot of water, from a hose. This will remove all the loose solids which may have stuck to the vehicle. It is important to flush these off in such a way as to prevent grit from scratching the finish. The wheel arches and underframe need washing in the same way to remove any accumulated mud which will retain moisture and tend to encourage rust. Paradoxically enough, the best time to clean the underframe and wheel arches is in wet weather when the mud is thoroughly wet and soft. In very wet weather the underframe is usually cleaned of large accumulations automatically and this is a good time for inspection.

3 Periodically, it is a good idea to have the whole of the underframe of the vehicle steam cleaned, engine compartment included, so that a thorough inspection can be carried out to see what minor repairs and renovations are necessary. Steam cleaning is available at many garages and is necessary for removal of the accumulation of oily grime which sometimes is allowed to become thick in certain areas. If steam cleaning facilities are not available, there are one or two excellent grease solvents available which can be brush applied. The dirt can then be simply hosed off.

4 After washing paintwork, wipe off with a chamois leather to give an unspotted clear finish. A coat of clear protective wax polish will give added protection against chemical pollutants in the air. If the paintwork sheen has dulled or oxidised, use a cleaner/polisher combination to restore the brilliance of the shine. This requires a little effort, but such dulling is usually caused because regular washing has been neglected. Always check that the door and ventilator opening drain holes and pipes are completely clear so that water can be drained out (photos). Bright work should be treated in the same way as paintwork. Windscreens and windows can be kept clear of the smeary film which often appears, by adding a little ammonia to the water. If they are scratched, a good rub with a proprietary metal polish will often clear them. Never use any form of wax or other body or chromium polish on glass.

3 Maintenance – upholstery and carpets

1 Mats and carpets should be brushed or vacuum cleaned regularly to keep them free of grit. If they are badly stained remove them from the vehicle for scrubbing or sponging and make quite sure they are dry before refitting. Seats and interior trim panels can be kept clean by wiping with a damp cloth. If they do become stained (which can be more apparent on light coloured upholstery) use a little liquid detergent and a soft nail brush to scour the grime out of the grain of the material. Do not forget to keep the headlining clean in the same way as the upholstery. When using liquid cleaners inside the vehicle do not over-wet the surfaces being cleaned. Excessive damp could get into the seams and padded interior causing stains, offensive odours or even rot. If the inside of the vehicle gets wet accidentally it is worthwhile taking some trouble to dry it out properly, particularly where carpets are involved. *Do not leave oil or electric heaters inside the vehicle for this purpose.*

4 Minor body damage – repair

The photographic sequences on pages 238 and 239 illustrate the operations detailed in the following sub-sections.

Repair of minor scratches in bodywork

If the scratch is very superficial, and does not penetrate to the metal of the bodywork, repair is very simple. Lightly rub the area of the scratch with a paintwork renovator, or a very fine cutting paste, to remove loose paint from the scratch and to clear the surrounding bodywork of wax polish. Rinse the area with clean water.

Apply touch-up paint to the scratch using a fine paint brush; continue to apply fine layers of paint until the surface of the paint in the scratch is level with the surrounding paintwork. Allow the new paint at least two weeks to harden: then blend it into the surrounding paintwork by rubbing the scratch area with a paintwork renovator or a very fine cutting paste. Finally, apply wax polish.

Where the scratch has penetrated right through to the metal of the bodywork, causing the metal to rust, a different repair technique is required. Remove any loose rust from the bottom of the scratch with a penknife, then apply rust inhibiting paint to prevent the formation of rust in the future. Using a rubber or nylon applicator fill the scratch with bodystopper paste. If required, this paste can be mixed with cellulose thinners to provide a very thin paste which is ideal for filling narrow scratches. Before the stopper-paste in the scratch hardens, wrap a piece of smooth cotton rag around the top of a finger. Dip the finger in cellulose thinners and then quickly sweep it across the surface of the stopper-paste in the scratch; this will ensure that the surface of the stopper-paste is slightly hollowed. The scratch can now be painted over as described earlier in this Section.

2.4A Check drain holes in lower body and doors are clear ...

2.4B ... and poke them through with a piece of wire to remove dirt

Repair of dents in bodywork

When deep denting of the vehicle's bodywork has taken place, the first task is to pull the dent out, until the affected bodywork almost attains its original shape. There is little point in trying to restore the original shape completely, as the metal in the damaged area will have stretched on impact and cannot be reshaped fully to its original contour. It is better to bring the level of the dent up to a point which is about $\frac{1}{8}$ in (3 mm) below the level of the surrounding bodywork. In cases where the dent is very shallow anyway, it is not worth trying to pull it out at all. If the underside of the dent is accessible, it can be hammered out gently from behind, using a mallet with a wooden or plastic head. Whilst doing this, hold a suitable block of wood firmly against the outside of the panel to absorb the impact from the hammer blows and thus prevent a large area of the bodywork from being 'belled-out'.

Should the dent be in a section of the bodywork which has a double skin or some other factor making it inaccessible from behind, a different technique is called for. Drill several small holes through the metal inside the area – particularly in the deeper section. Then screw long self-tapping screws into the holes just sufficiently for them to gain a good purchase in the metal. Now the dent can be pulled out by pulling on the protruding heads of the screws with a pair of pliers.

The next stage of the repair is the removal of the paint from the damaged area, and from an inch or so of the surrounding 'sound' bodywork. This is accomplished most easily by using a wire brush or abrasive pad on a power drill, although it can be done just as effectively by hand using sheets of abrasive paper. To complete the preparation for filling, score the surface of the bare metal with a screwdriver or the tang of a file, or alternatively, drill small holes in the affected area. This will provide a really good 'key' for the filler paste.

To complete the repair see the Section on filling and re-spraying.

Repair of rust holes or gashes in bodywork

Remove all paint from the affected area and from an inch or so of the surrounding 'sound' bodywork, using an abrasive pad or a wire brush on a power drill. If these are not available a few sheets of abrasive paper will do the job just as effectively. With the paint removed you will be able to gauge the severity of the corrosion and therefore decide whether to renew the whole panel (if this is possible) or to repair the affected area. New body panels are not as expensive as most people think and it is often quicker and more satisfactory to fit a new panel than to attempt to repair large areas of corrosion.

Remove all fittings from the affected area except those which will act as a guide to the original shape of the damaged bodywork (eg headlamp shells etc). Then, using tin snips or a hacksaw blade, remove all loose metal and any other metal badly affected by corrosion. Hammer the edges of the hole inwards in order to create a slight depression for the filler paste.

Wire brush the affected area to remove the powdery rust from the surface of the remaining metal. Paint the affected area with rust inhibiting paint; if the back of the rusted area is accessible treat this also.

Before filling can take place it will be necessary to block the hole in some way. This can be achieved by the use of zinc gauze or aluminium tape.

Zinc gauze is probably the best material to use for a large hole. Cut a piece to the approximate size and shape of the hole to be filled, then position it in the hole so that its edges are below the level of the surrounding bodywork. It can be retained in position by several blobs of filler paste around its periphery.

Aluminium tape should be used for small or very narrow holes. Pull a piece off the roll and trim it to the approximate size and shape required, then pull off the backing paper (if used) and stick the tape over the hole; it can be overlapped if the thickness of one piece is insufficient. Burnish down the edges of the tape with the handle of a screwdriver or similar, to ensure that the tape is securely attached to the metal underneath.

Bodywork repairs – filling and re-spraying

Before using this Section, see the Sections on dent, deep scratch, rust holes and gash repairs.

Many types of bodyfiller are available, but generally speaking those proprietary kits which contain a tin of filler paste and a tube of resin hardener are best for this type of repair. A wide, flexible plastic or nylon applicator will be found invaluable for imparting a smooth and well contoured finish to the surface of the filler.

Mix up a little filler on a clean piece of card or board – measure the hardener carefully (follow the maker's instructions on the pack) otherwise the filler will set too rapidly or too slowly.

Using the applicator apply the filler paste to the prepared area; draw the applicator across the surface of the filler to achieve the correct contour and to level the filler surface. As soon as a contour that approximates to the correct one is achieved, stop working the paste – if you carry on too long the paste will become sticky and begin to 'pick up' on the applicator. Continue to add thin layers of filler paste at twenty-minute intervals until the level of the filler is just proud of the surrounding bodywork.

Once the filler has hardened, excess can be removed using a metal plane or file. From then on, progressively finer grades of abrasive paper should be used, starting with a 40 grade production paper and finishing with 400 grade wet-and-dry paper. Always wrap the abrasive paper around a flat rubber, cork, or wooden block – otherwise the surface of the filler will not be completely flat. During the smoothing of the filler surface the wet-and-dry paper should be periodically rinsed in water. This will ensure that a very smooth finish is imparted to the filler at the final stage.

At this stage the 'dent' should be surrounded by a ring of bare metal, which in turn should be encircled by the finely 'feathered' edge of the good paintwork. Rinse the repair area with clean water, until all of the dust produced by the rubbing-down operation has gone.

Spray the whole repair area with a light coat of primer – this will show up any imperfections in the surface of the filler. Repair these imperfections with fresh filler paste or bodystopper, and once more smooth the surface with abrasive paper. If bodystopper is used, it can be mixed with cellulose thinners to form a really thin paste which is ideal for filling small holes. Repeat this spray and repair procedure until you are satisfied that the surface of the filler, and the feathered edge of the paintwork are perfect. Clean the repair area with clean water and allow to dry fully.

The repair area is now ready for final spraying. Paint spraying must be carried out in a warm, dry, windless and dust free atmosphere. This condition can be created artificially if you have access to a large indoor working area, but if you are forced to work in the open, you will have to pick your day very carefully. If you are working indoors, dousing the floor in the work area with water will help to settle the dust which would otherwise be in the atmosphere. If the repair area is confined to one body panel, mask off the surrounding panels; this will help to minimise the effects of a slight mis-match in paint colours. Bodywork fittings (eg chrome strips, door handles etc) will also need to be masked off. Use genuine masking tape and several thicknesses of newspaper for the masking operations.

Before commencing to spray, agitate the aerosol can thoroughly, then spray a test area (an old tin, or similar) until the technique is mastered. Cover the repair area with a thick coat of primer; the thickness should be built up using several thin layers of paint rather than one thick one. Using 400 grade wet-and-dry paper, rub down the surface of the primer until it is really smooth. While doing this, the work area should be thoroughly doused with water, and the wet-and-dry paper periodically rinsed in water. Allow to dry before spraying on more paint.

Spray on the top coat, again building up the thickness by using several thin layers of paint. Start spraying in the centre of the repair area and then, using a circular motion, work outwards until the whole repair area and about 2 inches of the surrounding original paintwork is covered. Remove all masking material 10 to 15 minutes after spraying on the final coat of paint.

Allow the new paint at least two weeks to harden, then, using a paintwork renovator or a very fine cutting paste, blend the edges of the paint into the existing paintwork. Finally, apply wax polish.

5 Major body damage – repair

Because the body is built on the monocoque principle and is integral with the underframe, major damage must be repaired by competent mechanics with the necessary welding and hydraulic straightening equipment.

If the damage has been serious it is vital that the body is checked for correct alignment, as otherwise the handling of the car will suffer and many other faults such as excessive tyre wear and wear in the transmission and steering may occur. Renault produce a special alignment jig and to ensure that all is correct a repaired car should always be checked on this jig.

6 Bumpers – removal and refitting

Front bumper

1   The front bumper unit must be detached together with the outer retaining brackets. The main brackets are mounted to the front body panel and the retaining nuts removed from within the engine compartment.
2   Detach the corner sections from the brackets inside the wing

panel on each side, within the engine compartment.
3   Remove the bumper with brackets.
4   Refitting is a reversal of the removal procedure.

Rear bumper

5   Unscrew and remove the bumper corner fixing bolts to the brackets on each side. If the brackets are also to be removed, remove the luggage compartment side trim to gain access to the bracket bolts through the panel box sections.
6   Unscrew the overrider bolts.
7   Detach the number plate wires at the connector and withdraw the bumper assembly.
8   Refitting is a reversal of the removal process.

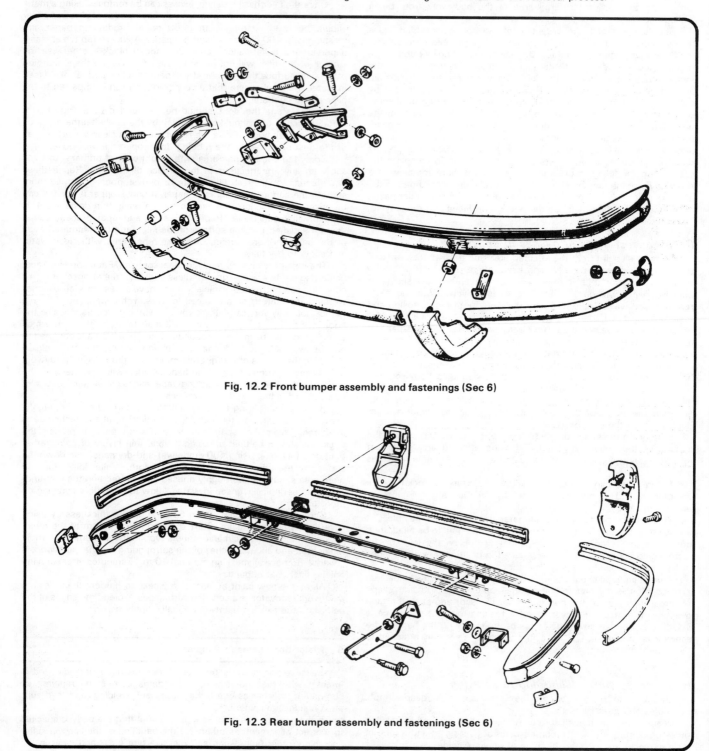

Fig. 12.2 Front bumper assembly and fastenings (Sec 6)

Fig. 12.3 Rear bumper assembly and fastenings (Sec 6)

7 Front grille and headlight panels – removal and refitting

1 Unscrew and remove the front grille retaining screws and then lift the grille clear from its bottom location peg.
2 Refitting is a reversal of the removal procedure.
3 To remove the headlight panels, remove the grille, then unscrew the panel retaining screws. Withdraw the panel(s).
4 Refit in the reverse sequence.

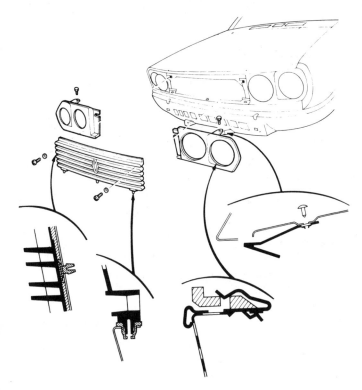

Fig. 12.4 Front grille and headlight surround panels showing fixing point locations (Sec 7)

8 Bonnet – removal and refitting

1 Raise the bonnet and get an assistant to support it whilst you unscrew the two retaining bolts from each hinge (photo). Mark around the hinges prior to removal, using a pencil to act as a guide for correct

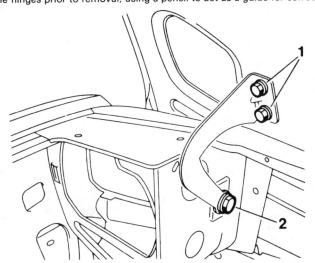

Fig. 12.5 Bonnet hinge showing the retaining bolts (1) and pivot bolt (2) (Sec 8)

8.1 Removing a bonnet hinge bolt

alignment when refitting. Alternatively, the pivot bolts can be removed if desired, but will be necessary to remove the front grille and headlight panels as given in the previous Section. Remove the bonnet.
2 Refitting is a reversal of the removal procedue, but check the bonnet for correct fitting adjustment on completion.
3 To adjust the bonnet for alignment, loosen the hinge retaining bolts and move the bonnet to adjust as necessary. Then retighten the bolts.

9 Bonnet lock release cable assembly – removal and refitting

1 If the release catch cable has broken, the bonnet can be raised and the catch released in the following manner.
2 Remove the front grille and headlight panels (see Section 7), and withdraw the inboard light unit on each side. Unscrew and remove the bonnet hinge pivot bolt on each side and raise and support the bonnet at the front sufficiently to pass a thin rod through to press onto the release catch at the point indicated (photo). Simultaneously, raise the bonnet at its rear edge and lift clear.
3 To renew the cable, unscrew and remove the catch retaining nuts and detach the cable.
4 Disconnect the cable from its sleeve stop on the bulkhead.
5 Prise the cable catch retaining pin C-clip and extract the pin.
6 From within the car, pull the cable through the bulkhead.
7 Unscrew the lower steering column surround, then unscrew the

9.2 Press catch lever at point arrowed to release

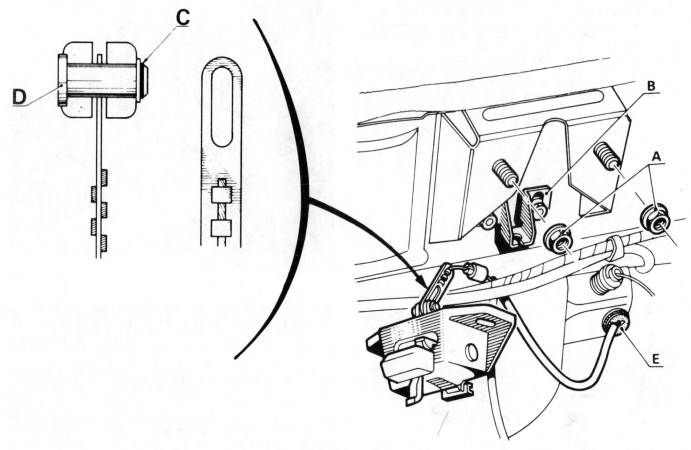

Fig. 12.6 Release catch assembly showing retaining nuts (A), cable sleeve stop (B), cable catch pin and retaining clip (C and D), and grommet (E) (Sec 9)

steering column catch release fixing screws. Remove the cable assembly.

8   Refitting is a reversal of the removal procedure, but check the bonnet for adjustment and security when closed and, if necessary, make further adjustment (see Section 8).

10 Door trim panel – removal and refitting

1   Disconnect the battery earth lead (on front door panels fitted with a radio speaker unit).
2   Unscrew and remove the door pull/armrest retaining screws, after

prising the caps free as necessary. Rotate the armrest and remove it (photo).
3   Where fitted, slide the front door pocket up and detach it from the retainers. Remove the retainer screws.
4   Prise the rubber seal free from around the lock indicator capsule.
5   Unscrew the door catch escutcheon retaining screw and remove it (photo).
6   On front door panels fitted with a radio speaker unit, prise free the speaker grille, unscrew the unit retaining screws, withdraw the speaker unit and detach its leads.
7   On doors fitted with a manual window winder, use a screwdriver blade to prise back the window winder handle plastic cover, as shown

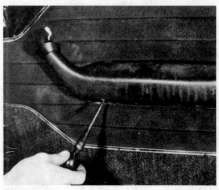
10.2 Removing the armrest/door pull retaining screw

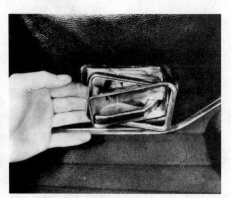
10.5 Remove the door catch escutcheon

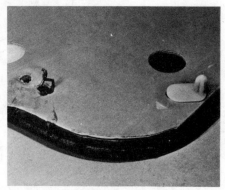
10.8 Door trim panel retaining clips

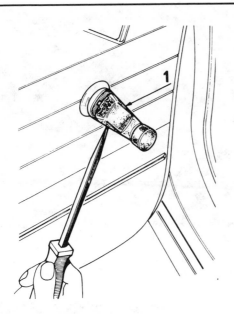

Fig. 12.7 Prise back the window cover (1) (Sec 10)

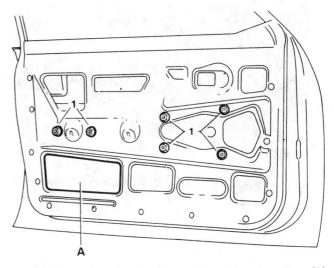

Fig. 12.8 Inner door showing the retaining plate nut positions (1) – withdraw counterbalance through aperture A (Sec 11)

in Fig. 12.7. Unscrew the retaining nut to remove the handle. On models fitted with a remote control door mirror unscrew the control sleeve (just forward of the armrest).

8   The trim panel can now be removed by prising it free from the various retaining clips around the door panel (photo). Start at the door lower edges and take care not to damage the panel or clips. When all the panel clips are released, lift the panel clear of the lock indicator capsule and remove it.

9   Access to the door panel inner mechanisms can be gained by peeling back the plastic dirt seal sheet.

10   Refitting is a reversal of the removal procedure.

11   Front door window and electric winder mechanism – removal and refitting

1   Lower the window about halfway and disconnect the battery earth lead.

2   Remove the front door trim panel (see Section 10).

3   Disconnect the window winder motor wiring.

4   Remove the six winder assembly retaining nuts as shown in Fig. 12.8.

5   Support the window in the half way position, then push the plate in to free it, and the counterbalance, from the lower window channel, and detach the rollers.

6   Pivot the counterbalance and extract it through the lower rear door inner panel aperture.

7   The window can now be lowered, tilted and then lifted out as shown in Fig. 12.9.

8   To refit, locate the outer rubber seal strip into position, engaging into the clips with a wooden dowel.

9   Insert the window into the door frame, locating it into the frame side channels.

10   Locate the winder mechanism and engage the slide and roller.

11   With the roller engaged, locate the fixed plate but do not tighten the retaining nuts fully before checking the window mechanism for correct engagement.

12   Reconnect the battery and motor feed wires, then test the window operation fully in both directions before refitting the trim panel.

12   Electro-magnetic door lock – removal and refitting

A description of the electro-magnetic locks system is given in Chapter 10.

1   Refer to Section 10 and remove the door trim panel.

2   Close the door window completely.

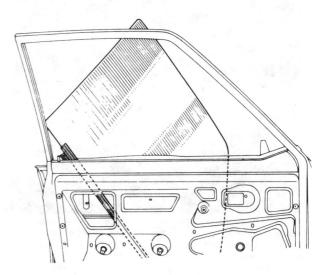

Fig. 12.9 Method of removing the window (Sec 11)

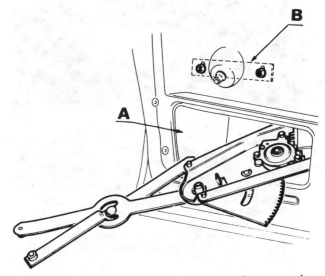

Fig. 12.10 Insert the winder mechanism through aperture A and locate fixed slide B (Sec 11)

This sequence of photographs deals with the repair of the dent and paintwork damage shown in this photo. The procedure will be similar for the repair of a hole. It should be noted that the procedures given here are simplified – more explicit instructions will be found in the text

In the case of a dent the first job – after removing surrounding trim – is to hammer out the dent where access is possible. This will minimise filling. Here, the large dent having been hammered out, the damaged area is being made slightly concave

Now all paint must be removed from the damaged area, by rubbing with coarse abrasive paper. Alternatively, a wire brush or abrasive pad can be used in a power drill. Where the repair area meets good paintwork, the edge of the paintwork should be 'feathered', using a finer grade of abrasive paper

In the case of a hole caused by rusting, all damaged sheet-metal should be cut away before proceeding to this stage. Here, the damaged area is being treated with rust remover and inhibitor before being filled

Mix the body filler according to its manufacturer's instructions. In the case of corrosion damage, it will be necessary to block off any large holes before filling – this can be done with zinc gauze or aluminium tape. Make sure the area is absolutely clean before...

...applying the filler. Filler should be applied with a flexible applicator, as shown, for best results; the wooden spatula being used for confined areas. Apply thin layers of filler at 20-minute intervals, until the surface of the filler is slightly proud of the surrounding bodywork

Initial shaping can be done with a Surform plane or Dreadnought file. Then, using progressively finer grades of wet-and-dry paper, wrapped around a sanding block, and copious amounts of clean water, rub down the filler until really smooth and flat. Again, feather the edges of adjoining paintwork

The whole repair area can now be sprayed or brush-painted with primer. If spraying, ensure adjoining areas are protected from over-spray. Note that at least one inch of the surrounding sound paintwork should be coated with primer. Primer has a 'thick' consistency, so will fill small imperfections

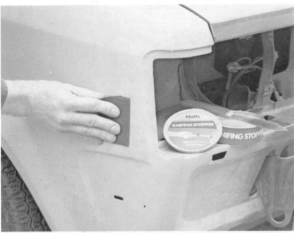

Again, using plenty of water, rub down the primer with a fine grade of wet-and-dry paper (400 grade is probably best) until it is really smooth and well blended into the surrounding paintwork. Any remaining imperfections can now be filled by carefully applied knifing stopper paste

When the stopper has hardened, rub down the repair area again before applying the final coat of primer. Before rubbing down this last coat of primer, ensure the repair area is blemish-free – use more stopper if necessary. To ensure that the surface of the primer is really smooth use some finishing compound

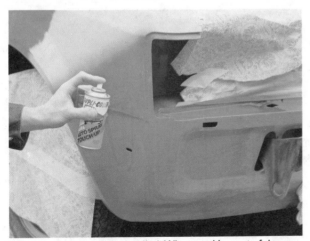

The top coat can now be applied. When working out of doors, pick a dry, warm and wind-free day. Ensure surrounding areas are protected from over-spray. Agitate the aerosol thoroughly, then spray the centre of the repair area, working outwards with a circular motion. Apply the paint as several thin coats

After a period of about two weeks, which the paint needs to harden fully, the surface of the repaired area can be 'cut' with a mild cutting compound prior to wax polishing. When carrying out bodywork repairs, remember that the quality of the finished job is proportional to the time and effort expended

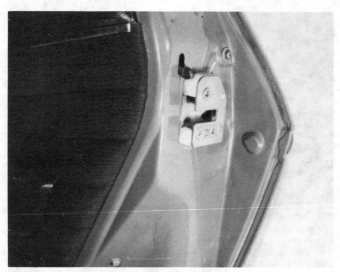

12.3 Door lock (rear) showing three retaining screws

3   Unscrew and remove the three lock retaining screws (photo) and the lower actioner securing bolt.
4   Detach the remote control rod, as shown in Fig. 12.11.
5   Referring to Fig. 12.12, remove the remote control rod bearing by rotating it 90°.
6   Pull the retaining clip from the lock barrel, then disconnect the junction block from the change-over switch. The lock barrel can now be extracted from the door.
7   Detach the pushbutton and, holding it in the vertical position, pass

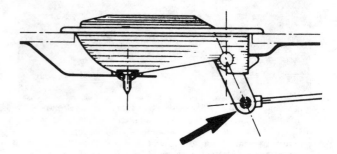

Fig. 12.11 Detach the control rod (Sec 12)

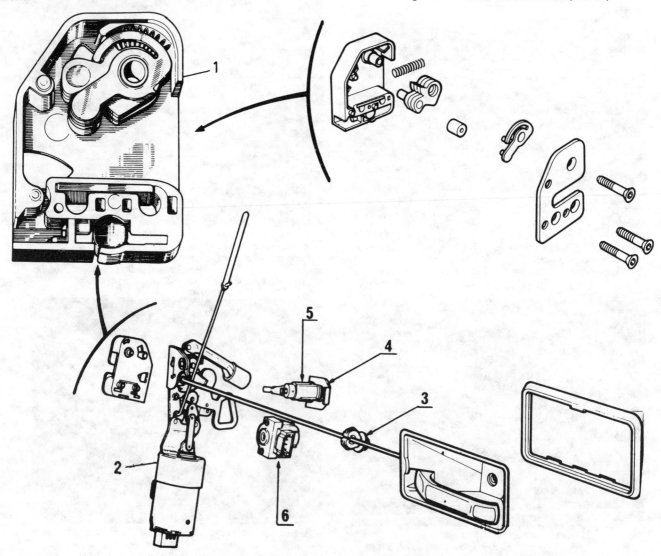

Fig. 12.12 Electro-magnetic door locking mechanism (Sec 12)

1	Door catch and components	2	Electro-magnetic actioner	3	Control rod bearing	5	Lock barrel
				4	Lock barrel retaining clip	6	Changeover switch

the lock round the window channel and extract the lock unit through the door frame aprture.

8   To remove the door lock indicator, prise the capsule retaining flange tab free, then turn the capsule 90° to release the lug and detach.

9   Refitting of the door lock mechanism components is a reversal of the removal procedure.

10 When checking the locks for operation, note that the childproof locks operate in the same manner as normal, being actuated when the lever is in the 'up' position.

13 Front door lock barrel – removal and refitting

1   Open the door and lock it, then remove the handle retaining screw from the rear edge, tilt the handle downwards and remove it.

2   Working through the aperture in the door, withdraw the barrel sleeve retaining clip. It is slotted and can be prised from the sleeve, but try not to drop it down into the door or you will have to remove the trim panel to retrieve it.

3   Withdraw the lock barrel assembly and disconnect the changeover block where an electro-magnetic door lock is fitted.

4   Extract the pin to remove the barrel from the sleeve.

5   Refitting is a reversal of the removal procedure. Ensure that the retaining clip is firmly in position over the sleeve, when fitted, and use a new clip if the old one has become defective or lost its tension on the sleeve. When finally assembled, test the lock mechanism for operation to ensure that it is satisfactory.

14 Doors – removal and refitting

1   Referring to Section 10, remove the door trim.

2   Disconnect the battery earth lead.

3   Take a note of the respective positions and detach the leads to the door lock switch unit, the window winder motor unit (when fitted), and the radio door speaker(s) (where fitted).

4   Position a jack or support under the door. Use a suitable punch drift and drive out the hinge pins from the top and bottom door hinges. An assistant would be helpful here, to hold the door and support it once the pins are removed.

5   Refitting is a reversal of the removal procedure. Always use new hinge pins and ensure that the respective wires are correctly reconnected. Lubricate the hinges with engine oil. Use the same number of shims on assembly to each hinge to adjust the door initially.

6   The door adjustment is made (if needed) by inserting or removing hinge shims (as applicable) to align the door to the front pillar. Height adjustment is gained by loosening the hinges and moving accordingly in the slotted holes.

15 External door handle – removal and refitting

1   Remove the inner trim panel (see Section 10).

2   Unscrew and remove the handle retaining nut on the inner panel face, as shown in Fig. 12.13.

3   Prise the forked retainer clip free and remove the handle.

4   Refit in the reverse order, but use a new retainer clip if the old one was damaged or defective on removal.

16 Window and window winder mechanism (manual type) – removal and refitting

1   Referring to Section 10, remove the door trim panel.

2   Open the window halfway, then unscrew and remove the three winder plate retaining screws. Press the plate inwards to detach it as shown in Fig. 12.14.

3   Remove the counterbalance from the lower channel, disengaging the rollers.

4   Pivot the counterbalance unit and extract it through the aperture in the lower door frame, as shown.

5   The window can now be lowered, tilted and pulled upwards to remove it from the door.

6   If a new glass is being fitted to the runner, ensure that when fitted, it is located as shown in Fig. 12.15, 75 mm (3 in) from the edge.

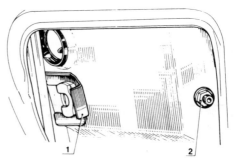

Fig. 12.13 External door handle retaining nut (2) and clip (1) (Sec 15)

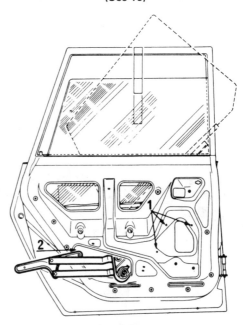

Fig. 12.14 The inner panel showing the three plate retaining screws (1) and counterbalance removal aperture (2) – note angle of window for removal (Sec 16)

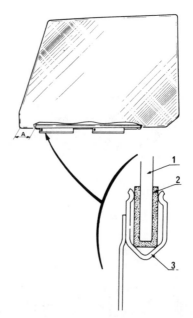

Fig. 12.15 Window bottom channel to be located as shown, distance A to equal 75 mm (3 in) – inset shows glass (1), seal (2) and channel (3) (Sec 16)

7   Fit in the reverse order. When the glass is located into the window slide at the bottom edge, insert the plate retaining bolts (hand tight). Lift the window fully, then tighten the three retainer nuts. Smear some light grease into the slide and check the operation of the winder before refitting the panel.

17 Tailgate – removal and refitting

1   The tailgate is hinged along its top edge at two points, and when opened, is retained by a counterbalance arm on each side. Remove as follows.
2   Disconnect the heated rear window wire and the rear screen wiper wiring harness connectors (where applicable).
3   Get an assistant to support the tailgate in the open position whilst you unscrew the counterbalance arms retaining screws each side (photo).
4   Unscrew the hinge nuts (photo) and lift the tailgate clear. Note the adjuster shims with each hinge.
5   Refitting is a reversal of the above procedure. If, when refitted, the tailgate needs adjustment to allow correct positioning, add or remove more shims at the hinges as applicable for height setting. To adjust the tailgate aperture frame alignment, loosen the hinge nuts and slide the tailgate in the desired direction. Retighten the nuts.

17.3 Counterbalance arm pivot bracket retaining screws to tailgate

17.4 Tailgate hinge and retaining nuts

18.4 Counterbalance arm body-mounted pivot pin and retaining circlip

18 Tailgate counterbalance arm – removal and refitting

1   It is not necessary to remove the tailgate when a counterbalance arm has to be detached.
2   Remove the main parcel shelf and the secondary parcel shelf.
3   Unscrew the tailgate arm retaining screws.
4   Prise the hinge pin retaining clip free (photo) and remove the counterbalance arm.
5   Refitting is a reversal of the removal procedure.

19 Scuttle grille – removal and refitting

1   The scuttle grille is the body panel directly in front of the windscreen lower edge, which must be removed to gain access to the windscreen wiper motor, heater matrix and associate components.
2   Remove the windscreen wiper arm and blade assembly on each side.
3   Prise the three ventilation grilles free, but take care as they are made of plastic.
4   Unscrew the three screws retaining the scuttle to the bulkhead and the two to the windscreen moulding.
5   Detach the windscreen washer tubes from the jets and lift the grille clear.
6   Refitting is a reversal of the removal procedure. The self-adhesive sealing strips should be renewed if defective or badly worn. Engage all the screws before tightening them. Align the windscreen wiper arms on the pivots and check alignment when operating and parked.

20 Windscreen and rear window – removal and refitting

Renewal of a broken windscreen, or of a perished windscreen surround, is one of the few jobs which the DIY mechanic is advised to leave to an expert. The fitting charge made by a windscreen specialist is less than the expense which will be incurred if the new screen is accidentally broken. For the owner who is determined enough, or who has some experience, the following procedure is given.
1   Remove the windscreen or tailgate wiper arms (as applicable).
2   Where the glass has shattered, the easiest way to remove the screen is to stick a sheet of self-adhesive paper or plastic sheeting to each side and push it from the inside outwards. Seal the air intake grille on the scuttle, and air ducts and radio speaker slots on the facia panel, to prevent glass crystals from falling into them during the removal operation. Protect the surfaces of the bonnet with a blanket to prevent scratching. On the rear screen disconnect the heater element wire.
3   Where the glass is to be removed in order to renew the rubber surround, make up two pads of cloth and with the aid of an assistant

press the two top corners of the screen from the inside outwards and at the same time pulling the rubber surround from the upper corners. Remove the rubber surround as soon as the screen is withdrawn and clean the edges of both the glass and the body screen frame.

4   Commence refitting by positioning the rubber surround round the edge of the windscreen glass. Place the assembly flat down on a bench or table.

5   Lay a length of string or thin cord (F) in the channel in the inner side of the rubber surround as shown in Fig. 12.16.

6   The string should be about 3 mm (0.125 in) diameter and the ends should overlap at the bottom edge by 100 mm (4 in) and leave a few inches to grip with the hands.

7   Place a bead of sealing mastic in the lower two corners of the screen frame.

8   Locate the lower edge of the screen surround in the body frame so that the two ends of the string hang inside the car, then pull both ends of the string while an assistant presses the glass and surround into position as the operation progresses.

9   The string will finally emerge from the top centre of the rubber surround and the screen and rubber surround lip should be in correct engagement with the screen frame.

10 Using either a sealing mastic gun or tube, insert the nozzle between the rubber surround lip and the outer surface of the screen frame and insert a thin even bead of sealer. Press the rubber surround

hard to spread the sealer and to ensure correct location. Wipe away any excess sealer with a paraffin moistened cloth.

11 The embellisher should be located round the seal before it is fitted. You will need to improvise here and fabricate a suitable tool to insert the embellisher strips. The official Renault tool for the job (No 438) is shown in Fig. 12.18. When the strips are fitted, locate the corner piece to complete.

21 Front wing panel – removal and refitting

1   Disconnect the battery earth lead.
2   Referring to Section 19, remove the scuttle grille.
3   Referring to Section 6, remove the front bumper.
4   Unscrew and remove the wing retaining screws at the points shown in Fig. 12.19. Unscrew them from the top edge (1), the wing to lower front and panel (2) and the rear vertical edge (3). Remove the wing panel.
5   Refitting the wing panel is a reversal of the removal instructions. Apply sealer to the rear edge joint (A) when fitting. Before tightening the fasteners fully, check the wing for alignment. When in position and secured, apply underseal to the wing underside. Apply sealer to the area around the front panel-to-wing joint.

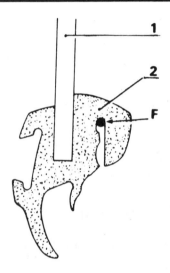

Fig. 12.16 The windscreen (1) and seal rubber (2) showing location for string (F) (Sec 20)

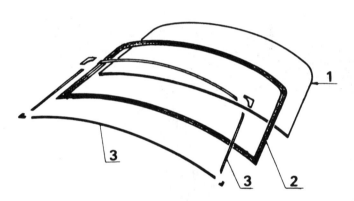

Fig. 12.17 Windscreen fittings, showing glass (1), seal (2) and embellishers (3) (Sec 20)

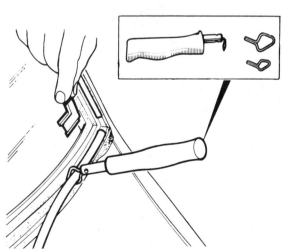

Fig. 12.18 Fitting the embellisher strip and corner pieces using special Renault tool No 438 (Sec 20)

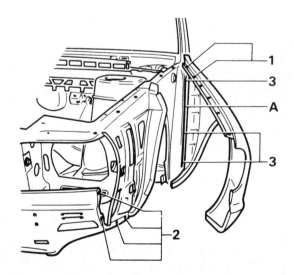

Fig. 12.19 Front wing panel fixing points. For key see text (Sec 21)

22 Front seats – removal and refitting

1   Slide the seat forward to gain access to the runner rear retaining bolts. Unscrew and remove the bolt from each runner.
2   Slide the seat rearwards and repeat the procedure with the front runner bolts.
3   Use a screwdriver and prise the two tensioner clips free underneath as shown in Fig. 12.20. Lift the seat out.
4   Refit in the reverse order and, if necessary, adjust the slide control by tensioning the control rod screw accordingly.

23 Remote control rear view mirror – removal and refitting

1   Remove the door trim panel as detailed in Section 10.
2   Lower the window so that its top edge is 100 mm (4 in) from the seal edge.
3   Remove the mirror control bracket and the plastic seal sheet as shown in Fig. 12.21.
4   Prise the mirror control cable retaining clip free within the door.
5   Remove the mirror retaining screws, then pull the mirror free from the outside and guide the control cable through the window channel.
6   To refit the mirror, pass the control and cable through from the outer door panel and guide the control and cable past the channel of the window and through the inner panel aperture as shown in Fig. 12.22.
7   Insert the mirror retaining screws and refit the control bracket. Locate the plastic clip to retain the cable, and check that the window and mirror operate satisfactorily. Refit the inner trim panel and adjust the mirror to complete.

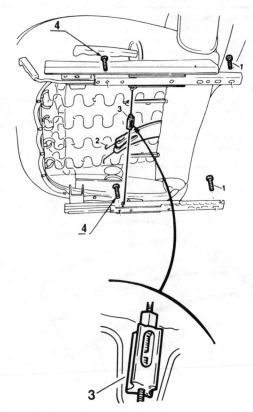

Fig. 12.20 Seat runner retaining screws (1 and 4), tensioner clips (2) and control rod screw (3) (Sec 22)

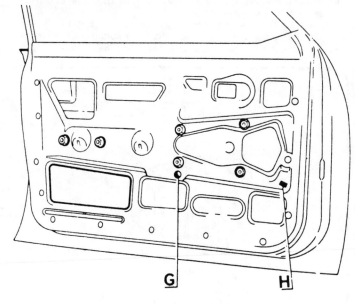

Fig. 12.21 Mirror control bracket (G) and plastic clip (H) that retains cable (Sec 23)

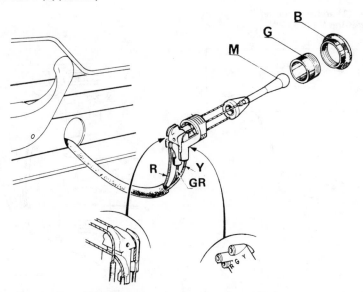

Fig. 12.22 The mirror remote control unit (Sec 23)

| B | Control sleeve | M | Cable knob | Gr | Green | Y | Yellow |
| G | Control bracket | R | Red | | | | |

Index

Printed by
Haynes Publishing Group
Sparkford Yeovil Somerset
England